Banking Terminology

THIRD EDITION

EDUCATION POLICY & DEVELOPMENT

AMERICAN
BANKERS
ASSOCIATION

1120 Connecticut Avenue, N.W.
Washington, D.C. 20036

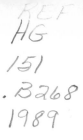
Certain terms included in *Banking Terminology* have been adapted from the glossary of *Recent Innovations in International Banking*, published by the Bank for International Settlements (1986), and are used with permission.

Library of Congress Cataloging-in-Publication Data

Banking terminology. -- 3rd ed.
    p. cm.
  ISBN 0-89982-360-2
  1. Banks and banking--Dictionaries.   I. American Bankers
Association. Education Policy and Development Group.
HG151.B268 1989
332.1'03--dc20   89-14963
                                                  CIP

This publication is designed to provide accurate and authoritative information in regard to the subject matter covered. It is sold with the understanding that the publisher is not engaged in rendering legal, accounting, or other professional service. If legal advice or other expert assistance is required, the services of a competent professional person should be sought.

From a Declaration of Principles jointly adopted by a Committee of the American Bar Association and a Committee of Publishers and Associations.

Printed in the United States of America

Contents

Introduction

Since the second edition of *Banking Terminology* was published in 1985, the banking industry has continued to undergo major change. As the industry has evolved, the language that bankers use to describe their industry has been refined. In some cases, this evolution has led to the development of new terms and expressions to help bankers communicate with each other as well as individuals outside the industry. In other cases, the traditional language used by bankers has changed to reflect competitive and regulatory developments within the industry.

The purpose of this third edition is to define the new terminology being used in the banking industry today. At the same time, this edition updates the existing language of bankers so that practitioners, students, and others interested in the banking industry can have a clearer basis for communication and understanding.

Major subject areas covered by this new edition include accounting, auditing, bank cards, commercial lending, consumer lending, economics, electronic funds transfers, funds management, general banking, human resources, insurance, international banking, law and regulatory compliance, marketing and sales, operations/automation/payment systems, real estate finance, securities and investments, and trusts.

The dictionary is organized in alphabetical order, by letter. In this manner, multiple-word terms are treated as single words. In cases where terms have more than one acceptable meaning, each alternative definition is numbered (1), (2), (3), and so on. Many terms are also cross-referenced to other terms in the dictionary with such expressions as *see, see also, distinguish from,* or *compare with.* By reading these additional definitions, the reader will gain a fuller understanding of the term in question. In cases where a term is fully defined by another entry, a cross-reference is provided instead of a definition.

Five appendixes appear at the end of the dictionary. One includes a list of acronyms and abbreviations used in the banking industry. Another presents common bank performance ratios used by bank analysts. The third presents a glossary of economic indicators. The remaining two appendixes provide the reader with addresses of the Federal Reserve banks and their districts, and the major regulatory agencies along with other addresses and telephone numbers useful to bankers.

This edition of *Banking Terminology* was made possible by the active cooperation and substantial efforts of many experienced and knowledgeable bankers and others who reviewed the entire second edition and contributed significantly to this third edition. The following individuals are to be commended for their commitment to this publication:

Roy M. Adams, Schiff, Hardin & Waite, Chicago, Illinois

Eric N. Compton, The Chase Manhattan Bank, N.A., New York, New York

Robert M. Duvall, Consultant, Yonkers, New York

Charles W. Hall, National City Corporation, Cleveland, Ohio

Garrett B. Hunter, Rhode Island Hospital Trust National Bank, Providence, Rhode Island

Gary L. Jewel, First American Corporation, Memphis, Tennessee

Richard L. Jones, SunBanks, Inc., Orlando, Florida

John W. Lanza, Manufacturers Hanover Trust Company, New York, New York

Suzanne Massey, York Associates, Bethesda, Maryland

Francis J. McNichol, NCNB Texas, Dallas, Texas

Pamela V. Mercurio, Bank of New England, N.A., Boston, Massachusetts

David M. Morris, The Chase Manhattan Bank, N.A., New York, New York

Samuel Newman, Manufacturers Hanover Trust Company, New York, New York

Mary Ann Pezzullo, Pezzullo & Associates, Marlton, New Jersey

Robert L. Schoonmaker, Provident National Bank, Philadelphia, Pennsylvania

Dr. Edmond J. Seifried, Lafayette College, Easton, Pennsylvania

W. Randall Stewart, NCNB Texas, Dallas, Texas

Kathy Trost-Norris, Texas Independent Bank, Dallas, Texas

John J. Vahey, Morgan Christiana Corporation, Newark, Delaware

Active support from the staff of the American Bankers Association was also essential to the completion of the project. Veida Dehmlow, Project Manager, handled most competently and enthusiastically the massive task of coordinating the development of this new edition. Cheryl Handel, freelance editor, very capably edited the manuscript.

I am very pleased to have played a role in the research and writing of many of the new definitions and revisions and to have worked with the staff of the Educational Development division in directing the project. Together with me, all of the individuals who worked on this dictionary hope it will continue to be a useful reference tool to readers interested in the banking industry.

> James F. Nielsen
> Professor of Banking & Finance
> College of Business
> Oregon State University
> Corvallis, Oregon

Dictionary of Banking Terms

abandonment (1) Relinquishment of possession or property rights. In banking, abandonment often refers to a borrower's turning collateral over to a bank instead of repaying the loan. In bankruptcy, abandonment is a term used to describe the trustee's relinquishment of claim over a debtor's asset, thus allowing the secured creditor to take possession of the collateral. (2) The refusal of a shipment, because of damage, by the person who is authorized to accept the shipment.

abatement The reduction of a gift under a will because there are insufficient assets to satisfy all the gifts after the legal obligations of the estate (debts, taxes, charges, and claims) have been fully paid. All gifts of the same class shall abate proportionately unless otherwise provided.

abrogation A declaration that an agreement or other item is legally null and void.

absolute gift A gift of property by will that carries with it possession of and complete dominion over the property. *Compare with* conditional gift.

absolute priority rule In Chapter 11 bankruptcy proceedings, if a class of creditors receives less than what is fully due to that class, no junior creditor or class may receive anything under the bankruptcy plan.

absolute title (1) The unqualified right of ownership for real property. (2) A legal document that indicates the unqualified right of ownership for real property.

absorption The total amount of internal and external resources that will be used in an economy.

abstract *See* abstract of title *and* chain of title.

abstract of title A written history of the title transactions and conditions of title affecting a given piece of land, covering the period from the original source of title to the present. An abstract of title summarizes the material facts that are a part of the public record. *Also called* abstract.

accelerated availability *See* expedited availability.

accelerated cost recovery system A method for determining depreciation using statutory percentages of the cost basis of property over a given life, as opposed to the declining balance method, straight-line depreciation, or sum-of-the-years-digits method. This method was created by the Economic Recovery Tax Act of 1981.

accelerated depreciation A method of depreciation in which a larger proportion of the asset's cost is written off in the early years of the asset's useful life. The declining balance method and sum-of-the-years-digits method are primary examples. *Compare with* straight-line depreciation.

accelerated remainder Property that passes to the remainderman through the failure of the income or preceding beneficiary.

acceleration The advancement of the interest where a trust is created for one beneficiary for life or for a term of years and for another in remainder, and the trust fails as to the interest for life or the term.

acceleration clause A clause in a loan contract stating that the entire loan balance shall become due immediately if a breach of certain conditions stated in the contract occurs.

acceptable paper The promissory notes, drafts, bills of exchange, and bankers' acceptances that the Federal Reserve will accept for discount or as collateral for an advance. *Compare with* eligible paper.

acceptance A time draft (bill of exchange) that the drawee, known as the "acceptor," is obligated to pay at maturity. The drawee writes the word "accepted," the maturity date, and his or her signature on the draft. A draft accepted by a bank is a bankers' acceptance; a draft accepted by the buyer of goods is a trade acceptance. *See also* bankers' acceptance; draft; trade acceptance.

acceptance credit An arrangement between an importer or exporter and a bank for the acceptance of bills of exchange.

acceptance liability The liability assumed by a bank when accepting drafts (bills of exchange) drawn upon it. The bank is unconditionally obligated to pay the drafts at maturity.

acceptance market The informal market in which bankers' acceptances are bought and sold.

acceptance sampling A method of statistical sampling in which a decision is made on whether a population is to be accepted or rejected.

accepted batch listing (ABL) An itemized list of each dollar amount that a computer system has accepted for any particular day.

accepted credit card Under the Truth in Lending Act, a credit card that a cardholder has requested and received, used, or authorized another to use, to obtain money, property, labor, or services on credit.

accepted debit card Under the Electronic Fund Transfer Act, a card, code, or other means of access to a consumer's account for the purpose of initiating electronic funds transfers when the person to whom such card was issued has requested and received, signed, used, or authorized another to use such card or other means of access to transfer money between accounts or to obtain money, property, labor, or services.

acceptor A person accepting a bill of exchange.

access (1) (Verb) To store or retrieve data; to communicate with or make use of any portion of an electronic data processing system. (2) (Noun) The ability and means to use an EDP system. (3) (Noun) The right of authorized parties to add to, reduce, or examine the contents of a safe deposit box.

access card The card used in an automated teller machine for deposits, cash withdrawals, account transfers, and other related functions.

access control The process of limiting access to an electronic data processing system (or to restricted files or areas) to authorized users, programs, and processes.

access time The amount of time a computer requires for retrieving or storing data.

accidental death and dismemberment insurance (AD&D) Insurance providing benefits in the event of loss of life, limbs, or eyesight as a result of an accident.

accommodation endorsement (1) The guarantee (endorsement) that one party gives to induce a bank or other lender to grant a loan to another party. (2) The banking practice whereby one bank endorses another bank's acceptances for a fee, so they can be sold in the acceptance market.

accommodation endorser A party who guarantees a note for a loan made to another party, thereby becoming liable in the event of default.

accommodation paper A promissory note that is signed on the back by one party to induce a lender to grant a loan to another party.

accord and satisfaction An agreement between two parties, one of whom has a right of action against the other, that the latter party should do or give, and the former party accept, something in satisfaction of the right of action different from, and usually less than, what might be legally enforced.

account (1) The credit established under a particular name, usually by deposit, against which withdrawals may be made. (2) A record of the financial transactions affecting the assets, liabilities, income, expenditures, or net worth of an individual or business entity. The financial transactions are dated and entered in an account as debits or credits. (3) In the Electronic Fund Transfer Act, a demand deposit, savings deposit, or other asset account established primarily for personal, family, or household purposes.

accountability (of a trustee) A major duty of a trustee. A trustee must maintain accurate records of income, disbursements, and other significant matters affecting a trust. A trustee must also inform beneficiaries (and a court, if involved) of its actions and honor reasonable requests for information from both.

account activity A summary of activity in an account, including previous balance, payments, credits, new credit extended, finance charges, late charges, and new balance owed.

account analysis (1) A systematic procedure of determining profit or loss from an account. (2) A monthly statement prepared by the bank, summarizing activity in one or more corporate accounts and evaluating the adequacy of balances for the purpose of compensating for account activity. The analysis may also take into consideration other services provided by the bank and their costs.

account conversion The changing of a person's account with one bank card plan to another--for example, from a merchant's to a bank's card plan or from one bank's plan to another. *Also called* account transfer.

account error *See* billing error.

account history The payment history of an account over a specified period, including the number of times the account was past due or over its limit.

accounting (1) A record showing the transactions in an account. (2) The submission of such a record to a court or to the beneficiaries of a trust or estate by the fiduciary. (3) The science of organizing, recording, and reporting all transactions that represent the financial condition and performance of a business, organization, or individual. *See also* accrual basis of accounting; cash basis of accounting; cost accounting; double-entry accounting; single-entry accounting.

accounting control A component of internal controls that comprises the plan of organization, procedures, and records that safeguard assets and maintain the reliability of financial records.

account in trust An account opened by one person and held in trust and maintained for the benefit of another. Unless this is a trust fund, the person who opened this account must approve withdrawals from it.

account maintenance The administrative or overhead cost incurred in compiling information about a depositor's account and sending out monthly or periodic statements.

account owner bank A bank that holds an account at another bank (the account servicing bank). *See also* due to account.

account reconcilement service A bookkeeping service offered to some bank customers to aid them in balancing their accounts. This service includes numerically sorting checks, itemizing outstanding checks, and actually balancing the account.

account representative A person responsible for resolving mail, telephone, and in-person inquiries for customers.

account servicing bank A bank that services an account for another bank (the account owner bank). *See also* due from account.

account servicing bank's reference A reference assigned by the account servicing bank to identify a transaction. This is the reference that the account owner bank will use to make inquiries to the account servicing bank.

accounts payable Those amounts due from a company to its vendors that must be paid within 1 year or less.

accounts receivable Amounts due to a company for goods or services sold on credit. These are generally short-term assets. *See also* uncollectible and execution-proof accounts.

accounts receivable acquisition Acquisition (through a purchase or other transfer) of outstanding charge balances and/or rights to the underlying accounts.

accounts receivable financing The process of obtaining funds for working capital, by selling or borrowing against accounts receivable.

accounts receivable insurance Insurance that protects against the loss of accounts receivable resulting from destroyed or lost records or nonpayment.

account status report A list of all cardholder accounts for which there has been activity within a specified period. *Also called* activity status report *or* daily status report.

account transcript A document, showing entries in an account, that a transfer agent may be asked to provide. The Securities and Exchange Commission's turnaround rules allow the transfer agent 20 business days to respond to the request.

account transfer *See* account conversion.

accretion The extension of boundaries or acquisition of land by the gradual or imperceptible action of natural forces, as by sand washing up from the sea or a watermark receding.

accretion account An account that records the difference between the acquisition value and the face value of bonds purchased at discount.

accretion of discount The gradual accumulation of capital gains on discount bonds, in anticipation of being paid par at maturity.

accrual basis of accounting A method of accounting in which revenue is recognized when earned, expenses are recognized when incurred, and other changes in financial condition are recognized as they occur, without regard to the timing of the actual cash receipts and expenditures. *Compare with* cash basis of accounting.

accrue (1) As applied to a right, to come into existence as an enforceable claim. For example, a cause of action has accrued when the right to sue becomes vested and exercisable. (2) To accumulate in anticipation of payment. (3) To recognize income or expense over time.

accrued dividends Dividends that are declared but not yet paid.

accrued income receivable Income earned but not yet received.

accrued interest Interest income (expense) that has been earned (incurred) but not yet received (paid).

accrued interest payable Interest expense that has been incurred but not yet paid.

accrued interest receivable Interest income that has been earned but not yet received.

accrued taxes and interest Taxes and interest expense that have been incurred but not yet paid.

accumulated income That portion of income from a trust that is retained in the account.

accumulation bond A bond that is sold at a discount. If it is held to maturity, interest is realized up to the difference between the face value and the original purchase price of the bond. If it is sold before maturity, interest is the difference between the purchase and sale price of the bond.

accumulation distribution The amount of income earned by a trust in a previous year that is distributed to a beneficiary and subject to the income-tax throwback rules.

acid test ratio A financial ratio that lenders use to measure a firm's ability to meet its current obligations. The ratio is calculated by dividing current assets minus inventory by current liabilities. *Also called* quick ratio.

acknowledgment (1) A wired or written notification that an item has been received. (2) A declaration or admission of the truth of a fact, act, or position. (3) The formal declaration made by a court official or notary public before one has executed a deed or other legal instrument.

acquirer (1) The institution within a transaction interchange network that receives identification and authentication information from a customer. (2) The financial institution or agent of a financial institution receiving information from the card acceptor.

acquiring bank (1) In interchange, a bank that maintains the merchant relationship and receives all transactions. (2) In a merger, the bank that absorbs the bank acquired.

acquisition The process of buying or acquiring some asset. The term can refer to the purchase of a block of stock or, more often, to the acquisition of an entire company.

acquisition costs The primary costs of establishing a new asset. Loan acquisition costs, for example, include the cost of the loan interview, credit investigation, loan committee process, and loan documentation process.

acquisition program An advertising campaign, solicitation, or promotion designed to encourage consumers to apply for a bank card.

acquittance (1) The discharge of an obligor from a legal obligation. (2) A legal document that gives written evidence of the discharge of, or freedom from, a specific financial or other obligation.

action to quiet title The legal process by which any person claiming an interest or estate in real property (not in the actual possession of another) may maintain a suit in equity against another who claims an adverse interest or estate in the property, to determine conflicting or adverse claims, interests, or estates.

activation program An advertising campaign or solicitation designed to activate inactive debit card, credit card, or revolving credit line accounts.

active account An account that has had financial activity during a specified period. *Compare with* dormant account.

active income Income earned through employment (wages and salary).

active trust A trust under which the trustee has some active duty to perform. *Compare with* passive trust.

activity charge (1) A service charge incurred by a customer whose account balance is not sufficient to offset the expenses incurred in handling transactions on the account. (2) A fee assessed on the number or type of transactions--for example, a per-check charge on a checking account, a cash advance charge on a credit card, or a withdrawal from an ATM.

activity file A list of the most recent transactions in a terminal, group of terminals, or system, used to detect fraudulent repetitive transactions.

activity limit The dollar value representing the maximum amount of a transaction or the maximum number of transactions that can be authorized.

activity ratio The number of active accounts expressed as a percentage of total accounts.

activity status report *See* account status report.

actuals The items being traded, as opposed to futures contracts for those items.

actual total loss In marine insurance, total loss of the insured material.

actuarial interest *See* simple interest.

actuary A statistician who computes insurance and pension rates and premiums based on experience tables.

add-on interest A method of calculating interest on a loan. The total interest due over the life of the loan is calculated by multiplying the original principal amount by the interest rate. This is added to the principal, and the total is divided into equal installments that are paid over the life of the loan. In consumer transactions, the add-on rate must be converted to an annual percentage rate.

ademption A willmaker's act that has the effect of extinguishing or withdrawing a legacy. For example, a person leaves an acre of land to his son in his will, but during his lifetime, the willmaker sells the land, thus extinguishing that legacy.

adequate notice A printed notice to a cardholder that sets forth the facts clearly and conspicuously, so that a person receiving the notice could reasonably have seen it and understood its meaning.

adequate protection In bankruptcy proceedings, the term used to describe the compensation, value, or lien granted to a secured creditor to compensate the secured creditor for the value of the property the debtor is using while under the protection of the bankruptcy court.

adjudication The decision of a competent court on matters in dispute. *Distinguish from* arbitration.

adjustable rate mortgage (ARM) A mortgage on which the rate is subject to periodic adjustment. The exact method, frequency, and basis for the change are fully disclosed to the borrower. ARM rates are usually tied to some widely published market rate of interest. *Also called* variable rate mortgage.

adjusted gross estate The value of an estate after all allowable deductions have reduced the gross estate, but before federal estate taxes have been paid.

adjusting entry A journal entry posted at the end of an accounting period to recognize changes in assets, liabilities, revenues, and expenses affecting the period that have not been recorded in the daily accounting pro-

cess. Examples include entries for depreciation, accruals, and uncollectible accounts receivable.

adjustment bond *See* income bond.

adjustment credit Credit extended by a Federal Reserve bank for brief periods to help borrowers meet short-term needs for funds when their usual sources are not reasonably available.

ad litem For the purpose of the suit.

administration (1) The care and management of an estate by a trustee or guardian, to be distinguished from the settlement of an estate by an executor or administrator. (2) The performance of management duties.

administrative control The procedures and policies that are concerned with management's authorization of transactions.

administrative expense The expenses pertaining to the management of an enterprise.

administrative fee (1) A fee to cover the overhead and other fixed costs incurred in connection with performing a customized service for a customer. (2) (Trust) A charge for establishing, periodically reviewing, and performing routine operations for a trust.

administrative provisions Provisions in a will or trust agreement setting forth the duties and powers of the executor or the trustee regarding the care and management of the property. *Distinguish from* dispositive provisions.

administrator (1) Any person who performs the functions of administration in a bank. *See also* administration. (2) An individual or trust institution appointed by a court to settle the estate of a person (a) if the person has died without leaving a valid will, (b) if the person has died without naming an executor, or (c) if the executor will not serve. If the individual appointed is a woman, she is known as an administratrix.

administrator ad colligendum An administrator appointed to collect foreign assets.

administrator ad litem An administrator appointed by the court to act as a party to an action at law, in which the decedent or his or her representative was, or is, a necessary party.

administrator cum testamento annexo A person or trust institution appointed by a court of probate to settle the estate of a deceased person according to the terms of the will when the will has named no executor or the one named has failed to qualify. Often abbreviated to administrator c.t.a. *Also called* administrator with the will annexed.

administrator cum testamento annexo de bonis non A person or trust institution appointed by a court of probate to complete the settlement of the estate of a deceased person according to the terms of his or her will, when the executor or the administrator with the will annexed has failed to continue in office. Often abbreviated to administrator c.t.a.d.b.n. or d.b.n.c.t.a. *See also* administrator cum testamento annexo.

administrator de bonis non A person or trust institution appointed by a court of probate to complete the settlement of the estate of a person who has died without leaving a valid will, when the administrator originally appointed has failed to continue in office. Often abbreviated to administrator d.b.n.

administrator de son tort A person or corporation charged with the duties and liabilities of an administrator, but not appointed as such because of his, her, or its own wrongdoing with respect to assets in his, her, or its possession.

administrator durante absentia An administrator appointed by a court to serve during the absence of an executor or another administrator.

administrator pendente lite A person or a trust institution appointed by a court to take over and safeguard an estate during a suit over an alleged will, or over the right of appointment of an executor or administrator.

administrator with the will annexed *See* administrator cum testamento annexo.

administratrix *See* administrator.

ad valorem taxes Real estate taxes based on property values. Literally translated as "taxes according to the value."

advance (1) A loan. (2) A partial payment to a borrower, for example, under a construction loan. *Also called* a draw. (3) A verb used to describe a general increase in prices in the securities market. *See also* overdraft.

advance commitment (1) An agreement by a private buyer to purchase a bond issue at some future date. (2) A written contract calling for the sale of a specified amount of mortgages, mortgage-backed securities, or other securities, at a given price or yield within a specified time.

advance-decline index An indicator showing the cumulative net difference between advances and declines in stock prices. *Also called* advance-decline ratio.

advance payments The funds paid by a purchaser for goods or services before they are received. Under the accrual basis of accounting, advance payments are a current liability on the books of the seller.

advance refunding (1) An operation that has not been used in recent years in which the Treasury offers the owners of a given issue of outstanding federal obligations the opportunity to exchange the securities for a longer-term issue that might bear a higher yield to maturity. (2) For a municipal bond, the sale of a refunding issue before the first call date of the issue that is to be refunded from the proceeds to be held in trust.

advancing market A market in which stock prices are generally rising.

adverse action Under the Equal Credit Opportunity Act (ECOA), and Regulation B, a creditor who denies a consumer's request for credit, who reduces an existing credit line (except for delinquency), or who changes the terms, rate, or amount of a request has taken "adverse action" and must advise the applicant in writing of the reasons for the denial of the request or change in terms.

adverse possession A method of obtaining title by asserting a hostile claim against the claim or title of someone else through possession of the property for a statutory period of time.

advice (1) A written form or verbal order from which an electronic entry may be posted to an account (that is, a credit or debit advice). (2) A written acknowledgment or notice of a particular transaction. (3) A notification confirming that a funds transfer or other transaction has been

executed. An advice does not contain instructions for payment orders.

advice information Information to a party to a transfer, such as (1) information on charging (whom to charge and how to apply the charges); (2) sending information (telephone number, cable address, and so forth); and (3) other appropriate information (bank's name, hours of availability, etcetera).

advice method A code that specifies the method used to notify a party to a funds transfer that the proper account has been credited and funds are available.

advice to receive An advance notice to an account-maintaining bank that it will receive funds to be credited to the account of the person giving notice.

advised line of credit An expression of a bank's willingness regarding the maximum amount it may lend to a customer, confirmed in writing to that customer. *See also* line of credit.

advising bank A bank that contacts the beneficiary of a letter of credit after it has been notified of the opening of that L/C. The advising bank reaffirms the terms and conditions involved.

advisory fee The fee that a trust department charges for managing an advisory account.

affiant A person who makes an affidavit or statement under oath or affirmation.

affidavit A sworn statement in writing before a proper official, usually a notary public. Under certain circumstances, the Federal Housing Administration and Veterans Administration require such statements from borrowers. An affidavit is also often required by a depository for the distribution of assets to which another claim might exist.

affiliate (1) A business organization sharing with another organization some aspect of common ownership and control. (2) Any organization participating in the issuance of cards and interchange of paper using either of the national bank card systems.

affiliate bank An issuing bank that is part of a processing or service association. *See also* agent bank.

affiliated company Companies with some degree of common ownership, officers, or directors.

affinity Relationship by marriage. *Distinguish from* consanguinity (relationship by blood).

affinity card program A credit card program designed for individuals having a common bond or sharing a common interest (for example, fans of a specific football team, alumni of a particular university, members of a specific trade union, ski enthusiasts). The card's graphic design reflects the group's interest, and a portion of the income derived by the card issuer may be shared by the organization to whose members the card is issued. The card is called an affinity card.

affinity group A collection of individuals with some form of common interest or relationship.

affirmation A response to a broker's confirmation, acknowledging that the records of the affirming party (investment manager, bank, and so on) agree with the trading details stated in the broker's confirmation.

after-acquired clause Legal language in a security agreement, mortgage, or deed of trust that subjects after-ac-

quired property to the lien of the instrument in which the clause is contained.

after-acquired property (1) Property acquired by a debtor as security, after the execution of a mortgage or other form of indebtedness, that additionally secures the indebtedness. (2) Property acquired by a testator subsequent to making a will.

after-born child A child born after the execution of the parent's will. *Distinguish from* posthumous child.

agencies *See* agency security.

agency The relationship between an agent who acts on behalf of another person and the principal in whose behalf the agent acts. *See also* fiduciary.

agency account An account in which the title to the property constituting the agency does not pass to the trust institution but remains with the owner of the property (who is called the principal) and in which the agent is charged with certain duties with respect to the property.

agency bank (1) An entity authorized to do limited banking. Foreign banks establish agency banks in the United States that cannot make loans or accept deposits but can act as agents for the parent bank. (2) Loosely, U.S. branches of foreign banks.

agency costs Reductions in the amount of return owners of a business receive because of the separation of ownership and control. Agency costs are caused by the different risk/ reward preferences of owners and managers.

agency coupled with an interest An agency in which the agent has a legal interest in the subject matter of the agency. Unlike other agencies, such an agency is not terminated by the death of the principal but continues in effect until the agent's legal interest is realized.

agency issues *See* agency security.

agency security A security issued by a U.S. government agency other than the U.S. Treasury. *Also called* agencies; agency issues.

agent A person who acts for another person by the latter's authority. The distinguishing characteristics of an agent are that (a) he or she acts on behalf, and subject to the control, of his or her principal; (b) he or she does not have title to the property of his or her principal; and (c) he or she owes the duty of obedience to the orders given by his or her principal.

agent bank (1) A bank that, by agreement, participates in another bank's card program--usually by turning over its applications for bank cards to the bank administering the bank card program and by acting as a depository for merchants. *Also called* affiliate bank. (2) A bank acting for a foreign bank to handle such affairs as bills of exchange or loan administration. (3) A bank acting on behalf of a group of banks in extending credit to a foreign or domestic borrower.

agent de change A stockbroker.

aging A procedure by which accounts are classified to determine collection time or delinquency (for example, current, 30 days past due, 60 days past due, and so on).

aging report *See* aging schedule; delinquent activity report.

aging schedule A table showing the age of accounts receivable for a firm.

agreement An arrangement between individual traders to honor market quotes within predetermined limits on outstanding size.

agreement corporation A corporate subsidiary of a bank, organized under Section 25 of the Federal Reserve Act to engage in international banking and finance. *See also* Edge Act corporation.

agricultural loan A specialized loan tailored to the needs of a farming business.

AIBD Association of International Bond Dealers.

alienation The transfer of title to property by legal conveyance. *See also* restraint on alienation of property.

alienation clause An acceleration clause that requires full payment of indebtedness if property has been conveyed or alienated either through sale or some other means. *Also commonly called* a "due-on-sale clause."

alien corporation *See* foreign corporation.

aligning edge The bottom edge of a check (to which MICR characters are parallel).

all-in cost (1) The cost of funds to a bank, including allowance for reserve requirements and the insurance assessments of the Federal Deposit Insurance Corporation. (2) In real estate, all the costs involved in completing a project.

all-in-one program A bank's program to provide a customer with multiple services as a package, such as a checking account, bank credit card, revolving credit line, traveler's checks, and other bank services. The bank may charge a monthly fee or require that a minimum level of balances be maintained to obtain all the services at low or no additional cost. *See also* systems selling.

allocate To designate funds or securities solely for a particular account or other purpose.

allocated transfer risk reserve (ATRR) A special reserve against the risks presented in certain international assets, required of banking institutions under the International Lending Supervision Act of 1983 when the Comptroller of the Currency, the Federal Reserve Board, and the Federal Deposit Insurance Corporation determined that such a reserve is necessary. At least annually, these regulatory agencies jointly determine which international assets are subject to risks warranting establishment of an ATRR, the size of the ATRR, and whether an already established ATRR may be reduced. In determining whether an ATRR is required, these agencies must decide (a) whether the quality of international assets has been impaired by protracted inability of the borrowers to make payments on their obligations and (b) whether there are no definite prospects for restoring orderly debt service.

allocation In accounting, the apportionment of an amount among several accounts according to some systematic rule.

allocation commitment An agreement or statement by a national or regional investor to purchase within a specified period a certain volume of mortgages, at a given price and specific location.

allonge Paper attached to a negotiable instrument, used for endorsements when there is no room for them on the instrument itself.

all-or-none A securities underwriting method. If the underwriter appears unable to sell the entire issue, none of the issue is sold. The sale may be made later at a more favorable time. The underwriter acts as an agent, receiving a fee.

allotment The allocation of securities to members of a syndicate involved in the Eurobond or U.S. securities markets. *See also* subscription.

allowable depreciation *See* allowed depreciation.

allowance The sum(s) awarded a fiduciary by a court as compensation for the fiduciary's services. *Distinguish from* charge; commission; fee. *See also* widow's allowance.

allowance for loan losses A balance sheet account designed to recognize the fact that all loans will not be repaid in full. The allowance is increased periodically by the aggregate amount of loans estimated to be uncollectible. The allowance is decreased when charge-offs actually occur. *Also called* loan loss reserve. *See also* provision for loan losses.

allowed depreciation The maximum amount of depreciation that the Internal Revenue Service allows during a year for the normal replacement of capital equipment.

alpha cardholder file A record of all cardholder accounts, with names arranged in alphabetical order, that includes name, address, and account number.

alpha cross-reference file A record of all cardholder accounts, with names arranged in alphabetical order, that includes name, address, account number, and types and account numbers of all accounts used.

alphanumeric (1) A method of filing using alphabetical and numerical codes. (2) Pertaining to a character set that contains letters, digits, and usually other characters, such as punctuation marks. *Also called* alphameric.

alpha risk In statistics, the risk of erroneously rejecting a good population (that is, one containing less than a material aggregate error).

alteration A change made on a note, check, or other instrument. The change may invalidate the document.

altered check A check on which a material change, usually in the dollar amount, has been made. The drawee bank is expected to detect alterations, and it is responsible only for paying checks as originally drawn.

altered sales draft A sales draft on which the dollar amount has been changed to read as something other than what the cardholder actually agreed to and signed.

alternate valuation date The date, usually 6 months after the date of the decedent's death, that an executor can elect to determine the value of the assets of the decedent's gross estate for federal estate tax purposes. This election can benefit an estate that holds an asset or assets that decline materially in value during the period immediately after the decedent's death.

alternative minimum tax An alternative to the regular income tax. The alternative minimum tax, sometimes referred to as the "ATM," was enacted to ensure that corporate and upper-income noncorporate taxpayers (including estates and trusts), who enjoy tax savings from certain deductions and exemptions, do not escape completely from paying income tax. It functions by taxing certain items, called "items of tax preference," not subject to regular income tax because of deductions and exemptions.

alternative mortgage loan (AML) A term occasionally used to describe alternatives to the fixed-rate, fixed-term, and fixed-amount mortgage. It includes variable rate mortgages, graduated payment mortgages, and others.

amalgamation The combining of two or more separate businesses into a new one, while dissolving the original businesses.

amendment An addition, deletion, or change in a legal document.

American Bankers Association (ABA) The national trade association for commercial banks, organized in 1875 to promote their general welfare. The ABA seeks to keep members aware of developments affecting the industry, to help educate bank personnel, to pursue improvements in bank management and services, and to represent the interests of commercial banks to government.

American Bankers Association (ABA) number *See* transit number.

American depository receipt (ADR) A negotiable instrument representing ownership in foreign securities that is dollar denominated rather than denominated in the currency of the issuer. U.S. banks serve as depositories for ADRs, while the underlying instruments are held by a foreign correspondent bank.

American Institute of Banking (AIB) A branch of the American Bankers Association that provides education to bank employees. AIB offers courses and other educational activities to bank employees through local chapters and study groups.

American Institute of Real Estate Appraisers (AIREA) A national professional association of real estate appraisers. Qualified members are designated M.A.I. (Member of Appraisal Institute).

American Land Title Association (ALTA) An organization composed of title insurance companies, abstracters, and attorneys specializing in real property law. ALTA has adopted certain title insurance policy forms to standardize coverage nationally for property owners and lenders.

American National Standards Institute (ANSI) A nonprofit organization engaged in developing national industry standards, including standards for bank cards and financial communication networks.

American rule *See* prudent-investor rule for trust investment.

American Stock Exchange (ASE) One of two major national stock exchanges. Companies whose securities are traded on the American Stock Exchange are generally smaller or newer than those whose securities are traded on the New York Stock Exchange. *Also called* AMEX.

American-style option An option that may be exercised at any time up to and including the expiration date. *Distinguish from* European option. *Also called* American option.

amortization (1) A systematic apportionment of the cost basis of intangible assets to future periods in which benefits accrue from such assets. Amortization is treated as an expense in the income statement for the period, while accumulated amortization is treated as a deduction from the asset category to which it relates. (2) As a tax concept, the recovery of the cost or other basis of an intangible asset over its estimated useful life in a manner similar to straight-line depreciation. (3) Depletion in value of tangible assets, such as oil wells and minerals, which are referred to as "wasting assets." (4) The name given to periodic reductions in a mortgage or other loan.

amortization of debt discount The noncash expenditures charged on a company's income statement to offset, over the life of a bond issue, the difference between the proceeds of bonds sold at a discount and the par value payable at maturity.

amortization of premium The charges made against interest received on bonds, to offset any premium paid for the bonds above their par value or call price. The premium may be gradually amortized over the life of the bond issue or repaid at one time.

amortization schedule A table showing the amounts of principal and interest due at regular intervals and the unpaid balance of the loan after each payment is made.

amortized mortgage loan A mortgage loan that provides for regular repayments at stated intervals, usually monthly, quarterly, or semiannually, to reduce the principal and to cover interest as it comes due.

amount The value of a transaction expressed in units of currency.

amount field An MICR field on a check that defines the boundaries within which amount data appear. The amount data always consist of 10 digits bracketed by two amount symbols.

amount financed In the Truth in Lending Act, the amount of credit that the customer is actually able to use. The amount financed may or may not be the same as the face amount of the note.

analog computer A computer that manipulates numbers representing data of such physical quantities as length. Electronic analog computers work on voltages instead of numbers.

analog recording A method of recording in which the signal can take any value between defined limits.

analysis *See* financial analysis; systems analysis.

analyst A person who defines problems and develops algorithms and procedures for their solution. *See also* financial analyst; systems analyst.

ancestor (1) One from whom a person is descended, whether through father or mother. (2) In law, one from whom an estate has descended. (3) In common law, applies only to a person in line of descent.

ancillary Subordinate or auxiliary to something or someone else. It is used in such terms as ancillary administration, and ancillary guardian.

ancillary letters testamentary Letters subordinate or auxiliary to letters testamentary, for example, those issued in a jurisdiction for probate of property owned by a nonresident decedent.

ancillary trustee A trustee that administers property located elsewhere than in the state of the decedent's or settlor's domicile. *Distinguish from* domiciliary trustee.

and interest A method of quoting bond prices by which the purchaser must pay the interest accrued since the last payment of interest.

anniversary year The 12-month period following an employee's date of hire or date of reemployment (after a break in service) and each succeeding 12-month period.

announcement effects Market reactions to announcements of borrowings by the U.S. Treasury, actions by the Federal Reserve, reports on money growth, or statements of government policy.

annual cap The maximum amount by which the interest rate on an adjustable rate mortgage may be raised in any one year. *See also* life cap; rate cap.

annual exclusion *See* annual gift tax exclusion.

annual fee A fee, usually assessed annually, that a bank charges for a particular product. The fee is charged most frequently for credit cards, but it may also be charged for maintaining overdraft banking, equity lines, or debit cards.

annual gift tax exclusion The amount of property (presently $10,000 for an individual, or $20,000 for a married couple) that may annually be given to a donee, regardless of the donee's relationship to the donor, free of gift tax. Only gifts of present interests qualify for the annual exclusion. *Also called* annual exclusion.

annual high The highest price paid for a stock or bond during the past 12 months.

annualize To convert statistics for a certain period into figures that would be represented if the statistics for the period continued for a year. For example, sales of 100 during a certain month might be expressed as sales of 1,200 on an annualized basis.

annual low The lowest price paid for a stock or bond during the past 12 months.

annual percentage rate (APR) The cost of credit on a yearly basis. Expressed as a percentage, the APR results from an equation that considers three specifically defined factors: the amount financed, the finance charge, and the term of the loan. The APR is usually expressed in terms of the effective annual simple interest rate.

annual report A formal financial report issued annually to shareholders by a corporation. The annual report generally includes a set of financial statements (balance sheet, income statement, cash flow statement, and footnotes), the auditor's report, and a review of the year's accomplishments.

annuitant (1) The person insured under an annuity plan. (2) The beneficiary of an annuity.

annuity (1) A fixed amount payable annually or at regular intervals for a given period, such as for a stated number of years or for the life of the annuitant. (2) An investment that yields such payments. *See also* deposit annuity.

annuity bond *See* consol.

annuity plan A type of retirement insurance from which, after making payments for a specified time, a person receives income for a given period or for life.

ante-nuptial contract An agreement with respect to property, made before marriage by the parties to the marriage.

Antiboycott Compliance Law A part of the Export Administration Act of 1977, which prohibits a U.S. resident from taking or knowingly agreeing to take certain actions with the intent to comply with, further, or support an unsanctioned foreign boycott of a nation friendly to the United States.

anticipated balance The end-of-period balance, including interest if applicable, projected for a savings account, assuming no deposits or withdrawals.

anticipated interest The interest that a given account is projected to receive by the end of an accounting period, assuming no additional deposits or withdrawals.

anticipatory auditing A proactive approach to auditing where techniques such as key indicators, call programs, and special reviews are used to ensure a continuous audit monitoring process.

Anti-Drug Abuse Act The act requiring that a bank's board of directors establish a currency transaction compliance program to monitor compliance with the Bank Secrecy Act.

antitrust laws Those provisions found in federal and state laws that prohibit certain forms of business activity considered harmful to vigorous competition and economic growth. Such practices include conspiracy to restrain trade, price fixing, or attempts to monopolize trade or commerce.

appellate courts Courts that hear appeals from lower courts.

applicable federal rate The statutory interest rate that must be charged for most loans and installment agreements to avoid imputation of income under the Internal Revenue Code. The Treasury Department determines three applicable federal rates monthly based on the current market yields on outstanding obligations of the federal government with similar maturities. The federal short-term rate is applicable to transactions having terms of 3 years or less, the federal mid-term rate is applicable to transactions having terms of 3 to 9 years, and the federal long-term rate is used for transactions having terms in excess of 9 years.

applicant Under the Equal Credit Opportunity Act, any person who requests or has received an extension of credit from a creditor, including anyone who may be contractually liable but not including a guarantor or endorser.

application (1) A printed form used by lenders to record necessary information concerning a prospective borrower and collateral. (2) Under the Equal Credit Opportunity Act, an oral or written request for an extension of credit that is made in accordance with procedures established by a creditor for the type of credit requested. (3) The problem to which a computer is applied. *See also* standby application.

application audit Detailed evaluation of the internal controls within a given application system. Areas reviewed include input, processing, and output control; program and user documentation; program and data integrity.

application program A data-processing program for a functional or service user, designed to perform specific tasks such as payroll, demand deposit accounting, or accounts receivable.

application software A program that defines and completes the specific task required of a computer.

appointment *See* nomination; power of appointment.

apportion To divide an amount among several different accounts or for other purposes.

apportionment The distribution of a receipt of property or a disbursement of property between two or more accounts, such as between principal and income.

appraisal A report containing an opinion of value based on a factual analysis.

appraisal report An oral or written report that leads the reader from the definition of the appraisal problem to a specific value conclusion.

appraised value An estimate of property value at a specific date reached by an appraiser.

appraiser A person trained and qualified to estimate the value of real property.

appreciating value collateral Assets pledged as collateral that increase in value over the life of the loan.

appreciation An increase in value; the opposite of depreciation.

appreciation (foreign exchange) An increase in the value of one country's currency in terms of another country's currency.

approval ratio The number of applications approved, expressed as a percentage of the number of applications processed.

approved list A list, statutory or otherwise, that contains the authorized investments that a fiduciary may acquire.

appurtenance An item belonging or attached to something else and incident to the principal thing. For example, a right of way is the appurtenance over land, which is the principal thing.

arbitrage The simultaneous purchase and sale of similar financial instruments in separate markets, in order to benefit from existing price differentials or from an assured future change in the price relationship of the instruments.

arbitration The hearing and determining of a controversy by a person or people mutually agreed on by the parties or chosen by the court or by someone under statutory authority. *Distinguish from* adjudication.

arithmetic unit The unit of a computing system containing the circuits that perform arithmetic operations.

ARM *See* adjustable rate mortgage.

arm's length transaction A transaction negotiated by unrelated parties, each acting in his or her own self-interest. It is the basis for a fair market value determination.

arrearages (1) Unpaid obligations that are past due, such as unpaid dividends on cumulative preferred stock or past-due interest on bonds. (2) The extent of, or amount in, arrears.

arrears (1) An unpaid, overdue debt. (2) The unpaid dividends on cumulative preferred stock or unpaid interest on bonds. (3) Collecting payments on loans in arrears refers to collecting interest after it has accrued.

Article 9 (1) The section of the Uniform Commercial Code that governs the documentation of loans secured by personal property. (2) SEC Regulation S-X, Article 9,

contains substantially all the requirements for bank holding company financial statements, related footnotes, and supplemental schedules required to be filed with the SEC and included in annual reports to shareholders.

articles of partnership *See* partnership agreement.

ascertainable standard For federal tax purposes, a standard of invasion or appointment of income of a trust that is basically limited to those amounts needed by the beneficiary for health, education, support, or maintenance. When a beneficiary of a trust has a power to invade trust income or principal for his or her benefit and that power is limited by an ascertainable standard, the beneficiary will not have a taxable general power of appointment.

Asia dollar The Asian version of the Eurodollar.

asked price The trading price proposed by a prospective seller of securities. *Also called* ask *and* asking price. *See also* bid and asked prices.

assemblage A group of properties such as a subdivision that are sold as a package. Assemblages are designed by homeowners in order to profit when building complexes or shopping centers invade their area, disrupt lifestyles, and threaten to lower property values.

assembler language A source language that includes statements in a symbolic machine language in which there is a one-to-one correspondence between the instruction formats and the data formats of the computer.

assembly language A computer instruction language that uses words, phrases, or statements. This is the programming language most closely related to the detailed instruction level at which the computer operates.

assessed valuation The value placed on property for the purpose of taxation.

assessment (1) The process of appraising property for the purpose of taxation. (2) A levy against property for a special purpose, such as a sewer assessment. (3) In insurance, the practice of requiring the insured party to pay charges for losses in excess of those anticipated. (4) In some circumstances, an amount levied against mutual owners of an enterprise to cover specified deficiencies.

assessment bond A type of special-tax municipal bond. Funds raised are used to build sewer systems, pave sidewalks, and so on. Assessment bonds are repaid from related taxes, such as real estate or property taxes.

assessment ratio The ratio of the assessed value to the full or true value of property for the purpose of calculating real estate taxes.

assessor A person who evaluates property for the purpose of taxation.

asset Anything owned by a business or individual that has commercial, exchange, or book value. Assets may consist of specific property or claims against others, in contrast to obligations due to others (liabilities). They may be tangible (physical in character), such as land, buildings, and machinery, or intangible (characterized by legal claims or rights), such as amounts due from customers (accounts receivable) and patents (a protected right). Under generally accepted accounting principles, an asset is defined as the probable future economic benefits obtained or controlled by a particular entity as a result of past transactions or events.

See also current assets; frozen assets; intangible assets; pledged assets; tangible assets.

asset account Any account listed on the asset side of a business firm's balance sheet.

asset-backed securities *See* securitization.

asset-based loan Any loan that is secured by the borrower's assets. The loan is generally short-term and the security is typically inventory or accounts receivable.

asset card *See* debit card.

asset cost In leasing, the actual property cost before any adjustments for a down payment or trade-in.

asset ledger An itemized bookkeeping system for a bank's or department's assets, including earning assets, such as interest-bearing bank deposits, securities held, loans, lease financing, cash due, or real estate acquired.

asset/liability management The management of a bank's assets and liabilities to maximize long-term wealth for the bank's shareholders. This requires planning to meet needs for liquidity, avoiding excessive risk of default, planning maturities to avoid unwanted exposure to interest-rate risk, and controlling interest rates offered and paid to ensure an adequate spread between the cost of, and the return on, funds.

asset/liability management committee The management committee in a bank responsible for asset/liability management.

asset maintenance requirements Loan provisions requiring a borrower to adhere to agreed conditions regarding asset holdings.

asset management (1) The management and control of asset maturities and rates to achieve the banking goals of profit, safety, and liquidity. (2) A service performed by full-service brokerage firms that involves tailoring an investment portfolio to meet the individual investor's specific needs and investment goals.

asset securitization The packaging of assets with similar characteristics into a security.

assets repriced before liabilities (ARBL) A measure of the gap between maturities of assets and liabilities. ARBL is used in the management of bank funds. *See also* gap.

asset utilization A measure of the gross yield earned on assets. It is calculated by dividing total operating income (interest and noninterest revenue) by average total assets.

asset valuation The process by which the worth of a company's assets is determined item by item.

asset value The value of assets.

assign To sign a document transferring ownership, or giving the right to transfer ownership later, on security or loan collateral.

assigned account An account that has been assigned to a lender as security on a loan.

assignee (1) One to whom an assignment has been made. (2) A person appointed by another or by a court to do some act or enjoy some right, privilege, or property.

assignment The transfer in writing by one person to another of the title to property, rights, or other interests. For example, the assignment of stocks or registered bonds may be effected by filling in the form printed on the reverse of the certificate or by executing a separate assignment form.

assignment (swap market) The sale of a swap contract by one party to another, usually for a lump-sum payment. Swap assignments are cumbersome because they require the approval of the remaining original party.

assignment guarantee agreement The agreement among a guaranteeing agency, a bank, and the holder of a note to whom the bank has assigned the guaranteed portion of a loan. The agreement sets forth the terms of the assignment.

assignment of mortgage A document evidencing the transfer of mortgage ownership from one person to another.

assignor (1) One who makes an assignment. (2) A person who transfers the title to property, a right, or other interest.

associate member A bank that participates in a credit plan administered by another bank or group of banks. *Also called* associate bank.

assumed bond A bond for which a corporation other than the issuer will pay the interest and principal, as they fall due.

assumption agreement *See* assumption of mortgage.

assumption fee A fee charged for permitting a home buyer to assume the mortgage loan already outstanding on a home.

assumption of mortgage A contract, by deed or other form, through which a buyer accepts the obligation of an existing mortgage. The seller remains liable for this mortgage unless released by the lender from this obligation. *Also called* assumption agreement.

ATRR *See* allocated transfer risk reserve.

attachment (1) A legal writ of process for seizing a person's property and bringing it into the custody of the law; or a process for seizing money in the hands of a third person who may become liable to pay it over. (2) The seizure of property by court order. Attachments are usually taken to provide security in a pending suit.

attest To bear witness to, to authenticate, or to affirm the truth of a document, for example, to attest a will.

attestation clause The clause of a document containing the formal declaration of the witnesses that the document has been executed before them. In the case of a will, the attestation clause immediately follows the signature of the testator and usually begins, "signed, sealed, published, and declared by the said. . ."

attesting witness One who signs his or her name to a document, for the purpose of providing and identifying the document. *Distinguish from* subscribing witness.

at-the-market In buying or selling securities, a transaction executed at the current market price, rather than at a predetermined price.

at-the-money An option is at-the-money when the price of the underlying instrument is very close or equal to the option's exercise price.

at-the-opening order A securities transaction that is to be executed at the opening of a market or not at all.

attorney at law A person who is legally qualified and authorized to represent and act for clients in legal proceedings. *Distinguish from* attorney-in-fact.

attorney-in-fact (1) An individual authorized by another to act on his or her behalf. (2) A person who, acting as agent, is given written authorization by another person to transact business for that person out of court. *Distinguish from* attorney at law. *See also* power of attorney.

attribute sampling Statistical sampling from an attributes population (that is, a population where every item has a particular attribute).

attribution For purposes of the Internal Revenue Code sections dealing with stock redemptions and stock ownership, attribution refers to particular situations in which one family member (or a trust or estate) is deemed to own stock held by another family member (or trust or estate). The attribution of ownership between family members or trusts or estates may have adverse consequences in a stock redemption.

auction (1) A public sale of property or property rights in which bidders bid against each other, with the bidder who offers the highest bid purchasing the property. (2) The type of market in a stock or other exchange. The term "auction" is appropriate, because sellers who cannot find buyers at their asked prices lower their prices until a buyer accepts, while buyers raise their prices until a seller accepts.

auction marketplace *See* auction.

auction rate securities Securities that use an auction, or bidding, mechanism to reset the rate periodically at which dividends or interest payments are to accrue.

audio response An automated voice response to a coded request for authorization, balance information, or other inquiry.

audit An official examination and verification of accounts. *See also* detailed audit.

audit charter A formal document that establishes the objectives and responsibilities of the internal audit department.

audit committee A committee made up of bank directors responsible for monitoring the internal audit organization and activities.

audit department The bank department responsible for providing the board of directors and senior management with reasonable assurance that the organization is in compliance with management's system of internal controls. The department is also responsible for evaluating the efficiency and effectiveness of those controls.

audited financial statement A financial statement that has been audited in conformity with generally accepted auditing standards by a certified public accountant and is accompanied by the auditor's opinion.

auditing The systematic examination of a company's records and documents to determine the legality of transactions and the accuracy of records. *See also* anticipatory auditing.

auditor The bank officer, usually appointed by and reporting to the board of directors, who is responsible for examining any and all phases of the bank's operations.

audit plan A detailed description of audit work to be performed by the internal audit department during an established time period (cycle).

audit program A detailed list of specific audit procedures to be performed during an audit.

audit risk The complement of that portion of assurance that comes specifically from audit procedures, audit risk is one of the components, along with inherent risk and control risk, that make up the final risk of undetected material error.

audit sample A segment of the population (for example, account holders) selected by a sampling method for the purpose of investigating the properties of the population. *See also* sample.

audit scope A definition of the limitations of the audit work to be performed.

audit software Internal audit computer programs designed to aid the auditor in accumulating audit evidence and/or detecting internal control deficiencies.

audit trail (1) A reporting or record-keeping method that presents a clear path for auditors to follow. (2) A chronological record of system activities that allows the reconstruction or review of the sequence of events for an electronic data-processing transaction from its inception to final output.

audit trail number A 10-digit number recorded on the top right-hand corner of a payment for tracing purposes.

authenticated copy A copy of a document whose similarity to the original has been evidenced in the manner required by law, as by the certification and seal of a specified public official.

authentication (1) The signing, by the trustee, of a certificate on a bond, to identify and validate the bond as being issued under a certain indenture. (2) Identification or verification of the eligibility of a station or person to access specific categories of information. (3) A measure designed to protect against fraudulent transmissions by establishing the validity of a transmission, message, station, or person. (4) Determination that a message comes from a source authorized to originate messages of that type.

authentication key A cryptographic key used for authentication. When this key is applied to the authentication algorithm, a message authentication code (MAC) will result. The MAC is a result of a bilateral agreement between the sender and receiver regarding the method of calculation.

authority to pay An advice indicating the place of payment but not requiring a bank to make the payment.

authority to purchase Permission received by a bank to purchase drafts drawn on an importer.

authorization The issuance of approval, by or on behalf of a card issuer, a merchant, or another affiliate, to complete a transaction. *Also called* credit authorization.

authorization center A facility established to authorize cash advances and merchant sales exceeding preestablished floor limits.

authorization code A number assigned by a bank to a merchant sale or cash advance that has received specific approval. The authorization code is used as proof that the trans-

action has been properly authorized. *Also called* authorization number.

authorization department The department responsible for providing telephone approval for purchases and cash advances.

authorization in float *See* authorization outstanding.

authorization message (1) A coded message used to access a computer authorization system. (2) The response generated by a computer authorization system in answer to an inquiry.

authorization number *See* authorization code.

authorization outstanding An authorization for a transaction that has been approved but for which the bank has not yet received and posted the sales draft. *Also called* authorization in float.

authorization request A request for approval of a financial transaction, by or on behalf of the card issuer.

authorization reversal A nonmonetary transaction, issued to reverse a previous authorization, that increases an account's available credit by the amount of the authorization.

authorized common stock (1) The maximum number of shares of common stock that a corporation can issue, as stipulated in its charter. (2) The total number of common shares that the board of directors has authorized a company to issue. The board of directors must vote on any increase in this authorized amount.

authorized dealer A bank that is permitted by its regulators to deal in foreign exchange.

authorized investment An investment that is authorized by the trust instrument. *Distinguish from* legal investment.

authorized settlement agent A bank in the United States that clears cash items either directly or indirectly through the Federal Reserve System and that a VISA International clearing member has authorized to prepare or honor clearing drafts for the settlement of interchange.

authorized signature The signature(s) affixed to a negotiable instrument of the party or parties who have the legal right to issue instructions for its handling.

authorizing member A member of a credit card clearing association that provides authorization facilities for its merchants and other members.

automated balance reporting service A service that provides balance data via a computer network for the purpose of managing balances and banking relationships.

automated clearing house (ACH) A clearing facility operated for the convenience of the banks in a particular region, generally through the regional Federal Reserve bank. Automated clearing houses electronically process interbank credits and debits. They may also handle the electronic transfer of government securities and customer services, such as the automatic deposit of customers' wages, direct deposit of Social Security payments, and preauthorized payments of bills by banks.

automated deposit reporting service (1) A deposit reporting service that typically involves a computer network. (2) A service in which a depository bank prepares a depository transfer check for either the daily

deposit or the excess over a minimum balance at a specified time.

automated funds transfer service A service that allows corporations and banks to initiate and confirm funds transfers via a computer network.

automated teller machine (ATM) A machine, activated by a magnetically encoded card or by the transmission of a code via a keyboard or keyset, that allows customers to perform routine banking transactions, such as withdrawal and deposit of funds, transfer of funds between accounts, and the payment of certain obligations.

automated transit The reading, calculating, accumulating, printing, and sorting of out-of-city MICR-encoded items by MICR sorters/readers, high-speed check listers, and computers.

automatic bill payment Payment by one check to many creditors or direct payment by the bank for specified recurring bills. *Also called* multiple payee checking.

automatic chargeback A transaction that does not meet the conditions for acceptance by a bank, as set forth in a merchant agreement.

automatic data processing (ADP) Data processing performed by a system of electronic machines interconnected to minimize the need for human involvement.

automatic deposit plan A plan by which the customer arranges for checks (payroll, Social Security, and so on) to be sent directly to a bank and deposited into a savings or checking account.

automatic dividend reinvestment A plan, offered by the issuer or by a mutual fund, in which the investor can instruct the other party to pay dividends in additional shares of stock rather than cash.

automatic investment The process by which dividends or interest earned by securities is automatically reinvested to purchase more of the same or other specified securities.

automatic stay The term used to describe the law that prohibits a creditor from taking further actions to collect a debt, repossess its collateral, or perfect its security interest after the borrower files a petition in bankruptcy.

automatic transfer of funds The movement of funds between accounts under prearranged conditions, according to an earlier agreement between a bank and a customer.

automatic transfer service (ATS) A service by which a bank moves funds from one type of account to another for its customer on a preauthorized basis.

automatic transfer systems (ATS) Electronic banking systems through which customers can make deposits, withdraw funds, and automatically transfer funds between savings and checking accounts.

auxiliary storage (1) A storage that supplements another storage. *Compare with* main storage. (2) In making a flowchart, an off-line operation performed by equipment not controlled by the central processing unit (CPU).

availability The unrestricted access of a depositor to an account balance. The available balance in an account is the amount subject to withdrawal. The Competitive Equality Banking Act of 1987 requires banks to make deposited funds available to customers within specified time limits.

availability factor A number expressing the average delay between date of deposit and date of credit to the depositor's collected balance.

availability schedule A list indicating the number of days that must elapse before deposited checks can be considered converted into usable funds. The time period is based on the location of the bank on which the deposited check is drawn. Posting of this schedule is mandated by the Expedited Funds Availability Act.

available balance The portion of a customer's account balance on which the bank has placed no restrictions, making it available for immediate withdrawal.

available credit The difference between the credit limit assigned to an open-end credit plan and the present balance outstanding, including any authorization outstanding.

available funds *See* same day funds (preferred term).

aval (From the French, meaning (1) guarantee or endorsement and (2) below, downward, or under.) An endorsement to the guarantee of a bill of exchange, usually placed at the bottom of an instrument. This guarantee is used occasionally to support weak credit risks.

average balance The average balance outstanding on a cardholder or other account within a specified period.

average collected balance The sum of the daily balances of an account, less uncollected items, divided by the number of days in the period being measured.

average collection period The average number of days required to collect accounts receivable. *See also* turn-over ratio (the reciprocal of the collection period).

average daily balance (1) The aver-age amount of money kept on deposit by a customer, determined by adding either all or selected daily balances and dividing by the number of balances taken. (2) The average daily credit card balance outstanding during a billing cycle or other specified peri-od. The average daily balance is calculated by dividing the aggregate of the balance outstanding at the close of each day during the billing cycle by the number of days in the billing cycle.

average daily float The portion of a customer's account balance that consists of deposited checks that are in the process of collection. The aver-age daily float is deducted from the average book balance for purposes of account analysis.

average draft size *See* average ticket, average sale.

average fixed cost The total fixed costs of an operation (those costs that are constant and do not change with output) divided by the total number of units produced.

average monthly balance The aver-age balance in an account within a specified period. The average month-ly balance is calculated by adding all of the monthly balances on an account within a specified period and dividing the total by the number of months within that period.

average outstanding balance The average balance outstanding on all cardholders or other accounts within a specified period. The average outstanding balance is calculated by dividing the total balance outstanding

by the number of accounts with balances.

average shares In an annual earnings report, the average number of shares outstanding.

average ticket, average sale The average amount on all sales drafts received by a bank during a specific period. This amount is calculated by adding the totals on all sales drafts received within a specified period and dividing the total by the number of sales drafts received within that peri-od. Cash advances can be similarly identified. *Also called* average draft size.

average total cost The total cost (total fixed costs plus total variable costs) divided by the total number of units produced. *Also called* average cost.

average variable cost The total vari-able costs (those costs directly related to output) divided by the total number of units produced.

averaging up or down The practice of purchasing the same security at differ-ent prices, thereby arriving at a higher or a lower average cost than the cost of the original purchase.

award An allowance by a judge or an arbitrator. *Distinguish from* decree *and* judgment.

away A secondhand quote. A dealer may refer to another dealer's bid as "away."

baby bond A bond with a face value of $100 or less.

back contracts The most distant futures contracts in the market, that is, those that will not soon mature.

back-to-back commitment A commitment composed of two commitments --one issued by a lender to advance a construction loan and another issued by the same lender to close and retain a permanent loan on the property.

back-to-back letters of credit Two letters of credit issued to cover the same shipment of merchandise where the first letter of credit is used as security to issue the second credit to another beneficiary. Typically, the beneficiary of the first credit is an agent, and needs the second credit to pay a supplier.

back-to-back loans Two parties in different countries make loans to one another of equal value, with each loan denominated in the currency of the lender and each maturing on the same date. The payment flows are identical to those of spot and forward currency transactions. Currency swaps have a similar structure, except that there is not necessarily any loan on the balance sheet.

back up (1) To shorten the maturity of one's investments. (2) (Verb) Used to describe bond or other markets that tend to become congested when prices fall.

backup procedures The provisions made for the recovery of data files and program libraries after a system failure or a disaster.

backup withholding The procedure by which a payor of interest must withhold a portion of the earnings under certain conditions. Backup withholding is required by the Interest and Dividend Tax Compliance Act of 1983.

bad debt *See* charge-off.

bad debt ratio *See* loss ratio.

bad debt recovery The collection of funds on an account that has been charged off for possible credit losses.

bail To deliver property in trust to another person or legal entity for a certain purpose and limited period.

bail bond A bond guaranteeing the appearance of a prisoner at a trial or whenever required.

bailee (1) An individual or other legal entity that receives and holds personal property under a contract of bailment. (2) A person who receives goods or money from another person in trust. *Also called* pledgee.

bailment The delivery of personal property by one person, the bailor, to another, the bailee, for a limited period and for some specific purpose, such as use, repairs, or safekeeping, but without passing title to the property. *See also* gratuitous bailment.

bailor A person who delivers property in trust to another person or legal entity for a certain purpose and limited period. *Also called* pledgor.

B.A.I. School of Bank Administration A school sponsored by the Bank Administration Institute for bank auditors, operating officers, and comptrollers.

balance The generic term referring to the amount of funds in an account. The book balance is a simple statement showing the posting of all debits and credits; the collected balance is the book balance minus all float; and the available balance is the amount that the depositor may withdraw.

balance as a whole In bookkeeping, a proof method in which each of several bookkeepers is responsible for a subset of the total accounts. At the end of a posting run, the bookkeepers add their combined totals and "balance as a whole" to the control total for their ledger group. If the total for the entire group of accounts balances, there is a balance as a whole.

balance certificate *See* transfer agent custodian (TAC) program.

balanced budget A budget in which projected expenditures and receipts are equal for a given period.

balanced funds Mutual funds that invest in a mix of common stock, preferred stock, and bonds. The companies selected are in different industries and different geographical regions.

balance due (on credit cards) The dollar amount representing the sum of the previous balance due plus cash advances and merchandise purchases for the billing period less credit for payments and/or merchandise credits received, plus any appropriate finance charge.

balance inquiry A nonfinancial transaction that permits a cardholder to obtain the current balance of his or her account. A balance inquiry can be performed at an unattended terminal only by the cardholder.

balance of account The amount needed to equate the total debits and credits posted to any given account.

balance of payments A system that records all of a country's receipts from and payments to foreign countries during a given period.

balance-of-payments table A summary of transactions (loans, investments, repayments, donations, and other transfers of funds) in a given period. It is published for the U.S. Department of Commerce.

balance-of-stores ledger A ledger used by a manufacturer's purchasing department to record production materials on hand, ordered, available, and apportioned against orders for finished products that have been received or are expected.

balance of trade The difference between a nation's exports and imports of merchandise over a given period.

balance-order settlement A process for settling securities trades through a clearing house. Accounting for the transaction concludes on settlement date, at which time due to and due from obligations are fixed. *See also* continuous net settlement (CNS); trade-for-trade (TFT) settlement.

balance sheet A detailed list of assets, liabilities, and owners' equity (net worth), showing a company's financial position at a specific time. A bank's balance sheet is generally called a statement of condition.

balance sheet management The management and control of quantities of and rates on all items in the balance sheet, including capital, in order to achieve the banking goals of profit, safety, and liquidity. *Also called* funds management.

balloon maturity (1) A loan requiring a much larger payment at maturity than on earlier payment dates. (2) A bond issue with substantially larger payments due at later maturity dates. (3) A mortgage in which installment payments do not fully amortize the loan. At the end of the term, the balance is due in a lump sum or "balloon" payment.

balloon mortgage A mortgage in which the debt service (interest and principal) that is paid regularly will not result in the complete payment of the loan at the end of the mortgage term. The payment that represents the amount of principal still due at the end of the term is called the balloon payment. "To balloon" a mortgage is to schedule the amortization payments over a longer period than the term of the mortgage.

balloon payment The last payment on a loan when that payment is substantially larger than other earlier payments.

band of investment A method of deriving rates of capitalization by weighting the return on various interests in real estate.

bank (1) As defined by the Bank Holding Company Act, an institution that accepts demand deposits and makes commercial loans, or that is insured by the FDIC. Commercial banks are described as full-service institutions because of the additional functions they handle, over and above those mentioned above. (2) Any organization under the laws of a foreign country that engages in the business of banking as defined by the applicable foreign law. *See also* central bank; correspondent bank; industrial bank; national bank; nonmember bank; savings bank; state bank; state member bank; trust company.

Bank Administration Institute (B.A.I.) An organization of bank and savings and loan officials that formulates and encourages the use of standard auditing and operating procedures. The B.A.I. was originally founded in 1924 as the National Association of Bank Auditors and Comptrollers (NABAC).

Bank Bribery Act A federal law amended in 1985 that makes it a felony for employees of federally insured banks to fraudulently give or receive anything of value in connection with any business of the bank.

bank card A card issued to anyone who satisfies a bank's credit criteria. This card may be used as a means of (a) identifying to participating merchants a person for whom funds are available at the issuing bank and (b) ensuring that the issuing bank will purchase sales drafts submitted by the merchants and bearing the imprint of the card. A bank card may be either a credit or debit card, and the specific financial arrangements with the issuing bank may not be discernible from the card.

bank card association A group of banks formed either to sponsor a single identity, for example, VISA or MasterCard, or to operate a credit or debit card plan jointly through the use of common processing and administrative facilities.

bank card processing center The physical facility where bank card operations are conducted.

bank certificate of deposit *See* negotiable certificate of deposit (CD).

bank charge plan A plan initiated by a bank to reimburse merchants for purchases made by the bank's credit card holders. Merchants and customers both pay a fee for this service.

bank check (1) Any payment document written against an account maintained by a financial institution for the transfer of a dollar amount from one party to another. The term includes variable-amount payment documents, such as personal, business, and government checks, and drafts. (2) A draft drawn by a bank against its own funds, or funds deposited to its account in another bank, and payable immediately on demand.

bank credit The total loans and discounts at all commercial banks. It also refers to the credit made available to a borrower.

bank credit card A credit card, issued by a bank, used to indicate to participating merchants that the issuing bank has established a line of credit for the cardholder and will purchase sales drafts submitted by the merchant.

bank debits Checks and other instruments charged against the funds deposited in a bank.

bank directors Those people responsible to the stockholders of a bank for its management, and to governing authorities for the sound and legal operation of the bank. The bank's stockholders elect the bank directors.

bank discount A bank's charge for discounting a promissory note or bill of exchange, usually equal to simple interest on the note or bill's face value.

bank discount rate The rate at which short-term market instruments without coupons are quoted. A bank discount rate is the net present value of the principal at maturity. It is less than the bond equivalent rate on coupon bonds, and a rate adjustment calculation must be made to compare rates.

bank draft A draft written by a bank against its funds on deposit with another bank, domestic or foreign.

bank elasticity The likelihood that customers will change banks in response to a change in the price of services.

bank eligible issues Securities that bank regulatory agencies consider to be of sufficient quality to represent sound investments for banks. Examples of bank eligible issues include U.S. Treasury securities, commercial paper, and federal agency securities. Banks are generally not permitted to invest in stocks of other companies or in state or municipal securities that are rated below the top four classifications.

bank endorsement An identifying inscription placed on the back of all items passing through a bank, except for cash letters, on-us checks, or checks from clearing house exchanges.

bankers' acceptance A time draft (bill of exchange) drawn on and accepted by the bank on which it was drawn (that is, stamped with the word "accepted" and signed by a representative of the bank). It usually arises from international trade transactions where there is an underlying obligation of a buyer to make payment to a seller at some future time. Many bankers' acceptances are created when payment is made by a letter of credit. In all instances, the bank accepting the draft assumes the obligation of making payment at maturity on behalf of the buyer or the buyer's bank.

bankers' and brokers' blanket bond A fidelity bond that provides protection against losses incurred by financial institutions. *Also called* financial institutions' bond.

bankers' bill *See* bankers' acceptance.

bank examination A detailed scrutiny of a bank's assets, liabilities, income, and expenses by authorized bank examiners representing a federal or state agency. The examination is performed to ensure the bank's sound operation, proper statement of financial condition, and proper following of applicable laws and regulations.

bank examiner An individual who represents a state or federal regulatory agency in performing a bank examination.

bank float Deposits credited to a depositor's account in one bank but not yet collected from the bank on which the items were drawn.

Bank for International Settlements (BIS) A financial institution in Basle, Switzerland, that acts as a type of central bank for the central banks of the western industrialized nations.

bank holding company (BHC) A corporation that owns, controls, or otherwise has the power to vote at least 25 percent of the voting stock in one or more banks. All BHCs come under the jurisdiction of the Federal Reserve.

Bank Holding Company Act The 1956 act that applied federal antitrust laws to the activities of multibank holding companies and gave the Federal Reserve the power to approve or deny applications from multibank holding companies that wanted to acquire additional banks or engage in new business activities. The act also limited activities of multibank holding companies to those directly related to banking. A 1970 amendment to the act embraced one-bank holding companies.

bank identification number (BIN) (1) The numerator of the fraction printed in the upper right-hand corner of a check, which identifies a particular bank and its location. (2) A series or group of digits used to identify card-issuing banks, bank card associations, or interchange groups.

Bank Insurance Fund (BIF) A fund created in 1989 under the Financial Institutions Reform, Recovery and Enforcement Act that receives the deposit insurance premiums that banks pay to the FDIC. *See also* Deposit Insurance Fund (DIF); Federal Deposit Insurance Corporation assessment.

bank investment contract (BIC) An investment instrument offered by banks and used primarily by pension and profit-sharing plans. The instrument is structured as a time deposit, open account that guarantees both the principal and the rate of return for a specified period. In addition, each participant's vested interest in the pension plan is guaranteed by FDIC insurance up to the current limit of $100,000. *See also* guaranteed investment contract.

bank line A preapproved agreement to lend up to a certain amount at the borrower's request if terms are agreeable.

bank note (1) A written promise to pay a certain sum of money to a bank that holds a note on or before a certain date. (2) Currency issued by a bank. Note issues of individual banks are no longer circulated.

Bank Protection Act of 1968 The federal law enacted to discourage bank robberies and other crimes against banks by setting minimum standards for a variety of security measures.

bank range The maturities of securities that are most attractive to banks, generally 2 to 7 years.

bank run A rapid loss of deposits precipitated by fear on the part of the public that a bank may fail.

bankrupt A corporation or other legal entity that is unable to meet its financial obligations. A person in bankruptcy proceedings is called a debtor.

bankruptcy The legal proceedings governed by the Bankruptcy Code.

Bankruptcy Code The law governing bankruptcy proceedings. The Bankruptcy Code was overhauled by the Bankruptcy Reform Act of 1978, and it was amended in 1984 and 1986. Chapter 7 is the traditional bankruptcy proceeding, in which a trustee is appointed who is charged with liquidating the debtor's estate and making a distribution to the debtor's unsecured creditors. Chapter 11 deals with business reorganizations. Unless circumstances warrant, there is no trustee appointed, but the business is allowed to put forth a plan that, if accepted, would allow the debtor to continue in business. Chapter 12 is a reorganization for family farmers, patterned after Chapters 11 and 13. Chapter 13 is often referred to as the wage-earner plan, because it allows persons to repay their creditors through future earnings in a plan not to exceed 5 years.

Bank Secrecy Act A federal act that requires banks to report cash transactions that exceed $10,000 in any one day. The act also requires that certain records be maintained (copies of checks paid, deposits, and so on). The act is intended to inhibit laundering of funds obtained through illegal activities. Every bank is required to name a Bank Secrecy Compliance Officer. *See also* laundered money.

bank service corporation A corporation owned by and providing special financial services to commercial banks.

banks for cooperatives (coops) Any of several banks that make loans to

farmers' associations. Coop bonds are issued to finance these loans. The bonds are not guaranteed by the U.S. Treasury, but they are secured obligations of banks operating with governmental supervision. Coops are supervised by the Farm Credit Administration.

bank statement A statement of a customer's checking account issued periodically by a bank, usually monthly. A bank statement shows the balance at the beginning of the period, all deposits and other credits, all checks and other debits, and the balance at the end of the period. A bank usually returns canceled checks and debits to the depositor with the statement.

bank statement period (Fed) The period (generally 14 days) over which a bank's reserve requirements are assessed or held.

bank-to-bank information A data element in funds transfers that specifies miscellaneous information pertaining to a transfer, including the bank(s) for which the information is intended.

barbell A portfolio in which maturities are concentrated in the short and long ends of the maturity spectrum, with no intermediate maturities.

bare trust *See* passive trust.

bargain and sale deed A deed that conveys title with no warranties.

bargain purchase option A provision allowing a lessee to purchase leased property for a price sufficiently lower than the expected fair market value of the property on the date the option can be exercised so that the exercise of the option appears, at the inception of the lease, to be reasonably assured.

bargain renewal option A provision allowing a lessee to renew the lease for a rental sufficiently lower than the fair rental value of the property at the time the option can be exercised so that the exercise of the option appears, at the inception of the lease, to be reasonably assured.

barometer stock A single stock whose price fluctuates with general economic conditions. It is therefore used as an index of trends in the market.

Barron's Confidence Index An index that compares yields on bonds that carry very high ratings with yields on bonds that carry low ratings. The spread between high- and low-rated bond yields supposedly reflects investors' confidence.

barter The trade of goods or services without the exchange of money.

BASE Central The operations center for VISA U.S.A. that provides BASE I, BASE II, and central computer services. *See also* BASE I; BASE II.

base data Data from which conclusions can be drawn, that a computer can internally access, and on which the computer performs operations.

base drift The shifting of base levels against which money supply targets are set. For a period of time, the Federal Reserve set its targets for money growth based on the average level of the money stock for an earlier period. As each new target was set, the base period was shifted forward. When the money supply exceeded the prescribed growth for one period, the base for the next period was accordingly higher (base drift). Thus, the actual growth rate for the two periods would be higher than the average of the reported growth rates for each period.

BASE I A data-processing network of VISA U.S.A., capable of providing message processing and authorization services, file services, and others, as may be specified by VISA's operating regulations.

BASE I activity file A file maintained at BASE Central that contains a record of cardholder account numbers for which authorizations have been given in the past 4 days.

BASE I exception file A file maintained at BASE Central that contains those cardholder account numbers for which the issuer has requested other than routine authorization.

BASE I user An authorizing member of VISA who, through a terminal or computer device, connects to BASE I for authorization and other services. BASE I users include those foreign affiliates who are identified on interchange data forms and all U.S. affiliates.

base period A period of time that is chosen as a base for measuring changes in data. For example, an analyst might say that a company's sales have risen 50 percent from those in an earlier (base) period.

base rate A rate used by banks to price loans. The actual loan rate is typically a predetermined markup over the bank's base rate, which is derived from one of several commonly used indices such as the federal funds rate or the London interbank offered rate (LIBOR). The markup reflects the perceived risk of the borrower. *See also* prime rate.

base rent In leasing terminology, the periodic payment required less the use or sales taxes.

BASE II An electronic draft data transmission system owned by VISA U.S.A. for the exchange of sales draft data by VISA U.S.A. and VISA International clearing members. The system includes all BASE II equipment, software, processes, techniques, programs, and information provided by VISA U.S.A. and used in connection with the system.

BASE II request A request sent by one bank card processing center through BASE II for a copy of a specific sales draft retained at another bank card processing center.

BASE II sales draft A purchase identified by a reference number that begins with "4."

base-year analysis The analysis of financial statements in which the figures for other years are compared with those of a common, earlier (base) year.

basic banking A term that refers to basic banking services for the underprivileged and elderly. This concept has been the subject of several proposed bills in Congress in the 1980s, but it has not been passed into law as of this writing. However, it is referred to in the Community Reinvestment Act (CRA) policy statements adopted by the Federal Deposit Insurance Corporation, Office of the Comptroller of the Currency, Federal Savings and Loan Insurance Corporation, and the Federal Reserve.

basic value The worth of rural property, derived from earnings under typical operation and from locational and home-usage features.

basing point price system A method of quoting prices for goods based on a hypothetical common location for production, regardless of where production actually occurs.

basis (1) The difference between prices of, or rates on, related but not identical assets. An example of basis is the difference between the cash price and a futures contract price for a commodity. The parallel term most commonly used in trading financial instruments is "spread." *See also* spread. (2) The number of days in a bond coupon period.

basis book A book of mathematical tables used to convert yields to maturity into equivalent prices at various interest rates.

basis point (bp) One one-hundredth (1/100) of 1 percent. Basis points are used in connection with interest rates or yields. *See also* pip; point.

basis price The price expressed in yield to maturity or in net return on an investment.

basket provision The laws and regulations governing savings institutions and life insurance companies that allow a certain percentage of the institution's total assets to be invested in investments not otherwise specified by the law. This percentage is known as the basket clause. *Compare with* legal investment.

batch header A process control document that is numbered serially and precedes a batch of items to be processed.

batch header ticket *See* merchant summary slip.

batch processing (1) A technique used to code and collect items into groups before processing. (2) A system that groups many similar input items for processing during the same machine run. *Also called* off-line batch processing.

batch proof A system for reconciling data on deposits. Deposits, checks, deposit tickets, and cash release tickets are first sorted separately and then the total deposits and other credits are compared against the total checks and other debits.

batch separator A control document that separates and organizes a group of records representing a single processing unit.

batch sheet The proof sheet used in the batch proof system.

Bayesian analysis A statistical method for assigning subjective probabilities to uncertain possible events. The analyst uses his or her best judgment to assign the probability of each alternative actually happening. As results become available, the assigned probabilities are revised to reflect the actual occurrences. The revised probabilities are then used to make new projections. This type of analysis is used to forecast sales of a new product.

bear An investor who believes the price of an asset is likely to decline and sells accordingly. *Compare with* bull.

bearer Any person or company that has physical possession of a check, security, or any negotiable financial instrument with no name entered on it as payee. Any bearer can present such an instrument for payment.

bearer bond A bond for which the owner's name is not registered on the issuer's books. Title passes by delivery, and interest and principal are payable to the bondholder. Coupons are usually attached to the bearer bonds to facilitate the payment of interest. In 1983, the Tax Equity and Fiscal Responsibility Act subjected bearer bonds to adverse tax consequences, and so they are no longer issued.

bearer form A type of instrument payable to the person in possession of it.

bearer security A security whose ownership is not registered in anyone's name. Thus, principal and interest or dividends belong to anyone who physically holds the security.

bearer stock Capital stock evidenced by certificates that are not registered in any name. The certificates are negotiable without endorsement and transferable by delivery. They carry numbered or dated dividend coupons.

bear market A market with generally declining stock (or other) prices. *Compare with* bull market.

below-the-line An extraordinary revenue or expense, or some other extraordinary and material nonrecurring item, that requires a separate grouping on a company's balance sheet or income statement.

below-the-market A price or rate lower than the prevailing level at which a security is currently quoted or traded.

benchmark A standard or rule to which other items or processes can be compared.

benchmark problem A hypothetical problem used to evaluate the performance of hardware or software.

benchmark program A sample program for comparing and evaluating computers or computer systems.

beneficial interest The profit, benefit, or advantage resulting from a contract or use of property, as distinct from legal ownership.

beneficial owner The true owner of a security. For the convenience or well-being of the beneficial owner, the name of a fiduciary may appear as the legal owner, but the fiduciary is bound to act always in the best interest of the beneficial owner. Under the securities laws, beneficial ownership may reside with any person who, directly or indirectly, has or shares voting power and/or investment power.

beneficiary The party legally entitled to receive the proceeds of an insurance policy, letter of credit, trust fund, or other transaction.

beneficiary deduct service A service in which commercial funds transfers, originated by a nonbank for ultimate payment to a nonbank beneficiary, are paid for by deducting the proceeds of the payment from the principal of the transfer. The service is common in foreign commercial payments, but relatively new to funds transfer payments in the United States.

beneficiary's bank A bank that acts as the financial agent for the beneficiary of a transfer. *Also called* account with bank.

beneficiary's bank information A data element in funds transfers that specifies miscellaneous information pertaining to the transfer and intended for the beneficiary's bank only.

beneficiary type A code that specifies whether the beneficiary in a funds transfer is a bank or a nonbank.

benefit-cost ratio The ratio of the marginal or incremental benefits associated with an investment project to the marginal or incremental cost of the same project.

benefit segmentation Categorizing the market according to the main product-related benefits sought by different groups of consumers (for

example, the cost-conscious, the convenience-oriented).

BEO (book-entry only) securities *See* book-entry securities.

bequeath To give personal property by will.

bequest A gift of personal property provided for in a will. *Distinguish from* devise.

best efforts *See* takedown method.

best interests of creditors' test In bankruptcy proceedings, the holding of law that prohibits a debtor from giving less to the secured creditors than the value of the collateral plus reasonable interest. Also, in a Chapter 13 proceeding, this rule requires the debtor to put forth a plan that would provide at least as much to the creditors as if the debtor were liquidated under Chapter 7 of the Bankruptcy Code.

beta (1) A coefficient that measures the effect of an independent (predictor) variable on the dependent variable (the one being predicted). (2) A measure of the relative volatility of the price of a stock. A stock with a high beta coefficient (greater than one) is more volatile than the market average. *Also called* beta coefficient.

beta risk The risk of erroneously accepting a bad population (that is, one containing a material aggregate error).

betterments Improvements to real property, other than mere repairs, that add to its value.

biased view *See* uncovered writers.

bid (1) A price offered by those wishing to buy given stocks, bonds, or other assets. (2) A price that a dealer is willing to pay for a security. (3) A competitive offer to obtain a contract for work.

bid and asked prices Prices quoted by market makers on over-the-counter stocks. The bid price is the price at which the market maker will buy the security. The asked price is the proposed selling price of the security.

Big Board The New York Stock Exchange.

bilateral contract An agreement, enforceable by law, between two persons or groups.

bilateral net credit limit The maximum amount of net transfers (that is, the value of receives in excess of sends) that each receiver determines it is willing to receive from each sender at any time, as is now the case on CHIPS.

billable currency The currency in which the bank card issuer bills the cardholder for transactions. A Canadian, for example, might be billed in U.S. or Canadian dollars.

bill adjustment An action taken either to correct a billing error on a cardholder account or to satisfy a cardholder's complaint.

bill-check A combination bill and check. The retailer sends the bill-check to the customer, who signs and returns it. The retailer then makes up a tape and sends it to the automated clearing house, which credits the retailer's bank and debits the customer's bank. The customer controls the time of payment, but actual payment is made electronically.

billing cycle The time interval between the dates on which regular periodic billing statements are issued.

billing date The month, day, and year when a periodic or monthly statement is generated and on which calculations for appropriate finance charges, minimum payment due, and new balance have been performed. The actual billing date is usually shown in a prominent location on each monthly statement.

billing error An inaccuracy in a periodic statement. The Fair Credit Billing Act and the Electronic Fund Transfer Act cover resolution of these inaccuracies. *Also called* account error.

billing-only account A bank card account set up with no cards issued on the account.

billing rights *See* Fair Credit Billing Act; Regulation Z.

bill of exchange A draft. A negotiable and unconditional written order, such as a check or trade acceptance, addressed and signed by one person to another. The person who receives a bill of exchange must pay a specified sum, on demand or at a specific future time.

bill of lading (b/l) A transport document, issued by a shipping company or its agent, that serves as a receipt for goods, as a contract to deliver goods to a specific location, and as title to the goods when issued in negotiable form.

bill of sale A legal document that conveys title to, or right of interest in, specific personal property from the seller to the buyer.

bill payment A checkless system for paying recurring bills with one authorization statement to a financial institution. Financial institutions use automated clearing houses to make necessary debits and credits.

bills payable (1) Notes and trade acceptances owed by a business to other firms, payable at maturity. (2) A sum borrowed from a Federal Reserve bank by a member bank, for which the bank has given its own collateral note.

bills receivable All notes and trade acceptances owed by customers of a business, usually for the purchase of merchandise.

bimetallism A government's commitment to exchange its currency on demand for stated amounts of either of two metals, usually gold or silver. *Also called* bimetallic standard. *Compare with* symmetallism.

binary (1) The most common form of counting used by computers. In the binary counting system only two digits, 0 and 1, are used. (2) The property of a choice or condition, in which there are exactly two possibilities.

binary cell (1) A cell having the capacity of one binary digit. (2) A one-bit register or bit position.

binary code (1) A code that makes use of exactly two distinct characters, usually 0 and 1. (2) A code in which each of the 10 decimal digits (0 to 9) is represented by its binary, radix 2, equivalent.

binary digit *See* bit.

binary number A number, usually consisting of more than one figure, representing a sum, in which the individual quantity represented by each figure is based on a radix of 2. The figures used are 0 and 1.

binder (1) A down payment for the purchase of real estate as evidence of a buyer's good faith. The accompa-

nying contract includes terms of sale as agreed by the buyer and seller. (2) The temporary document issued by an insurance agent that certifies insurance coverage of a particular risk.

bit A term, derived from binary and digit, that describes the capacity of one unit of information. A bit is the smallest unit of data in a computer. All data in a computer are coded as a combination of either a 0 or 1. *Also called* binary digit.

bit configuration The sequence in which bits are encoded. The least significant bit must always be encoded first and the parity bit last.

bit density The bit measurement in bits per inch, when measured along the line parallel to the longitudinal counterline of the signal within the information track of the magnetic stripe.

bit string A one-dimensional array of bits ordered by reference to the relations between adjacent numbers.

black light An ultraviolet or infrared light that can be used to verify signatures by revealing a signature printed in ultraviolet ink, for example, on a depositor's passbook. A customer's signature can be verified on another item by comparing it with the ultraviolet signature, which appears when placed under a black light.

Black-Scholes A widely used option pricing equation developed in 1973 by Fischer Black and Myron Scholes. It is used to price OTC options, value option portfolios, or evaluate option trading on exchanges. *Also called* Black-Scholes model.

blank A regimented place for storing data.

blank endorsement *See* endorsement in blank.

blanket bond A bond for which the security is a mortgage not on a specific asset but on all the assets of the issuing corporation.

blanket lien A security interest designed to cover every type of collateral owned by a debtor.

blanket mortgage A single mortgage lien covering all property, or more than one parcel of real estate, owned by an obligor. A blanket mortgage often includes any additional property that the obligor may acquire in the future, depending on the after-acquired property clause in the mortgage document.

blanket position bond A fidelity bond that protects a firm from liability due to the dishonesty of its employees in specified positions.

blanket rate A rate that is basic and applies to all categories of items being considered.

blanket rate increase A uniform and all-inclusive rate increase applicable to a large group of items, usually expressed as a percentage.

blind broker A broker who arranges a sale of securities without telling either party the identity of the other party.

blind-pool municipals Municipal bonds issued when interest rates are favorable to provide contingency financing for unspecified projects in the future. The funds received are invested in securities that provide a return roughly equal to the interest rate on the municipal bond.

blind trust A trust set up to prevent the owner from having detailed knowledge of assets in the trust. Govern-

ment officials frequently use blind trusts to avoid conflicts of interest between their official duties and personal financial transactions.

block (1) A status code that restricts or prohibits the use of a bank card. (2) A large amount of securities sold at one time. This term usually describes large sales by one institutional investor to another. *See also* large blocks. (3) In systems, a group of computer words that, by being stored in successive storage locations, are considered or transferred as a unit. (4) The set of locations or tape positions in which a block of words, as defined above, is stored. (5) A circuit assemblage that functions as a unit. (6) A group of consecutive computer words or characters considered or transferred as a unit, particularly with reference to input and output.

blockage (1) A discount from the established market for which a large block of stock of a single corporation would have to be sold if the entire holding were placed on the market at a given date. Blockage is used in connection with federal estate tax. (2) Placing an account under the U.S. Treasury's control because of enemy or suspected enemy interest.

blocked account Any account in a bank, the handling of which is closely circumscribed by government regulations. In this country, a blocked account designates any account whose administration is subject to the U.S. Treasury's license because of enemy or suspected enemy interest.

blocked currency A currency that by law or regulation cannot be converted into another foreign currency.

blockette The subdivision of a group of consecutive computer words transferred as a unit, particularly with reference to input and output.

block trader A broker who handles large securities transactions for institutional investors.

blotter (1) A banking journal usually used for the original handwritten entry of loans made. (2) A list kept by a bank bond or trust department of daily securities transactions, indicating each purchase and sale conducted. Items on the list include the customer's name, broker's name (if applicable), issuer, number of shares, price, and total amount to be paid or received.

blue chip A company, or the stock of a company, that has an excellent record in management, conservative financial structure, and regular dividend payments.

Blue List of Current Municipal Offerings A daily service published by Standard & Poor's Corporation listing municipal bonds offered publicly by dealers. This service covers approximately 40 percent of the municipal bonds available in the national market.

blue-sky laws State laws concerning the registration and issuance of securities. These laws may be different from federal laws and regulations and must be obeyed if a security is to be sold in that state.

board (1) Any stock exchange, but especially the New York Stock Exchange, which is also called the Big Board. (2) An electronic display of constantly changing ticker prices, located in a broker's office. (3) The directors elected by a corporation's stockholders to guide the overall operation of the company. (4) The general shorthand reference, in many consumer credit statutes and regu-

lations, to the Board of Governors of the Federal Reserve System.

Board of Governors of the Federal Reserve System A board of seven members appointed by the president of the United States and confirmed by the Senate. The Board of Governors of the Federal Reserve System supervises, coordinates, and formulates monetary policy and regulates member banks and bank holding companies.

bobtail statement An abbreviated statement prepared for holders of demand deposit accounts.

boilerplate legends Long standardized provisions, usually in very small print, contained in a document such as a deposit slip or contract.

bona fide (Adj.) In good faith; for example, a bona fide transaction.

bona fide error Under the Truth in Lending Act, an error that is unintentional and occurs notwithstanding procedures adopted to avoid such errors. Such errors can include clerical, calculation, printing, and computer-programming and malfunction errors. Bona fide errors are not subject to civil liability under the Truth in Lending Act.

bona fide purchaser One who purchases property in good faith, without having received notice of any defect in the title, and who pays a valuable consideration for the property.

bona fides (Noun) Good faith, honesty; for example, the bona fides of the transaction.

bond (1) A long-term debt instrument, generally with an original maturity of 5 years or more, issued in standardized format, that bears interest and promises repayment of the principal. A bond is issued under an indenture that specifies the issuer's obligations to the bondholder and the manner in which the debt is secured. The indenture provides for a trustee who is responsible for the bondholders' rights. (2) A formal written obligation in which the maker agrees to pay money either absolutely or upon certain conditions. *See also* bail. *See also* the following entries: accumulation bond; assumed bond, baby bond; bail bond; bankers' and brokers' blanket bond; blanket position bond; callable bond; called bond; consolidated systemwide bond; continued bond; contract bond; convertible bond; corporate bond; cost bond; coupon bond; current coupon bond; cushion bond; deep discount bond; definitive bond; discount bond; divisional bond; dollar bond; double-barrel obligation bond; dual-currency bonds; E bond; EE bond; equipment trust bond; estate tax bond; Eurobond; external bond; fidelity bond; fiduciary bond; first mortgage bond; flower bond; foreign bond; forgery and alteration bond; full-coupon bond; fully registered bond; general obligation (GO) bond; government bonds; guaranteed bond; H bond; HH bond; hospital and health care revenue bond; income bond; index bond; industrial bond; industrial development bond; internal bond; irredeemable bond; joint bond; junk bond; license and permit bond; limited tax bond; limited-tax GO bond; lost-instrument bond; mortgage-backed bonds; municipal bond; named-schedule bond; noncallable bond; open-end mortgage bonds; optional payment bond; original issue discount (OID) bond; participating bond; pay-through bond; performance bond; perpetual bond; petitioning on creditors' bond; plastic bond; pollution control bond; position-schedule bond; premium bond; profit-sharing bond; public housing bond; public official bond; public utility revenue bond; purchase-money bond; purchasing power bond; put bond; refunding bond; registered bond; revenue bond; savings bond; self-liquidating bond; serial bonds; series bonds; sheriff indemnity bond; short bond; sinking fund bond; special assistance bond; special tax bond; surety bond; tax-exempt bond; temporary bond; term bond; unlimited tax bond; unlimited tax GO bond; U.S. dollar bond; U.S. savings bond; Yankee bond; zero-coupon bond.

bond and coupon paying agent A corporate agent responsible for paying interest and repaying principal to bondholders from funds provided by the issuer.

bond and preferred stock funds *See* fixed-income mutual fund.

bond anticipation note (BAN) A municipal note maturing in less than 1 year issued in advance of a new bond issue. Proceeds from the bond issue will repay the note with interest.

bond averages Calculations of the mean price of selected bonds over a specific period. A series of such calculations reflects the general trend of the bond market.

bond broker A broker who arranges the sale of bonds but does not carry an inventory of bonds. Most bonds are traded by dealers who hold an inventory of bonds.

bond discount The difference between the face value of a bond and its selling price, where the latter is smaller. *See also* discount on securities.

bondholder An investor who lends money to an enterprise for a stated period and receives interest and repayment of principal. Any claims on a corporation's assets take precedence over the claims of preferred and common stockholders.

bond of indemnity *See* indemnity bond.

bond power A form of assignment, executed by the owner of registered bonds, that contains an irrevocable appointment of an attorney-in-fact to make the actual transfer of bonds on the books of the corporation. *See also* power; power of attorney; stock power.

bond ratings The classifications made by rating agencies that represent the relative financial strength of an issuer with respect to the issuer's ability to meet its bond obligations. For example, Standard & Poor's highest rating is AAA; its lowest is D.

bond register A book of original entry in which a firm records details about the purchase and sale of bonds for its investment accounts.

bond registrar A corporate agent responsible for recording changes in bond ownership. *See also* registrar.

bond resolution A legal order or contract, by the appropriate government agency, authorizing a bond issue. A bond resolution describes in detail the bondholders' rights and the issuer's obligations.

bond tables Mathematical tables that convert bond yields for different maturities into dollar values. These tables are employed for the pricing of municipal bonds, which frequently are quoted on a yield basis.

bond trustee A corporate agent that authenticates bonds. A bond trustee is responsible under the indenture for protecting a bondholder's interest if the issuer defaults on the issue.

bond yield The return on a bond to the bond investor as a function of the purchase price of the bond. The return equals the present value of the sum of interest payments received and any premium or discount paid or received, divided by the purchase price. The yield is generally expressed as a percentage of the purchase price of the bond.

bonus *See* stock bonus.

book To enter a loan on the records of the lender.

book balance The amount in an account on a bank's books. In deposits, a book balance includes funds that have been deposited but are still being collected.

book entry A method of transferring ownership in a security from one party to another, while the actual security document is kept in a depository.

book-entry securities Securities that are not in printed form but merely exist on the books of an agent of the issuer. The federal government and its agencies issue most of their debt in book-entry form. Federal Reserve banks keep the records for these debts in their computers.

book-entry settlement An accounting method for securities transactions, funds movements, and so on, in which no physical movement of the stocks, bonds, or funds is necessary. Instead, debits and offsetting credits (and vice versa) are posted to the accounts of the transaction's principals. These parties must be members of the same securities depository, clearing house, and Federal Reserve System, or they must maintain special accounts with a common bank or broker.

bookkeeping department The traditional name for the bank unit in which all records of depositors' accounts are maintained and updated. More recently, it has become known as the DDA (demand deposit accounting) unit.

book net worth *See* book value.

book-sort A preliminary and less refined process of alphabetically sorting all checks and deposits into the books or ledgers within the accounting department.

book transfer A transfer of funds between two accounts, both serviced by the bank executing the transaction.

book value (1) The equity of a company calculated by deducting from total assets all liabilities of the company. Book value represents the book net worth of the company's preferred and common stock. (2) For a trust account, the value of the trust assets at the time the trust becomes operative. The book value of a trust account is not the same, however, as the tax-cost basis of the account. (3) The amount at which an asset is carried on a firm's financial statement.

book value per share The value of each share of common or capital stock, based on the values at which a corporation's assets are carried on its balance sheet. Book value is obtained by deducting from total assets all the corporation's liabilities, including preferred stock, and dividing the remainder by the number of common shares outstanding.

boom A period of economic prosperity, characterized by a general expansion of market activity and also by a rapid rise in market prices.

bootstrap (1) A technique or device that brings itself into a desired state by its own action, for example, a machine routine whose first few instructions are enough to bring the rest of the routine into the computer from an input device. (2) A subroutine that, while in storage, gains control of and instructs the computer to read in other data, such as a loading routine.

borrowed funds All direct or indirect nondeposit liabilities of a bank. Borrowings may be accomplished through the use of promissory notes, bills payable, mortgages payable, a customer's paper rediscounted, the purchase of federal funds, and assets sold with the borrowing bank's endorsement.

borrower Any legal entity that obtains funds from another for a period of time. In the case of an extension of credit, the borrower usually signs a note as evidence of the indebtedness.

bottom line An informal term used to describe the end result, often used in place of net income.

bottomry In ancient Greece, an agreement applying to loans made on shipping vessels. In the event the ship was lost, the loan was canceled. *See also* respondentia.

bought-as-sold method A procedure whereby a dealer in commercial paper sells the paper at the best price available and delivers proceeds, less commission, to the issuer.

branch (1) In systems, the selection of one or more possible paths in the flow of control for the program. (2) A banking facility located away from the bank's main office.

branch banking Multioffice banking. The ability to operate branches is controlled by state law.

branch clearing account A general ledger account that reflects the flow of debit and credit items between local community offices or administrative units and processing centers.

branch expense The cost of activities performed by bank branches, such as receiving payments and merchant deposits and issuing cash advances.

branch pickup A method of distributing new bank cards to cardholders by notifying them that their new bank cards are available for them at a specified branch.

brassage A charge levied for coining bullion.

breach of promise The failure to perform a duty that has been agreed to by contract.

breach of trust The violation of a trustee's duty to a beneficiary.

breakdown An itemized list of all activity occurring on an account.

break-even analysis Calculation of the sales needed to cover costs (that is, to break even). Break-even analysis provides management with information necessary to determine whether a proposed new product can reasonably be expected to become profitable.

break-even chart A chart showing how total revenue and total costs vary with the quantity of goods or services produced and sold. The break-even point occurs at a production level where total revenue equals total costs.

break-even point The point at which total fixed and variable costs exactly equal revenues. *See also* break-even chart.

breakpoint A point in a computer program at which conditional interruption may occur to permit visual checking, printing out, or other analysis. Breakpoints usually occur in debugging operations.

Bretton Woods The site where the World Bank and the International Monetary Fund were founded in 1944. Rules were developed there regarding fixed exchange rates.

Bretton Woods System A system designed in 1944 at Bretton Woods to facilitate foreign exchange and stabilize exchange rates.

brick A package of new currency, banded by steel straps. New currency may be shipped to banks in this condition from a Federal Reserve bank.

bridge bank A bank that can be chartered by the FDIC for as long as 3 years to assist in the transfer of a failed bank from one owner to another.

bridge loan A temporary loan, used by issuers to bridge the time between redemption of one debt security and issuance of another. Brokers also grant bridge loans to investors for any purpose, through the investor's margin account. Bridge loans are also made to home buyers who need financing between the purchase of a new home and the sale of an old home. *Also called* swing loan.

broad form personal theft insurance Insurance that protects against loss by theft or mysterious disappearance of property placed with a bank, trust safe deposit company, warehouse, and so on.

broken date An unusual maturity (not the customary 30, 60, or 90 days) in the Euromarkets. *Also called* cock date.

broker (1) A licensed person or firm that buys and sells securities, commodities, property, or other assets for a commission. A broker is an agent, not a principal; a broker does not carry an inventory, as distinct from a dealer, who does carry an inventory. (2) A person or firm licensed to sell insurance.

brokerage (1) The business of arranging contracts for the purchase and sale of securities. (2) The fee charged by a broker.

broker confirmation (confirm) A receipt sent to a customer by a broker after trade execution. The "confirm" lists essential data, such as the customer's name, broker's account number, and description of the security, quantity, price, dollar amounts, and delivering and receiving parties. *Also called* trade confirmation *or* trade confirm.

broker-dealer A party that makes securities transactions on behalf of its customers, as well as for its own market position. A broker may not buy and sell from its own account and charges fees for services performed. A dealer may purchase and resell the securities to its customer and charges a markup, whenever possible, for its services. A broker-dealer may serve the customer as either a broker or dealer.

brokered deposit A deposit that is obtained when a bank pays a fee to an individual outside the organization (a broker) to solicit funds on the bank's behalf. These deposits are typically denominated in $100,000 amounts and are extremely rate sensitive.

brokered loan A loan that the originator sells to a third party for a fee. The buyer of the loan bears the interest rate risk and the default risk.

broker pledge A broker's deposit of securities as collateral for bank loans. A broker may also instruct a depository to set aside equivalent securities by book entry in the broker's collateral subaccount.

brokers' broker A firm that specializes in trading securities on behalf of other market professionals for a minimal commission. The firm distributes two-sided quotations showing offerings and request bids. Other dealers may use a brokers' broker to mask a buildup or disposition of a particular security.

broker's loan A customary type of loan made to brokers, usually by big city banks, secured by pledged securities. Brokers use these loans to finance underwriting and inventory or to secure funds for advances of credit to customers who maintain margin accounts.

budget (1) A statement of probable revenues and expenditures. (2) A statement of the projected level of assets, liabilities, income, and expenses to be attained over a period of time, usually a year. (3) A statement of funds available and needed for the payment of claims, taxes, and cash bequests in an estate.

budget calendar A schedule for completing segments of the budget process.

buffer An internal portion of a data-processing system that serves as an intermediate storage area between two storage or data-handling systems.

buffering A fraud scheme for bank cards that involves copying and storing magnetic stripe information, making a charge, and then restoring the original information. *Also called* refreshing.

building codes The state and local government regulations stating the physical requirements for the construction and repair of buildings.

building society The British term for a savings and loan association. *See also* savings and loan association.

bulk cash Rolled or bagged coins or banded currency.

bulk handling A method of financing collateral in bulk (that is, as a single package). This type of financing is used when the collateral is composed of a large number of small items, so individual invoicing would be impractical.

bull One who believes the price of an asset is likely to increase and invests accordingly. *Compare with* bear.

bullet loan A loan that has no amortization, but is payable in full at maturity.

bullion Unminted precious metals suitable for coining.

bull market A period of generally increasing market prices. *Compare with* bear market.

bundle of rights A theory that there are certain separate and distinct rights inherent in the ownership of property, such as the right to use real estate, lease it, sell it, and so on. Collectively, these are termed "bundle of rights."

burden of proof The duty of proving a position taken in a court of law. Failure in the performance of that duty calls for judgment against the person on whom the duty rests. Thus, the burden of proof that a paper writing is not the valid will of a testator rests with the person who contests the will.

business cycle A pattern of fluctuations in economic activity, characterized by expansion and contraction of repeating but very irregular length. Normally, this term indicates fluctuations of real gross national product.

business day Any day on which the offices of a financial institution are open to the public for carrying on substantially all of the institution's business functions.

business insurance trust A trust of life insurance policy contracts created in connection with a business. The term applies alike to a trust created for the liquidation of business interests and to one created for credit or other purposes for the benefit of the business enterprise.

business risk Risk that is uniquely associated with a particular firm, as opposed to risk that affects the total business community. For example, business risk might arise from the nature of a product sold.

business trust (1) In a Massachusetts trust or common-law trust, a business organization in which the assets are conveyed or transferred to a board of trustees for management and operation for the benefit of the holders of transferable trust certificates, representing shares that closely resemble the shares of a corporation's stock. (2) In a voting trust, a business organization in which the owners of part or all of a company's stock transfer their shares to trustees for the purpose of voting them. They receive in return transferable voting trust certificates that entitle them to any dividends on the stock. Some states require registration of voting trusts.

bus line (1) A circuit over which data or power is transmitted that often acts as a common connection among many locations. *Also called* trunk line. (2) A communications path between two switching points.

butterfly call spread An options strategy designed to profit from stable or decreasing volatility. The spread involves trades in four call options, all with the same expiration date: the purchase of an option with a low exercise price; the sale of two calls with an intermediate exercise price; the purchase of a call with a high exercise price. Profit is generated when the price of the underlying instrument remains within an established range. Loss is limited to the net premiums paid to set up the position.

buy-a-spread The simultaneous purchase of a near futures contract and the sale of a far futures contract.

buy back (Noun) A repurchase agreement.

buy contract A contract to buy an asset in the future. Note that the same futures contract is a buy contract for one party and a sell contract for another.

buydown (1) An arrangement in which a dealer rather than the manufacturer will make up the difference between the lender's buy rate and the rate charged to the customer. It is similar to subvention but does not involve the manufacturer. *See also* subvention. (2) The situation that exists when the developer or a third party in a real estate transaction provides an interest subsidy that lowers the monthly payments during the first few years of the loan.

buyer credit In export finance, a means by which the overseas importer uses a loan to pay the exporter.

buyers market A market in which supply exceeds demand at current prices, thereby giving buyers considerable influence over purchase price and terms of sale.

buy in (1) (Verb) To cover, offset, or close out a short position. (2) (Noun) The buying of securities through other sources at the prevailing market price if the selling party to a securities trade fails to deliver. The defaulting seller is liable for the difference in price. The buyer, however, must notify the seller of its intentions to buy the securities elsewhere before resorting to a buy in.

buying forward The purchase of an item for future delivery in anticipation of future demand.

buying on margin The use of borrowed funds, plus some equity, to purchase assets. The equity is the margin.

buying power (1) The value of money expressed as the amount of goods or services that it can purchase. (2) The spendable income of a specific group of purchasers. (3) The amount of money available in investors' margin accounts for the additional purchases of securities.

buying signals A progression of prices on a stock chart that exceeds the usual range. This progression is used as an indication that self-stabilizing forces will soon cause a reversal in trend.

buy rate The rate of interest a lender will charge a dealer to purchase retail contracts originated by the dealer for such items as automobiles, boats, or home improvements.

buy-sell agreement (1) An agreement wherein owners of a business arrange to transfer their respective ownership interests if one dies, or some other event occurs, so as to provide for continued control of the business or other desired end. (2) In real estate, an agreement among the borrower, construction lender, and permanent lender obligating the permanent lender to buy the loan from the construction lender after specific conditions have been met.

buy ticket A form prepared in multiple copies, used by a bank's investment department to instruct the order department to purchase a security.

bylaws Formal rules and regulations adopted by the board of directors governing the operation and internal management of a bank as a corporate entity. In contrast, resolutions are the formal actions of the board of directors of a bank on particular matters.

byte (1) A generic term used to indicate a measurable portion of consecutive binary digits (bits) that are operated on as a unit. A common use is to have a byte equal eight bits and represent a single character or two numbers. (2) A group of binary digits usually operated on as a unit and typically used to represent an alphanumeric character.

cable *See* wire.

cable transfer The transfer of funds domestically or internationally, the instructions for which are transmitted by cable, telex, or telegram. *Also called* wire transfer.

cafeteria benefits plan A flexible benefits plan that permits covered employees to select benefits they want from a package of employer-provided choices, some of which may involve employee contributions.

calendar The schedule of all known issues of certain classes of securities that will be offered for sale in the market at stated times in the future.

calendar call spread An options strategy designed to profit from the rapid decline in time value as options approach expiration. The position involves the sale of a near-term call option and the purchase of a call option with a more distant expiration date. Barring an increase in volatility, the time value on the nearby option will erode more quickly (as its maturity approaches) than will the time value on the more distant option. The trader expects that the cost of unwinding the position will be less than the net premiums received when it was established. *Also called* time call spread *or* horizontal spread.

call (1) To demand payment of a call (demand) loan. (2) To demand payment of a loan because of a debtor's failure to comply with the terms of the loan. (3) To ask for additional margin (collateral) when the value of existing collateral declines below a stated value. (4) (Noun) An option to buy a specific amount of stock (or bonds or other assets) at a specific price within a specified period.

callable Redeemable before maturity. The term describes a bond or preferred stock that is subject to redemption, usually within a specified period, under designated terms, and at a stated price.

callable bond A bond that the issuer can liquidate before maturity.

callable preferred stock Preferred stock that can be repurchased by its issuer at a specified price.

call back A procedure used to identify a terminal dialing into a computer system, in which the caller is disconnected and then reconnected once a computer operator has dialed the caller's verified telephone number.

call date The date on which a bond may be redeemed before maturity, at the option of the issuer.

called bond A bond that a debtor has declared to be due and payable on a certain date before maturity, according to the provisions of the bond indenture. If only part of an issue will be redeemed, the bonds to be retired are usually drawn by lot.

called preferred stock Preferred stock, containing call provisions, that is redeemed by a corporation.

call in To transfer control of a digital computer temporarily from a main routine to a subroutine that is inserted in the sequence of calculations to fulfill a subsidiary purpose.

call loan A loan payable on demand, at the discretion of either the lender or borrower. *Also called* call money and demand loan.

call money market A sector of the money market in which brokers borrow funds, using securities as collateral, and lend these funds to their customers to meet margin requirements.

call option An instrument that gives the holder the right, but not the obligation, to buy a specified financial instrument at a fixed price on or before a specified future date.

call premium The excess above the par value of a bond that is paid by the issuer of the bond when it is redeemed before maturity. The call premium is specified in the bond indenture.

call price The price at which a corporation or other obligor is permitted to redeem securities containing call provisions. To compensate for this privilege, the bond issuer usually pays a price above par upon redemption.

call program A business development technique used by banks in which corporate officers are required to make face-to-face contact with prospective and existing customers on a regular basis in order to make them aware of the types of services the bank provides.

call protection The specified period during which the issuer cannot call a security for redemption.

call provision (1) A feature of bonds or preferred stock that allows the issuer to repurchase part or all of an issue before it matures. Partial calls of an issue are conducted by lottery. (2) In a mortgage loan, this provision permits the lender to collect full payment when a specified event occurs.

call report A sworn statement of a bank's financial condition as of a certain date, submitted in response to a demand from a supervisory agency or authority. The quarterly Consolidated Reports of Condition and Income filed by a bank (in accordance with regulatory accounting principles established by the Federal Financial Institutions Examination Council) is commonly referred to as the call report. Consolidated financial statements filed by bank holding companies are reported to the Federal Reserve on Form FRY-9.

CAMEL (capital, assets, management, earnings, and liquidity) Factors considered by supervisory authorities in examining banks.

canceled check A check that has been presented to a drawee, charged to the drawer's account, and stamped, perforated, or mutilated to prevent its further use.

cancellation (1) The termination of an insurance (or other) contract before the end of the policy period. (2) Voiding of a document by defacement, perforation, or other means, making restoration impossible.

cancellation bulletin *See* restricted card list.

canon A rule or law. Under civil law, the rules by which the title to real property is traced are known as canons of inheritance; under common law, such rules are known as canons of descent.

canon law The law of the church, or ecclesiastical law.

canon of ethics Written and unwritten standards of conduct expected by certain groups, especially professional groups, in pursuit of their specialized activities.

canons of descent *See* laws of descent.

cap (1) The maximum daylight overdraft a commercial bank can incur on either the Federal Reserve Wire Network (Fedwire) or the Clearing House Interbank Payments System (CHIPS). *Also called* a sender net debit cap. (2) *See* interest rate cap.

capacity (1) The ability to pay a specific obligation when it is due. (2) In insurance, the financial ability to underwrite new insurance.

capacity cost The cost of operating a plant, process, department, and so on, at full capacity.

capacity utilization rate The percentage of the economy's total plant and equipment that is currently in production. Usually a decrease in this percentage signals an economic slowdown, while an increase signals economic expansion.

cap cost *See* capitalized cost.

capital (1) The funds invested in a company on a long-term basis. These funds are obtained by issuing preferred or common stock, retaining a portion of the company's earnings from the date of incorporation, and long-term borrowing. (2) The funds invested in a firm by the owners for use in conducting business. (3) The owners' original investment, plus any profit reinvested in the business, that appears on the balance sheet. (4) A factor of production, specifically referring to all goods used to produce other goods and services.

capital account (1) The net worth, capital investment, or owners' equity of an enterprise. The capital account is the difference between an entity's assets and liabilities. (2) Capital obligations, such as debentures, and stockholder equity (stock plus surplus). (3) The account used to record the flow of investment (long-term) capital to and from a nation.

capital adequacy One measure of the strength of a bank. Minimum capital ratios are set forth by the bank regulators. Previously, total capital was defined as primary capital and secondary capital, and it was required to be maintained at a specified percentage of total assets. However, a new risk-based capital (RBC) framework was agreed to by an international group of central banks and supervisory agencies (the Basle Committee). Each country establishes its own guidelines within the RBC framework. The U.S. federal banking agencies began implementation of these in 1989. The two components of RBC are Tier One (core equity) capital and Tier Two capital. Capital is required based on relative risk-weightings of assets (for example, more capital will be required for loans than investments in U.S. Treasury securities). Certain off-balance-sheet items are also factored into RBC. *See also* Tier One capital; Tier Two capital; primary capital; secondary capital.

capital asset An asset used to create a product or service, such as a factory, where the asset is intended for continued use rather than resale.

capital asset pricing model (CAPM) A theory that holds that the risk-free rate of return, plus a risk premium proportionate to the degree of risk unique to a particular asset, determines the appropriate return on that asset.

capital, assets, management, earnings, and liquidity *See* CAMEL.

capital budget That portion of a budget devoted to proposed additions and financing for capital assets.

capital budgeting Analysis of projects requiring capital outlays to determine which projects should be undertaken. The cash outlays are compared with the expected flow of future benefits derived from the investment.

capital debenture An unsecured note or bond that must be converted to common stock at or by a specified future date.

capital distribution *See* liquidating dividend.

capital expenditure An outlay intended to provide future benefits, usually by making an addition to capital assets or increasing the capacity, efficiency, or life span of an existing fixed asset.

capital gains The amount by which the proceeds from the sale of capital assets exceed their cost. *See also* long-term capital gains; short-term capital gains.

capital gains distributions Payments made to shareholders in mutual funds, representing their share of net capital gains received from the sale of securities in a mutual fund portfolio. *Also called* capital gains dividends.

capital gains dividends *See* capital gains distributions.

capital gains tax A tax levied on profits realized from the sale of capital assets. This tax may differ from the income tax rate.

capital gearing costs (UK) The costs of providing capital to meet requirements imposed by the Bank of England.

capital goods Assets that are expected to last a long time, used to produce other goods for sale.

capital impairment (1) The reduction of capital because of losses. (2) The reduction of capital below the level required by statute or by supervisory authorities.

capitalist A person who uses his or her privately owned capital or wealth to generate income.

capitalization (1) The total amount of equity and debt securities issued to finance the operations of a corporation. (2) An accounting procedure that treats certain expenditures as a long-term asset rather than an expense. *See also* capitalized expense.

capitalization rate A ratio of property income to property value expressed as a percentage. It is used in the income approach of the appraisal process; net operating income for a single year is divided by the capitalization rate to estimate property value.

capitalize To adjust a firm's or individual's estimated capital or worth to include the present worth of expected future earnings or expenses. The term also refers to the method in which an asset is booked as a capital item on a balance sheet.

capitalized cost The amount financed to a lessee. This may or may not be the actual cost to the lessor. If the lessor adds a markup to the actual cost, it will be included in the capitalized cost.

capitalized expense An expense that has been recorded as a long-term asset. For example, the costs incurred in overhauling a machine are capitalized, while minor repairs to the machine are typically expensed. The treatment depends on when the benefits will be received. Benefits from a major overhaul will be received for several years. As a result, the expenditure is added to the cost basis of the machine and allocated by means of depreciation charges. In the case of a minor repair, the benefits are derived in the current period. As a result, the expenditure is charged against current income.

capitalized surplus The transfer of a corporation's paid-in or earned surplus to capital stock by issuing a stock dividend, increasing the par or stated value of the capital stock, or issuing a resolution by the board of directors.

capital lease The classification of a lease on the lessee's books as an asset and a debt. A capital lease, from the lessee's viewpoint, is the same as a direct financing lease from the lessor's viewpoint.

capital loss The sale of a capital asset for less than its book value or purchase price.

capital market The market for buying and selling long-term loanable funds in the form of bonds, mortgages, and stocks. It is an informal market without any specific geographic location.

capital-output ratio The ratio of capital goods to total output for a firm or economy.

capital ratios Various ratios relating a bank's capital to its assets or liabilities, used as very rough measures of the bank's capital strength.

capital shares *See* dual-purpose fund.

capital stock (1) All the outstanding shares of a company's stock representing ownership, including preferred and common stock. (2) The total amount of stock, common and preferred, that a corporation is authorized to issue under its certificate of incorporation or charter.

capital structure The relationship between debt and the equity ownership of a company (that is, its long-term financing). A company financed primarily by stock issues generally has a more conservative capital structure than a company that issues debt securities. *Compare with* financial structure.

capped floating rate note A type of floating rate note, which sets an upper limit on the borrower's interest rate. The lender forgos the possibility of obtaining a return above the cap rate, should market interest rates exceed the cap rate, but in return receives higher than usual spreads over LIBOR. In essence, the note issuer obtains an interest rate cap--a form of option--from the buyer. *See also* floating rate note.

captive finance company A subsidiary of a large corporation whose primary business is to finance consumer purchases of the parent corporation's products.

card carrier *See* card mailer.

card code The combinations of punched holes that represent characters (for example, letters and digits) in a punched card.

cardholder A person to whom a card has been issued or who is authorized to use such a card.

cardholder account A record kept by a bank on each account for which a card has been issued.

cardholder accounting The posting of debits, credits, adjustments, and payments to cardholder accounts for the purposes of accounting and reporting to the cardholder.

cardholder agreement A written understanding stating the terms and conditions of card use and payment by the cardholder.

cardholder bank A bank that has issued a bank card to a person. The term is frequently used in conjunction with interchange arrangements to identify the card or the issuing bank.

cardholder base The total number of cardholder accounts belonging to a specific bank.

cardholder history file A record containing historical data on each cardholder account, including the current balance, credit limit, high (maximum outstanding) credit, and delinquency for the account.

cardholder master file A record of all cardholder accounts.

cardholder profile The demographics of a bank's cardholder base or a sample of that base.

cardholder statement The billing summary produced and mailed at specific intervals, usually monthly.

card image A representation in storage of the holes punched in a card, so that one binary digit represents the holes and the other binary digit represents the unpunched spaces.

card imprint The printing on a sales draft, credit voucher, or cash advance draft produced by a mechanical device called an imprinter. The card imprint includes the embossed characters of the credit card and the merchant's or bank's name and identification number.

card issuer Any bank or organization that issues, or causes to be issued, bank cards to people who apply for them.

card mailer A carrier used in mailing a card to a cardholder. A card mailer may contain specific instructions for the cardholder regarding use of the card. *Also called* card carrier *or* mailing holder.

card pickup An order to have outside agencies, a bank's own merchants, or bank personnel pick up a credit card that is being misused.

card-programmed (1) The ability of a computer to be programmed by punch cards. (2) The ability to perform sequences of calculations by following the instructions contained in a stack of punch cards.

card reader A device that translates holes in punched cards into electrical impulses and transmits the data to the memory of the computer for processing.

card reissue The process of preparing and distributing bank cards to cardholders whose cards have expired or will soon expire.

card security number (CSN) A hidden or difficult-to-reproduce number on or in the plastic of a card for purposes of deterring fraud.

carrier A company that provides communications services to the public and is subject to federal and state regulation.

carry (Noun) The interest cost of financing the holding of securities.

carryback Losses that can be carried back to reduce taxable income of earlier years.

carryforward Losses that can be carried forward to reduce taxable income in future years.

carrying charges (1) Expenses incident to the continued ownership or use of property, such as taxes on real property. (2) Charges made for carrying a debtor, such as interest charged on a margin account with a broker. (3) Charges added to the price of merchandise when payment is deferred.

carryover (1) In federal taxation, that portion of an individual or corporate operating loss that is deductible from the taxable income of following years. (2) The net capital loss of any taxpayer used to reduce capital gains or income in the future.

CARs Collateralized automobile receivables. *See also* securitization.

cartel A group of businesses united to attain some degree of control over a

market, for example, by setting prices, prescribing conditions of sale, or restricting production.

cash, cash market, cash commodities, cash securities The actual asset, as opposed to the futures contracts for the mentioned asset. *Also called* actuals.

cash accounts Coin and currency on hand or in transit, clearings, and cash items.

cash advance A cash loan obtained by a cardholder through presentation of the card at a bank office or automated teller machine, or through mail request. The loan is an advance from the line of credit underlying the credit card.

cash advance balance That portion of the total balance due on a credit card representing any unpaid portion of cash advance loans previously issued.

cash advance draft A document executed by a cardholder that evidences a cash advance obtained through the use of a bank card.

cash advance fee A fee received by a lender as compensation for granting a cash advance to a cardholder. *Also called* origination fee.

cash application systems Methods employed by corporations in conjunction with banks' receivable collection systems to expedite the posting of accounts receivable. Cash application systems generally involve the transfer of hard-copy information to machine-readable form (for example, punched cards or magnetic tape).

cash basis Income and expenses recorded when cash is received or paid out, regardless of when income was earned or expenses incurred. *See also* cash method of accounting.

cash basis of accounting An accounting system in which revenues and expenses are recorded and realized only when the accompanying cash inflow or outflow occurs, without regard to the actual period to which the transactions apply. *Also called* cash basis accounting. *Compare with* accrual basis of accounting.

cash budget A schedule of cash receipts and outlays, as opposed to accruals.

cash card A plastic card that is used to obtain cash from automated teller machines or point-of-sale systems. It involves immediate debiting of consumers' accounts and immediate crediting of merchants' accounts.

cash conversion cycle The length of time required for a firm to move through the production cycle, from cash to purchasing and processing materials, through collecting accounts receivables, and back into cash.

cash dispenser Equipment capable of automatically dispensing amounts of cash in an unattended environment. A cash dispenser is usually activated by the insertion of a specially prepared card or by the transmission of a code via a keyboard or keyset. It differs from an ATM in that it may not accept deposits or payments or transfer funds between accounts. *Also called* unattended banking terminal. *See also* automated teller machine.

cash dividend A dividend distributed in cash.

cash equivalent Short-term, highly liquid investments that are both (a) readily convertible to known amounts of cash, and (b) so near their maturity that they present insignificant risk of

changes in value because of changes in interest rates. Generally, only investments with original maturities of 3 months or less qualify under this definition. This definition is used for purposes of reporting a statement of cash flows under generally accepted accounting principles (GAAP).

cash flow (1) A company's funds available for working capital or expansion. (2) The expected timing and amounts of future net cash receipts from an investment. (3) The cycle through which a firm's cash passes as it is converted into raw materials, product, sales, receivables, and back into cash. (4) The income remaining from real estate operations after deducting operating expenses and debt service.

cash flow statement A statement of a company's cash receipts and payments during a given period.

cash forecasting A projection of a company's cash needs during an upcoming accounting period, used to determine the company's borrowing needs for that period.

cashier The officer of a national bank responsible for funds received and expended.

cashier's check A bank's own check drawn on itself and signed by an authorized official. It is a direct obligation of the bank. At a national bank, it is called a cashier's check; at a state bank, it may be called a treasurer's check. *Also called* official check.

cashing Strictly speaking, delivering money in exchange for a check drawn on another financial institution.

cash item Any item that a bank is willing to accept for immediate but provisional credit to a customer's account, thus increasing the book balance.

cash journal The original book of accounting entries, which records all details of a specific transaction. This journal serves as the source of later postings to detailed single-purpose accounting ledgers. A cash journal is a basic service provided to the customer in a master trust relationship.

cash ledger The ledger of a trust department that contains a detailed proof and record of all cash transactions in chronological order for a given personal trust account.

cash letter An interbank transmittal form, resembling a deposit slip, used to accompany cash items sent from one bank to another.

cash letter of credit A letter addressed by a bank to a correspondent asking that a specified amount of funds be made available to the party named in the letter within a certain time.

cash management Collection, disbursement (payment), concentration, and information services provided to corporate customers to speed collection of receivables, to control payments, and to manage cash efficiently.

cash management bill A U.S. Treasury bill issued with a maturity of less than 3 months to meet short-term needs.

cash method of accounting A system, used especially in computing income tax, in which income is not credited until it is actually or constructively received and expenses are not charged until they have been paid. The cash method is to be distinguished from the accrual method, in which income is credited when the legal right to the

income occurs and expenses are charged when the legal liability becomes enforceable. *See also* cash basis.

cash mobilization Centralizing cash balances to bring economies of scale to cash use. This demands precise knowledge of usable funds and the ability to mobilize those funds effectively.

cash-on-cash return A rate of return calculated by dividing the equity (or cash invested in the property) into the pretax cash flow received from the property. This is used as a measure of property performance.

cash on hand That cash in a person's or company's immediate possession, including bank deposits.

cash paid receipt A receipt given to a customer when he or she makes a bank card payment in cash. A cash paid receipt contains the identification number for the office receiving payment, the date of payment, and the initials of the teller accepting payment.

cash payment A payment made by cash.

cash price The price at which the creditor offers, in the ordinary course of business, to sell for cash any property or services.

cash reserve *See* overdraft banking.

cash settlement The settlement provision on some option and futures contracts that do not require delivery of the underlying instrument. For options, the difference between the settlement price on the underlying instrument and the option's exercise price is paid to the option holder at exercise. For futures contracts, the exchange establishes a settlement price on the final day of trading and all remaining open positions are marked to market at that price. *See also* marking to market.

cash statement The daily record of the opening and closing balances of cash on hand in each bank, a summary of the day's receipts and disbursements, and the details of deposits and withdrawals.

cash surrender value The equity accrued in a life insurance policy, which the policy owner receives if the policy is terminated before death. *See also* surrender value.

cash ticket The handwritten or machine-printed slip of paper on which cash deposits are recorded. The slip accompanies the cash deposits to a bank's proof department.

cash trade The purchasing or selling of foreign currencies or securities, which involves the delivery and settlement of a contract on the same day.

CATS (certificates of accrual on Treasury securities) Certificates that represent ownership in serially maturing interest or principal payments on specific underlying U.S. Treasury notes and bonds. Each CATS entitles the holder to receive a single payment at its maturity.

causal forecasting A prediction of the future success or failure of a bank's products or services, based on data collected to determine the cause of success or failure.

causa mortis *See* gift causa mortis.

caveat emptor Literally, "let the buyer beware." This legal term expresses the belief that a buyer is responsible for protecting him- or herself from unscrupulous sellers.

caveator An interested party who gives notice to some officer not to do a certain act until the party in opposition is heard, such as the caveator of a will offered for probate.

CD *See* certificate of deposit.

cemetery trust A trust established to maintain a grave, burial plot, or cemetery.

center *See* processing center.

central bank A bank responsible for controlling a country's monetary policy and serving as its lender of last resort. For example, the Federal Reserve bank is the central bank of the United States.

central file That location in a bank where alphabetic and numeric records of accounts are maintained.

central information file (CIF) (1) A record of each customer showing all the bank services used by the customer. (2) A computerized, electronic, or manual collection of data used by a business.

centralized management A plan of management in which most key decisions and managers are centrally controlled.

centralized retrieval (1) The consolidation of computer access for retrieval of data. (2) The functional unit responsible for centralized retrieval of data.

central liability The consolidated record of all a borrower's liabilities.

central processing unit (CPU) The computer component that contains the circuits controlling the interpretation and execution of instructions and input and output units. *Also called* central processor.

centrals Regional cooperatives formed by credit unions to lend to, and to provide clearing facilities for, members.

certainty equivalent The amount of cash that a person would accept in place of a larger but uncertain future payment.

certificate number The number assigned to each certificate within an issue.

certificate of analysis A certification by a third party, as may be required by a contract for sale and delivery of merchandise, that the merchandise has been inspected.

certificate of claim A contingent promise to reimburse the lender on an insured loan for certain costs incurred during foreclosure, provided that the sales proceeds on the acquired property can cover these costs.

certificate of compliance The certificate executed by a federal government official and given to a financial institution certifying that the government agency has complied with the federal Right to Financial Privacy Act.

certificate of deposit (CD) (1) A formal receipt for funds left with a bank as a special deposit. Such deposits may bear interest, in which case they are payable at a definite date in the future or after a specified minimum notice of withdrawal; or they may be noninterest-bearing, in which case they may be payable on demand or at a future date. These deposits are payable only upon surrender of the formal receipt, properly endorsed. (2) A certificate issued to the owners of bonds or stocks as evidence of the deposit of a stated number of shares or bonds when a corporation is reorganized. *See also* negotiable certificate of deposit.

certificate of incorporation A legal document issued by a state official evidencing the establishment of a corporation under the general corporate laws of the state.

certificate of indebtedness (1) A relatively short-term, interest-bearing, secured bearer obligation issued by a corporation to obtain temporary financing. (2) Any bond or evidence of indebtedness.

certificate of origin A document issued to certify the country of origin for goods traded internationally.

certificate of participation Evidence of pro rata ownership in a closed-end investment company. *Distinguish from* participation certificate. *See also* closed-end investment company.

certificate of quality A document issued by a recognized appraiser and used in connection with a letter of credit to certify that the goods being shipped conform to the buyer's specifications.

certificate of reasonable value A statement issued by the Veterans Administration (VA) establishing the maximum loan for a VA-guaranteed mortgage.

certificate on demand (COD) A depository service that delivers physical certificates upon request by a participant.

certificate on demand program *See* transfer agent custodian (TAC) program.

certificates Printed documents issued by a corporation as evidence of its obligation to the holders of the certificates. *Also called* securities.

certificates of accrual on Treasury securities *See* CATS.

certificates of lender and loan applicant A bank's certification to FmHA that it would not make a loan to an applicant without an FmHA loan guarantee, which is a necessary step in securing the guarantee.

certification A formal attestation of a matter of fact.

certification of disaster loss A statement of crop or other physical losses due to natural disaster. This statement is used by FmHA for the emergency disaster and emergency livestock loan programs.

certification teller A teller who certifies or accepts depositors' checks.

certified check A customer's check that has been presented to a bank for authentication and guarantee. By its certification, the bank guarantees that sufficient funds have been set aside from the customer's account to cover the amount of the check when payment is demanded. Generally, payment of a certified check is the bank's responsibility. However, if fraud was practiced on the bank, payment may be denied.

certified financial statement A corporation's financial statement that is accompanied by a public accountant's report; also, a claim that all items on the balance sheet, including inventory and receivables, have been verified by the accountant and that the statement was prepared in accordance with generally accepted accounting principles.

certified internal auditor (CIA) A professional designation awarded by the Institute of Internal Auditors to individuals who pass a written exam, subscribe to a code of ethics, and submit a qualified character reference in addition to meeting certain education and experience requirements.

certified public accountant (CPA) An accountant licensed to practice public accounting. To earn this title, a person must pass required CPA examinations and must meet requirements usually established by the state for age, education, experience, residence, and moral character.

cestui que trust (Plural, cestuis que trustent.) A person for whose benefit a trust is created. *Also called* beneficiary.

chain (1) Any series of items of any kind linked together. (2) A routine consisting of segments that are run through a computer in tandem, with only one in the computer at any given time and each using the output from the previous program as its input.

chain banking An individual or group of individuals with controlling interest in more than one bank. The control is most often informal rather than through a holding company framework.

chain code A series or group of digits used to identify numerically all outlets for a merchant having more than one outlet. *Also called* chain number.

chain merchant A merchant having more than one outlet.

chain of title The history of all the documents transferring the title to a piece of real property, from the earliest existing document to the most recent. *Also called* abstract.

Change in Bank Control Act of 1978 A federal law that requires an application to be filed with the federal agency regulating a particular bank if a group of people seek to acquire 25 percent or more of the voting stock of the bank, or if an individual seeks to acquire 10 percent or more of the bank's voting stock if no one else owns more than that percentage.

channels of distribution The sequence of firms involved in moving goods or services from a producer to a consumer.

Chapter 11 A chapter of the federal Bankruptcy Code dealing with corporate reorganizations.

character The number, digit, or symbol used to represent data or information in a computer language.

character density The number of characters that can be stored per unit of length.

character loan An unsecured commercial loan that is extended on the basis of the borrower's reputation.

charge *See* trust charge.

chargeback A transaction that a cardholder bank returns either to its own merchant or to the merchant bank because the transaction fails to meet certain established criteria.

chargeback rules The rules governing the right of a creditissuing bank to charge back to the signing merchant bank any sales that do not conform to agreed standards.

charge-off (1) An obligation, such as a loan or the balance on a bank cardholder account, that a bank no longer expects to be repaid and writes off as a bad debt. (2) The process of charging off accounts. A charge-off is generally recorded by a debit to the reserve for possible credit losses and a credit to the loan balance. *Also called* bad debt.

charges Fees associated with a funds transfer or other activities.

charges applied The amount of charges made by banks involved in the execution of a funds transfer.

charges to A stipulation as to which party in a transfer should pay charges. *Also called* details of charges.

charge wire *See* reverse money transfer.

charitable bequest A gift of personal property to a legal charity by will.

charitable devise A gift of real property to a legal charity by will.

charitable lead (or up-front) trust A trust for a fixed term of years in which a charity is the income beneficiary and the remainder goes to a noncharitable beneficiary.

charitable remainder annuity trust A trust that provides a certain sum, not less than 5 percent of initial fair market value of all property placed in trust, to be distributed at least annually to a noncharitable beneficiary, with the remainder to a qualified charity or for such use.

charitable remainder trust An arrangement in which the remainder interest goes to a legal charity upon the termination or failure of a prior interest.

charitable remainder unitrust A trust that provides a fixed percentage, not less than 5 percent of net fair market value of property (valued annually), to be distributed at least annually to a noncharitable beneficiary, with the irrevocable remainder interest to a qualified charity.

charitable trust A trust created for the benefit of a legal charity. *Also called* public trust. *Distinguish from* private trust.

charity An agency, institution, or organization in existence and operation for the benefit of an indefinite number of persons and conducted for educational, religious, scientific, medical, or other beneficent purposes.

chart *See* logical flowchart.

charter A document, issued by a federal or state supervisory agent, granting a bank the right to do business. *See also* corporate charter.

chartered bank auditor (CBA) A professional designation awarded by the Bank Administration Institute to individuals who pass a written exam, subscribe to a code of ethics, and submit a qualified character reference, in addition to meeting certain education and experience requirements.

chart of accounts A list of account names and numbers, used to record specific types of transactions.

chattel (1) An article of property that can be moved; personal property. (2) Any property, movable or immovable, except a freehold estate in real property. *See also* chattel personal; chattel real; freehold estate.

chattel mortgage A mortgage on movable goods or equipment (personal property) given as security for the payment of an obligation; a mortgage on personal property. *See also* mortgage.

chattel mortgage method A method of obtaining a security interest in a dealer's inventory and/or equipment, using a separate mortgage for each transaction.

chattel personal An article of personal property, as distinguished from an interest in real property.

chattel real An interest in land, such as a leasehold, that is more limited than a freehold estate. *See also* freehold estate; tenancy at sufferance; tenancy at will; tenancy for years.

cheap money The term applied to money during times of low interest rates.

check A demand deposit instrument (a draft) signed by the maker and payable to a person named or to a bearer upon presentation to the bank on which it is drawn. *See also* certified check; stop-payment check.

check authorization Authorization for cashing a check that can be accomplished by telephone or a point-of-sale or automated teller machine system. A customer's plastic card and personal identification number are used to verify his or her account.

check bit *See* parity bit.

check-cashing machine A single-purpose automated teller machine that accepts check deposits and issues coin and currency in the amount of the check.

check credit The granting of unsecured revolving lines of credit to individuals or businesses, using one of three basic methods: an overdraft, cash reserve, or special draft system. *See also* reserve checking/overdraft checking.

check-credit plan An installment loan plan, normally used along with a customer's regular checking account in a commercial bank, including a revolving line of credit and personal checking privileges. The customer may draw on the line of credit as needed and repay the amount in monthly installments.

check digit A suffix digit that a computer, by a programmed mathematical formula, can use to test the validity of an account number.

check guarantee service A bank service that guarantees to merchants and banks that a customer's check will be paid.

check kiting *See* kiting.

check list A list of checks that will be charged to the depositor's checking account. A check list summarizes a group of checks drawn on an account so that these subtotals, rather than each individual check, can be posted to the account.

check out The process of locating differences when deposits are checked under the batch proof system.

check overdraft protection *See* overdraft banking.

checkpoint A point in a machine run at which processing is halted to make a record on magnetic tape of the condition of all the variables, such as the position of input and output tapes and a copy of working storage.

check routing symbol The denominator of a fraction, of which the American Bankers Association transit number is the numerator, appearing on the upper right-hand corner of checks, and used for check processing. The check routing symbol consists of three or four digits, the first one or two of which identify the Federal Reserve district in which the drawee bank is located. The remaining digits identify the collection arrangement made for these checks and the immediate or deferred availability assigned to the checks by the Federal Reserve.

check safekeeping A method of handling checking accounts in which the depository institution retains the checks (or a copy of the checks) written by customers rather than returning the checks with the periodic statements sent to customers. The major incentive to institutions for offering such accounts is the savings often realized on the cost of sorting, filing, preparing, and mailing statements. *See also* check truncation.

check truncation A system that reduces the physical processing of a check. In a common form of truncation, the Fed forwards electronic information on checks to its drawees, instead of routing the actual checks.

check verification guarantee A system providing retail merchants with varying degrees of insurance against losses from bad checks by (a) verifying the authenticity of the check and its presenter or (b) guaranteeing payment of the check by the bank.

checkwriter A device used to imprint the amount of a check on its face in order to make alteration difficult.

Chicago Board of Trade (CBT) An organized futures market.

Chicago Board Options Exchange (CBOE) An exchange set up by the Chicago Board of Trade, using the facilities provided by the board for the open-market trading of certain stock options. Before the 1973 opening of the CBOE, trading in options was negotiated individually.

Chicago Mercantile Exchange (CME) An exchange organized in 1919 that provides a market for trading stock index futures and futures options contracts in various agricultural commodities.

Chinese wall A policy barrier between the trust department and the rest of a bank, designed to prevent use by the trust department of any material inside information that may come into the possession of other bank departments in making investment decisions. The purpose of the policy barrier is to comply with the Glass-Steagall Act, which requires separation of investment and commercial banking activities.

chip (1) A minute piece of semiconductive material used in the manufacture of electronic components. (2) A tiny piece of silicon on a piece of semiconductive material that contains one or more integrated circuits (an interconnected array of components) capable of performing specific functions in a computer system. These circuits make up the logic of today's computers.

chip card A card that carries an embedded computer chip with memory and interactive capabilities. It can be updated.

CHIPS (Clearing House Interbank Payments System) An automated clearing house of the New York Clearing House Association. CHIPS is used chiefly for interbank funds transfers for international customers of member and associate member banks, of which there are more than 130. The CHIPS member banks link to the CHIPS system via terminals located in New York City and handle large-dollar payment activity for thousands of accounts around the world. The system serves to facilitate the payment and settlement of large international transactions.

chose An item of personal property.

chose in action A personal right to receive or recover a debt, demand, or damages on a contract, but only by a

suit at law. Examples include a patent right, a copyright, a royalty right, a right growing out of a contract or out of damage to person or property, or a right under a life insurance policy. While the right itself is the chose in action, the evidence of the right (such as the life insurance policy) sometimes is referred to as if it were the chose in action. *Distinguish from* chose in possession.

chose in possession Any article of tangible personal property in actual, rightful possession, such as a watch, automobile, or piece of furniture. *Distinguish from* chose in action.

churning Creating an excessive volume of transactions in a customer's account, generally to benefit from sales commissions on the account.

circle To commit in principle to buy a security before it has been firmly priced.

circuitous routing A nineteenth-century banking practice of sending checks on long, circuitous collection routes across the country to avoid having to pay exchange charges.

Circular 79 A ruling by the Comptroller of the Currency that sets forth the conditions under which national banks may use futures markets.

citation A written order or summons by which a defendant is directed or notified to appear before a court.

city bank A commercial bank belonging to the Federal Reserve System and located in a city that has a Federal Reserve bank or branch.

city collections Items drawn on or payable by banks and businesses in the city where the bank is located.

civil law The legal system prevailing in European, Asiatic, Central American, and South American countries, which inherited their legal systems from Rome. Civil law prevails in practically all nonsocialist countries except English-speaking countries, that is, the United States of America and the British Commonwealth of Nations. *Compare with* common law.

Civil Rights Act of 1968 Legislation of the U.S. government prohibiting discrimination in employment on the basis of the race, color, religion, sex, or national origin of the applicant.

claim (1) A demand for payment or adjustment to compensate for injury, damage, or misrepresentation. (2) The right to any debts, privileges, or other things in another's possession.

claim against estate A demand made on an estate to do or to forbear doing something as a matter of duty. A common example would be the claim submitted by a creditor for payment of a debt owed by the decedent at the time of death.

claim letter A letter requesting compensation for injury, damages, misrepresentation, and so on.

class (options) The type (either put or call) of option on a particular asset.

class action An action brought on behalf of other similarly situated people. The lawsuit is usually originated by relatively few members of a group or class of claimants as representatives of the entire class.

class gift A gift to members of the same class, for example, the class consisting of the children of the same parents.

classified loan A loan that has been classified by supervisory authorities.

Classifications (from worst to least serious) are loss, doubtful, substandard, and special mention. Most major banks now have loan review functions that will classify their own loans without pressure from supervisory and regulatory authorities.

classified stocks Stock issues divided into different classes, each having different rights or privileges for the holder. For example, one class of stock may entitle the holder to voting privileges while another does not.

Clayton Act of 1914 Federal legislation directed against acts that decrease competition, result in unfair competition, or increase monopolistic power.

clean payment A payment unencumbered by documents.

clear (1) To collect funds on which a check is drawn and subsequently to pay these funds to the holder of the check. (2) To process securities transactions through a stock exchange clearing house. (3) (Adj.) Free from all encumbrances.

clear band A band, with a minimum width of 0.6250 inches, measured from the bottom reference edge of the check or other document, that must be free of any magnetic ink other than the characters in magnetic ink already on the document. This band extends the full length of the document. *Also called* MICR clear band.

cleared funds Funds available for withdrawal. *Also called* immediate funds *and* immediately available funds. (In the United States, immediate funds are same day funds in which settlement is simultaneous with the execution of the transaction.)

clearing (1) The interbank presentation of checks, the offsetting of counterclaims, and the settlement of resulting balances. The term may be used in a purely local operation or a regional or nationwide operation. (2) The exchange of mutual claims by financial institutions with settlement of the net balance.

clearing account An intermediate account through which transactions are processed before being transferred to other accounts. Groups of costs and revenues are often moved through such accounts before being totaled and summarized elsewhere.

clearing agency *See* securities depository.

clearing agreement An agreement between two countries that the value of all trade between them will be passed through special accounts in their central banks and kept approximately in balance.

clearing bank A bank that an interchange agreement has designated as the settlement bank for bank credit card transactions.

clearing corporation A mechanism for brokers and other parties to a securities trade to settle trades conveniently, with a minimum of paperwork and exchange of securities. The clearing corporation simplifies settlements by combining and netting transactions for each issue traded. Brokers settle in net amounts rather than by individual trades, normally on a book-entry basis. *See also* continuous net settlement.

clearing credit The total amount of checks presented by a clearing house bank to the other participating banks.

clearing debit The total amount of checks presented to a clearing house bank by the other participating banks.

clearing draft A draft drawn on a clearing member in settlement of a paper or electronic funds transfer entered into interchange by another clearing member.

clearing house (1) An establishment maintained by financial institutions for settling clearing claims. (2) A place where representatives of the banks in the same locality meet daily at an agreed time to exchange checks, drafts, and similar items drawn on each other and to settle the resulting balances. (3) An adjunct to a futures exchange through which transactions executed on the floor of the exchange are settled by matching purchases and sales. A clearing organization is also charged with the proper conduct of delivery procedures.

Clearing House Automated Payments System (CHAPS) A private telecommunication and payment system for interbank sterling payments operated by the London clearing house for banks in the London area.

clearing house funds A method of making payments, usually for cash letters and other exchanges, between banks. If an amount owed is paid in clearing house funds, one or more days may be required before the funds actually become available to the receiving bank. By contrast, payments in federal funds (balances on the books of Federal Reserve banks) represent funds available to the receiving bank on the same day that payment is initiated. *See also* next day funds.

Clearing House Interbank Payments System (CHIPS) *See* CHIPS.

clearing member (1) A firm that is a member of a clearing house or clearing organization. Each clearing member must also be a member of the exchange system. Not all members of the exchange system, however, are members of the clearing organization. All trading by a nonclearing member must be registered with, and eventually settled through, a clearing member. (2) A member of an interchange system who enters transactions into, and receives transactions through, interchange.

clearing number An alphanumeric number assigned by a clearing agency to each party that clears through that agency.

clear text Data in its original unencrypted form.

Clifford trust *See* short-term trust.

clipped coupon *See* coupon.

close *See* closing value.

closed corporation A corporation whose outstanding stock is held by a few people, often members of a single family. The stock of a closed corporation is not available for sale and thus is not traded publicly.

closed end A type of security issue, most commonly mortgage bonds, that prohibits any future sale of a junior issue with the same priority of lien on the corporate assets covered by the original indenture.

closed-end credit A type of credit, usually installment credit, that involves an agreement with a customer specifying the total amount involved, the number of payments, and the due date for each payment. *Compare with* open-end credit.

closed-end fund *See* closed-end investment company.

closed-end investment An investment fund that allows only the original prescribed number of shares to be distributed.

closed-end investment company A company whose primary business is investing its assets in securities of other companies. A closed-end company raises substantially all of its funds at the time it is established. Its stock certificates are traded on stock exchanges or over the counter. *Also called* closed-end fund. *Compare with* open-end fund.

closed-end investment trust An investment fund that allows only the original prescribed number of shares to be distributed. This kind of trust is generally organized for a specific purpose and liquidated from the proceeds of the initial investment.

closed-end mortgage A bond issue secured by real estate that does not permit the pledged assets to be used as collateral for any additional debt.

closed mortgage A corporate trust indenture under which bonds have been authenticated and delivered, such as an original issue, to the extent authorized under the indenture. *Compare with* open-end mortgage.

closely held company A corporation with a small number of owners, all living within one state at the time its stock is issued. The issue, therefore, need not be registered with the Securities and Exchange Commission.

closing The consummation of a real estate transaction that transfers certain rights of ownership in exchange for monetary and other considerations agreed upon. Closing includes the delivery of a deed, financial adjustments, and signing of notes, and the disbursement of funds necessary to the sale or loan transaction.

closing costs The costs to a borrower of closing a mortgage loan. These costs include an origination fee, title insurance, attorney fees, survey, and such prepaid items as taxes and insurance escrow payments.

closing entry In accounting, the transferring of balances in temporary accounts (for example, revenues and expenses for a particular period) into permanent accounts (for example, owners' equity) at the end of an accounting period, to prepare for drawing up financial statements.

closing price The trading price of any security for the last trade of the day.

closing statement A financial statement given the buyer and seller showing the proration of prepaid expenses, closing expenses, and the amounts due from the buyer and due to the seller.

closing the books (1) A custom prevailing among larger corporations to make no transfers of stock for a limited period in advance of a stockholders' meeting or a dividend or registered-interest payment date. Closing the books enables the management to determine who is entitled to receive notice of meetings, to vote at meetings, or to receive dividends or interest. *See also* record date. (2) The closing process in drawing up financial statements at the end of a period.

closing value The last trading price recorded on a specific day of trading. *See also* closing price.

cloud on title A defect in the owner's title to property arising from a written instrument, judgment, or order of court purporting to create in someone else an interest in or lien on the property and thereby impairing the marketability of the owner's title.

club account An account offered by banks to encourage customers to make periodic small deposits to be used for future expenditures, usually within a year (for example, Christmas, Hanukkah, or vacation club).

cluster sample A sample of observations or events drawn randomly from groups of events previously selected in a nonrandom manner. For example, a population being sampled could be divided nonrandomly into male and female. Then random samples could be drawn from each of the two groups and used to compare characteristics of the two groups.

CME *See* Chicago Mercantile Exchange.

CMO *See* collateralized mortgage obligation.

coapplicant *See* joint account.

COBOL A computer programming language designed specifically for the business data-processing industry.

cock date *See* broken date.

code (1) (Verb) To write a program. (2) (Noun) A symbol representing data or a computer program that a machine-readable device can accept.

co-debtor *See* co-maker.

co-debtor stay The section of the Bankruptcy Code that prohibits collection from a co-maker of a consumer debt while the maker is proceeding under Chapter 13 of the Bankruptcy Code.

code of accounts A chart of accounts classified by digits referring to account types.

code of ethics (conduct) A formal set of guidelines that represent a corporation's policies of corporate governance and individual conduct.

Code of Federal Regulations (CFR) A codification of regulations issued by various federal agencies, published and updated by the U.S. Printing Office. Most libraries carry this publication.

coder A person who prepares instructions from detailed flowcharts and other algorithmic procedures prepared by others, as contrasted with a programmer, who prepares the flowcharts and procedures.

codicil A document that is drawn after a will and serves to explain, add to, subtract from, qualify, alter, or revoke the provisions of the will. A codicil stipulates additional desires and bequests of the individual making the will.

codification The use of a number or other symbol to classify or to identify a record.

coding Transforming meaningful data from one character representation to another according to predetermined rules.

cognovit note A legal evidence of indebtedness in which the debtor acknowledges his or her liability and allows the creditor to take judgment without a suit.

coincident indicator An economic data series that consistently moves with overall economic activity, turning up or down at about the same time as the general economy.

coincident reserve requirements *See* contemporaneous reserve accounting.

coinsurance A sharing of the risk of an insurance policy by more than one insurer. Usually, one insurer is liable up to a certain amount and the other insurer is liable over that amount.

collateral Specific property, securities, or other assets pledged by a borrower to a lender as a backup source of loan repayment.

collateral heir A person not in the direct line of the decedent from whom he or she inherits real property, for example, a nephew of a decedent who receives a share of his uncle's estate. *See also* direct heir; heir. *Distinguish from* lineal descendant.

collateralize To secure a debt in part or in full by pledging collateral.

collateralized mortgage obligation (CMO) A mortgage-backed bond on which principal is repaid periodically. CMOs generally consist of several tranches or classes with various classes receiving principal repayments in a prescribed order. Principal in the first class is retired before the mortgage amortization and prepayments are used to pay down the principal in the second class, and so on. ·

collateral mortgage A document used in connection with a loan that effects a lien on real estate, where the purpose of the loan is not for the purchase of the property offered as security.

collateral note A promissory note that pledges certain property as security for a debt.

collateral trust bond A bond secured by other stocks and/or bonds owned by the issuer and deposited with a trustee.

collateral trust notes Notes secured by the deposit of other bonds or stocks, usually issued by holding companies, investment trusts, and rail-roads.

collected balance The cash balance in a bank account for investment, disbursement, or transmittal. Collected balances are ledger balances less checks in the process of collection. *Sometimes called* available balance, good funds, and usable funds, depending on bank policy.

collected funds Cash deposits or checks that have been presented for payment and for which payment has actually been received from the paying bank.

collectibility The lag between the time a check is deposited with the Federal Reserve and the time it is presented to the paying bank. Collectibility should not be confused with availability, which has a 2-day maximum. In instances where collectibility exceeds availability, Fed float is created.

collection (1) The presentation of a negotiable instrument and receipt of payment from the maker. (2) The procedures followed to collect past-due payments.

collection activity A process of collecting delinquent accounts by mail or telephone to obtain payment.

collection department (1) The department of a bank that handles the receipt of negotiable instruments and collects the funds before crediting the depositor's account. (2) The department responsible primarily for following up on past-due accounts. This department is also responsible for recourse, bankruptcy, and the accounts of deceased persons.

collection item Any item received by a bank for a customer's account and for which the bank does not or cannot give immediate, provisional credit.

Collection items receive deferred credit, often require special handling, usually are subject to special fees, and do not create float. *Also called* a noncash item.

collection manager The person responsible for collection activities on past-due accounts.

collection pattern A technique used to monitor and forecast the collection of accounts receivable. A 50-30-20 collection pattern means that, on average, 50 percent of a period's sales are collected in the first period, 30 percent in the following period, and 20 percent in the final period.

collection period The amount of time required to receive funds covering an item presented for payment. The collection period varies depending on the type of negotiable instrument and the distance between the banks involved.

collection ratio The percentage of dollars outstanding that has been repaid during a certain period. The collection ratio is calculated by dividing total payments received during a period, usually a billing cycle, by the dollar amount outstanding during or at the end of that period.

collection systems Systems that accelerate the receipt of cash by reducing processing or mail float through the use of field collection points and lockboxes.

collective investment fund A pooled fund, operated by a bank or trust company, for investment of the assets of separate trust accounts. Pooled funds help investors obtain diversification of investments, potentially improved earnings, and economies in investment procedure. The funds are used to purchase several different issues. Investors then receive units that represent ownership of these pooled securities. National banks and many state banks are authorized to invest trust assets in such funds.

collusion A secret agreement between two or more people to defraud another person of his or her rights or to obtain an unlawful objective.

co-maker The person who signs a note to guarantee a loan made to another person and who is jointly liable with the maker for repayment of the loan. Also referred to as cosigner or co-debtor, this person usually does not receive the direct benefit of the proceeds of the loan. Under Regulation AA, which applies to consumer loans, a lender must give an advance written statement to the co-maker warning that the co-maker is jointly liable for the debt. *See also* cosigner; endorser; endorsement.

combination *See* horizontal combination; vertical combination.

command (1) An electronic pulse, signal, or set of signals to start, stop, or continue some computer operation. (2) The portion of an instruction word that specifies the computer operation to be performed.

commercial account A checking account maintained for a business.

commercial bank *See* bank.

commercial bill A bill of exchange drawn by a seller of goods directly on a buyer.

commercial credit Loans and other short-term credit extended to business.

commercial finance company A company that specializes in making working capital or investment capital loans to small businesses.

commercial invoice A document listing goods sold and/or shipped, stating the price and terms of sale.

commercial law The whole body of substantive jurisprudence applicable to the rights, intercourse, and relation of people engaged in commerce, trade, or mercantile pursuits.

commercial lending Lending to businesses.

commercial letter of credit A letter of credit where the issuing bank's customer is a buyer of goods, and the bank promises to pay the seller upon presentation of certain documents representing shipment of the goods.

commercial loan A loan to a business to meet short- or long-term needs.

commercial mortgage A loan secured by real estate that is used or zoned for business purposes or multiunit dwellings.

commercial paper A negotiable, short-term, unsecured promissory note in bearer form, issued by well-regarded businesses. Commercial paper is generally sold at a discount and has a maximum maturity of 9 months. *Also called* paper.

commercial property Property used or eligible to be used for business purposes. The term does not usually include rental apartment houses or other residential uses, even though that kind of property is used in business. The term is often used to indicate office buildings, retail space, and other stores, but not warehouses or industrial property.

commercial teller The teller who handles transactions for commercial accounts.

commingled fund A common fund in which the funds of several accounts are mixed.

commission (1) The fee paid to a broker or financial institution for consummating a transaction involving sale or purchase of assets or services. (2) A percentage of the principal, or of the income, or of both that a fiduciary receives as compensation for services. *Distinguish from* allowance, charge, *and* fee.

commitment An agreement between a lender and a borrower to lend money at a future date, subject to specified conditions and terms. It may also mean the agreement by an investor to purchase or sell a loan, subject to specified conditions, at a future date. The fee that the borrower or the loan seller pays for the commitment is called a commitment fee. *See also* loan commitment; secondary market commitment.

commitment and disclosure statement A written acknowledgment by a real estate lender, required under the Truth in Lending Act, that stipulates under what conditions funds will be lent to an applicant under an adjustable rate mortgage.

commitment fee (1) Any fee paid by a potential borrower to a lender for the lender's promise to lend money, usually at a specified rate within a given time in the future. (2) A fee that a loan seller pays to an investor to purchase a loan, subject to specified conditions, at a future date.

commitment letter essentials A letter of intent that is customarily employed to reduce to writing a preliminary understanding of parties who intend to enter into a contract.

commitment overhang The maximum amount of money a bank has legally committed to lend to a borrower.

committee for incompetent A person or trust institution appointed by a court of law to administer the affairs of a person judged incompetent or unable to handle his or her own affairs. *Similar to* guardian, conservator, *and* curator.

Committee on Uniform Securities Identification Procedures (CUSIP) A uniform numbering system (named after the committee that designed it) widely used to identify specific securities and their issuers. This system includes corporate, municipal, state, federal, and some foreign issues. The CUSIP number appears on the certificate and in documents used in processing securities. *See also* CUSIP number.

commodities Basic products, usually but not always agricultural or mineral, that are traded on a commodity exchange.

commodities (commodity) futures contract A contract to purchase or sell a specific amount of a given commodity at a specified future date.

Commodity Credit Corporation A federal corporation formed to finance public price supports for agricultural commodities. The Commodity Credit Corporation purchases, sells, stores, transports, and subsidizes such commodities.

commodity exchange An organized market where commodity contracts are bought and sold for immediate and future delivery.

Commodity Futures Trading Commission (CFTC) The independent federal agency created by Congress to regulate trading in futures and options.

Commodity Futures Trading Commission Act of 1974 A federal law that created the Commodity Futures Trading Commission (CFTC) to regulate trading in futures and options. Previously, the Commodity Exchange Authority of the U.S. Department of Agriculture regulated the market.

commodity market The market or public demand for purchases and sales of commodity futures.

commodity trading The process of buying or selling contracts for spot or future delivery of a commodity.

common bond A requirement for membership in credit unions. The common bond is most often the fact that members share the same occupation or work for the same employer.

common disaster Sudden and extraordinary misfortune that brings about the simultaneous or near-simultaneous death of two or more associated persons.

common element The undivided interest held by the owner of a condominium in any portion of the condominium other than individual units.

common language for consumer credit A standardized system of terms and abbreviations for reporting the payment habits of credit users, developed by the Associated Credit Bureaus, Inc.

common law Law based on judicial decisions, or "case law." Common law is the legal system prevailing in English-speaking countries, that is, the United States of America and the British Commonwealth of Nations. It originated in England and its form of development was different from that of Roman (civil) law. *Compare with* civil law.

common-law trust *See* business trust.

common stock A security (or securities) that represents ownership in a corporation. Common stock is the one type of security that must be issued by a corporation. The two most important common stockholder rights are voting and dividend rights. Common stockholder claims on corporate assets are subordinate to those of bondholders, preferred stockholders, and general creditors.

common stock (special classes) Corporations typically issue only one class of common stock. However, some issue other classes, such as voting and nonvoting common class, or common class A, class B, or class C. These classes may have, for example, restricted voting rights or a different number of votes per share. Restricted stock, or letter stock that is not intended for resale to another investor, is another class of common stock.

common stock equivalent A security that in form is not a common stock but in substance is accounted for as if it were a common stock.

common trust fund A fund maintained by a bank or a trust company exclusively for the collective investment and reinvestment of money by the bank or trust company in its capacity as trustee, executor, administrator, or guardian. A common trust fund must conform to state statutes and regulations. It must also conform to the federal rules and regulations of the Comptroller of the Currency pertaining to the collective investment of trust funds by national banks. *Also called* collective investment fund *or* commingled fund.

communicating pair Two parties that have previously agreed to exchange data.

communication service A service that moves messages among subscribers, including funds transfer transactions that are subject to settlement by other means, for example, through the Federal Reserve.

communication system The means by which instructions and information pass between banks and between banks and their customers. These include S.W.I.F.T., telex, fax, cable, voice, video, and mail communications.

community bank A small local bank that serves the financial needs of one community.

community property Property in which husband and wife both have an undivided one-half interest by reason of their marital status. Community property is recognized in all civil law countries and in certain states of the Southwest and Pacific Coast area of the United States.

Community Reinvestment Act (CRA) A law passed in 1977 that requires financial institutions to meet the credit needs of their community, including the lowand moderate-income sections of the local community. It also requires banks to make reports concerning their investment in the areas where they do business. The act mandates that a statement be adopted by the board of directors every year, and this statement must be made available to the public. Also, the Federal Reserve Board is to consider the financial institution's CRA policies when the financial institution files a request for an expansion of business, such as a branch application. It allows consumers to object to such expansion if the institution has not invested in the community. A new policy statement was adopted in 1989 that expands the way regulators evaluate a bank's CRA program.

community trust A trust ordinarily composed of gifts made by many

people to a trustee for educational, charitable, or other benevolent purposes in a community. The property of the trust is trusteed. A selected group of citizens who act as a distribution committee control the distribution of the funds. There may be one trustee or, more often, several trustees, usually trust institutions of the community. In administering the property committed to its care and management, each trustee serves under identical declarations of trust. Some community trusts are called foundations. *See also* foundation.

commutation A power in a trustee or other individual to convert the interest of a beneficiary of a trust into the right to receive a fixed payment from the trust and thereby terminate that interest. Such a power, in particular situations such as a grantor income trust, could be used to reduce the value of the grantor's retained interest for federal estate tax purposes.

comparative disadvantage *See* law of comparative disadvantage.

compatibility A situation in which one machine may accept and process data prepared by another machine without conversion or code modification.

compatible systems Two computer systems that can be integrated without modification.

compensating balance The balance that a customer must keep on deposit with a bank in order to ensure a credit line, to gain unlimited checking privileges, and to offset the bank's expenses in providing various services.

compensation (1) The income or wages, bonuses, "perks," and other benefits received for services rendered. (2) A general term covering four different, specific terms: allowance, charge, commission, and fee.

compensation trading The act of offering goods rather than cash as partial or full payment to an exporter.

compensatory financing Short-term loans offered by the International Monetary Fund to compensate for fluctuations in a member country's exports.

competition *See* imperfect competition; perfect competition; unfair competition.

Competitive Equality Banking Act Legislation enacted by Congress in 1987 significantly affecting the operations of nonbank banks, the powers granted to commercial banks and bank holding companies, and the timeframe during which banks of deposit must make checks available to customers. Section 1204 requires that any adjustable rate mortgage must include a limitation on the maximum interest rate during the term of the loan. *See also* nonbank bank; rate cap; Regulation Z.

competitive profile A list of a firm's major competitors and a comparison of their growth, product mixes, and services. For banks, this profile would include a comparison of growth in deposit and loan volume.

compilation The degree of work performed by a public accounting firm in conjunction with the issuance of financial statements of a nonpublic entity that is less in scope than a review or audit. As such, the accountant does not express an opinion or any other form of assurance on the financial statements.

compile To prepare a program in a machine language from a computer program in another programming language.

compiler A computer system that translates high-level source data from a language such as COBOL into machine or assembly language that provides instructions that are easier to understand, read, and write.

complex capital structure Capital structure that exists when a corporation has securities that, if assumed converted, would cause a material dilution of earnings per share.

complex trust A trust in which the trustee (a) is not required to distribute income currently, (b) distributes amounts other than income, or (c) makes a charitable contribution. *Compare with* simple trust.

compliance examinations Specially designed examinations given by federal and/or state regulatory authorities as a comprehensive review of a bank's compliance with federal and state consumer credit statutes and regulations.

compliance inspection report A report issued by a designated compliance inspector indicating whether required repairs or replacements have been satisfactorily completed. These reports are often required by FHA, VA, and direct lenders in connection with the granting of a loan.

compliance program The policies and procedures that a financial institution follows to ensure it is obeying all federal and state laws and regulations.

compliance testing Audit testing whose objective is to (a) confirm the existence, (b) assess the effectiveness, and (c) check the continuity of operation of those internal controls on which reliance is to be placed.

composites Data that combine information from various sources to yield summary statistics concerning the securities industry.

composite tape A stock-ticker printout that reports transactions occurring in national, regional, and over-the-counter exchange markets.

compounding Adding interest accrued for one period to the principal at the beginning of the period and computing interest for the next period on the total interest plus principal. Compounding may be done at various intervals. The more frequent the compounding, the higher the actual rate of interest paid, or the "yield." Continuous (instantaneous) compounding yields the highest actual rate.

compound interest The method of interest computation in which the rate of interest is applied to a deposit for a specific period (1 day, 1 month, 1 quarter) and then in subsequent periods is applied to the principal plus previously earned interest.

comptroller *See* controller.

Comptroller of the Currency The official of the U.S. government, appointed by the president and confirmed by the Senate, who is responsible for chartering, examining, supervising, and, if necessary, liquidating national banks.

comptroller's call The term applied to the Federal Reserve Act requirement that national banks submit certain reports of their financial activities at least three times a year. These "call" reports also must be published in local newspapers.

computer balancing A section of the general accounting department responsible for balancing registers to accounting machine tapes.

computer crime Reference to a broad array of defalcations initiated via abuse of existing electronic data-processing systems.

computer output microfilm (COM) A process by which data are recorded on microfilm or microfiche directly from a computer file (for example, a magnetic tape) without printing hard copy (paper).

computer proof and transit The use of a computer to sort, move, and list transit items (checks).

computer word A sequence of bits or characters treated as a unit and capable of being stored in one location in the computer. *Also called* machine word.

concentration account A deposit account to which funds are periodically transferred from other accounts held in the same name.

concentration bank A bank that serves as a concentration point for corporate funds transferred from local depository banks and that usually performs disbursement services or provides credit.

concentration ratio An indicator of the degree of competitiveness that exists in a certain market. The ratio is calculated as the share of the market held by, for example, the top 4, 8, 10, or 20 firms.

concurrent jurisdiction The jurisdiction of several different tribunals, each authorized to deal with the same subject matter.

concurrent processing A method of processing in which two or more jobs appear to be processed at the same time. Actually, the instructions of all the jobs are processed one at a time, alternating to make the most efficient use of the system; that is, parts of one job are interspersed with parts of another job. *Also called* multitasking.

condemnation The appropriation of private property for public use under the right of eminent domain.

condensed balance sheet A balance sheet that combines individual balance sheet captions to eliminate unnecessary detail. Condensed balance sheets provide a brief overview of a firm's financial position.

conditional commitment for guarantee The notice by the Farmers Home Administration (or other guarantor) to a bank that a loan has been approved for guarantee, subject to the conditions set forth in the commitment.

conditional endorsement An endorsement that attempts to restrict the endorser's liability. Conditional endorsements place no legal obligation on either the paying bank or future endorsers to determine the validity of the restriction.

conditional gift A gift of property under conditions of a will that is subject to some condition specified in the will or in the trust instrument. *Compare with* absolute gift.

conditional sale A sale in which the transfer of title depends on the performance of some condition, for example, the payment of the balance of the purchase price.

conditional sales contract A contract for the sale of an asset, financed by installment payments, under which the title remains with the seller until all payments are made.

condition precedent A qualification or restriction that must happen or be performed before a contract or the estate dependent on it can arise or vest.

condition subsequent A condition whose failure or nonperformance defeats an already vested estate.

condominium The system of separate ownership of individual units in a multiple-unit building, with all the unit owners having a right in common to use the common elements. *Compare with* cooperative; cooperative apartment.

conduit theory Under U.S. tax law, certain forms of doing business are not subject to tax directly; rather, the liability is passed through (hence "conduit") to the investors or owners, who are taxed on any realized profits. For example, a regulated investment company (mutual fund) is not subject to tax directly, but the fund investors are taxed on interest or dividends earned or securities sold. Similarly with a partnership. Such entities are called pass-through entities.

confession of judgment An acknowledgment in a note by which the defendant, to save expense, permits judgment to be entered against him or her without trial in court.

confidence level The probability that a statistic will fall within a specific range of values. For example, to determine the percentage of checking customers who fall within a given age range, a random sample of one-tenth of these customers could be surveyed to learn what proportion of the sample falls in that age range. Assume the sample statistic is 55 percent. Consulting a table of confidence intervals, one could say with a 90 percent (or greater) confidence level that the population statistic (that is, what would be found if every customer were surveyed) would fall within a specific range of the sample statistic (for example, plus or minus 3 percent, or between 52 percent and 58 percent).

confirmation (1) A written or electronic message confirming an original telegraphic or telephone transmission, usually used in connection with fund transfers. *See also* broker confirmation. (2) The auditing process by which a bank or auditor contacts a customer to confirm the bank's records regarding the status of an account, loan, and so on. *See also* negative confirmation; positive confirmation.

confirmation of purchase or sale A message sent by the executing party providing the accounting in detail for securities and payments.

confirmed letter of credit A letter of credit where a second bank, in addition to the issuing bank, undertakes the responsibility to honor drawings made in compliance with the terms of the credit. This second bank is called the confirming bank.

confirming house A firm that acts as intermediary between an overseas customer requiring goods and a seller of those goods in the home market.

confirm only comparison option (COCO) An option for settling securities trades that generates receive and deliver tickets but does not generate automatic book-entry settlement. Trade settlement must be effected directly between the broker and the institution.

conflict of interest (1) A situation in which an action taken by an individual in an official capacity may benefit that individual personally. The benefit may be a gift, gratuity, commis-sion, discount, or future employment. (2) The term used by attorneys to describe a situation in which a lawyer may be representing two or more parties with discordant interests.

conflict of laws The branch of law that concerns the legal principles applicable when the laws of two or more jurisdictions are, or are claimed to be, in conflict with one another.

conformed copy A copy of an original document on which the signature, seal, and other such features are typed or otherwise noted.

conglomerate merger The process by which two businesses with unrelated product lines are combined into one corporation.

consanguinity Blood relationship. *Distinguish from* affinity (relationship by marriage).

consent to pledge A legal document signed by a party who owns a particular asset, giving permission for another party to pledge that asset as security for a loan.

consent trust A trust in which the consent of the settlor or some designated person is required before the trustee can take a specified action. *Distinguish from* consult account.

conservator (1) Generally, a person or trust institution appointed by a court to care for property. (2) Specifically, a person or trust institution appointed by a court to care for and manage the property of an incompetent person, in the same way that a guardian cares for and manages the property of a minor.

consideration Something of value given by one party to another in exchange for a promise or act by the other party.

consignee The recipient of a consignment shipment.

consignment note A document accompanying imported and exported goods detailing the contents and the names of the importer and exporter.

consignment shipment A shipment of goods that is not paid for until the goods are sold by the importer.

consol A bond that pays a fixed amount of interest but never repays the principal. Consols were first issued by the British government in 1814. *Also called* a perpetual bond, irredeemable bond, annuity bond, *and* continued bond.

console A device used by a computer operator to type in commands to the computer.

consolidated balance sheet *See* consolidated financial statements.

consolidated financial statements The combined financial statements of a parent company and its subsidiaries, showing assets, liabilities, and net worth for the total organization, net of any intercompany items that are eliminated in consolidation.

consolidated statement A statement that combines all personal banking services in one monthly report.

consolidated systemwide bond A bond issued by federal farm credit banks.

consolidated tape A record of trading volume and price per share for trades in stocks listed on the New York Stock Exchange (NYSE). This record includes all trades made in NYSE-listed stocks on seven stock exchanges and over the counter.

consolidation The surrender of two or more small denominations of a security for a larger denomination. Consolidation frequently follows the receipt of small lots of securities resulting from the exercise of rights or stock dividends.

consolidation loan An installment loan that enables a borrower to repay smaller outstanding loans, with one periodic payment rather than several smaller ones.

consortium bank A bank owned by several banks, frequently each from a different country.

constant (1) The percentage of an original loan, if paid in equal annual increments, that would provide for the reduction of the interest and principal over the life of the loan. (2) A quantity or message available as data in an EDP machine that will not change with time.

constant ratio investing A method of investing to maintain at a fixed level the ratios among different types of securities held in a portfolio.

constitutional court One of the federal courts as provided in Article III, Section I, of the U.S. Constitution.

construction A legal process involving the interpretation of ambiguous or inconsistent language in a document, for example, the interpretation of a will by a court.

construction loan A short-term loan to a contractor to finance the cost of construction. The lender makes partial advances (progress payments) to the builder or owner at specified stages of completion. The loan is repaid when construction is completed, usually by proceeds from a mortgage loan.

constructive notice Information (such as notice of intent to file a lien) delivered to the public at large by appearing in prescribed public records. The public is legally presumed to have been notified if the prescribed form of notice has been used.

constructive receipt doctrine Income, although not actually reduced to a taxpayer's possession, that is credited to his or her account, set apart for him or her, or otherwise made available so that he or she may draw on it at any time. The constructive receipt doctrine helps determine, using cash method accounting, what is included in a taxpayer's gross income.

constructive trust A trust imposed by a court of equity as a means of doing justice, without regard to the intention of the parties, in a situation in which a person who holds title to property is under a duty to convey it to another person. *Distinguish from* express trust *and* resulting trust.

consular invoice An invoice for merchandise shipped from one country to another, prepared by the shipper and certified at the shipping point by a consul of the country of destination. The consul's certification applies to the value of the merchandise, port of shipment, destination, and, in certain cases, place of origin of the merchandise.

consult account A trust in which the instrument requires the trustee to consult a designated party before taking action. *Distinguish from* consent trust.

consultant A person with whom a fiduciary must confer in administering a fiduciary account.

Consumer Advisory Council An advisory board of consumers established by the Equal Credit Opportunity Act to advise the Federal Reserve Board on a broad range of consumer issues.

consumer credit Loans extended to individuals. Consumer credit includes secured and unsecured installment and revolving credit. *Also called* personal loans.

consumer credit company *See* consumer finance company.

Consumer Credit Protection Act A 1969 federal statute covering consumer credit activities. Popularly known as the Truth in Lending Act, this act applies to all lenders that extend credit to consumers. It requires disclosure of certain pertinent facts about loan rates and charges. For example, it requires that the annual percentage rate (APR) and the total finance charges be stated. *See also* Regulation Z, which is issued under Title I of this act.

consumer finance company A firm whose primary business is making small loans to individuals. *Also called* consumer credit company.

consumer lease A contract in the form of a bailment or lease for the use of personal property by a natural person, primarily for personal, family, or household purposes.

Consumer Leasing Act Legislation passed in 1976 requiring lessors to disclose specified information about payment, trade-in allowances, and estimated value of property at the end of the lease. *See also* realized value; Regulation M; total lease obligation.

consumer loan *See* personal loan.

consumer price index (CPI) An index measuring the cost of a hypothetical basket of goods and services purchased by consumers. Although different indexes are computed, the index generally used is the CPI(U), which measures the prices paid by an urban wage-earner family. *Also called* cost-of-living index.

consummation The time when a contractual relationship exists between the parties to a transaction.

consumption The purchase or use of a product or service by a consumer.

contemplation of death The act of considering and acting on the possibility of death. For federal estate taxes, transfers made within 3 years of the date of death are considered transfers in contemplation of death and, as such, along with gift taxes paid, are taxable in an estate.

contemporaneous reserve accounting (CRA) A system that requires depository institutions to hold reserves against deposits currently outstanding. The Federal Reserve now allows contemporaneous reserve requirements, with some modification. *Also called* coincident, simultaneous, *and* synchronous reserve requirements.

contest of a will An attempt by legal process to prevent the probate of a will or the distribution of property according to the will.

contingency (1) An event, the occurrence of which is somehow dependent on another event happening, not happening, or on chance. (2) In accounting, contingencies relate to possible gains or losses to an enterprise. Depending on whether the contingency is probable, reasonably possible, or remote, and whether the contingency is reasonably estimable, different accounting treatments are prescribed.

contingent beneficiary A beneficiary whose interest is conditioned on a future occurrence that may or may not occur. Unless or until the condition occurs, the beneficiary interest is only contingent.

contingent executor An executor named in a will whose authority depends on the action or nonaction of the principal executor.

contingent interest A future interest in real or personal property that is dependent on the fulfillment of a stated condition. Thus the interest may never come into existence. *Distinguish from* vested interest.

contingent liability (1) The contingent obligation of a person or business that guarantees a payment. (2) A liability that will exist only if a specific event occurs.

contingent life tenant A person whose life interest in an estate depends on certain events occurring.

contingent order An order issued to a broker that is effective only when a specific price is reached or a specific price difference occurs between two securities.

contingent payment order A payment order that is executed by a bank only on receipt of a stipulated covering payment that provides the funds with which to make the payment.

contingent remainder A future interest in property that is dependent on the fulfillment of a stated condition before the termination of a prior estate. *Distinguish from* vested remainder. *See also* remainder.

contingent reserve A part of earnings set aside for an unexpected need or for a need where the magnitude of the payment cannot be ascertained in advance.

contingent trustee A trustee whose appointment is dependent on the original (or a successor) trustee's failure to act.

continued bond *See* consol.

continuing guarantee A guarantee of one party's debts by another party that is not limited to a specific loan but may also be applicable to later debts.

continuous audit A constant audit of all entries affecting a particular account.

continuous-form checks Checks manufactured by a method that results in many checks being joined together for automatic feeding and printing in data-processing printers.

continuous net settlement (CNS) A process for settling securities trades that summarizes multiple transactions into single figures for net security and net money settlement. After trade affirmation, the identity of the contra side is lost. The bank and broker settle all security and money transactions with the clearing corporation. *See also* balance-order settlement; trade-for-trade (TFT) settlement.

contra (1) The opposite side. (2) The opposite party to a security trade.

contra account An account that partially offsets the entries in another account. Examples are accumulated depreciation accounts (which offset fixed asset accounts) and reserves for possible credit losses (which offset receivables accounts).

contract (1) An agreement between two or more people to perform, or to refrain from performing, some acts. (2) A unit of trading for a commodity, exchange, or financial future. (3) The actual bilateral agreement between the buyer and seller of a future transaction, as defined by an exchange.

contract bond A bond that assumes the liability for the principal's failure to perform a designated task.

contract in foreign currency An agreement to buy and sell an amount of one currency for another at an agreed exchange rate.

contract month The month in which futures contracts may be satisfied by making or accepting delivery.

contract of guarantee (line of credit) A contract issued by the Farmers Home Administration (FmHA) to a lender testifying that FmHA agrees to guarantee the bank's loan.

contract of sale An agreement between a buyer and a seller of real property describing the property to which title will be conveyed upon the satisfaction of certain conditions, including the payment of an agreed price.

contract sheets Daily reports provided by a clearing corporation to brokerage houses, listing all transactions on stock exchanges reported into the clearing system involving a specific brokerage house.

contractual accumulation plan An installment method of purchasing shares in a mutual fund. The investor agrees to invest a set amount in the shares periodically.

contractual income The income determined by contract before a service is rendered. Rent, wages, and interest payments are examples of contractual income.

contractual intermediaries Financial institutions that obtain their funds by entering into long-term contracts. Examples of contractual intermemediaries include insurance companies and pension funds.

contractual liability An express obligation to repay all debts arising on an account.

contribution (1) A sum paid by an employer to an unemployment or group insurance fund or to a retirement benefit plan for employees. (2) A sum paid by employees under such a fund or plan.

contributory benefit plan A benefit plan that requires employees to pay a portion of the cost.

control (1) In data processing, part of a digital computer or processor that determines the execution and interpretation of instructions in proper sequence. *See also* master control. (2) The components in any mechanism responsible for interpreting and executing manually initiated directions. (3) In some business applications, a mathematical checking of computations performed. (4) In corporate management, the percentage of ownership of a corporation needed to control its management. Theoretically, this is 51 percent. However, in large corporations where stock ownership is widely diffused, this percentage can be much lower. A bank holding company must obtain Federal Reserve approval before acquiring more than 4 percent of the voting shares of a bank. (5) In management, the process by which managers ensure that instructions are carried out.

control account An account that summarizes the totals of various subsidiary accounts.

control data Data used to identify, select, execute, or modify other routines, records, files, operations, or data.

control field A constant location where information for control purposes is placed.

controller A senior accounting officer of an organization. *Also called* comptroller.

control number An alphanumeric identification field used by a submitter to identify a transaction.

control risk The risk that the system of internal control will fail to detect or prevent an error.

convenience amount The amount in figures on a payment document that shows the valid payable amount of the document.

convenience amount clear area An area above and below the convenience amount scan band held clear of printing that would interfere with the convenience amount.

convenience amount constraint area A rectangular area within the convenience amount scan band that restricts the location of the convenience amount to a fixed position.

convenience amount scan band An imaginary band across the face of a payment document, parallel to the bottom edge of the document, used by equipment to read the convenience amount.

conventional loan A mortgage that is not insured by the Federal Housing Administration or guaranteed by the Veterans Administration.

conventional mortgage *See* conventional loan.

conversational mode The mode of operation that maintains real-time communications between humans and machines. In this mode, the system is used only for servicing remote terminals.

conversion An arbitrage strategy in options involving the purchase of the underlying instrument offset by the establishment of a synthetic short position in options on the underlying instrument (the purchase of a put and sale of a call). The overall position is unaffected by price movements in the underlying instrument. This trade would be established when small price discrepancies open up between the long position in the underlying instrument and the synthetic short position in the options. *See also* arbitrage; reverse conversion; synthetic positions.

conversion agent A corporate agent that exchanges new securities for old when an issuer replaces one type of security with another.

conversion charge The fee an investor pays to move his or her funds from one mutual fund to another managed by the same company.

conversion feature A feature of mutual funds that permits an investor holding shares in one of several funds all operated by one investment company to switch his or her investment readily from one fund to another in the group.

conversion parity The price at which common stock has the same value as bonds convertible into that stock. The holder of a convertible bond will usually not exercise the privilege until the market price of common stock reaches conversion parity.

conversion premium (bond) A price concession offered to the holder of an outstanding bond to encourage the

holder to buy a new bond being offered in exchange for the outstanding bond.

conversion price The price at which one common share will be valued if a security (such as bonds, debentures, or preferred stock) is exchanged for common stock. *See also* convertible (conversion) feature.

conversion privilege The right of an individual covered by a group insurance contract to purchase individual insurance of a stated type and amount, when all or part of the group insurance is canceled, without meeting any medical requirements, provided that application is made within a stipulated period (normally 31 days).

conversion rate The rate at which one currency is exchanged for another.

conversion ratio The number of common shares that will be issued for each $1,000 bond or preferred share. *See also* convertible (conversion) feature.

convert (1) To change numerical data from one number base to another. (2) To transfer data from one recorded medium to another. (3) To exchange one security for another.

convertibility The degree to which a currency can be exchanged for gold or another currency.

convertible A bond, debenture, or preferred stock that can be exchanged by the owner for another class of securities, according to the terms of the issue.

convertible bond A bond that gives the holder the right to exchange it for some other type of security, usually common or preferred stock, within some specific period.

convertible debenture An unsecured note or bond that must be converted to common stock at or by a specified future date.

convertible (conversion) feature A feature offered on some bonds, debentures, or preferred stock that allows the holder to exchange the security, usually for common stock, at a stated exchange ratio. The interest or dividend rate may be lower than the market rate on a comparable nonconvertible security, but the market value of the convertible security will rise if the common stock price rises sufficiently.

convertible preferred stock Preferred stock that is convertible into common stock under specified conditions.

conveyance (1) The transfer of title or interest to real property from one person to another. (2) The document that effects the transfer of real property, such as a deed, lease, or mortgage.

cooperative The multiple ownership of property in which a central party holds title to the property and grants the right of occupancy for particular units to shareholders by means of proprietary leases or similar arrangements.

cooperative apartment A dwelling unit in a multidwelling complex in which each owner has an interest in the entire complex and a lease on his or her own apartment. The owner does not own his or her apartment, however, as in the case of a condominium, but owns a share in the corporation that holds actual title.

coops *See* banks for cooperatives.

copy (1) (Noun) Carbon copy, photocopy, microfilm or microfiche copy, or copy produced by any accurate information retrieval system. A creditor who uses a computerized or mechanized system need not keep a written copy of a document if the creditor can regenerate the precise text of the document on request. (2) (Verb) To reproduce data, unchanged, in a new location or at another destination.

copyright To register a writing, work of art, or design with the Library of Congress upon publication, in order to claim exclusive right to reproduce, publish, and sell the material.

core In a computer, the working memory immediately available for accessing.

core allocation The provision of core space (a) for programs permanently or temporarily in core; (b) for data permanently or temporarily in core; and (c) for working space.

core deposits (1) That portion of a bank's deposits that is relatively stable and has a predictable cost. Deposits fluctuate seasonally and cyclically, but even in adverse circumstances do not fall below some minimum level. That minimum level is referred to as the bank's core deposits. (2) A specific deposit account that a bank feels will be relatively stable in adverse circumstances.

core equity *See* capital adequacy; Tier One capital.

core storage The fundamental and most important storage of the central processing unit. The core storage is usually composed of magnetic cores that are uniquely arranged in matrices on digit planes, each core of which can store one binary digit.

corporate agency services Services performed for corporations, in connection with their corporate stock and bond issues, by outside parties such as corporate trust departments. Services may include issuing and recording ownership, transferring stock from one owner to another, and paying dividends and interest.

corporate bond Long-term debt financing by a corporation to raise outside capital. The conditions of the financing are spelled out in an indenture. *See also* corporate indenture.

corporate campaign A marketing campaign intended to benefit the image of a particular corporation.

corporate card A bank card issued to companies for company employees to use for business expenses. The liability for abuse of the card typically rests with the company, not the employee.

corporate charter A corporation's constitution, granted by the state in which it is incorporated, that specifies, for example, rules and limitations of ownership, operation, funding, and security issuance.

corporate depository A trust institution that serves as the depository of funds or other property. *See also* depository.

corporate fiduciary A trust institution that serves in a fiduciary capacity, such as executor, administrator, trustee, or guardian.

corporate income tax A federal or state tax levied on a corporation's profits.

corporate indenture An agreement by a bank to act as an intermediary between a corporation offering public bonds and the purchasers of those bonds. The bank agrees to act as a trustee by protecting the bondholders' interests.

corporate investment program A plan for the investment of a corporation's assets.

corporate note A debt instrument in which a corporation promises to pay a specific amount at a stated future date, plus stated interest, if any. Unlike a corporate bond, a corporate note requires no indenture.

corporate raider A company or person who has a history of attempting to acquire corporations by means of unfriendly takeovers. *See also* greenmail; tender offer.

corporate reorganization (1) A major change in the capital structure and financial operation of a corporation, often requiring new issues and exchanges of securities. (2) A major change in the management structure of a corporation.

corporate resolution An official document, issued by a corporation and bearing the corporate seal, establishing the authorities of officers as approved by the directors and authorizing certain actions (such as the opening of a bank account).

corporate seal A company's official seal (an emblem or a device that imprints that emblem). The corporate seal is sometimes required for authentication of legal documents, although many states have done away with corporate seals.

corporate shell A corporation that exists legally but is not active.

corporate trust A trust created by a corporation (for example, a trust to secure a bond issue).

corporate trustee A trust institution serving as a trustee.

corporation A business organization that is treated as a single legal entity and is owned by its stockholders, whose liability is generally limited to the extent of their investment. The ownership of a corporation is represented by shares of stock that are issued to people or to other companies in exchange for cash, physical assets, services, and goodwill. The stockholders elect the board of directors, which then directs the management of the corporation's affairs. *See also* sole corporation.

corporeal hereditament *See* hereditament.

corpus (body) (1) The principal or capital of an estate, as distinguished from the income. (2) The property within a trust account, the title to which vests in the person entitled to the future estate. *Also called* the principal of the trust account.

correction entry (1) The functional unit responsible for correcting transactions and logging batches into the computer system. (2) An entry to correct an error.

correlation (1) The degree of relationship between two sets of data. A correlation near plus or minus 1 indicates that movements in one set of figures tend to be closely associated either directly or indirectly with movements in the other set. (2) The degree to which a change in price or yield of one financial instrument varies with a change in price or yield of another financial instrument (for example, in constructing a hedge).

correspondent (1) A bank, securities firm, or other financial institution that performs services for another such firm. (2) A lender who sells to and services mortgage loans for a secondary market investor under the terms of an agreement.

correspondent balances Deposits one bank keeps in another bank to compensate that bank for services rendered or to provide a balance for clearing transactions through that bank.

correspondent bank A larger bank that sells its service(s) to other, small respondent banks or financial institutions from which it receives fees or compensating balances. *Also called* upstream correspondent.

correspondent bank balance *See* due from account.

correspondent delivery and collection service One of the envelope settlement services offered by clearing corporations. This service provides facilities for the delivery and collection of securities for banks and brokers located outside clearing house centers.

cosigner A person who signs an instrument along with another person and becomes responsible for the obligation. A cosigner can be either a co-maker or an endorser. *See also* co-maker; endorser.

cost *See* direct cost; fixed cost; marginal cost; standard cost; variable cost.

cost accounting A branch of accounting that deals primarily with classifying, recording, allocating, summarizing, and reporting current and expected costs of materials, labor, and overhead of producing and distributing a commodity or rendering a service.

cost and freight (C&F) A shipping term indicating that the quoted price of a good includes the cost of the good and handling and freight charges up to delivery at a foreign port.

cost and insurance (C&I) A shipping term indicating that the quoted price of a good includes the cost of the good and insurance only and excludes freight charges.

cost approach to value One of the methods used in estimating property value. It is based on the assumption that the worth of a property can be indicated by adding together the current cost to construct the improvements (less depreciation), the land value, and entrepreneurial profit.

cost basis The original price or cost of an asset. The cost basis is usually based on the purchase price of the asset or, for assets received from an estate, on the appraised value of the asset at the death of the donor or at some anniversary or other fixed date.

cost-benefit analysis A method used to determine whether a particular investment project is worthwhile. The analysis compares the total cost associated with a project to the total benefits. The project is acceptable if total costs are less than total benefits.

cost bond A bond that guarantees the payment of costs in any legal action.

cost center A unit in a bank that does not generate income. In a profit-planning system, that unit budgets only its expenses. Compare with a profit center, which generates income and budgets both income and expenses. *Also called* expense center.

cost containment Methods for controlling the rising cost of insurance or other business expenses.

cost, insurance, freight (CIF) A shipping term indicating that the quoted price of a good includes the cost of the good, the insurance charges, and the freight charges to the named destination.

cost of capital An overall rate, typically determined by calculating the weighted average of a firm's costs of debt and equity. As used in capital budgeting, it directs a firm not to make investment outlays unless the outlays promise a return greater than the overall cost of capital to the firm.

cost-of-living adjustment An increase in wages linked to inflation.

cost-of-living index An index intended to measure what it costs to maintain a given living standard. There is no regularly published index that correctly provides a measurement of the cost of living. Sometimes the consumer price index is used as an approximation for the cost of living. *See also* consumer price index.

cost of money A figure calculated from the respective costs of the several sources of bank funds to establish a cost of total funds that is charged to the bank's profit centers. The cost of money must be covered by a bank's return on loans and other assets, if the bank is to make a profit.

cost or market, whichever is lower *See* lower of cost or market.

cost plus fixed fee (CPFF) A contract used for some types of construction, development programs, and research programs for which costs cannot be estimated beforehand. The compensation is the sum of all expenses incurred plus a specific fee.

cost-plus pricing The practice of setting a selling price by adding a fixed amount or percentage to costs.

cost-push inflation An inflationary cycle that results from the increasing costs of supplies and labor. These increased costs lead to increased prices for goods. As the cost of living rises, workers demand wage increases and the cycle repeats itself.

cost-volume-profit relationship The relationship between output and the fixed and variable costs associated with production. The relationships are depicted in break-even charts and are used as planning and forecasting tools.

co-transfer agents Regional agents that are appointed by some issuers to serve cities in which stock exchanges are listed, to speed the transfer process. Co-transfer agents cancel certificates and issue replacements. The principal transfer agent, however, maintains the centralized records of cancellation and issuance.

counterfeit card (1) A device or instrument that has been printed, embossed, or encoded like a bank card but that has not been authorized by an issuer. (2) A card that has been validly issued by an issuer but that has been changed or added to without the issuer's authorization.

counterfeit money Any spurious currency or coins made to appear genuine. Creating counterfeit money is a felony under law.

counterfeit paper Paper arising from the use of a counterfeit credit card, evidencing a cash advance or the purchase of goods or services from a merchant.

counterfeit securities Any spurious securities made to appear genuine. *See also* Rule 17f-1.

counteroffer An offer to extend credit on a term, rate, or amount different from those requested by the applicant. Unless the applicant accepts the terms offered, the counteroffer is considered

adverse action and requires the notice set forth in Regulation B.

country bank (1) Any bank not located in a city having a Federal Reserve bank or branch. (2) In check clearing, a bank that neither is in a Federal Reserve city nor has its items processed in a nearby Federal Reserve city. Country banks do not receive overnight processing of their items.

country club billing A billing system by which copies of transactions are mailed to the cardholder with a monthly statement.

country collections All items sent for collection outside the city where the collecting bank is located.

country limit A bank's internal guideline specifying the maximum credit exposure it will accept within a particular country, including its government. *Also called* sovereign risk limit.

country risk The risk that borrowers within a country cannot repay their obligations to foreign creditors because of political or general economic factors, such as lack of exchange, prevailing in their country. *See also* sovereign risk.

coupon (1) One of a series of promissory notes of consecutive maturities attached to a bond or other debt certificate and intended to be detached and presented on the respective due date for payment of interest. (2) The rate of interest a debtor promises to pay on a debt issue. *See also* remittance coupons.

coupon bond A bond to which coupons are attached that the bearer remits in exchange for interest payments.

coupon rate The stated annual interest rate on a debt instrument, as a percentage of its face value. Because bonds do not often trade at face value, the coupon rate seldom equals the yield on the bond. *Also called* nominal rate rate *and* coupon yield.

coupon stripping The process of producing single-payment (zero-coupon) instruments from existing conventional bonds. It can be accomplished either by separating the coupons from the principal or by selling receipts representing the individual coupons and principal on a security held by a trustee.

coupon yield *See* coupon rate.

court account An account that requires a court accounting and approval in its normal conduct. Probate, guardianship, conservatorship, and testamentary trust accounts are the most common examples of a court account.

court of equity A court applying a system of jurisprudence more flexible than common law, when common law by reason of its rigidity fails to recognize or is unable to enforce a right.

court of general jurisdiction A court whose authority extends to any case, regardless of its nature.

court of limited jurisdiction A court that cannot hear all disputes and whose authority is limited by statute or state constitutional provisions.

court of probate *See* probate court.

court order A written direction by a court or judge not included in a decree or judgment and not establishing the rights of parties.

court trust A trust under the immediate supervision of a court (such as a trust by order of court or, in some states, a trust under will).

covenant A legally enforceable promise by one party to another regarding the performance or nonperformance of certain acts, or a promise that certain conditions do or do not exist.

covenant of equal coverage *See* negative pledge clause.

cover The purchase of futures to offset a previously established short position, or the sale of futures to effect a purchase.

coverage ratio A measure of a corporation's financial ability to meet recurring expenses. Earnings are compared to interest or other routine expenses, and the resulting ratio is referred to as the coverage ratio.

covered arbitrage, covered interest arbitrage A basic form of arbitrage in foreign markets with minimum risk. It involves the simultaneous purchase of a currency at the spot rate with the proceeds invested in an asset denominated in that currency, and the forward sale of that currency with a maturity matching that of the asset. This transaction would be undertaken when the yield on the asset purchased was better than the yield available on a comparable domestic security. Thus the arbitrageur secures a better yield but has no exchange risk.

covered option An option written by an investor who owns and pledges enough securities to cover the option if it is eventually called.

cover payment The reimbursement of a correspondent bank for a payment.

coverture The legal status of a married woman.

CRA *See* Community Reinvestment Act.

cram down A confirmation of a reorganization plan resulting from the court's forcing the plan on dissenting classes of creditors, as long as at least one impaired class consents to the plan and the plan does not discriminate unfairly.

crash A severe and sudden decline in stock prices.

credit (1) An agreement to deliver something of value (goods, services, or money) before payment is received. (2) The power to buy or borrow on faith. (3) The right granted by a creditor to defer payment of a debt, to incur debt and defer its payment, or to purchase property or services and defer payment on them. (4) An addition to a bank deposit account or a payment on a credit card account or other debt. (5) An accounting entry made on the right-hand side of an account (the credit side) that decreases the balance of an asset or expense account or increases the balance of a liability, income, or equity account. *See also* line of credit.

credit A & H insurance *See* credit disability insurance.

credit adjustment A transaction posted to a loan account that reduces the balance. A similar transaction posted to a deposit account would increase the balance.

credit analysis A critical appraisal of the economic and financial condition of a potential borrower. A credit analysis evaluates the borrower's ability to meet its debt obligations and the suitability of such obligations for the purposes of underwriting or investment. *See also* five Cs of credit.

credit analyst One who performs the function of reviewing applications for credit, together with pertinent credit data, and who decides whether to approve or to reject the applications.

credit approval department The aspect or department of a bank card operation that is responsible for processing and approving or declining new cardholder applications. The credit approval department may also be responsible for limit control.

credit authorization *See* authorization.

credit balance An account on which payments have exceeded the balance owed. The credit balance is what remains on a cardholder account when credits posted during a billing cycle exceed the previous balance plus debits posted. A credit balance is usually indicated by Cr. after the dollar figure.

credit bureau An agency that gathers and maintains information on the debts and repayment records of individuals and businesses.

credit card A plastic card (or its equivalent) to be used upon presentation by the cardholder to obtain money, goods, or services, possibly under a line of credit established by the card issuer. The cardholder is billed for any outstanding balance. *See also* debit card.

credit card center The physical facility where credit card operations are conducted--that is, where charges and payments to individual cards are processed.

Credit Control Act of 1969 An act that empowers the president to authorize at any time complete control over all forms of credit. The act has been used once, in 1980.

credit criteria The standards applied to loan or credit card applications to determine whether to approve or deny an applicant's request for an account or an increase in an existing line or loan.

credit department The unit within a bank in which all information regarding borrowers is obtained, analyzed, and kept on file. The department's work may also include answering inquiries from outside sources. A bank's credit files contain the history of each account relationship and include all correspondence, memorandums, financial statements, and other material that must be retained.

credit disability insurance Insurance offered, for a fee, to a borrower or a cardholder that will pay the monthly payment on a debt in the event of the borrower's disability. These plans usually require a minimum of 14 days disability before the insurance takes effect. *Also called* credit A & H (accident and health) insurance.

credit facility A formal agreement to extend credit.

credit for tax on prior transfers A tax credit allowed for federal estate tax already paid on the transfer of property to the present decedent from a transferor who died within 10 years before, or within 2 years after, the present decedent's death.

credit history The financial background of a person, business, or other prospective borrower.

credit history file A historical record of an account such as current balance, credit limit, number of times 30-60-90 days past due, late charges collected or owed, and so on.

credit information system A method for providing credit information about individuals.

credit insurance Insurance to insure a lender against losses on a particular consumer loan product. Service companies often offer this type of insurance to a lender as an incentive for the lender to buy the loans originated by the service company.

credit investigation A process used to check a borrower's ability to repay a loan, in which the following information about the borrower is examined: employment history, vocational stability, financial capacity, character, and personal qualifications.

credit life insurance Life insurance supplied by a bank to a borrower in an amount equal to the borrower's outstanding balance. Upon the death of the borrower, the insurance is payable to the bank. If the lender requires the insurance, the premium for the insurance coverage must be included in the annual percentage rate disclosed to the borrower.

credit limit The dollar amount assigned to an open-end credit account. The borrower should not be allowed to exceed this amount.

credit line An agreement by a bank to make a specific amount of funds available to a certain borrower when needed.

credit list *See* envelope settlement services.

credit losses Loan amounts written off as bad debts.

credit manager The person responsible for supervising credit plans, including the approval of new applications and the establishment or increase of credit lines. *Also called* credit officer.

credit memo (1) An authorization for a certain credit to be posted to a specific account. (2) A notification from one party to another granting credit for overpayment on returned merchandise or for a similar reason.

credit officer *See* credit manager.

creditor (1) Any party to whom money is owed by another. (2) A person who, in the ordinary course of business, regularly extends or arranges for the extension of consumer credit, or who offers to extend or arrange for the extension of such credit. The credit is payable by agreement in more than four installments and the payment of a finance charge is or may be required, whether in connection with loans, sale of property or services, or otherwise.

creditor's notice In probate, the notice published stating the decedent's death and the name of the executor or administrator to whom claims should be presented for payment.

credit party The party to be credited or paid by the receiving bank.

credit rating A formal evaluation of a person's loan repayment history or potential.

credit report A factual data report from an independent agency that verifies the applicant's current employment and income and provides information on previous debts and liabilities. It is used to help determine creditworthiness.

credit review *See* limit control.

credit risk The probability that a debtor cannot or will not repay a debt. Credit risk also relates to the amount of risk that exists with any individual credit, whether the risk is high or low.

credit sale Any sale for which the seller extends or arranges consumer credit.

credit scoring (1) A formula for predicting the creditworthiness of credit applicants. (2) The use of such a formula.

credit-scoring plan *See* credit system.

credit slip A document evidencing (a) the return of merchandise by a cardholder to a merchant or (b) some other refund made by the merchant to the cardholder. The bank uses a copy of this document to credit the cardholder's account. *Also called* refund slip *or* credit voucher.

credit system A system for evaluating credit risk by assigning values to borrowers' characteristics--income or home ownership, for example. Under the Equal Credit Opportunity Act (ECOA), a creditor may use a demonstrably and statistically sound, empirically derived credit system obtained from another person or may obtain credit experience from which such a system may be developed. *Also called* credit-scoring plan, credit-scoring system, *or* credit-rating system.

credit transaction Every aspect of the dealings between an applicant for credit and a creditor regarding an application for credit or an extension of existing credit.

credit union A savings institution whose depositors share a common bond, such as the same employer. A credit union is owned by its depositors, and most of its funds are lent to members for consumer purchases.

credit voucher *See* credit slip.

creditworthiness The ability and willingness to repay debt, largely demonstrated by a credit history.

criminal referral forms Under banking regulations, reports that are required to be filed when bank officers suspect a criminal activity.

criticized loan A loan that bank examiners believe is unlikely to be collected or has been poorly documented. Such loans are typically cited during a bank examination.

cross-border outstandings A term developed by the Securities and Exchange Commission for bank holding companies to use to report their exposures to less developed countries (LDCs). It includes total loans (including accrued interest), acceptances, interbank placings, other interest-bearing investments, and other monetary assets denominated in U.S. dollars or other nonlocal currency.

cross-collateralize To secure a debt with collateral from another separate debt. When two loans are cross-collateralized, the individual collateral from each loan serves as collateral for both.

cross-currency exposure A situation existing when a company's debt-servicing requirements in a currency cannot be met by its revenues in that currency.

cross-hedge A hedge in some asset other than the one being hedged. For example, T-bill futures might be used to hedge commitments in other money market instruments, such as commercial paper.

cross-intermediation Moving deposits from one financial institution to another to take advantage of higher interest rates or better services.

cross-rates The exchange rates between each pair of three or more currencies.

cross-remainder Dispositive provisions of a will or trust agreement, providing that surviving life beneficiaries shall be entitled to receive or share in the income of the deceased beneficiary.

cross-selling The practice of promoting financial services in addition to the one a customer is currently using.

cross-subsidize To use profits from a product or service that is generating net earnings to subsidize a product or service whose costs exceed earnings. Cross-subsidization allows a bank to place a low price on a high-cost service in order to retain customers and market share.

crowding out The preemption of the available supply of loanable funds by the federal government, thereby crowding private businesses and consumers out of the market. Government borrowing is an absolute demand that will be filled regardless of the level of interest rates, in contrast to private borrowing, which is choked off by rising interest rates.

crown loan An interest-free demand loan. Under the tax laws, these loans are now grouped into categories--gift loans, corporation/shareholder loans, employer/employee loans, and tax avoidance loans. Gift and income tax consequences will result from any of these loans. For example, if a parent makes a crown loan to a child, the parent will be deemed to have made an annual gift of the forgone interest (determined by reference to the applicable federal rate) to the child for gift tax purposes, and the child will be deemed to have retransferred annually that amount to the parent as interest for income tax purposes. Previously it was thought that crown loans could be made free of gift and income tax consequences.

Crummey power A limited, usually noncumulative power of withdrawal over trust property that ordinarily lapses within a specified period. This power gives a trust beneficiary a present interest over property transferred to a trust. Because property transferred to a trust may not otherwise create a present interest in a beneficiary, a Crummey power is used to secure an annual exclusion for the donor of the property, permitting trust management of the property for the benefit of the beneficiary, as contrasted with an outright gift.

Crummey trust A trust granting a beneficiary a limited power to withdraw income, principal, or both. This power is exercisable during a limited period each year and is noncumulative. The power of withdrawal is generally limited to the amount excludable from gift tax liability under the annual gift tax exclusion or to the greater of $5,000 or 5 percent of the trust property.

cryptographic equipment A device in which cryptographic functions (for example, encryption, authentication, and key generation) are performed.

cryptographic key A parameter that determines the transformation from plain text to cipher text or vice versa. *Also called* key.

cryptoperiod The time during which a specific key is authorized for use or in which the keys for a given system may remain in effect.

CSV *See* cash surrender value.

cumulative An arrangement in which a dividend or interest, if not paid when due or received when due, is added to that which is to be paid in the future.

cumulative dividends or interest Dividends or interest to be added, if not paid when due, to the next or a future payment. Cumulative charges in arrears must be paid before payments can be made on junior securities.

cumulative preferred stock Preferred stock that is entitled to receive at a later date those dividends that accumulate (dividends in arrears) during profitless years. During profitless years, common stock and regular preferred stocks generally are paid no dividends. *See also* arrearages; cumulative dividends or interest.

cumulative voting A method of voting in which each stockholder has one vote per candidate per share held. When electing a board of directors, these votes can all be cast for a single individual or distributed among the candidates.

cumulative voting system (or rights) A provision of some common stock issues that allows the stockholder to cast all of his or her votes for one director, instead of splitting the votes among the several directors who may be standing for election. This privilege may give minority shareholders greater influence over the board of directors.

curator A person or trust institution appointed by a court to care for the property, person, or both of a minor or an incompetent person. In some states, a curator is essentially the same as a temporary guardian.

currency (1) Technically, any form of money that serves as a circulating medium, including both paper money and metallic money (coins). In banking, however, currency generally refers only to paper money. (2) Money of a nation, including its paper money, coins, and deposits. In this sense, currency is an abstract term. The U.S. dollar and the British pound are currencies.

currency basket A composite of several currencies in which international transactions are sometimes denominated. *Also called* currency cocktail.

currency code A data element in funds transfers that identifies the currency in which the transaction amount is stated. The three-letter International Organization for Standardization (ISO) code is recommended.

currency risk The risk of loss from unfavorable movements in foreign exchange rates.

currency swap A transaction in which two counterparties exchange specific amounts of two different currencies at the outset and repay over time according to a predetermined rule that reflects interest payments and possibly amortization of principal. The payment flows in currency swaps (in which payments are based on fixed interest rates in each currency) are generally like those of spot and forward currency transactions.

currency transaction report (CTR) A report required by the Bank Secrecy Act for transactions involving more than $10,000, unless exempted under one of the provisions of the act.

currency union A group of nations that maintain fixed exchange rates with each other but permit the group of currencies to float against other nations' currencies.

currency warrants Usually, detachable options included in securities issues giving the holder the right to purchase from the issuer additional securities denominated in a currency different from that of the original issue. The coupon and price of the securities covered by the warrant are fixed at the time of the sale of the original issue. It can also be a currency option in negotiable form.

current account (1) The value of all invisible and visible trade between nations (goods, services, income, and unilateral transfers). (2) A cardholder account that has been paid up to date and on which there is no amount past due. (3) In the United Kingdom, a noninterest-bearing demand deposit account.

current assets Cash and other items readily convertible into cash, usually within 1 year or within the normal operating cycle of the business, whichever is longer.

current coupon bond A bond that is selling at par. The coupon rate on the bond is the same as that on new issues of the same quality and maturity. *Also called* par bond.

current liabilities The short-term debts of a business. Current liabilities are those expected to be paid within the coming year or within the normal operating cycle of the business, whichever is longer.

current market price The most recently reported price at which a stock or bond is sold.

current ratio A ratio used to analyze the financial stability of a business. It is computed as current assets divided by current liabilities.

current returns The interest or dividend income an investor expects from a given company.

current yield A percentage rate calculated by dividing the annual interest or dividends by the current price of a bond or stock. For stocks, the figure for annual dividends is the latest quarterly dividend times four.

cursor A movable character (an underscore, hyphen, or box) on a display screen, used to indicate where the next character keyed by the operator will appear.

curtailment A reduction in the amount owed on a particular piece of inventory by a dealer engaged in floor plan financing. For example, when new model cars are introduced, the dealer may be required to "curtail" the amount owed on the prior years models remaining in inventory.

curtesy (1) The life estate of a widower in the real property of his wife. *See also* dissent. (2) At common law, curtesy took effect only if a child capable of inheriting the property had been born of the marriage. *See also* dower.

cushion bond A bond that pays unusually high interest rates.

CUSIP (Committee on Uniform Securities Identification Procedures) number A 9-digit code that uniquely identifies a security issue. The American National Standards Institute (ANSI) adopted it as a national standard in 1988.

custodial receipt The principal or interest component of a Treasury security sold to investors by broker-dealers. The security is held intact in a trust account for the dealer, and holders are paid from the account.

Therefore, the instrument is not guaranteed by the government. The stripped security is known as a zero-coupon Treasury security receipt. Examples include Lehman Investment Opportunity Notes (LIONs), Treasury Investment Growth Receipts (TIGRs), and Certificates of Accrual on Treasury Securities (CATS).

custodian An agent, usually a bank, that performs services for the safekeeping of its customers' securities and the collection of dividends and interest. A custodian also buys, sells, receives, and delivers securities if so instructed by its customers.

custodian account *See* custody account.

custodian to a minor The supervisor of securities or other property held for a minor under the Uniform Gifts to Minors Act or similar laws.

custody The banking service that provides safekeeping for a customer's property under written agreement and also calls for the bank to collect and pay out income and to buy, sell, receive, and deliver securities when so ordered by the principal.

custody account An agency account for which the custodian (agent) safeguards, preserves, and performs ministerial acts for the property, as directed by the principal, but has no investment or managerial responsibilities. *Distinguish from* managing agency account *and* safekeeping account.

customer-bank communication terminal (CBCT) A remote terminal (that is, one located away from a financial institution's office), either attended or unattended, that permits customers to conduct a variety of routine banking transactions, such as making transfers or inquiries, receiving cash, or making deposits.

customer profile A description of the distinctive attitudes and personal characteristics of the typical consumer who buys a product.

customer profitability analysis A method of analyzing income and expenses associated with maintaining a customer's total banking relationship. It is designed to show whether the relationship is profitable for the bank.

customer relations (1) The policies, programs, and processes to which the total organization is committed in its relations with customers. (2) The area of the bank that is responsible for processing and resolving customer inquiries and complaints. It may be called the customer service department.

customer's net debit balance *See* debit balance.

customers' trading room A reception area in a brokerage office where customers can consult with their brokers and can also watch the electronic "ticker" for news of the stock market.

customs invoice A document that contains a declaration by the seller, the shipper, or the agent of the value of the goods covered.

cutoff date The date, selected for auditing or closing purposes, on which a period to be reported on shall end. *See also* statement cutoff date.

cycle mailing (1) The practice of dividing bank depositors' accounts into groups whose statements are mailed at staggered intervals during the month. (2) The mailing of credit card or overdraft checking or check

credit statements at staggered intervals during a month.

cycle period A specified period of time during which both debit and credit transactions are accumulated for billing.

cyclical A description of an industry that displays swings in the demand for its product over the business cycle.

cy pres doctrine Literally, "as nearly as may be." The equitable doctrine is applied in English and Scottish law and in some areas of the United States when a testator or settlor makes a gift to or for a charitable object that cannot be carried out to the letter. The court will then direct that the gift be made as nearly as possible, in its judgment, to conform with the donor's intention.

daily balancing Procedure by which all monetary transactions processed within a given 24 hours are balanced.

daily interest (1) Interest earned daily from the date funds are deposited to the date they are withdrawn. (2) Interest compounded daily and credited to the depositor's account at monthly, quarterly, or other intervals.

daily reserve calculation The daily calculation done by a bank to determine whether its reserves meet legal minimum requirements.

daily status report *See* account status report.

daily transaction tape In fully automated demand deposit accounting, the magnetic tape record of each day's debits and credits to all accounts, usually by account number.

D & O insurance Directors' and officers' liability insurance. D & O provides protection against losses arising out of negligence or alleged negligence on the part of directors or key officers of a business.

data (1) In statistics, the quantitative information used in any study. (2) In systems, any facts, concepts, or instructions represented in a formal manner suitable for communications, interpretation, or automatic processing. *See also* control data; master data; raw data.

data base management system (DBMS) A set of computer programs or languages that structures the makeup of records or data and provides for controlled methods of input, updating, and output.

data capture In point-of-sale systems, the function performed by a terminal or computer in capturing data relative to a sale. This function is performed in addition to the authorization function of approving or disapproving a sale. Captured information is stored in a data base. *Also called* data entry.

data center audit Detailed evaluation of the data center's overall system of internal control (central controls). Areas reviewed include management, systems and programming, computer operations, data integrity, and teleprocessing.

data check The capacity built into a computer program to detect a flaw when reading data on tape or disk.

data concentrator A device used in data communications to multiplex or simultaneously transmit numerous

low-speed lines on a single high-speed line.

data control That part of a data-processing operation that is responsible for inputting, reconciling, and balancing all transactions and for distributing all reports generated by the computer system. Data control usually consists of both an input and output section.

data conversion The process of changing data from one form of representation to another.

data encrypting key A key used to encrypt and decrypt, or to authenticate data. Only in the case of a cryptographic service message may a data key be used for encryption, decryption, and authentication.

data encryption algorithm (DEA) The encryption algorithm specified by ANSI X3.92-1981, "Data Encryption Algorithm." *See also* data encryption standard.

data encryption standard An algorithm placed in electronic hardware devices for the cryptographic protection of computer data.

data entry The writing, reading, or posting of data to a code form or to a terminal or processing medium. *See also* data capture.

data file utility (DFU) A common program that copies or maintains a data file.

data integrity (1) The degree to which stored data match source data. (2) The degree to which data have been protected from accidental or malicious alteration or destruction.

data library A collection of data bases.

data processing The gathering, interpreting, and transmitting of data for reference or decision making, and the relaying of instructions on how the decisions should be implemented.

data-processing center A computer installation that provides data processing to customers. It usually charges a fee for the service.

data-processing system A network of machine components capable of accepting information, processing it according to a plan, and producing the desired results.

data reduction The process of transforming raw data or experimentally obtained data into useful, simplified, and condensed information. *See also* on-line data reduction.

data set (1) A collection of similar and related data records that is recorded for use by a computer. (2) A recordable medium such as a data file.

data universal numbering system A numbering system designed and maintained by Dun & Bradstreet, Inc., to identify commercial businesses.

dated date The month, day, and year that an issuer originally issued a certificate.

date of acquisition The effective date for the purchase of an asset.

date of message The date on which the sender computed the message authentication code (MAC). This date is used to synchronize the authentication process through selection of the proper key.

date of record *See* holder of record date.

daylight exposure (1) The dollar amount of foreign exchange needed to cover transactions cleared through the bank during business hours. (2) The amount of time a bank's foreign exchange department is permitted to operate in a business day.

daylight overdraft (1) An overdraft in a bank's reserve account at the Federal Reserve during business hours that must be cleared by the close of business. (2) Any temporary overdraft in an account, when payments made during business hours exceed incoming funds actually received, that is cleared by the close of business.

day loan A loan made and repaid during the business hours of the same day, to facilitate the purchase of securities. The securities are delivered and pledged as collateral to secure a call loan that finances the purchased securities for a few hours of the business day.

day order An order to buy or sell securities on a specific day. If not executed, it expires at the end of that trading session.

day points The number of days required to send transit letters to distant geographical points. When transit letters are sent out, the bank calculates how many days will pass before the items are collected. *See also* transit item; transit letter.

days of grace The period of time allowed beyond the due date for paying obligations or presenting certain financial documents for payment.

day trading The establishment and liquidation of the same position or positions in the same trading day.

DBA An abbreviation for "doing business as." Some entities may have one name but conduct business under another name.

DEA device The electronic hardware part or subassembly that implements only the data encryption algorithm (DEA), as specified in ANSI X3.92-1981, and is validated by the National Bureau of Standards.

dead hand The continuing hold of a settlor or testator who has been dead for many years upon living people or organizations confronted with conditions that the settlor or testator could not have foreseen. *See also* statutes of mortmain.

DEA key A secret 64-bit input parameter of the DEA standard, consisting of 56 bits that must be independent and random and 8 error-detecting bits set to make the parity of each 8-bit byte of the key odd.

dealer An individual or firm that buys and resells securities or other assets for profit. A dealer carries an inventory, as distinct from a broker, who does not carry inventory.

dealer activities The activities of a bank operating as a securities dealer by underwriting, trading, or selling securities.

dealer financing An arrangement made by a bank to purchase loans from a dealer who sells automobiles or other durable goods to the public. Customers purchase from the dealer on credit, the dealer sells the loans to banks, and the dealer's customers effectively become borrowers of the bank. *See also* indirect loan.

dealer loan (1) A loan to a securities dealer. (2) A loan to a firm that sells automobiles or other durable goods. *See also* dealer financing.

dealer market A nationwide telephone market for trading government securities, centered primarily in New York City.

dealer market maker A firm that trades in the over-the-counter market. These firms hold inventories of the stocks they trade but do not expect to make profits from speculation or investment in these issues. Instead, their profits are based on a large, rapid turnover at a favorable price.

dealer paper A term used to describe all loans made in an indirect manner. *See also* dealer financing.

dealer participation *See* dealer reserve.

dealer rebate A portion of interest that a bank receives on a dealer-financed loan and pays to the dealer for arranging the loan through the bank.

dealer recourse *See* recourse plan.

dealer reserve (1) A reserve account set up by a bank containing the interest rate differential that accrues to dealers when they sell or discount installment sales contracts to a bank. (2) In leasing, the amount by which the dealer's markup exceeds the normal markup. The lessor usually holds this as a reserve until the lease expires. It may also include the excess charge when the dealer calculates the rental payment at a higher money factor than the lessor's stated factor. The difference accumulates monthly in the reserve account and may be disbursed periodically.

death benefits The proceeds received by a beneficiary of an insurance policy when the insured party dies.

death certificate The legal document presented as evidence of death.

death duties *See* death taxes.

death taxes Taxes imposed on property or on the transfer of property at the owner's death. This general term includes estate taxes, inheritance taxes, and all succession or transfer taxes associated with the death of the owner of the property. *Sometimes called* death duties.

debasement A reduction in the quality, purity, or content of precious metal in a coin, thereby reducing its intrinsic value.

debenture A bond or promissory note backed by the general credit of the issuer but not secured by specific assets of the issuer.

debit (1) An accounting entry made on the left-hand side of an account (the debit side) that increases the balance of an asset or expense account or decreases the balance of a liability, income, or equity account. (2) A charge against a customer's balance or bank card account.

debit adjustment A correction, posted to a credit card holder's account, that increases the balance owed.

debit balance The lack of funds in an account, indicating an excess of total debits over total credits.

debit card A plastic card enabling the cardholder to purchase goods or services, or withdraw cash, the cost of which is immediately charged to his or her bank account. Debit cards are used to activate point-of-sale terminals in supermarkets, gas stations, and stores. Together with credit cards, they are commonly referred to simply as bank cards.

debit party The source of funds for a payment on the receiving bank's books.

debit ticket The form used to describe a debit entry for a general ledger account.

debit transfer An instruction that specifies, and in which the sender is authorized to make, a debit to a party other than himself or herself. A debit transfer is usually used in conjunction with a draw down.

debt A sum of money owed to another person.

debt coverage ratio A ratio used as a measure of risk in underwriting income-producing property loans. The commonly used ratio is annual net operating income divided by annual debt service.

debt discount The difference between the proceeds of a loan and the face value of a note or bond.

debt financing The process of raising funds by issuing bonds or other forms of debt rather than stocks. *Compare with* equity financing.

debt-for-equity swap In international lending, an exchange of a loan for local currency in the debtor's country, whereupon the currency is used to make equity investments. The currency exchange is handled by the debtor nation's central bank, and the loan may be valued at a discount.

debt-funded leases Leases that are titled and owned in the name of the originating dealer. The financing is treated as a loan with interest and principal. Otherwise, all postings are identical to those of a direct financing lease.

debt instrument A written promise to repay a debt. Examples include bills, notes, and bonds.

debt limit The statutory or constitutional maximum borrowing power of a government entity.

debt management The control of maturities and timing of issuance for securities by business or government.

debtor (1) A person or entity that has filed bankruptcy. (2) A term often used in security agreements referring to the customer.

debt ratio A leverage ratio (total debt divided by total assets) showing the percentage of a business that is financed by creditors. *Also called* total-debt-to-total-assets ratio. A similar ratio used for the same purpose is the debt-to-worth ratio (total debt divided by total equity).

debt rescheduling Postponement or restructuring of debt repayments.

debt service (1) The outlay of funds necessary to pay all interest and principal payments owed on borrowings during a given period, usually 1 year. (2) A budget for paying interest on bonds and retiring matured bonds. (3) The periodic payment of principal and interest due on loans.

debt-service ratio As used in international finance, foreign debt repayments (including interest and other servicing costs) made by a country as a percentage of the country's export earnings.

debts written off *See* credit losses.

debug To locate and to correct any errors found either in a particular computer program or in the computer itself.

decal An emblem placed on merchants' windows and doors to identify their affiliation with a credit card plan, the Federal Deposit Insurance Corporation, the Federal Reserve System, or for other purposes.

deceased account An account held in the name of a deceased person. A bank holds that account until a court-appointed legal representative of the estate is named.

decedent A deceased person.

decentralize (1) To delegate authority and responsibility to the lower levels of an organization. (2) To structure an organization such that day-to-day decisions are made in smaller segments of the organization.

decentralized management A plan of management in which key decisions are made and personnel operate fairly independently, reporting their performance to upper management. Decentralized management allows a high degree of independence for middle managers.

decimal digit In decimal notation, one of the characters from 0 through 9.

decision rule Any guidelines set up to help a person make decisions in the face of uncertainty.

deck A collection of computer cards, frequently a complete set of cards, that have been punched for a definite service or purpose.

declaration An instrument under state statute that provides for the ownership of condominiums.

declaration date The date on which the directors of a corporation authorize the payment of a dividend. *Distin-*

guish from the date of payment of the dividend.

declaration of trust An acknowledgment, usually but not necessarily in writing, by a person who holds property or takes title to property being held in trust for another person's benefit.

declaratory judgment A court's judgment or decision that interprets an instrument or declares the meaning of the law on a given matter under a statutory proceeding that authorizes the court to enter such a judgment in a case not being litigated.

declared dividends Dividends that have been voted by the board of directors to be paid at a stated future date.

decline The downward movement of a business cycle, characterized by a slowdown in production, a slackening of investment, easing credit conditions, and rising unemployment.

declining balance depreciation A method of depreciating property on an accelerated basis in which the percentage of depreciation each year is based on the depreciation that has not yet been written off for the property.

declining yield curve A yield curve in which rates on long-term maturities are lower than rates on shorter maturities. A declining yield curve is common during periods when rates on all maturities are felt to be relatively high.

decode (1) To apply a code to reverse some previous encoding. (2) To determine the meaning of characters in a message. (3) To determine the meaning of an instruction from the set of pulses that describes the instruction, command, or operation to be

performed. (4) To translate a coded language into clear language.

decoder (1) A device that determines the meaning of a set of signals and initiates a computer operation accordingly. (2) A matrix of switches that selects output channels according to the input signals present.

decree The decision of a court of equity, admiralty, probate, or divorce. *Distinguish from* judgment *and* award.

decryption A process of transforming cipher (unreadable) text into plain (readable) text.

dedicated portfolio A portfolio of securities designed and managed to keep its cash flows equal to that of a specific group of liabilities or schedule of payments.

dedicated system (1) A computer system designed or used for a specific function or user. (2) Programs, machines, or procedures with specific applications.

dedication Establishing and maintaining an asset portfolio that has a duration equal to that of a specific group of liabilities or schedule of payments. *See also* duration.

deductible (1) An amount that can be subtracted from a total amount for some specific purpose. For example, in income taxation, some mortgage interest expense is deductible from gross income in arriving at taxable income. (2) In insurance, the dollar amount of each claim for which the policyholder is responsible. In health insurance programs, the deductible is applied up to a specified sum and must be met only once each calendar year. A higher deductible reduces the cost of insurance to the policyholder, as the policyholder is assuming more of the risk.

deed A written instrument, signed, sealed, and delivered according to the applicable law, containing some transfer, bargain, or contract with respect to property. A deed is the common term for an instrument transferring the ownership of real property. *See also* warranty deed.

deed of trust A sealed instrument in writing duly executed and delivered, conveying or transferring property to a trustee. A deed of trust usually but not necessarily covers real property. A deed of trust is used in many states instead of a mortgage. Property is transferred to a trustee by the borrower, in favor of the lender, and reconveyed to the borrower upon payment in full.

deed restriction A limitation placed on a deed to restrict the use of the subject property.

deemed transferor The parent of the transferee of property who is more closely related to the grantor of the trust than the other parent of the transferee. When neither parent is related to the grantor, the deemed transferor is the party who has a closer affinity to the grantor.

deep discount bond A bond selling far below its face value. A bond will sell below par when current interest rates are higher than the nominal rates paid on the bond.

de facto "In fact."

defalcation Embezzlement or other misappropriation of funds or property.

default (1) The failure of a borrower to make a payment of principal or interest when due. (2) The state that exists when a borrower cannot or does not pay bond- and noteholders

the interest or principal due. (3) A breach or nonperformance of any of the terms of a note or the covenants of a mortgage. (4) The failure to meet a financial obligation.

default risk premium The extra interest paid to lenders as compensation for risking default by the borrower. The standard way of measuring the default risk premium is to compare the rate on a security with the rate on a U.S. Treasury security of comparable maturity.

default time line *See* due diligence.

defeasance The term generally connotes a debtor's release from liability. For financial accounting purposes, an "in-substance defeasance" occurs under conditions specified under GAAP. It involves placing assets in trust and irrevocably restricting their use solely to satisfying a specific debt. While the assets and related debt may be presented in the financial statements, net disclosure of the amount defeased is required.

defeasible Capable of being annulled or rendered void, as in a defeasible title to property.

defensive issues The securities of a company whose business is basically stable even in a period of declining economic activity (for example, the securities of variety chain stores).

defensive open market operations Purchases and sales of securities in the open market by the Federal Reserve to offset factors, such as Treasury borrowing or tax payments, that would otherwise have an undesired effect on the volume of reserves and the nation's money supply. *Compare with* dynamic open market operations.

deferred availability (1) Postponement of payment for checks for 1 or more days after they have been received by a Federal Reserve bank, to allow time for collection. The deferred availability represents an average collection time or a maximum deferral (currently 2 days). Thus the funds may be credited to the presenting bank before they are actually collected by the Federal Reserve bank. (2) A delay in the timeframe in which deposited checks are available for withdrawal. The delay is necessary to prevent a bank customer from withdrawing or using deposited checks before the checks are cleared. Under the terms of the Expedited Funds Availability Act, limits have been placed on the time period that banks can hold depositors' funds to prevent abuses. *See also* Regulation CC.

deferred compensation The postponement of payment for services rendered until a future time.

deferred credit Credit given to a bank depositor for items that cannot be or are not given immediate, provisional credit when deposited.

deferred income Income that has been received but not yet earned. Deferred income appears on a balance sheet as a liability.

deferred payment letter of credit A commercial letter of credit where payment is deferred for a specified number of days after goods are shipped. These credits are often used to allow time for the independent inspection of food entering the country, with a provision that payment will not be made if the food is rejected.

deferred posting A method of posting bank transactions to accounts after the day of receipt.

deferred tax The tax consequences attributable to items that are included in book income but excluded from computations of taxable income during that period. The tax consequences of the event will be recognized in a future period.

deficiency judgment A judgment for the balance of a debt remaining after the collateral security has been exhausted, for example, a deficiency judgment following the foreclosure of a mortgage.

deficit An excess of expenditures over receipts for a given period.

deficit financing (1) The financing of government spending by borrowing. (2) The process of spending more money than is brought in over a given period.

deficit spending unit (DSU) An economic unit that currently spends more than its income.

defined-benefit plan A pension plan that guarantees the payment of a specified benefit at retirement age and provides annual contributions equal to an actuarially determined amount sufficient to produce the specified benefit.

defined-contribution plan A pension plan that provides for an individual account for each participant and for benefits based on the amount contributed to the participant's account, including any income, expenses, gains, or losses.

definition (1) The resolution and sharpness of an image, or the extent to which an image is brought into sharp relief. (2) The degree to which a communications system reproduces images of sound or messages.

definitive bond A permanent bond issued by a corporation. It is distinguished from a temporary bond, which is issued pending the preparation of the definitive bond. *Compare with* temporary bond.

deflation (1) A decrease in prices, which usually results from a decrease in total demand relative to the supply of available goods and services. (2) A decrease in the money supply, which causes an increase in the value of money and a resulting reduction in prices.

de jure "By right" or "under authority of law."

delete *See* purge.

delimiter In data processing, a character that limits a string of characters and therefore is not a member of the string.

delinquency A loan principal and/or interest payment that is not paid when due. *See also* default.

delinquency percentage The percentage of either dollar amount or number of loan accounts in a bank that are past due. The delinquency percentage is calculated for dollar amount by dividing dollars delinquent by total dollars outstanding. It is calculated for the number of accounts by dividing the number of accounts delinquent by the total number of active accounts. *Also called* delinquency ratio.

delinquency ratio *See* delinquency percentage.

delinquent account (1) Any account that remains past due beyond a fixed period. In some banks, this period is 5 to 10 days; in others, it is 15 to 30 days. (2) A cardholder account on which one or more payments have not been made according to the terms and conditions of the cardholder agreement.

delinquent activity report A periodic report displaying all of the activity on past-due accounts. *Also called* aging report.

delisting The removal of a security issue from the list of those traded on an exchange.

delivering party The selling broker who originated the trade and who will deliver the securities. If a correspondent clearing broker issues the broker confirmation, the delivering party is identified in the confirmation.

delivery The tender and receipt of an actual financial instrument or cash in settlement of a futures contract or other financial agreement.

delivery against payment *See* delivery versus payment (DVP).

delivery against receipt The delivery of securities in exchange for a signed receipt.

delivery date The date on which securities and funds are to be exchanged.

delivery month The month in which a futures contract matures and the contract must be covered or delivery made.

delivery notice A written notice of the seller's intention to make delivery against an open, short futures position on a particular date.

delivery point The location nominated by a futures exchange for the actual delivery of the commodity or financial instrument on fulfillment of the contract.

delivery price The price of a delivery on a futures contract fixed by a clearing house or the price at which a futures contract is settled when delivered.

delivery versus payment (DVP) A delivery of securities whose terms require payment. Normally, payment is due on a scheduled settlement date, even if delivery of the securities is delayed.

delivery-versus-payment (DVP) privilege A privilege given a large investor, such as an institutional investor, allowing it to defer payment until securities are actually delivered to the investor or its agents. This privilege protects the institutional investor and its agent from error, delays, and failure to deliver. With some exceptions, the DVP privilege is confined to customers who use an electronic confirmation and institutional delivery system for their transactions.

Delphi technique A method of technological forecasting that involves analyzing the independent opinions of experts on the future technological and economic trends of the market or on other matters. One set of opinions is grouped and analyzed and then referred without identification to the participants, who express second opinions in light of the previous group of opinions. The process is repeated until a substantially common opinion is reached. This technique is named after the ancient Greek temple of Apollo, at Delphi, whose oracle made obscure, ambiguous pronouncements.

delta The change in an option's price divided by the change in the price of the underlying instrument. An option whose price changes by $1 for every $2 change in the price of the underlying instrument has a delta of 0.5. At-the-money options have deltas near 0.5. The delta rises toward 1.0

for options that are deep-in-the-money, and it approaches 0 for deep-out-of-the-money options. *See also* at-the-money; in-the-money; out-of-the-money; delta hedging.

delta hedging A method option writers use to hedge risk exposure of written options by purchase or sale of the underlying asset in proportion to the delta. For example, a call option writer who has sold an option with a delta of 0.5 may engage in delta hedging by purchasing an amount of the underlying instrument equal to one-half of the amount of the underlying instrument that must be delivered upon exercise. A delta-neutral position is established when the writer strictly delta-hedges so as to leave the combined financial position in options and underlying instruments unaffected by small changes in the price of the underlying instrument.

delta-neutral *See* delta hedging.

demand The quantity of goods or services buyers will purchase at a given price. *See also* elastic demand; inelastic demand.

demand curve A graphic representation of the quantity of a product or service that will be purchased at different prices.

demand deposit Funds that a customer may withdraw from a bank with no advance notice, usually by writing checks or using an automated teller machine. Checking accounts are the most common form of demand deposits.

demand deposit accounting (DDA) The automated demand deposit bookkeeping function in banks.

demand deposit accounting (DDA) system A system used by a bank to record demand deposit transactions (that is, deposits, checks, and other transactions).

demand draft A written order to pay at sight upon presentation. A check is a demand draft drawn on a bank or other financial institution.

demand for money The relationship among incomes, interest rates, and the quantity of money needed to support a given level of economic activity. The demand for money is the amount of money the public wants to hold, given the level of incomes and interest rates.

demand loan A loan that has no specified maturity date but is due for payment on demand by the creditor or at the initiative of the borrower. *Also called* call loan. *See also* secured demand loan.

demand mortgage A mortgage that is due whenever the holder demands payment.

demand note A promissory note payable on demand of the note holder as payee or transferee.

demand-pull inflation A general rise in the prices of goods and services that results when demand exceeds supply at current prices.

demarket To act to decrease demand for a product or service.

demise (1) The conveyance of an estate, usually for life or for a fixed number of years. (2) Death.

demographic Pertaining to the study of data on population groups in terms of certain characteristics, such as income, occupation, age, and race. Market research often entails demographic studies of pertinent markets.

demonstrative gift A gift by will of a specified sum of money paid from a designated fund or asset. For example, a gift of $1,000 paid from a specified bank account would be a demonstrative gift.

denial letter The notice given to a bank by the Farmers Home Administration (or other guarantor) refusing to guarantee a loan under the proposed conditions.

denomination The face amount of a financial instrument in units of the currency in which it is issued, such as a $1,000 bond or a $10 note.

de novo New. A de novo branch or subsidiary is one that is started, rather than purchased.

density *See* character density.

departmental overhead Those overhead expenses that are charged directly to a specific department. They may include a portion of the bank's general overhead as well as the specific department's overhead.

Department of Housing and Urban Development (HUD) A department of the federal government responsible for administering government housing and urban development programs. *See also* Federal Housing Administration (FHA); Government National Mortgage Association (GNMA); HUD public housing notes and bonds.

Department of the Treasury The department of the U.S. federal government that is responsible for managing the nation's finances. Its responsibilities include formulating and recommending tax and fiscal policies; serving as the government's financial agent; manufacturing coins and currency; and enforcing laws pertaining to its functions.

dependent Under the tax laws, a person who is dependent for support on another person. A dependent is distinguished from a person who merely derives a benefit from another person's earnings.

dependent variable A variable whose value is determined by other variables within a mathematical expression.

depletion A noncash amount charged to current operating expenses over time in order to write off the value of a wasting asset, such as a mine or an oil well. *See also* economic depletion; physical depletion.

depletion (for tax purposes) The dollar value assigned for the purpose of taxation to assets extracted and sold. Cost depletion and percentage depletion are two types of depletion for tax purposes.

deposit (1) Funds (cash, checks, drafts, and so on) left with a bank to be used according to banking practice. A deposit balance in a bank is a credit, representing the depositor's right to receive an equivalent sum of money from the bank. (2) The crediting of cash, checks, or drafts to a customer's account at a financial institution.

deposit account *See* deposit.

deposit analysis The process of analyzing account deposits to determine whether a portion of the deposit must be considered float and cannot be immediately credited to an account.

deposit annuity A group annuity in which the contributions are held by the insurer, usually at a guaranteed rate of interest, until an employee's retirement, when the employee purchases the annuity.

depositary (1) A person or group responsible for safekeeping or preserving an asset. (2) One who receives a deposit of money, securities, instruments, or other property. *Distinguish from* depository.

depositary bank A term used in Regulations J and CC to denote a bank in which a check is first deposited. The bank may also be the paying bank if the check is drawn on, payable at, or payable through the bank. The bank is also considered the depositary bank for checks it receives as payee. *Also called* receiving depository institution.

deposit base The total dollar amount of customer deposits held by a financial institution.

deposit correction slip A form sent to notify a depositor of an error that the depositor made.

deposit date (1) The date on which a bank receives funds for deposit. (2) The date on which a bank receives paper from a merchant.

deposit envelope An envelope merchants use to transport sales drafts and credit vouchers to banks for credit to their deposit accounts. *Also called* sales draft envelope.

deposit expansion The extent to which all financial institutions can create deposits at any given time. Since depository institutions are required to hold reserves equal to a specified proportion of their deposit liabilities, deposit expansion is limited by both the amount of reserves available and the percentage of reserves required. Deposit expansion relates to the ability of depository institutions to create liabilities (deposits) as part of the asset acquisition (lending) process. *See also* fractional reserve banking.

deposit expansion multiplier The multiple of reserves by which deposits expand whenever more reserves are made available.

deposit function The traditional banking function of accepting funds for credit to a demand or time account. In the case of checks, the deposit function includes converting them into usable, available funds.

Deposit Insurance Fund (DIF) The combined deposit insurance funds from commercial banks (the Bank Insurance Fund) and savings and loan associations (the Savings Association Insurance Fund) that guarantee depositors' funds in financial institutions up to a current limit of $100,000.

deposition The written testimony of a witness under oath before a qualified officer. Under certain conditions, a deposition may be used in place of oral testimony of the witness at a trial or other hearing, such as the deposition of a nonresident subscribing witness to a will.

depository (1) A bank designated by the U.S. Secretary of the Treasury to receive public funds. *Distinguish from* depositary. *See also* securities depository. (2) A place where something is deposited, such as a safe deposit vault. (3) A corporate agency established to safekeep customers' securities in its nominee name. Depositories simplify securities trading by immobilizing the securities and offering bookentry settlement between participants. They also collect dividend and interest payments, forward proxy material to the beneficial owners, and offer a variety of related services. (4) In automated teller machines, the mechanism for receiving and storing deposited funds.

depository agent An agent retained by the maker of a tender offer to receive securities forwarded to the agent by the owners, to hold the securities, and to make payment to the owners when so authorized by the maker of the tender offer. A depository agent may be a trust company or another financial service. This agent is not affiliated with a securities depository.

Depository Institutions Act of 1982 (Garn-St Germain) Major financial regulatory legislation. By permitting thrift institutions to offer demand deposits and to make commercial loans in limited amounts, this act expanded the powers of thrift institutions. It set up a list of priorities to use in considering merger candidates from different states or from different financial industries and authorized the interstate merger of troubled institutions according to those priorities. It permitted the use of money market deposit accounts (MMDAs) without rate ceilings or reserve requirements for accounts over a minimum size. It provided for federal infusion of capital into troubled thrifts. It also gave banks authority to form subsidiaries that could band together to offer joint services to participants.

Depository Institutions Deregulation and Monetary Control Act of 1980 (DIDMCA) Major financial regulatory legislation. The act authorized the use of transaction accounts (which compete with checking accounts) by financial institutions on a national basis. These accounts include NOW accounts, accounts accessed through remote service units, and ATS accounts. The act created the Depository Institutions Deregulation Committee and required that it eliminate ceilings on interest rates over time. The statute overrode state usury ceilings, some permanently. It gave all depository institutions equal access to Federal Reserve discount facilities. It required that the Federal Reserve price competitively, charge for clearing and funds transfer services, and make those services available to all depository institutions. It also extended reserve requirements to all depository institutions.

depository interface Securities depositories, as members of the Federal Reserve System, receive access to the Fed's book-entry system through the depository interface to settle government and agency securities trades for participants. Member banks may also use their own interface with the Fed's book-entry system to settle such trades.

depository intermediaries Financial institutions that obtain funds by accepting demand or time deposits and that invest those funds in market instruments and other assets.

depository receipt A receipt issued by a depository institution in exchange for foreign securities deposited with it. The receipt is generally used when the underlying securities do not fulfill requirements for listing on the local stock exchange. The receipt is traded locally instead of the securities.

depository transfer check (DTC) A cash-management service that facilitates cash concentration. A DTC is a demand deposit instrument used to effect transfers of cash from the account of a corporation in one bank to the account of the same corporation in another bank. The DTC may be paper-based or electronic.

Depository Trust Company (DTC) The New York depository serving institutional participants, such as banks, brokers, insurance companies, and other high-volume securities traders. *See also* depository.

deposit receipt The printed receipt issued to a person who makes a deposit.

deposit slip A list of items that a customer gives to a bank to be credited to an account, a copy of which may be returned to the customer as a receipt.

depreciable A term used to indicate that an asset may be depreciated. *See also* depreciate; depreciation.

depreciable cost The portion of the cost of a fixed asset that will be depreciated over the useful life of the asset. The depreciable cost equals the cost minus the salvage value of a fixed asset.

depreciate (1) In accounting, to reduce periodically a fixed asset's book value by charging a portion of the asset's cost as an expense to the period in which it provides a service. (2) To decrease in service capacity or usefulness.

depreciated cost The net book value of a particular fixed asset. The depreciated cost equals the cost less the accumulated depreciation of a fixed asset.

depreciation (1) In accounting, a process of allocating the cost of a fixed asset less salvage value, if any, over its estimated useful life. A depreciation charge is treated as a noncash expense. *See also* accelerated depreciation; declining balance depreciation; double declining balance depreciation; straight-line depreciation; sum-of-the-years-digits (SYD) depreciation. (2) In economics, a loss of value in real property caused by age, physical deterioration, or functional obsolescence. (3) In foreign exchange, a decline in the value of a nation's currency in terms of another nation's currency or gold because of market factors. *Distinguish from* devaluation.

depreciation fund The funds or securities set aside to replace depreciating fixed assets.

depreciation method The arithmetic procedure for reducing the book value of an asset over its useful life. *See also* accelerated depreciation; declining balance depreciation; double declining balance depreciation; straight-line depreciation; sum-of-the-years-digits (SYD) depreciation.

depression A prolonged period during which business activity, production, capital investment, and income all decline, resulting in massive unemployment and business failures. A depression is a severe recession.

deputy An individual authorized to act for another in certain transactions. *See also* agent; attorney-in-fact; power of attorney.

derived PIN A personal identification number (PIN) generated from a customer's account number or some other nonsecret value uniquely associated with the customer.

derogatory information Data received by a lender, usually from a credit reporting agency, indicating that an applicant or existing borrower or cardholder has not paid accounts with other creditors as agreed.

descendant A person who is descended in a direct line from another, however remotely (for example, a child, grandchild, or great-grandchild). *Also called* issue.

descent The passing of property by inheritance.

descriptive billing A method of billing in which each monetary transaction posted to an account during a billing period is identified and described on the bill.

descriptive entry An entry in an account that uniquely identifies the transaction, for example, the serial number and dollar amount of a check, the name of the direct payee and dollar amount, or the serial number and amount of a charge receipt.

descriptive statement A bank account statement that lists one or more descriptive entries for which no separate items giving supporting details are enclosed. Bill-checks, preauthorized payments, and direct payroll deposits require the use of some form of descriptive statement unless the bank encloses an additional document describing the entries.

descriptive statistics The branch of statistical studies that summarizes the group characteristics of particular sets of observed data.

detailed audit The examination of all or many accounting entries in the books of account.

detail file A file that contains relatively temporary data. A master file contains more permanent data.

details of charges *See* charges to.

details of payment *See* originator-to-beneficiary information.

devaluation A lowering of the value of a nation's currency relative to gold or other nations' currencies. Devaluation can help a country reduce its balance of payments deficit by increasing demand for the country's exports while reducing domestic demand for imports. *Distinguish from* depreciation.

development mortgage A loan to develop vacant land for the construction of buildings.

devise A gift of real property by will. *Distinguish from* bequest.

devisee One who receives a gift of real property by will.

devolution The transfer from one person to another of a right, liability, title, estate, or office by process of law.

diagnostics Programs that detect and isolate a malfunction or error in a computer system.

difference account *See* over and short account.

digital computer A computer that primarily uses numbers. A digital computer performs sequences of arithmetic and logical operations both on data and on its own program.

digital recording A method of recording in which the signal can take only one of two defined values. In magnetics, the values are large enough to saturate the particles in either direction.

dilution of common stock The decrease (dilution) in earnings and book value per share of common stock when the number of shares increases. This occurs because the net income and assets are divided among more shares.

diminishing balance accrual An accrual method for recognizing earned income by applying the rule of 78s to the unearned interest balance on an account.

diminishing returns *See* law of diminishing returns.

direct access The retrieval or storage of data by reference to its location on a disk so that the speed of access does not depend on the location of the data.

direct claim A loan by the ultimate lender to the ultimate borrower with no intermediaries. A direct claim is a financial claim sold in the market by the entity that will use the funds to the entity that is the ultimate lender. *Compare with* indirect claim.

direct cost A cost that is traceable to the production of certain specifiable goods.

direct debit A method of collecting certain generally repeated claims in which a debtor authorizes a bank to debit his or her account on sight when the bank receives a direct debit from a creditor. *See also* reverse money transfer.

direct deposit account (DDA) An account in which funds from the paying source are automatically deposited to a checking or savings account. *Note:* DDA is more commonly used as an abbreviation for demand deposit accounting.

direct deposit merchants Merchants that deposit directly into a bank through the U.S. Postal Service. The incoming processing unit in the bank's accounting department is responsible for servicing the merchants.

direct deposit program The process in which the issuer of a payment delivers information regarding the payee and the amount of the payment directly to the payee's bank for credit to his or her account. This information may be hard copy (that is, paper based), contained on magnetic tape, or transmitted electronically through an automated clearing house (ACH) system. Examples include the federal government's direct deposit of Social Security payments and a company's direct deposit of payroll.

directed account *See* directed trust account.

directed trust account A nondiscretionary trust account in which investment decisions are made by the trustor. The trust department, however, must exercise discretion in carrying out investment instructions.

direct expense That category of expenses--including operations, advertising, cost of funds, and losses--that are directly attributable to specific operations. *Also called* operating expense.

direct financing The purchase of direct claims by the ultimate lender, without the services of a financial intermediary. *Compare with* indirect loan (credit).

direct financing lease A lease other than a leveraged lease that does not give use of the manufacturer's or dealer's profit to the lessor but that meets one or more of the criteria in paragraph 7 and both of the criteria in paragraph 8 of FAS 13.

direct heir A person in the direct line of inheritance from the decedent (for example, father, mother, son, or daughter). *See also* collateral heir; heir.

direction *See* mandatory.

direct kill A method of sorting, listing, and sending transit and clearing items to their respective destinations with one handling.

direct lease financing A form of term debt financing for fixed assets. Lease and loan financing are similar because banks must consider a business's cash

flow, credit history, management, and projections of future operations.

direct liability An obligation to pay a sum of money either now or at some specific future date.

direct loan A bank loan directly to a customer for personal reasons or for specific purchases. This kind of loan generally involves only two parties, a bank and a borrower. It allows a bank closer control over its credit policies and a better opportunity to evaluate prospective borrowers than an indirect loan.

direct marketing The promotion and selling of goods and services through the mail, over the telephone, and in advertising that provides a customer response mechanism (for example, a coupon or application).

director A person elected by shareholders at corporate annual meetings to look after their interests. Directors are the highest authorities in a corporation. They choose the management team, determine when to declare dividends, and make other important corporate decisions.

direct or private placement The direct sale of a new security by the issuer to life insurance companies, banks, or other institutional investors, thus bypassing the underwriter or middleman.

directory An index used by a control program to locate programs stored in separate areas of a disk library.

direct paper Commercial paper placed directly in the market rather than through a dealer. Only large institutions with good credit can sell their paper in this manner.

direct-pay letter of credit *See* letter of credit.

direct quotation An exchange rate expressed in fixed units of a foreign currency and variable amounts of a domestic currency.

direct reduction mortgage An amortized mortgage for which principal and interest are paid at the same time, usually monthly, with interest computed on the remaining balance.

direct send program The method of check collection in which deposited checks are presented directly to their drawee banks for settlement.

direct skip An outright generation-skipping transfer, either by gift or at death, to a recipient (known as a skip person) who is two or more generation levels below the transferor. A direct skip also occurs on a transfer by gift or at death to a trust, all of the beneficiaries of which are skip persons.

direct verification An auditing procedure in which a bank confirms account balance, loan, or other information by directly contacting the bank's debtors or creditors. *See also* positive confirmation.

dirty float A currency that supposedly is free to float in the market against other currencies without intervention by government authorities, but is in fact supported or pegged more or less flexibly by its government. *Also called* managed float.

disability insurance *See* credit disability insurance.

disbursement A payment in cash or by check; funds paid out. *Compare with* distribution.

disbursement deceleration systems Programs designed to delay the presentation of disbursement checks without violating the terms of normal trade credit.

disbursement float The lag between the time a check is prepared and the time it is presented for payment.

disbursement systems A collective term that includes check preparation systems, zero-balance accounts, concentration accounts, treasurer's drafts, and other disbursement-related services.

discharge of mortgage *See* satisfaction of mortgage.

disclaimer A denial or disavowal of any interest in or claim to the subject of the action, such as renunciation of any title, claim, interest, estate, or trust.

disclosure A fact, condition, or description that is clearly shown in financial statements or the appended notes, loan agreements, deposit account agreements, and in bank advertising in footnotes, sideheads, or in the text of the document.

disclosures Under Regulation Z, which implements the Truth in Lending Act, the notices that must be given to a consumer borrower pertaining to the credit terms and containing other facts relevant to the loan. Disclosures are given when the application is made, when the loan is consummated, and sometimes when the loan or account is renewed or extended. *See also* Consumer Credit Protection Act.

discount (1) For debt discount, the difference between the par value of bonds sold by the issuing company and the below-par price at which they are sold. (2) For security prices, a term used in two expressions: (a) "at a discount" refers to a security selling below par value, in contrast to one selling above par (at a premium); (b) "has been discounted" refers to certain factors that are believed to be already reflected in the current market price of a security, by either a lower or a higher price than might have prevailed without these factors. (3) The fee paid by a merchant that delivers and receives immediate credit on sales drafts. (4) A currency of one country selling for less than its stated par value relative to another currency. (5) The interest withheld when a note, draft, or bill is purchased. (6) The interest collected in advance at the time a loan is made. (7) (Verb) To sell a note or other asset at less than face value.

discount bond A bond selling below par.

discount brokerage A brokerage service for the purchase and sale of securities that does not include the offering of investment advice. Rates may be considerably lower for this type of service than for full-service brokers.

discounted bill A promissory note or bill of exchange from which a bank has deducted, in advance, its fee or interest charge for lending the funds.

discounted cash flow A method of calculating the present worth or present value of an income stream. *See also* discount rate.

discounted cash flow analysis A technique used in the income approach of the appraisal process. It is a procedure of converting future benefits (that is, income from real estate investments) to their present worth based on a required rate of return *on* and return *of* capital.

discount from face value The way in which Treasury bills and other discount securities are sold. They have no stated interest rate but are sold at a discount price and redeemed at maturity for full face value.

discount house An institution in the London money market that borrows short-term funds from banks and invests the funds in money market instruments.

discounting (1) Selling financial instruments at a discount from their face value. (2) Calculating the present value of a future payment. Discounting is the reverse of compounding.

discount loan A loan for which the interest is deducted from the proceeds when the loan is made.

discount on securities The amount or percentage by which a security is bought or sold for less than its face value.

discount paper A money market instrument that carries no coupons and that is traded at less than face value.

discount rate (1) "The" discount rate is the rate of interest charged by the Federal Reserve on loans it makes to banks or other financial institutions. It is sometimes referred to as the rediscount rate because banks historically borrowed from the Federal Reserve by discounting short-term negotiable debt instruments (such as bankers' acceptances) a second time. (2) The rate used to determine the present value of a future cash flow. *See also* discounted cash flow analysis.

discount register A bank's book in which original entries are made. It includes a daily record of all loan department transactions, such as loans made, payments received, and interest collected.

discounts and advances The loans made to depository institutions by Federal Reserve banks. Discounts are loans sold to (discounted by) Federal

Reserve banks, while advances are secured loans made by Federal Reserve banks. Discounts have rarely been used in recent decades.

discount securities Securities that carry no coupons and are sold at less than face value but are redeemed on maturity at full value.

discount window The lending facility of the regional Federal Reserve bank through which depository institutions may borrow short-term from the Federal Reserve to meet temporary liquidity needs and to cover reserve deficiencies, as an alternative to selling money market securities or borrowing federal funds. The Federal Reserve monitors discount window borrowing to ensure that funds are not misused.

discovery proceedings (1) The disclosure of facts and documents in another party's exclusive knowledge or possession that are necessary to the conduct of a legal proceeding. (2) In trusts, the legal proceedings by which an executor or administrator procures rightful possession or control of wrongfully concealed or withheld estate assets.

discovery sampling A method of sampling in which the sample size is such that it will provide a specified level of assurance of detecting at least one error if a certain rate of error actually exists.

discrepancy (1) A difference between two records of the same transaction. (2) Any difference observed between opinions and facts, implying an error in one or both.

discretionary account An account for which the customer has given the broker or other professional manager the authority to make transactions at his or her own discretion.

discretionary fiscal policies Federal tax and/or spending changes aimed at reducing fluctuations and/or changing the levels of national income, prices, and employment.

discretionary income The income remaining after taxes and other essential outlays, such as debt repayments, are made. A person may spend discretionary income on travel, hobbies, savings, food, and so on. *Distinguish from* disposable income.

discretionary investment agency A relationship in which the trust department serves as an agent (but does not take title to trust assets) and the investment adviser or manager selects all investments and manages all assets.

discretionary order An order placed by a broker when empowered to act on behalf of a customer in a securities transaction.

discretionary powers Powers left to the trustee's judgment under the terms of the trust. Discretionary powers give the trustee the right, but not necessarily the duty, to perform or omit certain actions.

discretionary trust A trust that entitles the beneficiary to only as much of the income or principal as the trustee's uncontrolled discretion shall see fit to give, or to apply for the use of, the beneficiary.

discrimination Discrimination against an applicant for credit because of race, color, age, religion, marital status, national origin, or receipt of public assistance is prohibited under the Equal Credit Opportunity Act. To discriminate against an applicant means to treat that applicant less favorably than other applicants who have similar characteristics (in other respects) or are in similar circumstances. The term also applies to other activities of an organization, such as employment.

diseconomies of scale The tendency for certain classes of costs to increase as an institution's size or volume of business increases.

dishonor The refusal of the maker or a drawee to accept or pay a check, draft, or other instrument presented.

disintermediation The withdrawal of money from financial institutions, for example, when short-term interest rates (on Treasury bills, commercial paper, and so on) exceed the interest rates paid by the institutions. *Compare with* intermediation.

disk A flat, circular metal plate with a magnetic surface on both sides that stores data files and programs for use in a computer. A disk's capacity is measured in millions of bytes. *Also called* magnetic disk.

disk drive A device that holds and reads or writes data on a stack of recordlike disks.

diskette A form of magnetic disk storage that uses an inexpensive flexible plastic disk.

disk pack A stack of recordlike disks that contain data and can be removed from a disk drive.

disk storage Direct access storage that uses rotating magnetic disks to store programs and data files.

dispersion The distribution pattern of measurements of frequency. The standard deviation is the most commonly used measure of dispersion.

display The visible representation of data.

disposable income (1) The income remaining after all taxes are paid. (2) Under Chapter 13 of the Bankruptcy Code, the debtor's income remaining after paying for maintenance and support of the debtor or a dependent and, if the debtor is engaged in business, the amount remaining after paying the expenses necessary for the continuation, preservation, and operation of the business. *Distinguish from* discretionary income, which is disposable income remaining after fixed expenses have been met.

dispositive provisions The provisions of a will or trust agreement relating to the disposition and distribution of the property in an estate or trust. Dispositive provisions relate to the handling of the property while it is in the hands of the executor or trustee. *Distinguish from* administrative provisions.

dispute (dispute letter) *See* letter of dispute.

dissave To spend more in a year than one earns.

dissent The act of disagreeing. Thus a widow's refusal to take the share provided for her in her husband's will and assertion of her rights under the law are known as her dissent from the will.

dissolution right Any special right or privilege guaranteed to a security's holder when the issuing corporation considers going out of business.

distributable net income (DNI) All income generated by a trust, less all deductible expenses paid by a trust, whether charged against principal or income.

distributed system An arrangement of computers in which a large central computer is connected to smaller local computers.

distributee A person to whom something is distributed. A distributee is frequently the recipient of personal property under intestacy and is known as next of kin. *Distinguish from* heir.

distribution (1) The remittance of stock, cash, or property to stockholders, including any form of dividend. (2) The process of moving goods or services from producer to consumer. (3) The spread of observations over a series of measurements. (4) The division of a society's income among factors of production (functional distribution) or among people (personal distribution). (5) The apportionment of personal property or its proceeds among those entitled to receive it, according to the applicable statute of distribution or under the terms of a will or trust agreement. *Compare with* disbursement.

distribution in kind The distribution of the property itself, to be distinguished from the conversion of property into cash and the distribution of the proceeds of such a conversion.

distribution strategy A plan to make a product available at the time and place most desired by the target market.

distributive share A person's share in the distribution of an estate.

diversification (1) A method of decreasing the total risk of investments by investing funds in assets of different kinds. Diversification can be achieved through different maturities, geographic locations, types of business, or types of securities. (2) The manufacture or distribution of different products in the hope that depressed conditions in one market will not carry over to other products,

thus helping to stabilize the longer run position of the firm.

diversified common stock fund A mutual fund whose portfolio consists of the common stocks of many companies.

diversified holding company A corporation that controls several dissimilar companies. A diversified holding company does not directly manage the operations of its subsidiaries.

diversified investment company A company that combines funds of many investors and invests these funds in a variety of securities.

divest (1) To sell or decrease an asset. Divest is the opposite of invest. (2) To annul or remove a vested right.

dividend A payment made periodically, usually quarterly, by a corporation to its stockholders as a return on investment. Dividends can be paid in cash, stock, or property. *See also* cash dividend; extra cash dividend; property dividend; scrip dividend.

dividend check A dividend payment to a stockholder.

dividend claim A dividend claim arises when a purchase or sale of stock occurs between the record date and the ex-dividend date. *See also* dividend declaration date.

dividend declaration date The date on which directors declare (state that the bank will pay) a dividend. The dividend will be paid on the payment date to the owner of the stock on the holder-of-record date, which is specified at the time of the dividend declaration. On the fourth day before the holder-of-record date, the stock begins to trade ex-dividend; that is, the dividend belongs to the buyer if the stock is sold before the ex-dividend date, and it belongs to the seller if the stock is sold after the ex-dividend date.

dividend order A form that, when properly filled out, instructs a corporation to forward dividend checks to a specified address.

dividend paying agent The agent of a corporation charged with the duty of paying dividends on the stock of a corporation from funds supplied by the corporation. If this corporate agent also serves as a transfer agent, the dividend paying agent pays dividends and files tax reports with government authorities. If the two agencies are separate, the dividend paying agent prepares and mails checks based on a list of holders submitted by the transfer agent. For a stock dividend, the transfer agent issues new certificates.

dividend reinvestment agent An agent of the issuer that will arrange for the automatic reinvestment of a customer's dividends in additional shares of the company.

dividend reinvestment plan A plan in which dividends paid to a shareholder are reinvested in shares of the company through an agent for the shareholders, normally a bank.

dividend right The right that entitles a stockholder to receive dividends when declared by the issuer's board of directors.

dividends in arrears *See* arrearages.

dividend yield The ratio between a firm's annual dividend and the market price of its stock.

divisional bond A bond secured by a lien on a branch or division, but not the main line or entire mileage of a railroad.

dk (don't know) The result when a purchaser's clearing house or bank refuses to accept a delivery of securities simply because it "doesn't know" about, nor is expecting, the delivery. Disagreement between the parties (for example, on sale price or quantity) can be avoided by adequate communication between the customer and clearing agent before the delivery of securities.

document (1) (Noun) A form, voucher, or written evidence of a transaction. (2) (Verb) To instruct, as by citing references. (3) (Verb) To substantiate, as by listing authorities.

documentary collection A service banks provide exporters in which the bank arranges for the shipment documents to be turned over to the importer in exchange for payment, which is forwarded to the exporter.

documentary draft A written order to pay, accompanied by securities or other papers, to be delivered against payment or acceptance.

documentary stamp A state tax imposed on the transfer of real property.

document of original entry A basic document providing details for entering records of a transaction into an accounting system. For securities trades involving a bank, the fanfold or security ticket is the document of original entry.

documents (international) Items presented with a draft under a letter of credit or collection. These may include a bill of lading, commercial invoice, marine insurance policy or certificate, packing list, certificate of origin, and inspection certificate (certificate of analysis).

documents against acceptance (D/A) draft A time draft to which title documents are attached. The documents are surrendered to the drawee when the drawee has accepted the corresponding draft, thereby acknowledging his or her obligation to pay the draft when it matures.

documents against payment (D/P) draft A sight draft to which title documents are attached. The documents are surrendered to the drawee only when the drawee has paid the corresponding draft.

document truncation The termination of routing of the paper evidence of transactions at some predetermined point. The transaction is then completed through an electronic system.

doing business as *See* DBA.

dollar bond A municipal revenue bond, quoted and traded in dollars rather than on a yield basis.

dollar-day A dollar in collected balances for 1 day. As a unit of measure for quantifying the benefit of alternative cash management systems, a dollar-day is used with an opportunity cost to determine the value of a particular program.

dollar unit sampling A method of sampling in which the sampling units are defined as the individual dollars, with each individual dollar being given an equal chance of selection in the population.

domicile The place that a person regards as his or her permanent home and principal establishment. A domicile is a place to which, whenever a person is absent, he or she intends to return. A person's domicile may or may not be the same as his or her residence at a given time. *See also* residence.

domiciliary Relating to the place that a person regards as his or her permanent abode.

domiciliary administration The settlement of the portion of a decedent's estate that is located in the state of his or her domicile. A domiciliary administration should be distinguished from ancillary administration, which relates to property located elsewhere than in the state of the decedent's domicile.

domiciliary trustee The trustee of that portion of a decedent's or settlor's property that is located in the state of the decedent's or settlor's domicile. *Distinguish from* ancillary trustee.

dominant estate A parcel of land whose owner enjoys an easement or privilege to use another parcel of land for a special purpose.

donation (1) A return of stock to the issuing corporation, without requiring payment. (2) Any gift.

donative interest An interest in property that is subject to gift tax.

donee One who receives a gift.

donor One who gives a gift. *See also* grantor; settlor; trustor.

dormant account A customer's account for which activity has not occurred for a specified time. *Compare with* active account. *See also* escheat.

double-auction principle A principle that describes trading in an exchange market, in which many buyers and sellers compete simultaneously for the best price through their agents. The lowest price asked and the highest price bid define the range of prices within which the subsequent trade will fall and determine the buyer and seller for the trade.

double-barrel obligation bond A municipal bond whose interest and principal repayment are derived from a special tax or source of revenues. If such revenues fail to provide adequate funds, the bond is further backed by the full faith and credit of the municipality and becomes a general obligation bond.

double declining balance depreciation A method for depreciating an asset in which twice the straight-line rate of depreciation is applied to the asset's remaining book value each year.

double-entry accounting An accounting system in which each transaction is entered in two accounts. This permits a constant checking of accuracy, since in double-entry accounting the left side of the balance sheet (assets) always equals the right side (liabilities plus equity). *See also* single-entry accounting.

double-entry bookkeeping An accounting system based on the premise that for every debit entry there is an equal, corresponding credit entry. *Also called* dual posting.

double exemption The exemption of certain municipal bonds from both state and federal income taxation.

double financing A fraudulent action in which a dealer or other borrower submits a credit application and receives a loan for the same customer from two different banks.

double indemnity The provision in an insurance policy that doubles the benefits when death is caused by specified causes.

double taxation Taxing the same income twice. As an example, earnings of corporations are subject to the corporate income tax. When the earnings are paid out as dividends to stockholders, they are taxed again as personal income. *Compare with* conduit theory (of taxation).

Douglas Amendment An amendment to the Bank Holding Company Act of 1956 that effectively extended the provisions of the McFadden Act to holding companies. It prohibits a holding company from acquiring more than 5 percent of the shares of a bank located outside the company's home state unless authorized by applicable state law. *See also* McFadden Act.

dower The life estate of a widow in the real property of her husband. At common law, a wife had a life estate in one-third (in value) of the real property of her husband if he died without leaving a valid will or from whose will she dissented. In many states, common law dower has been abolished by statute or never has been recognized. *See also* curtesy; dissent.

Dow Jones Industrial Average A composite of the prices of 30 major industrial stocks. The Dow Jones is cited as a principal indicator of conditions in the market.

Dow Jones Industrials The 30 large industrial corporations whose stock prices are included in the Dow Jones Industrial Average.

downside risk The probability that the price of an investment will fall.

downstairs merger The merger of a parent corporation into its subsidiary.

downstream correspondent *See* respondent bank.

downstream loan Funds borrowed by a parent or holding company for its subsidiary, because the subsidiary cannot borrow the funds directly at the same favorable interest rate.

draft (bill of exchange) A signed order by one party (the drawer) addressed to another (the drawee) directing the drawee to pay at sight or at a definable time in the future a specified sum of money to the order of a third person, the payee. A draft is the basic financial instrument used in international trade to buy goods or services from abroad in a similar way that a check is used in domestic trade. *See also* bankers' acceptance.

draft envelope A wrapper merchants use to transmit sales drafts and credit slips to a bank for credit to their deposit accounts.

draft number The sequential number printed on sales draft form sets.

dragnet clause A clause, usually found in security agreements and mortgages, providing that the collateral pledged to secure the debt also secures other indebtedness owed to the holder by the maker of the security agreement or mortgage.

drawback A return of previously collected customs duties, when the imported goods are subsequently exported.

draw down An instruction to a receiver to reduce the balance of a sender's account, serviced by the receiver, by making a payment to the sender's account at another financial institution.

drawee The party on whom a draft is drawn and who is directed to pay the sum specified.

drawer The party who instructs the drawee to pay funds to the payee. *Also called* maker.

drive-in window (drive-through window) A convenience offered to the public, via a teller's window facing the outside of a bank building, so that customers can transact their business without leaving their cars.

drop location A facility convenient to a securities exchange that enables an out-of-town transfer agent to take physical delivery of securities.

dry trust *See* passive trust.

dual banking system The banking system in the United States, in which all banks are chartered either by the state in which they are domiciled or by the federal government through the Office of the Comptroller of the Currency. The side-by-side existence of both state-chartered and nationally chartered banks creates a dual banking system.

dual control A security technique that uses two or more separate entities, usually people, operating together to protect sensitive functions, information, or assets. Both entities are equally responsible for physically protecting materials involved in vulnerable transactions; no single entity can access or use the materials. For manual key generation, conveyance, and loading, dual control requires split knowledge of a key among the entities so that none of them can ever know the actual key.

dual-currency account An account kept by a bank with a bank in a foreign country, denominated in that foreign currency.

dual-currency bonds Long-term securities denominated in two currencies. The most common types have been bonds with initial payment and interim coupon payments in a nondollar currency, for example, Swiss francs or yen, and a fixed final principal payment in U.S. dollars.

dual dating A practice of embossing two dates on the face of credit cards, the first being the effective date and the second being the expiration date.

duality Full or partial participation by any one bank in two competing national bank card systems.

dual posting *See* double-entry book-keeping.

dual-purpose fund A closed-end mutual fund whose portfolio is half preferred stock and half common. Income shares issued by these funds receive as dividends all the net investment income of the fund. Capital shares of these funds reflect capital gains or losses of the funds. Both classes of shares trade in the market, rather than having the fund itself sell or redeem investors' shares.

dual-purpose tests Tests designed to fulfill simultaneously both compliance testing and substantive testing objectives.

due (1) Matured and payable, if referring to an obligation owed to others. (2) Receivable, if referring to an obligation to be received from others.

due bill An assignment or similar instrument given by the seller in a trade to transfer title to dividends, interest, or other rights legally due the buyer.

due bill check A check that follows a due bill, such as a check covering cash dividends due the buyer in a securities trade, payable on the date the issuer pays the dividend. The seller must deliver this check to the buyer within 5 days after the record date.

due-date analysis A review of a corporation's adherence to a policy of not paying accounts-payable items until they are due, as opposed to when they have been processed and cleared for payment.

due diligence (1) Procedures required by the U.S. Department of Education that a lender participating in the Guaranteed Student Loan Program must follow before filing a default claim. The regulation details the collection procedures that must be followed and the time sequence within which these procedures must be met. (2) Implication that the auditor must exercise reasonable care and competence when conducting an audit. (3) Procedures undertaken by experts such as auditors and attorneys in connection with examining valuations, disclosures, and assertions of management. Due diligence is used, for example, in new securities issuances and acquisitions.

due from account An account held by a bank (account owner bank) with another bank (account servicing bank) that represents funds "due from" the other bank on demand. This term is used in U.S. domestic banking. In international banking, the common terms are reciprocal and nostro account.

due from banks An asset balance owed by another bank to a bank, classified in the financial statements as the equivalent of cash.

due-on-sale clause A clause in a mortgage permitting the lender to demand full payment of the outstanding balance when the property is sold. The intent is to prevent the transfer of the mortgage, which may bear a relatively low interest rate, to a new buyer.

due to account An account serviced by a bank (account servicing bank) on behalf of another bank (account owner bank) that represents funds due to the other bank on demand. This term is used in U.S. domestic banking. In international banking, the common terms are loro account and vostro account.

due to banks A liability balance owed to another bank by a bank, which is classified in the financial statements as the equivalent of demand deposits.

dump (1) Under trade law, the sale of goods at less than fair value that causes injury, threatens to cause injury, or substantially retards the development of an industry in the importing country. A sale at less than fair value occurs when the sale price of goods in the importing country is lower than the price in the exporting country; however, this circumstance alone may not necessarily constitute a dump. (2) To copy all or part of the data into storage, usually from internal into external storage.

Dun & Bradstreet, Inc. A credit reporting agency that primarily supplies credit information on businesses.

dunning The process of contacting delinquent cardholders by mail or telephone to obtain payment.

duplicate statement A photocopy of the actual billing statement.

DuPont System A system widely used to analyze a firm's financial position. With this system, the analyst breaks down total returns and total costs into return on investments, asset turnover, and profit margins.

durable consumer goods Goods purchased by individual consumers that are normally more expensive and longer lasting than nondurable goods.

durable power of attorney A power of attorney that remains effective despite the disability or incompetence of the person granting the power.

duration Used in asset/liability management to reduce interest rate risk. Duration is the average time needed to recover an initial cash outlay. It is the time-weighted present value of an asset or liability (or a group of assets or liabilities) divided by its unweighted present value. Duration is computed by summing the present value of all future payment flows, multiplying each by the time to receipt, and dividing by the summed present value of all those flows (not weighted by time to receipt). If the duration of an asset equals the duration of a liability of equal size, interest rate risk is minimized (and under certain assumptions eliminated). For banks, a major weakness of the duration concept is the difficulty of determining the duration of some balance sheet items such as demand deposits.

duress Compulsion or constraint by force or fear of personal violence, prosecution, or imprisonment, which induces a person to do what he or she does not want to do or to refrain from doing something he or she has a legal right to do. Sometimes the word is used with reference to the making of a will, such as that it was made under duress.

Dutch auction An auction technique, sometimes used for selling securities, in which progressively lower bids are accepted until the entire issue is sold. This technique is also used in tender offers, in which progressively higher bids are accepted until the desired number of securities is acquired.

duty card A record in chronological order of actions to be taken. A duty card is used in many trust departments. *Also called* tickler.

dwelling (1) As used in the Fair Housing Act, any building, structure, or portion of one that is occupied, designed for occupancy, or intended for occupancy as a residence by one or more families. (2) As used in Regulation Z, a residential structure that contains one to four family housing units. A residential condominium unit is included in the definition. In some instances, dwelling is nearly identical with residence.

dwelling unit The living quarters occupied or intended for occupancy by one household.

dynamic open market operations Purchases and sales of securities in the open market by the Federal Reserve, designed to achieve objectives of monetary policy. *Compare with* defensive open market operations.

early warning system A system designed to identify a financial institution likely to fail.

early withdrawal penalty An interest penalty incurred by a depositor for withdrawing funds from an account before maturity.

earned income (1) The income received for work or services performed, as opposed to income from investments, rents, and so on. (2) In a lease, the portion of the rental payment that is equivalent to interest on a loan. It may also be called lease service charge.

earned surplus The profits of an enterprise that have been made through normal operations that remain undistributed.

earnest money A portion of a down payment delivered to a seller or an escrow agent by the purchaser of real estate, along with a purchase offer, as evidence of good faith in negotiating the final sale. Earnest money is forfeited if the final sale is aborted through the fault of the purchaser.

earning assets Loans, investments, and other interest-bearing (or dividend-bearing) assets. Earning assets should be distinguished from nonearning assets, such as cash and legal reserves.

earnings (1) The income derived from the work or services performed by an individual or business. (2) The net profit after all expenses and taxes are deducted.

earnings allowance The earnings on a compensating balance, which may be used to pay for account activity. An earnings allowance is usually computed by multiplying the average daily collected balance net of reserves by an arbitrary interest rate intended to approximate the interest rate of a no-risk security that could be sold on 1 day's notice.

earnings credit An allowance to a customer, offsetting part or all of the service charges on an account and calculated on the basis of the average balance in the account during a period and the earnings credit rate in effect at the time.

earnings per share (EPS) The most common method of expressing a company's profitability. Its purpose is to indicate how effective an enterprise has been in using the resources provided by common shareholders. In its simplest form, EPS equals the net income divided by the number of outstanding shares of common stock. The difficulty in computing EPS arises because of the existence of instruments that are not common stock but that have the potential of causing additional shares of common stock to be issued (for example, convertible preferred stock, convertible debt, options, and warrants). *See also* primary earnings per share; fully diluted earnings per share.

earnings ratio *See* price-earnings (P/E) ratio.

earnings report A statement of earnings, expenses, and profit or loss incurred during a period of time.

earnings statement An analysis and written presentation of the earnings of an enterprise. An income statement is an earnings statement.

easement An acquired right of use or enjoyment, falling short of ownership, that a person may have in the land of another (for example, one person's right of way over another person's land).

easement appurtenant An easement granted by deed that "runs with the land" and is necessary for the use of the land.

easement by prescription An easement acquired by the open, continuous, and hostile use of real property for a period required by statute.

easement in gross The right to use another's land for a special purpose, representing a personal right. This easement does not "run with the land."

E bond A savings bond issued by the U.S. government to the general public

from 1935 to 1980. The bonds were available in small denominations, were purchased at a discount, and earned interest at a prescribed rate.

econometric model An empirical method of economic forecasting that uses an equation based on the statistical relationship among economic variables, such as housing starts and equipment purchases.

econometrics A branch of economics that involves studying and testing economic theories by using mathematical and statistical analysis. By measuring the interrelation of economic variables, econometrics is also used to make economic forecasts. For example, loan volume might be forecast from capital spending plans of business.

economic depletion The decrease in value (of mineral or gas rights, timberlands, and so on) caused by production operations.

economic forecast A projection of the level of economic activity for a particular period. The most common measure of economic activity is the gross national product.

economic indicators (1) Factors in the economy that measure general economic activity. Common indicators include average hours worked per week in manufacturing, common stock prices, and corporate profits. (2) A group of measures of economic activity developed by the National Bureau of Economic Research that changes in close conformity with the business cycle. The economic indicators are divided into leading, coincident, and lagging indicators, which fairly consistently turn up or down before, coincident with, or after a turn in general business activity.

economic life (1) The length of time during which a fixed asset can yield services useful to its owner. (2) The estimated time during which a property can be used profitably.

economics The study of production, distribution, consumption, and the allocation of scarce resources among competing needs. Economics is divided into many specialized areas, including macroeconomics, microeconomics, labor economics, international economics, banking and finance, econometrics, and public finance.

economies of scale The tendency for certain classes of costs to decrease as an institution's size or volume of business increases.

ECP *See* Eurocommercial paper.

ECU *See* European currency unit.

Edge Act Legislation enacted in 1919 allowing banks' subsidiaries located anywhere in the United States to engage in international banking. The Board of Governors of the Federal Reserve System charters Edge Act corporations under this act.

Edge Act corporation A nationally chartered corporate subsidiary of a bank established under Section 25(a) of the Federal Reserve Act to engage in international banking and investment.

EDP *See* electronic data processing.

EE bond A savings bond issued to the general public by the U.S. government. EE bonds are sold at a discount from face value in amounts that are limited for each purchaser. They are nontransferable and may not be used as collateral for a loan. They may also be exchanged for HH bonds.

effective annual yield The return on an investment, expressed in terms of the equivalent rate of simple interest.

effective date The date on which a bank card becomes valid.

effective gross income Gross income, less an allowance for vacancy and bad debts.

effective income Income that is reasonably certain, less nonrecurring income earned infrequently.

effective interest rate The rate of interest earned on a security. It is based on the actual price paid for the security and the security's coupon rate, maturity date, and purchase date. *Compare with* nominal interest rate. *See also* effective rate of interest.

effective rate of interest The rate of simple interest paid on a loan.

effects test A standard imposed by the Equal Credit Opportunity Act to determine whether lenders are guilty of credit discrimination. Lenders are legally responsible for evaluating their policies and procedures to be certain they do not adversely affect the ability of nine protected classes of loan applicants to obtain credit.

efficient market A market that immediately incorporates all available information into the price of the asset being traded.

efficient portfolio A portfolio that cannot be improved in the sense that no other portfolio provides as high a return at as low a risk.

EITF *See* Emerging Issues Task Force.

either-way market A market in which bid and asked quotes are the same. This term is used in the Eurodollar market.

elastic demand A measure of the relationship between changes in the price for a product or service and changes in the quantity demanded. The demand for a firm's product is elastic if the percentage change in quantity sold is greater than the percentage change in price (both expressed in absolute values). Under such circumstances, a relatively small price increase will cause a comparatively large decline in the quantity of a product purchased, reducing total revenue received by the firm. *See also* inelastic demand.

elasticity *See* bank elasticity.

election The choice of an alternative right or course. For example, the right of a widow to take the share of her deceased husband's estate to which she is entitled under the law, despite a contrary provision in the will, is known as the widow's election.

electronic data capture The electronic process of obtaining authorization and creating the debit transaction to post to a cardholder account.

electronic data interchange (EDI) The electronic exchange of data pertaining to routine business transactions, using standard industry formats. EDI allows the customers and suppliers of corporations to transmit purchase orders, invoices, and other common business documents from computer to computer. EDI is based on a series of standard formats for common business transactions developed by ANSI X-12, a working group of the American National Standards Institute.

electronic data processing (EDP) The use of electronic equipment to sort,

classify, identify, record, and summarize data.

electronic data transfer (EDT) The transfer of any data, initiated through an electronic terminal, telephonic instrument, or magnetic tape.

electronic funds transfer (EFT) An electronically based rather than paper-based system of transferring funds to and from accounts.

electronic funds transfer system (EFTS) A system designed to facilitate the exchange of monetary value by electronic means. Objectives include expanding the times when, and places where, basic financial services are available and reducing the present growth in the volume of paper (cash and checks).

electronic giro Payments that customers initiate from their own financial accounts and control in an electronic payment environment. (Giro is not an acronym, but a term taken from the Italian "giro," meaning turn or transfer.)

electronic spreadsheet A large worksheet on a computer divided into cells where data are stored.

electronic terminal An electronic device, other than a telephone, operated by a consumer to initiate an electronic funds transfer. The term includes, but is not limited to, point-of-sale terminals, automated teller machines, and cash-dispensing machines.

eleemosynary Pertaining or devoted to legal charity, such as an eleemosynary institution.

eligible bankers' acceptance (1) An acceptance that is eligible for discount by the Federal Reserve in accordance with Federal Reserve Regulation A.

(2) An acceptance that can be sold without subjecting the proceeds of the sale to reserve requirements.

eligible borrower A borrower who meets eligibility standards for participating in a guaranteed loan program.

eligible lender Any lending institution for which a guaranteeing agency will consider guaranteeing loans. For the Farmers Home Administration, for example, this includes any federal or state-chartered bank, Federal Land Bank, production credit association, or other approved lending institution.

eligible paper The promissory notes, drafts, bills of exchange, and bankers' acceptances that the Federal Reserve is permitted by law to accept for discount at its lowest rate of interest. *Compare with* acceptable paper.

embezzlement The fraudulent use or appropriation of funds or other property that has been entrusted to one's care.

emboss To print identifying data on a bank card in the form of raised impressions.

embossed character reader (ECR) A device that reads embossed characters on a bank card.

embosser A device that produces characters in a raised impression on bank cards.

embossing The mechanical raising of data from the otherwise flat surface of a bank card, for subsequent automatic or manual reading.

emergency credit Credit extended by a Federal Reserve bank to entities other than depository institutions where failure to obtain credit would adversely affect the economy.

Emergency Home Owners Relief Act of 1975 An act authorizing the secretary of Housing and Urban Development to make payments of repayable emergency mortgage relief on behalf of distressed homeowners.

emergency provision The provision of a will or trust agreement that empowers the trustee to pay principal or accumulated income to meet emergencies in the life of the beneficiary caused by illness, accident, or other unforeseeable events.

Emerging Issues Task Force (EITF) Formed by the Financial Accounting Standards Board in 1984 to identify and define emerging accounting issues on a timely basis. The task force has 15 members, including the chief technical partners of the Big Eight accounting firms. Approximately half the issues dealt with have related to financial institutions and financial instruments. Consensus positions of the EITF are viewed as authoritative accounting guidance by the Securities and Exchange Commission.

eminent domain The inherent sovereign power of the state over all the private property within its borders, which enables it to appropriate all or any part of the property to a necessary public use by making reasonable compensation.

empirical information Information derived from observation or experience.

empirically derived credit system A credit-scoring system that evaluates an applicant's creditworthiness, primarily by allocating points or weights to key characteristics that describe the applicant or various aspects of the transaction.

employee-benefit plan A plan established or maintained by an employer, employee organization, or both, to provide employees a certain benefit or benefits such as a pension, profit sharing, thrift plan, stock bonus, and health, accident, and disability insurance.

employee-benefit trust A pension or profit-sharing plan set up by an employer, usually a corporation, for its employees. The plan is managed by a trustee, usually a bank, which pays out funds to employees during employment, at retirement, or at death, as designated. These institutional investors are major holders of securities.

employee relations The policies, programs, and processes that bank managers use in relating to employees.

Employee Retirement Income Security Act of 1974 (ERISA) An act that set federal minimum standards for private employee benefit plans, including standards regulating the conduct of a plan's fiduciaries and trustees. The act added to the prudent-man rule the requirement that trustees adhere to the investment standards of a person knowledgeable and experienced in investments. Thus the prudent-man rule became the prudent-expert rule under ERISA. The act also established an insurance program designed to guarantee workers some pension benefits if their defined-benefit pension plan should end. In addition, this act established requirements for reporting, disclosure, and vesting.

employee savings plan An employee group investment plan. Employees contribute to this plan voluntarily, and the employer may match all or part of the employees' contributions. The amount that an employee can eventually realize from the plan

depends solely on contributions and the fund's investment performance. A trust department often administers these plans.

employee stock ownership plan (ESOP) A plan in which an employer or employee makes contributions to purchase the company's stock for the account of the employee. An ESOP may be either a stock-bonus or stock-purchase plan.

employees' trust or employee-benefit trust A trust established to hold the assets of an employee-benefit plan.

Employment Act of 1946 Law that established the Council of Economic Advisers and required the federal government to promote, through fiscal and monetary policy measures, full employment, economic growth, and price stability.

emulate To use one system to imitate another so that the imitating system accepts the same data, executes the same programs, and achieves the same results as the system being imitated.

emulator (1) A device or computer program that emulates. (2) The combination of programming techniques and special features of a machine that permits a computer to execute programs written for another computer.

encode To use a code to represent individual characters or groups of characters in a message.

encoder A device capable of translating from one method of expression to another.

encoding (1) The process of inscribing or imprinting MICR characters on checks, deposits, or other bank documents. (2) The magnetized recording of data in the magnetic stripe on a bank card.

encoding strip On bank checks, the clear band in which magnetic ink will be deposited to represent characters.

encroachment An improvement to property that intrudes illegally on another's property or easement rights.

encryption A process of transforming plain (readable) text into cipher (unreadable) text for security or privacy.

encumbered Property against which some claim, such as a mortgage, lien, or easement, has been given.

encumbrance Any claim, interest, or right in property, such as a lien, mortgage, dower right, or easement. Such encumbrances generally do not prevent a property from being bought or sold, but they generally reduce its value.

end-of-text character A character that signals the end of a message or information in the magnetic stripe on a bank card. *Also called* end sentinel, stop character, *or* sentinel.

endorsement (1) The signature, placed on the back of a negotiable instrument or in an accompanying power, that transfers the instrument to another party and legally implies that the endorser has the right to transfer the instrument. (2) The placement of an endorsement stamp on bank card sales and credit slips to identify the originating bank and the date processed. *See also* qualified endorsement; restrictive endorsement; special endorsement.

endorsement areas Spaces on the reverse of a check reserved for endorsements according to functional roles in the collection of cash items.

endorsement date (1) The date appearing on the interchange advice and endorsed on paper by the clearing member that first enters the paper into interchange. The endorsement date must be the same date the paper is mailed to the card issuer's clearing member. *See also* interchange; advice; clearing member. (2) The date placed on the back of a check by each processing bank to identify when the bank handled the item.

endorsement guarantee The term used to describe the method of guaranteeing the endorsement of a stock certificate or investment security in all respects. *Distinguish from* signature guarantee.

endorsement in blank The signature of an authorized person on the back of a negotiable instrument, or on a separate power, that is not accompanied by the specific name of the party to whom the instrument is being transferred. Endorsement in blank makes the instrument as transferable as if it were in bearer form.

endorser One who endorses. *See also* endorsement.

endorsing machine A device used to cancel checks, passbooks, and so on.

endowment fund A fund arising from a bequest or gift, the income from which is earmarked for a specific use, such as sponsoring a cultural or educational program.

endowment insurance Life insurance that pays the face amount of a policy when the insured party dies or at the end of the contractual period.

end sentinel *See* end-of-text character.

end-user (swap market) A counterparty that engages in a swap to change its interest rate or currency exposure, in contrast to a swap-trading institution. End-users may be nonfinancial corporations, financial institutions, or governments.

engagement letter A letter submitted by an external auditor specifying the scope of an intended audit, the time required, procedures to be followed, and reports to be submitted.

enhancement The improvement or upgrading of a computer system to make it better suited to user needs.

enter To record a transaction in a journal or data in a computer.

entity That which exists as separate and complete in itself. For example, a corporation is a legal entity, separate and distinct from its stockholders.

entree card A debit card program currently used by some member banks of an interchange system, in which the transactions are posted to the customer's checking account.

entrepreneur A person who invests in a business, at some risk, in order to make a profit.

entry The original records of a particular transaction made in the books of account.

entry date A date on which entries are made in the records of an account. *Also called* posting date, execution date, payment date, *and* transaction date.

envelope settlement services Delivery services offered by clearing corporations when the physical delivery of certificates is necessary. The delivering participant drops off envelopes containing the securities and a credit list indicating the dollar amount

chargeable to the recipient's account. The clearing corporation forwards the envelopes to the addressees and enters charges or credits on participants' accounts, as directed in the credit list.

en ventre sa mere The term describes a child conceived but not yet born.

environmental liability That series of federal or state environmental statutes that impose liability (or a superior lien) for environmental clean-up costs on the owner or operator of the site, including lenders with security interest who foreclose on the site or control the owner or operator.

Equal Credit Opportunity Act (ECOA) A federal law passed in 1974 that requires lenders and other creditors to make credit equally available without discrimination based on race, color, religion, national origin, sex, age, marital status, receipt of income from public assistance programs, or past exercise of rights under the Consumer Credit Protection Act. ECOA specifies actions and questions that are prohibited when obtaining information relative to credit applications. *See also* Regulation B.

equalization reserve An account credited at regular intervals with funds used to cover irregular expenses. The reserve is set up to distribute those irregular expenses uniformly over accounting periods. The equalization reserve is no longer allowed under GAAP.

equalizing dividend A dividend paid to correct irregularities in the payment of dividends when the regular date for dividend payment is changed.

equilibrium price The price of goods determined in the market by the intersection of a supply and demand curve.

equipment *See* off-line equipment; on-line equipment; peripheral equipment.

equipment dealer (ED) draft *See* household equipment draft.

equipment trust A corporate trust established to finance the purchase of equipment. Railroads often use equipment trusts to purchase rolling stock.

equipment trust bond A bond issue secured by machinery and equipment. For example, railroads, airlines, and truckers may back these issues with locomotives, planes, or trucks. Investors may favor such bonds because, if the issuer defaults, the equipment may be sold to a competitor.

equipment trust certificate An interest-bearing document issued to purchase new equipment. Until the notes are paid off, a trustee holds title to the equipment.

equitable apportionment A doctrine that requires all recipients of probate and nonprobate assets to pay their proportionate share of death taxes. A tax clause in a will or trust can override this doctrine.

equitable charge A charge on property imposed by and enforceable in a court of equity, as distinguished from a charge enforceable in a court of law. A conveyance of real property, absolute on its face but intended only as security for a loan, may constitute an equitable charge on the property.

equitable conversion The change of property from one form to another, as from real to personal property or the reverse, which is considered to have occurred even though no actual exchange has occurred.

equitable ownership The estate or interest of a person who has a beneficial right in property, the legal ownership of which is in another person. For example, a beneficiary of a trust has an equitable ownership in the trust property. *Distinguish from* legal ownership.

equitable title A right to the benefits of property that is recognized by and enforceable only in a court of equity. *Distinguish from* legal title.

equities Securities that represent owned rather than borrowed capital. This term is used synonymously with common stock or capital stock. The stockholders' equity in a company may be stated inclusive or exclusive of preferred stock.

equity (1) The value of the stockholders' ownership of a corporation, which equals the difference between the company's total assets and its total liabilities. Equity includes preferred stock, common stock, retained earnings, and other surplus reserves. *Also called* book net worth *or* total proprietorship. (2) In real estate, the interest or value an owner has in the property, less the amount of existing liens. (3) A system of principles and rules developed to supplement and correct a system of law that had become too narrow and rigid in scope and application. Its characteristic is flexibility and its aim is the administration of justice.

equity annuity *See* variable amount note.

equity financing The process of raising funds for a company's expansion by selling stocks rather than bonds. *Compare with* debt financing.

equity line An open-end line of credit secured by a mortgage on the borrower's home. It generally has a high credit limit. The open-end provision may allow advances for as long as 10 years and be renewable at that time. After the open-end provision expires, the borrower may repay over a period of 10 to 20 years. Some banks permit interest only to be paid for up to 5 years. *See also* home equity line.

equity multiplier (EM) A measure of financial leverage. It is calculated by dividing average total assets by average shareholder's equity.

equity of redemption The right under common law in which a defaulted borrower can redeem property during foreclosure, upon payment of the debt plus the lender's expenses. In some states, the mortgagor even has the statutory right to redeem property after a foreclosure sale.

equity participation An agreement with a lender to let the lender share in the gross income, net income, or cash flow of income-producing real estate; also, an ownership interest by an investor. The term "equity kicker" refers to an equity participation by a lender that provides additional compensation above the interest charged on the loan.

equity participation mortgage The partial ownership of income property, conveyed by the owner to the lender as part of the consideration for making the loan.

equity securities Securities that represent ownership in a corporation. Total equity includes preferred and common stock; common equity includes only common stock.

equivalent bond yield The yield on a Treasury bill is computed on the basis of a 360-day year. The price of a bond is computed on the basis of a 365-day year. To compare the yield on the two, the yield on a 91-day bill

can be converted into an equivalent bond yield by the following formula:

$$\frac{\text{Amount of Discount}}{\text{Price of Bill}} \times \frac{365}{91}$$

erase To obliterate information from a storage medium, for example, by clearing or overwriting.

error-correcting codes Special codes, such as Hamming codes, allowing at least single-error correction and double-error detection.

error rate In market research, the amount by which a sample statistic might vary from the true population statistic because of the size of the sample. For instance, in a sample of consumers, 45 percent might have a certificate of deposit. However, with a 3 percent error rate, the true statistic (if everyone in the population were interviewed) would lie in the 42 to 48 percent range.

escalation clause (1) A clause in a loan contract that permits the lender to increase or decrease the rate of interest charged if economic conditions change substantially during the life of the contract. (2) In purchase contracts, a provision for unforeseen changes in basic costs (for labor or materials), which require an increase in the final price.

escape clause A provision that allows one or more of the parties to a contract to withdraw under stipulated conditions, or to somehow modify a previously agreed performance.

escheat The reversion of property to the state when there are no devisees, legatees, heirs, or next of kin. It was originally applicable to real property only, but it is now applicable to all kinds of property, including dormant accounts whose owners cannot be located.

escheat law The statutory provisions governing the reversion of property to the state when unclaimed by the owner for a specified number of years or under other specified conditions.

escrow An agency service trust departments offer to individuals and corporations. The escrow agent provides safekeeping for cash, securities, or documents until certain conditions required by the escrow agreement between two parties are met. The escrow agent then surrenders the assets, as required by the agreement. The subject matter of the transaction (the money, securities, instruments, or other property) is the escrow.

escrow account A deposit account maintained in connection with a mortgage loan, into which a borrower deposits regular amounts for payment of taxes, insurance, special assessments, and so on.

escrow agreement A document, agreed to by two or more parties, that appoints and authorizes an agent to perform certain acts on their behalf. As used in real estate transactions, an escrow agreement authorizes the disbursement of funds on the satisfaction of certain requirements.

escrow payments Payments into an escrow account.

estate The right, title, or interest that a person has in any property, to be distinguished from the property itself. The term is often used to describe the property of a decedent.

estate account Funds managed by an appointed legal representative for an individual who is deceased.

estate for years A lease that continues for a definite period.

estate in common *See* tenancy in common.

estate in fees *See* fee.

estate in fee simple The absolute right to ownership in real estate.

estate management The professional management of estates. Management and settlement of estates is a principal personal trust activity. A court periodically reviews and approves the trustee's actions.

estate of inheritance *See* freehold estate.

estate plan A definite plan for the administration and disposition of one's property during one's lifetime and at death. An estate plan is usually set forth in a will and in one or more trust agreements.

estate planning (1) Determining how to maximize the after-tax value of an estate and taking steps to accomplish that end. (2) Measuring a person's estate before the person dies and determining how it will be distributed.

estate pur auter vie *See* life estate.

estates A functional unit in a trust department. Management and settlement of estates is a principal personal trust activity. A court periodically reviews and approves the acts of the trustee.

estate tax A tax imposed on a decedent's estate as such and not on the distributive shares of the estate or on the right to receive the shares. *Distinguish from* inheritance tax.

estate tax bond A designated government bond redeemable at par that accrues interest to pay federal estate taxes if the decedent owned the securities at the time of death. *Commonly called* flower bond.

estate trust A trust that is required to pay to a surviving spouse or to accumulate all of its income, and whose property passes to the surviving spouse's estate at his or her death. The estate trust will qualify for the marital deduction and will be treated as a separate taxpayer for income taxes.

estimated gross income The total anticipated earnings from property without deductions for vacancies, uncollectible rents, and so on.

estimated residual value The estimated fair market value of leased property at the end of the lease term.

estimation sampling A method of statistical sampling in which an estimate is made of some characteristic (such as the frequency or total value of error) in the population on the basis of a sample drawn from that population.

estoppel The preclusion of a person from alleging in an action what is contrary to his or her previous action or admission. Estoppel bars a person from denying a misrepresentation of a fact when another person has acted on that misrepresentation to his or her detriment. The person so precluded or barred is said to be estopped.

estoppel certificate (1) A statement from a lender showing the remaining balance of an outstanding mortgage. (2) A written statement made by a tenant, lender, or other party setting forth the facts pertaining to the relationship between the parties and/or the real estate in question. It is often used in real estate lending as evidence that the tenant is complying with the terms of a lease.

Eurobond A corporate bond denominated in a currency different from that of the country where it is sold.

Euro CD *See* Eurodollar certificate of deposit.

Eurocheque A system that enables citizens of certain countries traveling abroad to cash checks for limited amounts by presenting a card meeting certain requirements.

Eurocommercial paper (ECP) Paper similar to commercial paper sold by U.S. firms but issued by foreign corporations in the Eurosecurities markets.

Eurocommercial-paper facility A facility for issuing short-term notes with or without a backup line and generally with flexible maturities.

Eurocredit Any extension of credit that is made in one country and denominated in the currency of another country.

Eurocurrency A deposit denominated in a currency other than that of the country where the bank holding the deposit is located.

Eurocurrency deposits Deposits denominated in a currency other than that of the country where the bank accepting the deposit is located.

Eurocurrency market The market for issuing or trading bank deposits and debt instruments that are denominated in currencies other than those of the country in which they are issued.

Eurodollar A deposit in any branch or bank outside the United States, but especially in Europe, denominated in U.S. dollars and providing a readily available short-term source of funds to banks.

Eurodollar bond *See* Eurobond.

Eurodollar certificate of deposit (Euro CD) A dollar-denominated, short-term bearer certificate that represents deposits in foreign banks or foreign branches of U.S. banks.

Eurodollar market A currency market in which deposits of U.S. dollars are accepted by banks in other countries, generally in Europe and Japan, and made available for lending or investing as U.S. dollars.

Euroequities Dollar-denominated foreign equity securities traded in international markets.

Euro Feds Eurodollar deposits transmitted by Fedwire. Most Euro Feds are transferred through the Clearing House Interbank Payments System.

Euro line A line of credit set up in Eurocurrencies.

Euro-note A short-term note issued under a note issuance facility (NIF) or Eurocommercial-paper facility. *See also* note issuance facility; Eurocommercial-paper facility.

European currency unit (ECU) A composite currency based on a basket of European currencies.

European-style option An option that may be exercised only on the expiration date. It is an alternative to an American option, which can be exercised on any business day prior to expiration, or on the expiration date. *Also called* European option.

evening up Buying or selling to offset an existing market position. *Also called* liquidation *or* offset

evergreen letter of credit A standby letter of credit providing for continuous automatic renewals beyond the stated expiration date, usually for 1 additional year.

evergreen loan A loan in which no provisions have been made to pay off the principal. *Also called* a "standing" loan.

evidential matter Supporting accounting data and confirmatory information used by the auditor during the discharge of his or her duties.

examination *See* bank examination.

examination objectives A subsection in the Comptroller's Handbook describing, for each banking activity, the goal of primary importance to the examiner. Some objectives define the scope of specific areas of the examination, while others ensure compliance with laws, rules, and regulations.

examination of title A review of the chain of title for a piece of real estate, as revealed by an abstract of title to the property from the public records.

examination procedures A subsection in the Comptroller's Handbook describing, for each banking activity, the procedures an examiner is required to perform. These procedures are supervisory and help the examiner achieve the objectives for each subject area.

examine for bank endorsement The examination of the back of checks to see that the bank forwarding the checks has properly endorsed them.

exception item An item that cannot be paid by a drawee bank for one reason or another, such as a stop payment or insufficient funds.

exceptions Transactions, either monetary or nonmonetary, that fail to meet the parameters of the system and require special handling. Exceptions are usually displayed periodically on a listing called an exception report.

excess-benefit plan A nonqualified plan maintained by an employer solely to provide for certain employee benefits in excess of those that can normally be provided by the employer's qualified plan because of Internal Revenue Code limitations on contributions and benefits.

excessive purchases Credit card purchases in excess of some control number. When the number of purchases electronically posted to an account in a day exceeds a certain number, the account is listed on a printout for manual attention. When the account file is accessed, the authorization system may display a code indicating excessive purchases.

excess reserves Funds held by depository institutions in excess of the legal minimum required by the Federal Reserve. Banks hold these funds in their own vaults, on deposit at a Federal Reserve bank, or in a pass-through account in a bank approved by the Federal Reserve.

excess retirement accumulation In general, the amount by which the federal estate tax value of a decedent's qualified retirement benefits (including individual retirement accounts) included in the decedent's gross estate exceeds the present value of an annuity, payable for a period equal to the decedent's normal life expectancy based on his or her attained age at death, or whichever is greater, (a) $150,000, or (b) $112,500, indexed for inflation. A 15 percent supplemental estate tax is imposed on estates of decedents dying after 1986 on excess retirement accumulations.

excess retirement distributions The aggregate amount of distributions

from qualified plans to a taxpayer during the year to the extent they exceed whichever amount is greater, (a) $150,000, or (b) $112,500, indexed for inflation. A 15 percent excise tax is imposed for taxable years after 1986 on excess retirement distributions. If a taxpayer receives a lump-sum distribution for which special lump-sum income tax treatment is elected, the limit is increased by five times and separately applied to the distribution.

exchange agent The party who receives securities of a company being acquired in a merger and replaces the securities with stock of the new company. In the recapitalization of a company, this agent may exchange one class of securities for another.

exchange bureau A cooperative consumer-reporting agency operated by banks engaged in installment credit activities.

exchange charge A service charge made by a drawee bank for paying checks and other instruments presented to it.

exchange controls Government-imposed monetary exchange rates that establish the relative price between two or more currencies.

exchange member A person who has purchased a seat on one of the various stock exchanges from a former member who was willing to sell his or her seat. A seat on the exchange entitles the bearer, and the firm with which he or she is affiliated, to trade on that exchange, that is, to have a broker on the floor of the exchange.

exchange rate The price at which one currency can be bought with another currency or gold. *Also called* rate of exchange.

excise tax A tax levied on the manufacture, sale, or consumption of consumer goods, usually luxuries, within a country.

exculpatory provision A provision in a will or trust instrument relieving, or attempting to relieve, an executor or trustee from liability for breach of trust. *Sometimes called* immunity provision.

ex-dividend When a dividend is declared by a corporation, it is payable on a designated date to stockholders of record as of a stated date. When stock is sold before the stated date, the dividend belongs to the buyer and not to the seller. When the stock is sold subsequent to the stated date and before the date of payment, the dividend belongs to the seller and not to the buyer. It is then said to sell ex-dividend. The New York Stock Exchange has a special rule to the effect that the stock becomes ex-dividend 4 business days before the stated date. Most other exchanges follow the New York rule.

ex-dividend date The day on and after which the right to receive a current dividend is not transferred automatically from seller to buyer. *Also called* ex-date. *See also* ex-dividend.

execution (1) A formal judicial order that directs a public officer, usually a sheriff, to execute a final judgment or decree of a court. (2) The act of signing an instrument by the parties involved, usually witnessed or notarized for recording purposes. (3) For a securities trade, execution occurs when a buyer and seller (through their brokers) agree on quantity and price.

execution date *See* entry date.

executive officer Under Regulation O, an officer of a bank or its parent who participates or has the authority to participate in major policy-making functions.

executor A party, frequently a bank or trust company, named in a will to carry out its terms. The executor gathers the assets of the creator of the will, pays all taxes, debts, and expenses, and distributes the net estate as ordered in the will. A female executor is called an executrix.

executor de bonis non The person or corporation named in a will to take over and complete the settlement of an estate in those cases in which the original executor, for some reason, has failed or cannot do so. Unless the testator names such a successor executor, the court of probate appoints an administrator de bonis non.

executor deed A deed, executed under court approval, that warrants title only against acts by the executor.

executor de son tort A person who, without legal authority, assumes control of a decedent's property as if he or she were executor and thereby makes himself or herself responsible for what goes into his or her possession.

executrix *See* executor.

exemplified copy A copy of a record or document that is witnessed, sealed, or certified, as required by law for a particular transaction.

exempt employee A person who, under the Fair Labor Standards Act, does not have to be paid additional compensation for overtime hours worked.

exemption (1) The designated amount of gross personal income exempt from taxation for a taxpayer and each person the taxpayer supports. (2) In bankruptcy, the amount and kind of property that is exempt from claims of creditors. (3) Under state law, the property that is exempt from execution by creditors holding a judgment against a person.

exemption equivalent The amount of property that can be given away or descend at death, without a transfer tax being imposed pursuant to the federal unified credit. *See also* unified credit.

exemption list A list of persons or entities exempt from having to file currency transaction reports pursuant to the Bank Secrecy Act. Banks must follow strict procedures before adding to this list and must produce this list for the government, if requested. They must also justify each name on the list under the law and regulations.

exempt securities (1) Securities that do not require registration with the Securities and Exchange Commission. Exempt securities include private placements, governments, agencies, and municipals. (2) Securities that are not subject to margin requirements under Federal Reserve regulations G, T, and U.

exercise price The price set in an option. The owner of an option has the right to buy (or sell) the security named in the option at the exercise price, within a set time period. *Also called* strike price.

Eximbank *See* Export-Import Bank of the United States.

exoneration (1) The act of relieving one of what otherwise would be or might be a liability or a duty. (2) The act of freeing one from a charge.

expansion (1) The act of enlarging a business by developing new markets, enlarging facilities, hiring new

employees, and so on. (2) A period of general growth in business or economic activity.

expectations hypothesis The assumption that the yield curve reflects the net present value of all expected future interest rates. Under this hypothesis, the yield curve points in the direction that rates are expected to move; for example, a rising yield curve indicates that the market expects rates to rise. *Compare with* liquidity preference hypothesis.

expected volatility The degree of volatility that option pricing formulas assume will prevail over the remaining life of an option.

expedited availability The reduced timeframe within which a bank must make deposited checks available to a depositor, as mandated by Regulation CC of the Federal Reserve System. *Also called* accelerated availability.

Expedited Funds Availability Act (EFAA) A law passed by Congress in 1987 that requires financial institutions to make deposited items available for withdrawal on an expedited basis. Implemented by Regulation CC issued by the Federal Reserve Board, the act also requires lobby notices and special notices to a customer if funds will not be made available on the scheduled basis.

expense (1) A charge against revenue or the incurrence of a liability (or a combination of both). (2) The using up of capital assets (for example, depreciation expense).

expense account (1) A statement of costs incurred in the execution of a firm's affairs. (2) An account that reimburses expenses incurred on behalf of a business. (3) An account in which expenses are entered for accounting purposes.

expense center *See* cost center.

expert system A computer system that has attempted to capture the experience of experts in a field of study. The system operates by means of a series of heuristic rules that an expert would use in making decisions.

expiration date (1) The date on which a contract terminates, after which it is no longer valid. (2) The date (month and year) after which a bank card is considered invalid.

explicit interest Real interest, as opposed to implicit interest; stated interest.

export Any product or service sold to a foreign country.

Export-Import Bank of the United States (Eximbank) An independent U.S. government agency formed in 1934 to promote U.S. trade by offering financial aid to U.S. exporters and by extending loans to foreign countries, the proceeds of which must be spent on U.S. goods and repaid in U.S. dollars.

exporting The practice of charging the rates permitted in the home state of a bank to its borrowers or cardholders who reside in other states. Many banks have moved certain loan products to states with permissive banking laws covering rates, fees, and terms.

export trading company (ETC) A large, fully integrated trading organization with many suppliers and markets. An ETC provides most, if not all, of the marketing and servicing functions needed to support export trade. An ETC may buy and sell as a commission agent or as a principal taking title to export goods, with or without purchase orders. It may warehouse, ship, finance, and insure goods, as well as provide its clients with marketing information and communications. Depending on the nature of the product and the ETC's arrangement with the exporter, the ETC may also provide follow-up services after delivery. Under the Bank Export Services Act of the Export Trading Company Act of 1982, U.S. banking organizations are now permitted to own and to operate export trading companies.

exposure The amount of loss that could be taken should a borrower default. It excludes all unearned amounts such as finance charges, insurance premiums, and dealer reserves. It is essentially the net principal amount. *Also called* loss exposure.

express duties (of a trustee) The duties of a trustee spelled out in an agreement or document that establishes the trust account. It also includes those duties contained in a state or federal law.

express trust A trust stated orally or in writing, with the terms of the trust definitely prescribed. *Distinguish from* constructive trust, implied trust, *and* resulting trust.

express warranty A specific statement by a seller that the product or service for sale is of a certain quality.

expropriation The takeover of private property by a government. *See also* eminent domain.

ex-rights The sale of a security without the rights it carries to the purchase of a new issue of the stock at a discount.

extend credit; extension of credit The granting of credit in any form. Under certain consumer statutes, these terms are important for disclosure purposes.

extended credit Lending by a Federal Reserve bank to help depository institutions meet longer-term needs for funds. Extended credit includes seasonal loans to assist in meeting liquidity needs and special difficulties.

extended credit facility *See* extended credit.

extended product A fundamental product accompanied by many related intangible or tangible offerings, such as packaged services.

extension agreement (1) A written authorization by creditors to postpone the due date of their bills, with the hope that the debtor can improve his or her financial condition and honor the debts later. (2) An agreement to extend the maturity of a note.

extension fee A charge made on an installment loan for postponing the due date of a payment.

extension swap A sale of a security and purchase of a similar security with a longer maturity, made to lengthen the maturity of a portfolio.

external audit A periodic review by outside auditors to verify the accuracy of the bank's financial statements, conduct in-depth reviews of various departments, and evaluate controls.

external bond A bond issued by one country, sold in another country, and payable in the second country's currency. *Distinguish from* internal bond.

external evidence Evidence that comes from an independent outside source (that is, positive confirmation).

external security audit A security audit conducted by an organization or individuals independent of the organization being audited.

extra cash dividend A dividend exceeding the regular dividends.

extraordinary item Under generally accepted accounting principles, an item that is both unusual and infrequent. The item, if material, is separately identified on the income statement and the notes appended.

401(k) plan A form of qualified retirement plan under which an employee can elect to have the employer contribute an amount to the plan (subject to a ceiling determined annually by the Internal Revenue Service) or pay the amount to the employee in the form of taxable cash compensation. For this reason, these plans are sometimes referred to as qualified cash or deferred profit-sharing plans.

face-amount certificate company An investment company whose primary business is investing its funds in the securities of other enterprises. A face-amount certificate company issues certificates that repay a set amount at maturity.

face value The principal of a security, insurance policy, or unit of currency, expressed in a monetary sum and somehow marked on the item. For securities, the face value and market value are usually different until the point of maturity; the difference is called the premium or discount.

facility fee A fee charged by a lending institution for establishing a line of credit or making a loan.

facsimile An exact copy of something, such as a signature or a document, by a duplicating process.

facsimile draft A computer-produced document providing information to identify a transaction. A facsimile draft includes the account number; merchant name, city, and state; reference number; transaction date; amount; and authorization code.

facsimile transmission The transfer, electronically, of a photographlike reproduction of an original document. *Also called* fax *and* image transmission.

factor A financial organization that primarily purchases the accounts receivable of other firms at a discount and assumes the risk and responsibilities of collection.

factoring The short-term financing obtained by selling accounts receivable to a factor.

factors of production The resources required to produce a product, usually categorized as land, labor, or capital.

fail (Noun) The failure of the seller to deliver securities to the buyer on the settlement date or the failure of the buyer to accept and pay for the securities. A "don't know" is the most common fail, in which one party to the trade was not notified that the trade was being made. Errors in type of security, number of units, price, or other facts of the trade also cause a fail. *Also called* settlement fail.

failure of issue Lack, by nonexistence or death, of lineal descendants (children, grandchildren, and on down the line).

Fair Credit and Charge Card Disclosure Act of 1988 A federal law that requires financial institutions to disclose information on annual interest rates, fees, balance computation methods, and grace periods on credit card applications and solicitations.

Fair Credit Billing Act of 1974 An amendment to the Truth in Lending Act that requires creditors to resolve billing errors in a prescribed manner within a specified period. Lenders must furnish customers a detailed description of their rights and the procedures they must follow in making complaints about billing errors. *See also* Regulation Z.

Fair Credit Reporting Act A federal law that guarantees an individual the right to examine all of his or her information on file with a credit reporting agency. The act also specifies procedures for rectifying errors in those files. A bank must either tell an unsuccessful consumer applicant why credit was denied, or give the name and address of the credit bureau that provided information on which the denial was based. The Fair Credit Reporting Act became effective April 1971.

Fair Debt Collection Practices Act A federal law that regulates the collection of debt by third-party debt collectors. Most banks are exempted; however, if a creditor violates some portions of the act, it could trigger coverage of the act and become liable to the debtor for damages.

fair employment practices The compliance by an employer with government regulations concerning relationships between employers and employees.

Fair Housing Act The federal law that requires an Equal Housing Lender poster to be posted in the lobby of each branch that offers home loans or home improvement loans.

**Fair Labor Standards Act of 1938
(Wage-Hour Law)** The basic federal
law governing pay standards for
covered employees. This law sets
requirements for minimum wages and
overtime pay, prohibits discrimination
by sex in pay rates, and limits
employment of children.

fair market value The price at which
property would be transferred
between a willing buyer and a willing
seller, each of whom has a reasonable
knowledge of all pertinent facts and is
not under any compulsion to buy or
sell.

fair value The legal concept of
reasonable or equitable value, usually
used as the basis of valuation when
service rates for public utilities are
being determined.

family allowance The allowance from
the estate, stipulated by statute and
made by the court, to provide for the
family during the period when a
deceased person's estate is in the process of settlement.

**Family Farmer Bankruptcy Act of
1986** The federal law that added
Chapter 12 to the bankruptcy laws. It
provides for the rehabilitation of
family farmers by allowing them to
file a reorganization plan with the
court without all the requirements of
the more complicated Chapter 11
proceedings.

fanfold (1) A security ticket, also
called a document of original entry.
A bank uses a fanfold to track the
receipt and movement of delivered
securities. (2) A printout of computer
data in hard copy. (3) An abbreviated
reference to the specialized data
included on that printout. For example, in a bond department, a list of
bonds might be called the fanfold.

Fannie Mae *See* Federal National
Mortgage Association.

Farm Credit Administration
A federal agency that oversees the
Farm Credit System which is
composed of the Federal Land Banks,
the Federal Intermediate Credit
Banks, and the banks for cooperatives.

**Farmers Home Administration
(FmHA)** An agency of the U.S.
Department of Agriculture. The
FmHA aids loan programs in rural
areas. Its outstanding securities are
guaranteed by the U.S. government.

FAS 13 The abbreviation for Statement of Financial Accounting Standards No. 13 Accounting for Leases,
which explains the accounting rules
applicable to leases.

fast/TAC *See* transfer agent custodian
(TAC) program.

favor of *See* beneficiary (preferred
term).

fax *See* facsimile transmission.

feasibility study An in-depth investigation and report on the desirability
of undertaking a specific project or
task. A feasibility study generally
breaks down the costs and benefits
involved in the project or task.

Fed *See* Federal Reserve System.

Fed (clearing) float *See* Federal
Reserve float.

federal agencies Interest-bearing
obligations of a U.S. government-
sponsored sponsored enterprise or
federal agency. Securities sold by
government-sponsored enterprises and
federal agencies to the investing
public are not direct obligations of the
United States but involve federal
sponsorship and in some cases guarantees. Funds raised by the sale of
these securities provided specialized
credit for large groups of U.S. citizens

and businesses in competition with private lenders. This credit aids, for example, housing and urban renewal, farmers, small businesses, the shipping industry, and U.S. foreign trade. *Also called* federal agency issues *and* federal agency securities.

federal agency An executive department, an independent federal establishment, or a corporation or other entity established by the Congress that is owned in whole or in part by the U.S. government.

federal agency issues *See* federal agencies.

federal agency securities *See* federal agencies.

Federal Agricultural Mortgage Corporation (FAMC) A federal agency created by the Agricultural Credit Act of 1987 to develop a secondary market in farm and rural housing mortgages. FAMC guarantees the principal and interest payments on securities backed by pools of farm mortgages, which are sold to the investing public. Only securities sold by loan poolers certified by FAMC will be eligible for the guarantee. *Also called* Farmer Mac.

federal box A format suggested by the Federal Reserve Board to inform applicants of the significant details of a loan transaction. These include the annual percentage rate, the finance charge, the amount financed, and the total payments.

federal court of appeal One of 11 courts established to hear appeals in federal cases.

federal court system Federal courts may hear cases pertaining to the U.S. Constitution and federal statutes, cases between two or more states, and cases involving ambassadors or admiralty (maritime cases).

federal credit union A cooperative association organized under the Federal Credit Union Act to accept deposits from members and provide loans and other financial services from the proceeds.

Federal Credit Union Act of 1934 Federal legislation providing for the federal chartering of credit unions.

federal debt The total of all past federal deficits. *Also called* national debt.

federal deficit The amount by which the federal government's outlays exceed its receipts in a fiscal year. An important facet of fiscal policy, the size of the deficit profoundly affects economic conditions.

Federal Deposit Insurance Corporation (FDIC) A federal agency organized in 1933 that insures depositors' accounts up to a certain amount (currently $100,000) at most commercial banks and saving associations. All Federal Reserve member banks must be insured by the FDIC. The FDIC supervises insured state-chartered commercial banks that are not members of the Federal Reserve System and state-chartered savings associations.

Federal Deposit Insurance Corporation assessment Under the Financial Institutions Reform, Recovery and Enforcement Act of 1989, the annual premium financial institutions pay for deposit insurance. Commercial banks will pay 12 cents per $100 of deposits in 1990 then 15 cents per $100 of deposits from 1991 into the Bank Insurance Fund. Savings associations will be assessed 20.8 cents per $100 of deposits in 1990, then 23 cents from 1991 through 1993, which will go in the Savings Association Insurance Fund. *See also* Deposit Insurance Fund (DIF).

federal district court One of the 88 courts established as the first trial court for federal claims.

Federal Financial Institutions Examination Council An organization of regulatory agencies responsible for U.S. depository institutions. It is designed to promote more uniform supervisory and examination policies. The agencies include the Federal Deposit Insurance Corporation; Federal Home Loan Bank Board; Federal Reserve Board; National Credit Union Administration; and Office of the Comptroller of the Currency.

Federal Financing Bank (FFB) A bank established by the Federal Financing Bank Act of 1973 to coordinate the financing activities of federal agencies whose obligations are guaranteed by the federal government. The FFB is authorized to purchase any obligations of any federal agency. It does not purchase securities issued by the government-sponsored agencies (the Farm Credit System, the Federal Home Loan Bank system, the Federal Home Loan Mortgage Corporation, and the Federal National Mortgage Association), but it usually obtains funds by borrowing from the U.S. Treasury. FFB obligations are general obligations of the United States.

federal funds Loans of funds immediately available (same day funds) from reserve accounts at Federal Reserve banks. Federal funds are generally 1-day loans from one bank to another. The term "loans of fed funds" is not used. Instead, loans are described as sales and borrowings are described as purchases of fed funds.

A bank buys (borrows) or sells (lends) fed funds. For financial accounting purposes, the transaction is treated as a borrowing or lending, not a sale.

federal funds bought *See* federal funds purchased.

federal funds check A check drawn against a reserve account with the Federal Reserve bank.

federal funds market The market for day-to-day lending of excess reserve funds, largely among commercial banks.

federal funds payment or transfer A payment by check or wire transfer against an account with a Federal Reserve bank. Immediate credit is given for the payment.

federal funds purchased Short-term borrowing of reserves from another bank. *Also called* federal funds bought.

federal funds rate The interest rate charged on loans by banks that have excess reserve funds, above the level required by the Federal Reserve, to those banks with deficient reserves. The federal funds rate is a key rate in the Federal Reserve's monetary policy. It provides an early indication of major changes in the national economy.

federal funds sold Short-term (usually overnight) loans of reserves to another bank.

Federal Home Loan Bank (FHLB) system A system of banks created by authority of the Federal Home Loan Bank Act and approved July 26, 1932. The 12 regional Federal Home Loan Banks are under the oversight of the Federal Housing Finance Board (which replaces the Federal Home

Loan Bank Board abolished by the Financial Institutions Reform, Recovery and Enforcement Act of 1989). Commercial banks and savings and loan associations, federally or state chartered, may join the system upon meeting certain housing finance tests. The purpose of the FHLB system is to promote the availability of funds for home loans and mortgages.

Federal Home Loan Mortgage Corporation (FHLMC or Freddie Mac) A corporation authorized by Congress in 1970 to facilitate secondary mortgage market activity. It sells participation certificates secured by pools of conventional mortgage loans. The federal government, through Freddie Mac, guarantees the principal and interest on these loans. Freddie Mac simultaneously buys loans and loan participations from lending institutions. In 1989, Freddie Mac became a stockholder-owned corporation.

Federal Housing Administration (FHA) A federal agency that is part of the Department of Housing and Urban Development. It was established by the National Housing Act of June 27, 1934. FHA insures residential mortgages and settles claims for defaulted mortgages in cash or registered transferable debentures that have an unconditional U.S. guarantee.

Federal Housing Finance Board (FHFB) A federal agency created in 1989 to replace the Federal Home Loan Bank Board, which oversees housing lending by the regional Federal Home Loan Banks.

federal income tax In the United States, a progressive tax on individual and corporate income levied by the federal government.

Federal Intermediate Credit Banks (FICB) Established by the Agricultural

Credits Act of 1923, which provided for 12 Federal Intermediate Credit Banks--one in each farm credit district--and supervised by the Farm Credit Administration. All of the stock in these banks is owned by farmers through local production credit associations. The banks make loans to and discount agricultural paper for production credit associations, state and national banks, agricultural credit corporations, livestock loan companies, and similar lending groups.

Federal Land Bank (FLB) A federal agency responsible to the Farm Credit Administration, Federal Land Banks arrange long-term loans to farmers and ranchers secured by mortgages on farm or ranch properties. FLB bonds are issued to finance these loans.

federally sponsored enterprises Enterprises whose capital may originally have been owned by the U.S. Treasury but is now owned by the investing public or by the organizations served by the enterprises. They sell securities to raise funds to supply credit for farmers, ranchers, the housing market, and student loans. Federally sponsored enterprises include the Farm Credit System, Federal Home Loan Bank system, Federal Home Loan Mortgage Corporation, and Federal National Mortgage Association.

Federal National Mortgage Association (FNMA or Fannie Mae) A federally chartered and stockholder-owned corporation, chartered on February 10, 1938, and presently deriving its authority from Title VIII of the Housing and Urban Development Act of 1968. Fannie Mae adds liquidity to the residential mortgage market by buying mortgages from lenders, such as savings and loans, banks, and mortgage banking companies. Fannie Mae buys mortgages guaranteed or insured by government agencies, as well as conventional mortgages. To raise funds, it sells corporate debentures, notes, and mortgage-backed securities to the investing public and occasionally to the U.S. Treasury.

Federal Open Market Committee (FOMC) A committee of the Federal Reserve System that has complete charge of open-market operations, through which the Federal Reserve influences the growth of the U.S. money supply. The committee includes the members of the Board of Governors of the Federal Reserve System and five representatives from the 12 Federal Reserve banks serving in rotation.

Federal Reserve Act of 1913 The statute that established the Federal Reserve System.

Federal Reserve bank *See* Federal Reserve System.

Federal Reserve bank note A form of U.S. paper money issued by Federal Reserve banks and backed 100 percent by government securities. These notes are no longer actively circulated.

Federal Reserve city A city in which a Federal Reserve bank or branch is located.

Federal Reserve currency Paper money that is issued by Federal Reserve banks, is circulated as a medium of exchange, and is legal tender (must be accepted in payment of a debt). *See also* Federal Reserve bank note; Federal Reserve note.

Federal Reserve float The difference between uncollected cash items in the process of collection by Federal Reserve banks and the deferred availability credits made by the Federal Reserve. The Federal Reserve credits

banks for cash items on a deferred availability schedule based on average collection times, but it receives payment for the cash items only after they have been presented to the bank on which they were drawn. Federal Reserve float exists from the time after the sending bank has been credited until the time funds have been received from the paying bank.

Federal Reserve note A form of U.S. paper money issued by Federal Reserve banks. Originally, these notes had to be backed by 25 percent gold and 75 percent government securities. The gold backing is no longer required, and most assets held by the Federal Reserve can be used as collateral. Federal Reserve notes are by far the largest part of the nation's currency.

Federal Reserve regulations The regulations issued and administered by the Federal Reserve Board pursuant to various statutes. These regulations deal with the functions of the Federal Reserve System, its relationship to financial institutions, the administration of commercial banks and bank holding companies, and many consumer interests.

Federal Reserve requirements *See* reserve requirements.

Federal Reserve System The central monetary authority for the United States, created by the Federal Reserve Act of 1913. The Federal Reserve System is divided into 12 districts, each with a Federal Reserve bank owned by the member banks in that district. The principal policy groups are the Board of Governors and the Federal Open Market Committee. *Also called* the Fed.

Federal Reserve Wire Network (Fedwire) A payment service operated by the Federal Reserve System for the transfer of funds between financial institutions that have either reserve or clearing accounts at Federal Reserve banks. Funds transfers over Fedwire are immediate and irrevocable, with the Federal Reserve guaranteeing the payment received by the financial institution. Federal securities, economic statistics, and general administrative information are also transferred over this system, which connects the 12 regional Federal Reserve banks, their 26 branches, and several government offices.

federal savings and loan association A financial institution, federally chartered and supervised by the Federal Home Loan Bank Board, that accepts deposits and finances home mortgages and other loans to businesses and consumers.

Federal Savings and Loan Insurance Corporation (FSLIC) An organization created by federal authority in 1934 to insure the shares and accounts of all federal savings and loan associations and state-chartered associations that applied for insurance and met the corporation's requirements. The agency was abolished under the Financial Reform, Recovery and Enforcement Act of 1989, and a new fund, the Savings Association Insurance Fund (SAIF), was established to receive deposit insurance assessments from savings and loans associations.

Fed funds *See* federal funds.

Fedwire *See* Federal Reserve Wire Network.

fee (1) A fixed amount that a trust institution receives as compensation for its services. *See also* allowance; commission; trust charge. (2) An estate of inheritance in real property, sometimes referred to as an estate in fee or fee simple estate. (3) A charge or payment for services.

fee-based service A service provided by a bank to a customer for which the payment is an explicit fee rather than the collection of interest or the value of compensating balances.

fee income Income from fees.

fee simple An estate of inheritance without limitation to any particular class of heirs and with no restrictions on alienation. A fee simple is the largest interest or estate in real property a person may own. *Sometimes called* fee simple absolute.

fee simple absolute *See* fee simple.

fee simple determinable A fee simple estate that terminates once a stated event occurs.

fee simple estate An estate in real property in which the owner is entitled to the entire property, free from title restriction or encumbrances, over which he or she has an unconditional power of disposition.

fee splitting (1) The illegal practice of paying someone to refer potential loan customers. (2) In law, the illegal practice of dividing legal fees with a nonattorney.

fee subject to condition subsequent A fee simple estate that terminates once (a) a stated event occurs and (b) the owner acts to reenter and repossess the estate.

fee tail An estate limited to a person and the heirs of that person's body. Most states have abolished estates in fee tail, generally by converting them into fee simple estates.

FHA-insured loan A loan insured by the Federal Housing Administration against default.

FHA loan *See* FHA-insured loan.

fiat money Money whose value is not related to the inherent value of the metal or other material from which it is made. It is a medium exchange mandated by the government and backed by the law of the state.

fictitious loans The name given to the fraudulent practice by automobile dealers and other borrowers of submitting loan applications from nonexistent people or real people who do not have a sales contract with the dealer.

fictitious registration A document issued by a county or state official to identify the exact ownership of a firm when the firm's name does not do so.

fidelity bond Insurance that protects an employer against losses due to the deliberate misappropriation of the firm's assets.

fiduciary A person or trust institution charged with the duty of acting for the benefit of another party on matters coming within the scope of the relationship between them. A fiduciary relationship between two parties with regard to a business, contract, or piece of property requires that one party place trust and confidence in the other and exercise a corresponding degree of fairness and good faith. The relationships between a guardian and ward, an agent and principal, an attorney and client, one partner and another, and a trustee and beneficiary are examples of a fiduciary relationship.

fiduciary account A customer account involving a fiduciary relationship.

fiduciary bond A bond that guarantees that an estate entrusted to a fiduciary will not be lessened because of the fiduciary's dishonesty or negligence.

fiduciary return An income-tax return prepared by a fiduciary for a trust or estate, as distinguished from an individual income tax return.

fiduciary risk Potential losses associated with the failure to discharge fiduciary or trust duties properly.

field (1) In a record, a specified area used for a particular category of data, for example, a group of card columns used to represent a wage rate or a set of bit locations in a computer word used to express the address of the operand. (2) On a bank card, a defined area of fixed or variable length in one of the information tracks within the magnetic stripe. *See also* control field.

field separator *See* separator.

field warehouse financing *See* field warehousing.

field warehousing A method of financing inventories. The inventory is placed in the custody of the lender's agent, at the place of the borrower's business. The inventory is then held as collateral for the loan. As the inventory is sold, the inventory is released and the funds are transferred to the lender. *See also* warehouse financing.

fieldwork Audit work, that is, evidence gathering, performed at the auditee's location.

file identification The coding required to identify each physical unit of output in electronic data processing.

file maintenance The activity of keeping a file up to date by adding, changing, or deleting data.

filing The process of giving public notice of a lender's assignment of collateral, which includes presenting certain information to the appropriate government agency.

filing fee A charge made for the official recording of documents (with the appropriate municipal clerk's office or in another appropriate court of record) required for evidencing a security interest or lien.

fill or kill A price order that will be executed in its entirety as soon as it is entered. If it is not so executed, it will be canceled.

finance (1) (Verb) In financial terms, to raise capital by selling equity or by borrowing. (2) (Noun) The theory of investments, speculation, credit, and securities.

finance bill A long-term bill of exchange, secured or otherwise, drawn by one bank on a foreign bank, usually for nontrading purposes.

finance charge (1) The total costs, including interest, that a consumer must pay for obtaining credit. (2) The cost of credit as defined by the Truth in Lending Act, expressed in dollars and cents. One component of the finance charge is the interest charged. (3) The interest charge computed on an outstanding balance.

finance company A company that specializes in making small loans to consumers or small businesses. *See also* captive finance company; commercial finance company; consumer finance company; sales finance company.

finance paper Commercial paper sold directly to large investors by the issuer. The terms are negotiable. *Also called* directly placed paper *or* direct paper.

financial accounting The field of accounting concerned with external financial reporting. *Distinguish from* management accounting.

Financial Accounting Standards Board (FASB) A private-sector body authorized to establish financial accounting and reporting standards, commonly referred to as generally accepted accounting principles (GAAP). *See also* Emerging Issues Task Force.

financial analysis The application of analytical techniques to financial information. Examples include ratio analysis such as leverage and turnover.

financial analyst A person who performs financial analysis. *See also* financial analysis.

financial audit A method of auditing where the objective is to verify the reliability of the accounting records and to appraise the related system of internal control.

financial counseling An information service for customers, including but not limited to short- and long-term budgeting, investment advice, financial analysis, financial modeling, retirement planning, and other financial strategies.

financial futures Contracts traded on an exchange that call for the future transfer of financial instruments on a given date at a specified price. Financial futures may be used to hedge or speculate. Foreign currency futures, interest rate futures (based on U.S. Treasury securities, Ginnie Maes, Eurodollars, and CDs), and stock index futures are traded. In the case of stock index futures, the entire value of the contract does not change hands; instead, a cash settlement procedure is used. Certain other futures contracts may employ cash settlement. Financial futures may be contrasted with commodity futures (for example, wheat, cocoa, oil). *See also* futures contract.

Financial Industry Numbering Standard (FINS) number A five-digit code used to identify financial institutions taking part in securities transactions. The American National Standards Institute (ANSI) adopted it as a national standard in 1988.

financial institution (1) A firm that handles financial transactions or gives financial advice. (2) A depository institution, or its agent or service bureau. (3) An establishment responsible for holding in custody, lending, exchanging, or issuing money; for extending credit; and for facilitating transmission of funds.

financial intermediary A financial institution that transfers funds from savers to investors, by issuing its own liabilities to savers and using the funds thus acquired to make loans and investments for its own account. For example, a commercial bank issues deposit liabilities and uses the funds to make loans and investments.

financial lease A lease that cannot be canceled, is fully amortized, and does not provide for maintenance. *Compare with* operating lease.

financial leverage The use of debt or fixed-income securities, as opposed to common equity, in financing. *See also* leverage.

financial management (1) The process of ensuring that funds are available in adequate amounts when needed. (2) The process of raising and providing funds for capital purchases and operating expenses. (3) A field of study dealing with the raising and investment of funds.

financial markets The markets, both organized and informal, in which financial assets are traded.

financial planning The development and implementation of coordinated plans to achieve one's overall financial objectives.

financial position The relationship among a business firm's (or individual's) assets, liabilities, and owners' equity as of a specific date. *See also* balance sheet.

financial ratios The ratios of various items on a firm's financial statements, used to analyze the firm's financial position. Managers, creditors, and stockholders all use financial ratios to help them make decisions. *See also* ratio analysis.

financial risk The risk caused by a firm's use of leverage.

financial sector That part of the economy that includes financial institutions, markets, and instruments.

financial statement A written record of a firm's financial position at a point in time, as well as that firm's performance over a period of time. Financial statements include an income statement, balance sheet, and statement of cash flow.

financial structure The way in which a firm finances its activities, that is, the firm's liabilities and capital. In contrast, capital structure refers only to a firm's long-term sources of financing (that is, debt and equity).

financial uncertainty The probability of financial changes occurring in a company, the impact of which is unknown.

financing Providing funds for a specific purpose. *See also* short-term financing; wholesale financing.

financing statement A statement, filed with the appropriate public official by a creditor, recording a security interest or lien on the debtor's assets.

finder's fee (1) A fee charged by a company or person for referring new business to a lender. (2) A fee paid to a broker for obtaining a mortgage loan for a client, or for referring a mortgage loan to another broker. (3) A commission paid to a broker for locating a property. (4) A fee paid by a borrower to a person or company for locating a lender or investor.

fine sort Off-line manual sorting of bank documents.

firm (1) (Noun) A proprietorship, partnership, or corporation. (2) (Noun) Any business organization. (3) (Adj.) Describes a bid, offer, or order made for a security that will not change in price for a specific period.

firm commitment (1) For loans, a lender's agreement to make a loan to a specific borrower under specific terms and conditions within a given time. (2) In the secondary mortgage market or the securities market, a buyer's agreement to purchase loans (securities) under specified terms. (3) A Federal Housing Administration or mortgage insurance company agreement to insure a loan on a specific property with a designated borrower.

firm holder An owner of a security who is not expected to sell it in the normal course of events.

firming A period during which interest rates rise and the supply of money becomes less plentiful.

firming of the market A period in which security prices rise from a depressed level or stabilize at current levels.

firmware A permanent computer program, halfway between software and hardware, whose instructions are used by all other programs in the computer. This program cannot be changed or removed from the computer.

first in, first out (FIFO) A system of inventory valuation that assumes that a firm's operations will use first those items purchased earliest. Thus, on the firm's financial statements, the cost of the items purchased most recently is assigned to ending inventory. In a period of rising prices, FIFO accounting overstates earnings.

first mortgage (1) A real estate loan that creates a primary lien against a specified piece of real property. (2) A mortgage having priority over other mortgage liens against certain property. In the event of default, a first mortgage takes precedence over a second mortgage, which takes precedence over a third mortgage, and so on.

first mortgage bond A bond that is secured by a mortgage on the property of a person or corporation. The bond is not subordinate to any other claim.

first notice day The first date, varying by contracts and exchanges, on which notices of intention to deliver actual financial instruments against futures are authorized.

first-use notice An announcement sent to a cardholder when a debit transaction is posted to an account for the first time. The purpose of this notice is to thank the cardholder for using the account and to act as a security measure if the cardholder of record never received the bank card.

fiscal (1) Pertaining to the public treasury. (2) Pertaining to financial matters in general.

fiscal agent (1) An agent for a corporation who handles its taxes in connection with an issue of bonds. (2) An agent for a national, state, or municipal government who handles payment of its bonds and coupons or other financial matters.

fiscal drag A recurring fiscal budgetary surplus that may have a depressing effect on economic output.

fiscal policy (1) The planning of a government's spending and revenue-producing activities to achieve specific economic goals. (2) The financial policy of a business.

fiscal year The 12-month period selected by a business or government as an accounting period. This 12-month period may or may not correspond to a calendar year.

Fisher effect The effect of inflation on nominal interest rates, named after economist Irving Fisher. Fisher held that nominal interest rates have two components: real interest and a premium for expected inflation. The Fisher effect is the increase in nominal rates that occurs when investors expect an increase in the rate of inflation.

fit currency Currency that has been in circulation and returned to the Federal Reserve and that is deemed to be of sufficient quality (that is, not too wrinkled or dirty) to be recirculated.

"five and five" power A noncumulative general power of the donee to appoint in each calendar year the greater of $5,000 or 5 percent of the value of the trust at the end of the year.

five Cs of credit A method of evaluating a potential borrower's creditworthiness, including his or her character, capacity, capital, collateral, and conditions. Other versions are the three, ten, or twenty Cs of credit.

fixed assets Those items of a long-term nature required for the normal conduct of a business and not converted into cash during a normal operating period. Fixed assets include furniture, buildings, and machinery.

fixed capital The funds invested in fixed assets.

fixed charges Those overhead expenses paid on a regular basis, usually including interest costs, depreciation, debt amortization, lease rentals, and so on, but also sometimes including factory overhead expenses.

fixed cost A cost that does not change with the volume of output, within a given range.

fixed-dollar security A nonnegotiable security redeemable according to a fixed schedule, so that the dollar redemption value for any particular date is known in advance.

fixed exchange rate A fixed rate, relative to other currencies or gold, at which a government supports the price of its currency. *See also* pegged exchange rate.

fixed expenses The operating expenses of a company that do not change in relation to the volume of sales, production, or other activity, within a given range.

fixed income A steady level of income, such as income from retirement payments or a security that pays a constant amount at specific intervals.

fixed-income mutual fund A mutual fund whose portfolio consists of bonds and preferred stock, thus providing a set amount of income to the fund.

fixed-income securities Interest-bearing securities and preferred stock.

fixed liabilities The liabilities that will not mature during the next accounting period.

fixed-rate loan A loan whose rate does not vary with market conditions but is constant over the life of the loan.

fixed trust An organization created by a trust indenture between investors and a trustee for jointly investing funds.

fixture Any personal property so affixed to the land as to become part of the realty.

flat Used after a market quotation for a bond, a term indicating that no accrued interest will be paid by the purchasers to the seller. Issues in default and usually issues for which interest payments are contingent on earnings are quoted on a flat basis.

flat bed imprinter A device that leaves an image of embossed characters from a credit card on all copies of a sales draft form as a result of a manual horizontal movement of the imprinter head.

flat yield curve A yield curve in which rates on long-term maturities are substantively equal to rates on shorter maturities.

flexible budget A budget containing projected revenues and expenses for various outputs or levels of business activity.

flexible exchange rates Rates of exchange between currencies that are permitted to fluctuate in response to supply and demand for the currencies. *Also called* floating exchange rates.

float (1) The difference between deposits credited to an account and the amount of those deposits that has been collected. (2) The difference between amounts credited by the Federal Reserve to depository institutions and the amount of those items that has been collected by the Federal Reserve. (3) The amount of deposited cash items in the process of collection from drawee banks. *Also called* uncollected funds. (4) The time interval between the creation of a check and its ultimate payment by the bank on which it is drawn. Float is simply a means of quantifying the efficiencies or inefficiencies of the "cash in-cash out" cycle and focusing on the associated opportunities and costs. By minimizing the float associated with collection of accounts receivable and extending the float on the accounts payable side, corporations can increase cash flow and improve their working capital position. (5) (Verb) To place an issue of securities on the market.

floater A type of property insurance policy in which the property is insured wherever it is located.

floating debt A temporary short-term debt that has not been permanently funded. The term is generally used in connection with a municipality's current cash deficit or tax anticipation warrants.

floating exchange rates *See* flexible exchange rates.

floating lien A legal claim or attachment against similar property that a debtor may acquire in the future. For example, if inventory is being used as collateral in a loan, the claim is against any inventory of the same type that the borrower acquires after the loan has been made.

floating prime A variable rate loan. The interest rate floats up and down with a bank's prime rate.

floating rate (1) An interest rate that is not a fixed percentage of principal but fluctuates with market conditions. The issuer typically pegs the future rate it will pay to the future rate of a basic short-term financial instrument (such as a specific U.S. Treasury issue) and pays a small stated percentage above that rate. (2) An exchange rate that is not pegged by its government. Instead, the rate floats against other currencies.

floating rate note A note whose rate of interest is reset, or floats, at regular intervals, based on a predetermined reference rate (for example, LIBOR).

floating supply (securities) The total amount of a security issue held by owners who are willing to sell immediately if offered an acceptable price. These owners are generally dealers or speculators, as contrasted with firm holders. *See also* firm holder.

Flood Disaster Protection Act of 1977 The federal law that requires lenders to notify borrowers securing their loan by improved real estate as to whether the property is located in a flood zone. If so, the law requires the borrower to purchase flood insurance if the community participates in the National Flood Insurance Program.

flood zone An area designated as a flood zone on the flood maps of each community pursuant to the Flood Disaster Protection Act. Lenders may not make a loan secured by real estate within this area unless flood insurance is provided.

floor (1) The trading area of a stock exchange. (2) *See* interest rate floor.

floor broker A stockbroker who works on the floor of a stock exchange, taking orders to buy and sell stock by telephone from the central office of his or her firm and bringing the orders to the specialist for execution.

floor limit The maximum amount permitted for a single bank card transaction without requiring specific authorization. *Also called* floor release limit.

floor loan A mortgage loan providing that the proceeds be funded in two (or occasionally more) separate amounts. The initial amount, or floor loan, is funded on completion of construction in accordance with the terms and conditions of the loan. The balance of the loan is disbursed based on a specified event, such as the fulfillment of an occupancy requirement or the achievement of a level of income flow. *Also called* floor to ceiling loan.

floor planning A form of inventory financing. The bank advances funds to a dealer, who holds specific goods in trust for the bank and issues a trust receipt to the bank. When the goods are sold, the funds are paid to the bank. *Also called* trust receipt financing. *See also* inventory financing.

floor release limit *See* floor limit.

floor trader A member of an exchange who trades only for his or her own account or an account that he or she controls, or who has such a trade made. *Also called* local.

flotation costs The costs of bringing securities issues to the market.

flowchart (1) A graphic representation of the steps involved in a computer process. (2) Any chart that represents the steps in any procedure or task. *Also called* block diagram. (3) A method of documenting the internal control environment by depicting the flow of transactions throughout the system.

flower bond A certain U.S. Treasury bond that normally may be bought at a discount and used at par to pay the federal estate tax of a decedent in whose estate the bond is included. These bonds are no longer issued, and the last outstanding issue matures in 1998.

flow of funds A matrix showing the funds that flow into the market from suppliers and are taken from the market by borrowers. The matrix permits analysts to determine who borrowed how much from which suppliers. Summary tables are published in the *Federal Reserve Bulletin;* more detailed tables are also available from the Federal Reserve.

flow of work The path by which materials or work passes through a plant or office.

fluctuating value collateral Assets pledged as collateral that rise and fall in value over the life of a loan.

focus group A market research technique for obtaining qualitative (as opposed to quantitative) information about consumer feelings, attitudes, behavior, and concerns. A focus group generally consists of 8 to 12 individuals led by a professional through a discussion of topics about which the research sponsor is seeking consumer feedback. Results of this type of research are not statistically projectible to a market at large, but rather help identify key issues that might be addressed in larger scale quantitative research.

footings Balance sheet totals, either total assets or total liabilities plus capital.

footnotes A detailed explanation attached to and considered an integral part of financial statements.

forbearance (1) The act of postponing legal action when a mortgage is in arrears. Forbearance may be granted when a mortgagor satisfactorily arranges to bring mortgage payments up to date. (2) The act of postponing the filing of a claim on a student loan; granting an extension of time to a student before he or she must begin repayment.

for deposit only A restriction to the endorsement of a check, limiting its negotiability.

foreclosure A legal procedure undertaken to permit a creditor to sell property that is collateral for a defaulted loan.

foreclosure by action and a sale A method of foreclosure provided by state statute requiring foreclosure by court order.

foreclosure by entry and possession A method of foreclosure by a procedure of peaceable possession or by writ of entry.

foreclosure by power of sale Foreclosure by a written agreement granting the lender power of sale when a default occurs on a mortgage.

foreign bond A bond issued in the domestic market by a foreign borrower.

foreign card A bank card issued by a bank from a different geographical area. *Also called* out-of-area *or* out-of-plan card.

foreign corporation (1) A corporation organized under the laws of a state other than the state in which it does business. *Sometimes called* an out-of-state corporation to distinguish it from an alien corporation. (2) A corporation organized under the laws of another country. Such a corporation is more frequently called an alien corporation.

Foreign Corrupt Practices Act The federal act that prohibits the offering or payment of bribes to foreign officials. It requires management to maintain a complete set of accounting records and an effective system of internal controls.

foreign currency The money of another country.

foreign currency account An account maintained in a foreign bank, denominated in the currency of the country where the bank is located.

foreign currency futures Contracts for future delivery of a fixed amount of a specific foreign currency. These contracts are used for hedging as well as speculation.

foreign deposits Funds held in foreign currency accounts.

foreign draft A draft drawn by a bank on a foreign correspondent bank. *See also* draft.

foreign drawings and remittances service A service through which foreign exchange banks make their due from accounts available to their correspondents for use in arranging foreign exchange transfers.

foreign exchange (1) The currency of another nation. (2) Trading in or exchange of foreign currencies for U.S. funds or other foreign currencies. It is often abbreviated as FX.

foreign exchange desk (1) The physical area in a bank where foreign exchange is traded. (2) The personnel who do the trading of foreign exchange.

foreign exchange futures Contracts for the delivery of a specified amount of foreign currency at a specified price on a specified date.

foreign exchange market The market in which foreign exchange is traded. It is an informal worldwide market, linked by various kinds of direct and rapid communications equipment.

foreign exchange option An option to purchase or to deliver, within a specified period, a specified amount of foreign exchange at a specified price.

foreign exchange rate The price of one currency relative to another currency.

foreign exchange trading The buying and selling of foreign currencies.

foreign items (1) Bills of exchange, checks, and drafts payable at banks outside the country in which they are presented. (2) Checks payable on out-of-town banks.

foreign trade financing Any method of payment used to settle transactions between buyers and sellers in different countries.

foreign transaction An interchange item or an international transaction either originating in or routed to a point outside the United States or Canada.

forged check A demand draft drawn on a bank that has been fraudulently altered or on which the maker's signature has been forged.

forgery (1) The alteration of a document or instrument with intent to defraud. (2) Signing another's signature to a document with intent to defraud.

forgery and alteration bond A fidelity bond that protects against losses caused by the forgery or alteration of commercial instruments.

format The arrangement of data. With increasing technology and a desire to take advantage of the benefits it has to offer, there has been increasing interest in formats. For example, arranging data in standard formats was behind the success story of S.W.I.F.T. Users have been able to receive and process formatted S.W.I.F.T. messages in an automated fashion. This has enabled the receiving banks to enjoy the efficiencies of automation.

formula clause The provision of a will or trust agreement that states a formula by which the executor or trustee can determine the federal estate tax value of property. The formula clause is usually employed in connection with the marital deduction under the Revenue Act of 1954.

forward contract A nonstandardized transaction that involves a trade in an asset at some future date. A forward contract contrasts with a futures contract, which is standardized and traded on an organized exchange.

forward cover An arrangement protecting a buyer or seller of foreign currency from fluctuations in exchange rates.

forward deal The purchasing or selling of foreign currencies, with settlement to be made at a future date.

forward delivery (1) The transfer of foreign exchange or a commodity at a specified future date, not at the time of the contract. (2) The delivery of mortgages or mortgage-backed securities to satisfy earlier sales transactions.

forward discount The amount by which the spot exchange price of a currency exceeds its forward price.

forward exchange rate The price of one currency in terms of another currency, sold for delivery on a specified future date.

forward fed funds An agreement to deliver federal funds at a specified future date and rate.

forwarding agent A party who receives securities during a tender offer and forwards them to the appropriate depository agent daily, along with an accounting record.

forward market The market in which participants agree to deliver an asset (for example, a currency or a commodity) at a specified price on a specified date.

forward premium The amount by which the forward price of a currency exceeds its spot exchange price.

forward rate agreement *See* future rate agreement.

foundation A permanent body of property established by contributions from one source (such as the Carnegie Foundation) or from many sources (such as the Cleveland Foundation) for charitable, educational, religious, or other benevolent purposes. *See also* community trust.

founders The originators of a corporation; its first stockholders. They often advance further funds in exchange for stocks, bonds, or notes until the corporation is successful enough to attract outside financing. They may also receive special founders stock certificates.

fourth-generation language A high-level computer language having words and syntax similar to English.

fourth market A market in which institutional investors, buying and selling directly, execute block transactions of securities without brokers. Institutions wanting to sell list their securities in NASDAQ, an electronic quotation system sponsored by the National Association of Securities Dealers. Buyers can access those listings on their own terminals and contact the sellers to purchase the securities.

FRA *See* future rate agreement.

FRABBA terms Standard terms agreed to by the British Bankers' Association for interbank trading of FRAs. *See also* future rate agreement.

fraction A term generally applied to holdings of less than one share, resulting from rights and stock dividends. Because holdings of less than one share are not entitled to dividends, they are usually disposed of by sale or rounded out to full shares by the purchase of additional fractions.

fractional reserve banking A banking system that requires banks to maintain reserves of specified assets in proportion to their deposits, equal to a fraction of those deposits. Under a fractional reserve system, banks can expand their assets and liabilities by a multiple of their legal reserves. Conversely, a contraction of reserves forces a multiple contraction of assets and liabilities.

fractional rights In a rights offering, the residual portion of the total rights received by a stockholder that is too small to allow the purchase of a full share.

fractional share bequest A bequest of property, often made in connection with the establishment of a marital deduction trust, that is expressed in terms of a proportion of the assets involved rather than a specific dollar amount. *Distinguish from* pecuniary bequest.

franchise A business operated in association with other similar businesses, under common arrangements affecting certain aspects of the business (for example, common pricing, trademark, merchandise, advertising, and general policies). A central company sells the right to use these common arrangements to a purchaser of the franchise.

franchise plan A bank card plan for which one bank or association has granted right of use to another for a fee.

franchise tax A duty levied on the amount of outstanding or authorized capital stock of a domestic corporation.

fraud Common-law fraud contains five elements: (1) a false representation, (2) with respect to a material fact, (3) made with knowledge of its falsity, (4) with intent to deceive, and (5) with action taken in reliance on that representation. State law may have modified this doctrine to some extent.

fraud account (1) An account that the borrower had no intention of repaying. Fictitious data appear on the application. (2) A credit card account that has been used by someone other than the cardholder without his or her knowledge or consent, frequently, the result of cards that are lost, stolen, or never received.

fraud loss (1) A loss (charge-off) resulting from a fraudulent application. (2) A loss resulting from the fraudulent use of a credit card.

fraud risk Potential losses associated with the dishonesty or misconduct of employees or customers.

Freddie Mac *See* Federal Home Loan Mortgage Corporation.

free alongside (F.A.S.) A shipping term indicating that the quoted price of goods includes the cost of delivering the goods alongside the overseas vessel and within reach of its loading tackle.

free and open market A market in which supply and demand determine the prices for goods or services. A free and open market is not controlled or regulated by government.

free banking laws The statutes passed by various states during the nineteenth century, making it possible for banks to open and operate with very little supervision and minimum requirements.

free checking A service offered by banks in which customers with demand deposit accounts do not pay a fee for the privilege of writing checks.

freedom shares Nonmarketable U.S. Treasury savings notes. Freedom shares were not issued after 1970, but many will be outstanding until 1994. They are payable on presentation to certain banks, as well as to the

Bureau of Public Debt. *Also called* U.S. savings notes.

freehold estate A legal estate in land, commonly referred to as an estate of inheritance. There are three freehold estates: fee simple, fee tail, and life estate.

free item An item received by a processing bank that is not listed on the cash letter or deposit where it is enclosed.

freely convertible currency A currency that may be converted into other currencies and used by citizens and foreigners without restriction.

freely fluctuating exchange rate An exchange rate not controlled by governments, as it is in the gold standard, but allowed to fluctuate in a free market.

free on board (F.O.B.) A shipping term under which the price quoted applies only at inland shipping points. The seller arranges for loading the goods on to railway cars, trucks, barges, or other conveyances furnished for transportation.

free period That period for which no finance charges will be levied, provided that payment is made in full. A free period usually runs from the billing date to 25 days later.

free period cost of funds A charge, expressed as a percentage, for funds used to finance outstandings from the time a merchant account is credited for sales deposited until finance charges on these sales are billed to a cardholder.

free reserves Excess reserves (of the banking system) minus borrowings from the Federal Reserve banks.

frequency distribution The arrangement of data to display how often certain values or events occur.

frictional unemployment That part of total unemployment that is temporary and caused by labor market conditions. Frictional unemployment is not caused by changes in economic output.

fringe benefit Income or other benefit in addition to a basic wage or salary. The term may apply to one person, a group, or the entire staff.

FRN *See* floating rate note.

front-end fee A fee charged before a service is delivered.

front-end load contract funds Funds that charge a sales commission (load) and "front-end" the load by charging a high percentage of the load against the investor's first-year deposit. This results in a penalty for early withdrawal.

frozen account Funds on deposit for which a court order has suspended payment.

frozen assets Any assets that cannot be used by their owner because of legal proceedings.

full-bodied money Currency that is as valuable as a commodity as it is in its use as money. Gold coins are an example of full-bodied money.

full-cost broker A sales-oriented agent who arranges for the purchase and sale of securities and advises clients about what securities to buy. The full-cost broker works on commission. *See also* discount broker.

full-cost pricing The practice of setting a price that allows for the recovery of all costs incurred in providing services to the customer.

full-coupon bond A current coupon, that is, a bond that is selling at par. *See also* current coupon bond.

full-employment unemployment rate The rate of unemployment that would exist if all available resources in the economy were utilized, and only normal, frictional unemployment remained.

full payment The amount of money owed on a single account that, if paid, will reduce the account to a zero balance.

full recourse A type of dealer financing in which a dealer sells or assigns to a bank an installment sales paper with an unconditional guarantee. Should the purchaser become delinquent, the dealer accepts full responsibility for the paper.

full-service bank A name given to commercial banks because they perform a wide variety of financial services.

full-service banking The offering of a wide range of financial services to customers by banks.

full-service brokerage A brokerage service that includes a full line of services to investors, from investment advice to asset management. This type of firm generally has a large research department that produces reports for institutional clients and a "buy" or recommended stock list for all clients and internal use. In contrast, a discount brokerage firm only executes orders to buy and sell securities.

full-service financial institution An institution that services all of its customers' financial needs, including investment advice and asset management.

full value The fair market value of property on the bid side of the market, less a reasonable allowance for sales and other expenses.

fully diluted earnings per share Earnings per share recomputed to allow for the hypothetical conversion of all convertible securities and the exercise of all warrants.

fully discretionary trust account A trust account for which the trust department makes its own investment decisions.

fully guaranteed obligations Obligations of some federal agencies that the U.S. Treasury fully guarantees as to both principal and interest.

fully registered A term generally applied to bonds registered as to principal and interest. In this form, a bond is not negotiable, and interest is remitted by the disbursing agent to the registered owner.

fully registered bond A bond that has the holder's name and address recorded in the issuer's books. Bonds may be registered only as to principal or interest, or fully registered.

functional approach An approach to the study of jobs or people from the standpoint of what they do rather than what they or who they are.

Functional Cost Analysis Program A study based on data submitted by individual banks to the Federal Reserve System to compare various asset, income, and cost ratios.

functional organization An organizational arrangement based on specialized jobs performed by employees.

function code A data element in funds transfer that is a component of the message code that defines the class of business being requested (for example, collection and foreign exchange). *Also called* category code.

fund (1) (Noun) Cash or currency, to be distinguished from other kinds of property. (2) (Noun) An asset or group of assets segregated for some specific purpose, as distinguished from a reserve. (3) (Verb) To provide funding (money) needed to accomplish some purpose or objective.

fundamental product An offering to the market that is immediately recognized as what is being sold, such as a savings account.

funded debt (1) Debt formalized by bonds or notes and ordinarily having a maturity of more than 1 year. (2) Debt, generally intermediate or long term, with a formalized plan of repayment.

funded insurance trust A personal trust whose assets will be the proceeds of a life insurance policy. The trust becomes operative when the insured person dies. The maker of the trust provides cash or other assets to a trustee when the trust is created to ensure payment of the premiums during his or her lifetime. *Distinguish from* unfunded insurance trust.

funding (1) Financing. (2) The refinancing of an indebtedness on or before its maturity date, usually to extend the maturity to take advantage of a lower interest rate or to consolidate several issues.

funding (of a trust account) The original deposit of assets into a trust account.

funding gap The dollar difference between a bank's rate-sensitive assets and its rate-sensitive liabilities. *See also* gap.

funds management (1) The continual rearrangement of a bank's balance sheet to maximize profits, to maintain adequate rate spreads and liquidity, and to make safe investments. (2) The management and control of all items on a balance sheet, including assets, liabilities, and capital, to optimize a bank's earnings without taking excessive risk or liquidity exposure. *Also called* balance sheet management.

funds matching A financial term used to describe the funding strategy that uses short-term (generally interest-sensitive) deposits to fund short-term (generally interest-sensitive) loans, long-term funds for long-term loans, and so on.

funds rate The interest rate charged on federal funds.

funds transfer (1) The internal movement of funds between accounts. (2) The external movement of funds between banks. The complete movement of funds between the originator and the beneficiary may consist of one or more funds transfer transactions. *Also called* transfer; wire transfer.

funds transfer transaction The movement of funds directly between two parties, involving no intermediaries other than a payment or communication service. *Also called* transaction.

funds type The characteristics of funds within a given currency type, pertaining to availability and mobility/usage or exchange regulation (for example, in the United States, same day funds and next day funds).

funds type code A data element in funds transfer that is a code identifying the funds type.

fungibility The extent to which one asset can be used in place of another asset of equal part in the satisfaction of an obligation, that is, the interchangeability of money.

future estate or interest Any fixed estate or interest except a reversion, with the right of possession and enjoyment postponed until some future date or until some future event occurs. *See also* remainder interest; reversion.

future rate agreement (FRA) An agreement between two parties wishing to protect themselves against a future movement in interest rates. The two parties agree on an interest rate for a specified period from a specified future settlement date based on an agreed principal amount. No commitment is made by either party to lend or borrow the principal amount; their exposure is only the interest difference between the agreed and actual rates at settlement. *Also called* forward rate agreement.

futures Contracts covering the sale of any financial instruments or physical commodities on an exchange for future settlement. *See also* financial futures.

futures commission merchant (FCM) A firm or person who handles orders for the purchase or sale of futures contracts, subject to the rules of a futures exchange, and who, in connection with such solicitation or acceptance of orders, accepts any money or securities as margin collateral for the trades or contracts. An FCM must be licensed by the Commodity Futures Trading Commission.

futures contract An exchange-traded contract generally calling for delivery of a specified amount of a particular grade of commodity or financial instrument at a fixed date in the future. Contracts are highly standardized and traders need only agree on the price and number of contracts traded. Traders' positions are maintained at the exchange's clearing house, which becomes a counterparty to each trader once the trade has been cleared at the end of each day's trading session. Members holding positions at the clearing house must post margin, which is marked to market daily. Most trades are unwound before delivery. The interposition of the clearing house facilitates the unwinding since a trader need not find his or her original counterparty, but may arrange an offsetting position with any trader on the exchange. *See also* margin; marking to market.

futures exchange *See* futures market.

futures market The market for trading contracts for the future settlement of foreign exchange, commodities, or financial instruments.

FX (foreign exchange) position A bank's net holdings in foreign exchange in any particular currency at any given time.

GAAP *See* generally accepted accounting principles.

gain The excess of value received (paid) over the book value of an asset given up or a liability extinguished.

gamma The sensitivity of an option's delta to small unit changes in the price of the underlying instrument. Some option traders attempt to construct "gamma-neutral" positions in options (long and short) such that the delta of the overall position remains unchanged for small changes in the price of the underlying instrument. Using this method, writers can produce a fairly constant delta and avoid the transactions costs involved in purchasing and selling the underlying instrument as its price changes.

Gantt chart A graphic comparison of a production schedule to an employee's actual performance, or an employee's performance to a predetermined standard.

gap (1) The difference between repricing of a bank's assets and liabilities. Gaps are usually computed for each of several different ranges of maturity. A positive gap exists when short-term assets exceed short-term liabilities. A negative gap exists when short-term liabilities exceed short-term assets. (2) An interval of space or time indicating the end of a word, record, or file of data on a tape.

gap loan A temporary loan to finance the difference between a minimum loan and the maximum permanent loan as committed.

gap management The control of maturities of assets and liabilities to maintain the desired relationship between them. Although objectives can change over time, gap management may involve gapping or attempting to maintain a balanced maturity position.

gapping A policy of carrying a gap. The term is generally used to describe negative gapping.

garnishee The party on whom a garnishment is served.

garnishment A legal procedure in which some portion of an individual's wages are withheld and paid to his or her creditors. Permission for garnishment must be provided by court order.

Garn-St Germain *See* Depository Institutions Act of 1982.

gearing (U.K.) The relationship between capital funds and liabilities.

general average In marine insurance, agreement that, if one shipper's goods are jettisoned to save the ship, the other shippers must share the loss.

general examination A detailed overall examination of a bank by its regulator. National banks, for example, are examined at least every 2 years by the Office of the Comptroller of the Currency. *See also* specialized examination.

general gift *See* general legacy.

general ledger The consolidated, summary book of accounts for an entire bank or other enterprise. All changes in a bank's financial position and all subsidiary ledgers, such as branch and department totals, are recorded in the general ledger. It also provides the basis for all call reports and published statements of condition.

general legacy A gift of personal property by will that is not a particular thing distinguishable from all others of the same kind. *Distinguish from* specific legacy.

generally accepted accounting principles (GAAP) The rules, conventions, practices, and procedures that form the foundation for financial accounting.

generally accepted auditing standards (GAAS) The standards that govern the practice of external auditing. They comprise general standards, fieldwork standards, and reporting standards.

general obligation (GO) bond A municipal bond backed by the full faith, credit, and taxing power of the issuer. (GO is pronounced gee-oh.)

general operating expense An expense incurred by a firm's normal business activity.

general partnership A firm formed by two or more people joining as co-owners. All coowners are liable for company debts to the full extent of their personal assets.

general plan A statement of a local community's goals, covering the physical development of the community according to social, economic, and political objectives.

general power of appointment The power of a donee (the one who has received the power) to pass on an interest in property to whomever he or she pleases, including him- or herself or his or her estate. *Compare with* limited power of appointment. *See also* power of appointment.

general property taxes The taxes levied on real estate and personal property.

generation-skipping tax A tax imposed on any generation-skipping transfer. This tax is intended to be substantially equal to the transfer tax that would have been payable if the property had actually been transferred outright to each generation.

generation-skipping transfer Any taxable distribution or termination with respect to a generation-skipping trust or any skip from a transferor.

generation-skipping trust Any trust having beneficiaries who are younger than the grantor by two or more generations.

generic identification A common identification of all members of a group of cardholders as a single unit, for example, all VISA cardholders or all MasterCard cardholders.

generic product The essential benefit that a buyer expects to receive from a fundamental product. A customer who opens a checking account is not buying paper checks but a bill-paying convenience.

genuine and valid A term indicating the acceptability of a check that bears an authorized and genuine signature, is completed properly, and is drawn against sufficient funds.

gift causa mortis A gift of personal property made by a person in expectation of, and contingent on, death, completed by actual delivery of the property and effective only if the donor dies. *Distinguish from* gift inter vivos.

gift inter vivos A gift of property by one living person to another. Actual delivery of the property must be made during the lifetime of the donor and without reference to his or her death. *Distinguish from* gift causa mortis.

gift tax A tax imposed by the federal government since 1932 and by some states on transfers of property by gift during the donor's lifetime. For the purpose of this tax, gifts may include irrevocable living trusts.

G.I. loan A loan to a veteran, guaranteed by the government under the Serviceman's Readjustment Act of 1944.

Ginnie Mae *See* Government National Mortgage Association.

giro An instrument used widely in Europe for paying bills. In giro systems, a single payment order can implement money transfers from a customer's account to many other accounts on the books of the same institution. The giro system is characterized as a credit transfer system, while the U.S. check system is characterized as a debit transfer system. Some electronic funds transfer systems for paying bills in this country are similar to European giro systems.

give up Credit for the execution of an order given at the request of a customer to a brokerage house other than the one that performed the service.

Glass-Steagall Act A portion of the federal Banking Act of 1933 primarily concerned with the separation of commercial and investment banking. *See also* Chinese wall.

globalization A process in which financial institutions and markets evolve to the point where geographic boundaries place little or no restriction on financial transactions between parties.

global risk The total amount of risk a bank encounters in worldwide lending.

global risk analysis The system that examines all the sources and conditions of risk that must be considered in international lending.

GNMA mortgage-backed securities Securities whose principal and interest are guaranteed by the Government National Mortgage Association. GNMA securities are collateralized by pools of mortgages that are insured by the Federal Housing Administration or guaranteed by the Veterans Administration. GNMA securities are pass-through in nature (principal and interest payments and all prepayments are passed directly through to the holder, not reinvested). Because the securities are backed by the full faith and credit of the U.S. government, they can be sold at a lower yield than their issuer could obtain, based on its own net worth or the loans comprising the pool. *See also* Government National Mortgage Association.

go-around A survey by the Federal Reserve's Open Market Desk at the New York Federal Reserve Bank requesting quotes from all primary dealers. The best quote is then taken.

going concern (1) A company actively conducting a business, as opposed to one that merely holds assets. (2) For accounting purposes, a firm is assumed to be a going concern in the absence of evidence to the contrary.

going-concern concept Under generally accepted accounting principles, the assumption that, in the absence of evidence to the contrary, a company will not go out of business in the near future. The significance of this concept is that the company can be expected to realize value from its assets though normal use or sale, instead of having to dispose of them under emergency or forced circumstances (for example, liquidation).

going-concern value The value of a single asset or all assets of a business, based on the assumption that the business will continue to operate.

gold bullion Gold in the form of ingots.

gold card A preferred credit card, usually gold in color, issued to customers who meet higher standards than required for a regular credit card. This card usually has a higher credit limit. Many lenders have a minimum line of $5,000. It will

frequently have free additional services, such as luggage insurance, free rental car collision insurance, discount travel reservations, and so on.

gold clause A statement in a financial agreement linking payment to the value of gold.

gold exchange standard A monetary standard in which a nation will redeem its currency at a stated value in terms of a second currency that in turn will redeem its currency in gold. Thus the first currency is redeemable in exchange that is itself redeemable in gold.

gold standard An international monetary system in which individual nations agree to buy and sell unlimited amounts of gold at specified prices in terms of each nation's currency.

good delivery A term referring to all conditions of a securities' delivery that the seller must meet. These conditions include correct type of security, issuer, quantity, denomination of certificate(s), presence of any outstanding interest coupons, proper endorsement of the power of assignment, and timeliness of delivery.

good faith A standard of conduct between parties, meaning honesty in the conduct of a transaction. As an element of a defense to violations under several statutes, a good faith effort to comply means that the defendant did not know about the violation and took reasonable steps to avoid it.

good faith check The check that must be included with a bid on the sale of a bond. Ordinarily under a bidding notice, if bonds are awarded to a syndicate that does not claim them as agreed, the good faith check will be held as damages. However, the good faith checks of unsuccessful bidders are returned.

good faith estimate A listing of each service for which the customer will be charged in connection with a real estate loan, and the estimated cost of each. This must be given to the applicant at the time of the application or delivered or mailed within 3 business days after the loan application.

good funds *See* collected balance.

goods and chattels All of the tangible personal property in an estate, such as jewelry, furniture, tools, and equipment.

good-'til-canceled order An order to buy or sell at a specified price that remains in effect until it is filled, canceled, or changed by the customer.

good trader A U.S. Treasury bond that trades well. A good trader trades in such a volume that its price is more stable than the price of other issues.

good value An expression used to request the application of a defined retroactive value date to a funds transfer transaction.

goodwill (1) An intangible asset that is the present value of expected future income in excess of a normal return on an investment. Goodwill arises from such considerations as a firm's strong reputation, favorable location, and good relations with its customers. (2) Under GAAP, goodwill is *not* recorded unless it is purchased as part of a business combination transaction and represents the excess of the cost of an acquired company over the sum of identifiable net assets. Treatment of goodwill for regulatory reporting and tax purposes differs from GAAP.

go private The process by which a corporation buys up its own publicly held stock.

go public The process by which a company changes from a privately held corporation, in which all stock was held by a family or a few shareholders, to a public corporation.

government bonds Debt securities issued by the U.S. government. Bonds usually refer to debts with an original maturity in excess of 10 years, as distinct from shorter-term notes or bills. Government bonds include Series EE, Series HH, and Treasury bonds.

government check A check drawn on the U.S. Treasury and collected through the Federal Reserve banks.

Government National Mortgage Association (GNMA or Ginnie Mae) A corporation wholly owned by the U.S. government and administered by the U.S. Department of Housing and Urban Development. GNMA guarantees the principal and interest of pools of residential loans that are insured by the Federal Housing Administration or guaranteed by the Veterans Administration. GNMA-approved lenders who have accumulated a pool of such loans with similar rates and maturities can issue a mortgage-backed security in the amount of the loans in the pool. *See also* GNMA mortgage-backed securities.

governments An abbreviation frequently used to describe bonds issued by the federal government.

grace period A formally specified extension of time beyond a due date or maturity date for paying insurance premiums, taxes, or other obligations, or for redeeming certificates of deposit.

grading (rating) of securities The classification of securities according to several criteria, including the level of risk and the financial strength and stability of the issuer. The best-known rating services are Standard & Poor's and Moody's Investors Service.

graduated payment mortgage (GPM) A mortgage in which the payments are gradually stepped up, usually during the first several years of a mortgage term. The Federal Housing Administration insures several types of GPMs that permit various percentages of increase each year for periods ranging from 5 to 10 years. The lender defers the need to pay part of the interest and the amortization until later in the mortgage term.

grandchild exclusion For generation-skipping tax purposes, a limited special exclusion that applies to certain direct skips to grandchildren made before January 1, 1990. It allows an individual to transfer up to $2 million to each of his grandchildren without incurring a generation-skipping tax. *Also called* the Gallo exclusion.

grandfathering The practice of including special provisions in legislation to permit those already engaged in an activity prohibited by the legislation to continue, even though newcomers are prohibited from starting the activity.

grandfather tape A magnetic tape that contains data that have been copied onto a second tape. This second tape is then updated according to the latest transactions or changes. When this second tape is copied, it becomes the new grandfather tape. A series of grandfather tapes becomes the historical record or statistical base for further manipulating, analyzing, or developing an audit trail.

grantee A person to whom an interest in real property is conveyed.

grantor (1) A person conveying an interest in real property. (2) The creator of a living trust. *Also called* settlor, trustor, *or* donor. *See also* trustor.

grantor annuity trust A trust in which the grantor retains the right to a set annual dollar amount (the annuity) for a fixed term and gives the principal to others, such as the grantor's children, at the end of that term. If the grantor survives until the end of the annuity term, all of the trust principal will be excluded from the grantor's estate for death tax purposes. *Sometimes called* a GAT.

grantor income trust A trust in which the grantor retains the right to all of the trust income for a fixed term and gives the principal to others, such as the grantor's children, at the end of that term. If the grantor survives until the end of the income term, all of the trust principal will be excluded from the grantor's estate for death tax purposes. *Often called* GIT *or* GRIT (grantor retained income trust).

grantor trust For purposes of the income taxation of trusts and estates, a trust in which the grantor or a third party, because of certain rights to income or principal or certain power over the disposition of income and principal, is treated as the owner of the trust and taxed on income from the trust. Consequently, a grantor trust is not treated as a separate entity for income tax purposes.

gratuitous bailment A bailment for which no fee is charged.

greenmail The practice of profiting from an unfriendly takeover bid by forcing up the price of a corporation's stock using the following method. A corporate raider quietly buys large blocks of stock in the target company. When rumors surface that a tender offer is imminent, the price of the stock rises. The tender offer is made. To avoid acquisition, the corporation buys back its own stock from the raider at a price higher than the stock's current trading price. The raider abandons its offer and sells back the stock, profiting handsomely in the process. *See also* corporate raider; tender offer.

Gresham's Law A principle formulated by Sir Thomas Gresham during the sixteenth century, known as "Bad money drives out good money." Gresham's Law states that, when two or more currencies are circulating, the one with the higher intrinsic value will tend to be hoarded and, therefore, driven out of circulation.

gross (1) Whole, entire, total. (2) Without deductions.

gross book value The amount at which an asset is carried on a firm's books, without deducting accumulated depreciation or any other contra accounts.

gross debt A debtor's total obligations.

gross estate All of a person's property before debts, taxes, and other expenses or liabilities are deducted. *Compare with* net estate.

gross income The total amount of income from all sources. *See also* estimated gross income.

gross income multiplier A quantity multiplied by the effective gross income to obtain the capital value of a property.

gross margin The average percentage of markup on goods sold.

gross national product (GNP) A country's total output of goods and services from all forms of economic activity measured at market prices for a calendar year.

gross national product deflater An index designed to measure inflation in the nation's gross national product. It is computed by calculating the inflation rate for individual parts of the gross national product and then combining them into one overall figure.

gross potential income The annual gross income, assuming 100 percent occupancy.

gross private domestic investment The total value of private spending for capital assets plus the change in inventories for a particular year.

gross profit Sales revenues less the cost of goods sold, excluding selling, general, and administrative expenses.

gross sales A business's total sales before subtracting any deductions.

gross spread The spread between the price a purchaser pays and the price the issuer receives for a security. The difference is the selling cost.

gross volume The total amount of all merchant sales and cash advances.

gross yield The return on an investment before deducting the costs of procuring and managing the investment.

ground lease A contract for the long-term rental of land.

ground rent A price paid each year, or for a term of years, for the right to occupy a parcel of real property.

group annuity A pension plan providing annuities at retirement to a group of people under a master contract. A group annuity is usually issued to an employer for a group of employees.

group banking A holding company, formed by a group of banks, that supervises and coordinates all its members' activities.

group insurance Annual renewable insurance covering a class (or classes) of employees in accordance with a stipulated schedule of benefits.

group of ten The ten industrial countries that consult on monetary policy for the International Monetary Fund.

growing equity mortgage (GEM) A fixed-rate mortgage in which the monthly payments increase according to an agreed schedule or index to provide rapid payoff of principal.

growth stocks The common stocks of companies that are expanding more rapidly than the general economy or, because of some particular characteristics, are likely to expand in the future irrespective of the trend of the general economy. Usually, growth stocks pay few or no dividends. Investors buy them for potential capital gains.

GSL Guaranteed Student Loan. *See also* Guaranteed Student Loan Program.

GST exemption An exemption from a generation-skipping tax of $1 million in the aggregate for transfers by an individual either during life or at death.

guarantee (1) To give assurance that something is as represented. (2) To pledge to make good a note or security in case of default by the borrower.

guaranteed bond A bond for which a person other than the debtor has undertaken the responsibility to repay. The guarantee can appear as an endorsement, a contract with the issuing corporation, or a contract with the creditors.

guaranteed dividend A dividend on the capital stock of a firm, for which payment at specific intervals is guaranteed.

guaranteed interest certificate (GIC) A registered negotiable instrument, covering the guaranteed portion of a Small Business Administration loan, that lenders can sell in the secondary market.

guaranteed investment contract (GIC) An investment vehicle offered by insurance companies to pension and profit-sharing plans that guarantees the principal and a fixed rate of return for a specified (often multiyear) period. *Compare with* bank investment contract.

guaranteed loan (1) A loan guaranteed by a federal agency against loss because of default by the borrower. (2) A mortgage loan guaranteed by the Veterans Administration.

guaranteed mortgage certificate A certificate backed by mortgages and also by a guarantee. The Federal Home Loan Mortgage Corporation issues certificates of this type in registered form backed by conventional residential mortgages.

guaranteed stock A form of stock on which a company other than the issuer guarantees the dividend. These stocks are confined almost entirely to the railroad business.

Guaranteed Student Loan Program A U.S. Department of Education program that guarantees loans made by banks to students attending qualified schools and colleges. In most cases, the interest is paid by the federal government while the student is in school.

guarantee fee report A report to a guarantor of the guarantee fee due.

guarantee of signature A certificate affixed to the assignment of a stock certificate or registered bond or to other documents by a bank or stock exchange house vouching for the genuineness of the registered holder's signature.

guarantor The person or legal entity who makes a guaranty. *See also* guaranty.

guaranty A term used to refer to a contract in which one person becomes liable to perform a specific act or duty for another upon that person's failure to perform. A guarantor promises either that another person will perform his duty or that, if the other person does not perform his duty, the promisor will. Nonperformance by the other person is a condition precedent to the guarantor's duty to pay or perform.

guardian A person or trust institution appointed by a court to care for the property, person, or both of a minor or an incompetent person. When the guardian's duties are limited to the property, he or she is called a guardian of the property or guardian of the estate. When the guardian's duties apply only to the person, he or she is called a guardian of the person. When the guardian's duties apply to both the property and person, he or she is merely called a guardian. In some states, the terms committee, conservator, curator, or tutor designate a person who performs substantially the same duties as a guardian.

guardian ad litem A person appointed by a court to represent and defend a minor or an incompetent person in connection with court proceedings. *Sometimes called* special guardian.

guardian de son tort A person who, although not a regularly appointed guardian, takes possession of and manages an infant's or an incompetent person's property as if he or she were a guardian, thereby making himself or herself accountable to the court.

guardian of the estate *See* guardian.

guardian of the person *See* guardian.

guardian of the property *See* guardian.

guardianship A personal trust relationship, in which a court appoints a party, frequently a trust company, to hold in safekeeping and maintain the property of a minor or an incompetent person. The guardian must manage the property for the benefit of the beneficial owner of the securities or other property involved. The guardian is then held accountable to the court for its action.

guidance line The in-house limit on the amount of funds a bank feels it should lend to a borrower. *See also* line of credit.

haircut (1) The amount retained by brokers on repurchase agreements to pay for their services. A haircut is the difference between the bid and contract price for a repurchase agreement. (2) The difference between the market value of a security being used as collateral for a loan and the amount of money that a lender will advance against the security.

handle That part of a quote on a security price that is not mentioned by traders. To save time, traders give their quotes only in 32nds and ignore the whole numbers that precede the fractions. Traders assume that other traders know what the whole numbers are.

handling charge *See* interchange fee.

hanging power of appointment or withdrawal A Crummey power of withdrawal that lapses only when the lapse will not result in a release of a general power of appointment. A hanging power can permit more property to be transferred to a trust and to qualify for the annual exclusion than if the donee were given a "five and five" Crummey power. *See also* Crummey power.

hard copy Paper containing data (for example, sales drafts, credit memos, payment slips, computer printouts, or interpreted punch cards). Such documents may be used for input or output.

hard money Metallic money, as distinguished from paper money.

hardware (1) A computer and its peripheral equipment. (2) The physical components of a computer, as opposed to the computer program or method of use (for example, the mechanical, magnetic, electrical, or electronic parts of a computer). *Compare with* software.

hash total For checking purposes, a sum of one or more corresponding fields of a file that ordinarily would not be summed.

Hawthorne studies Studies conducted on the relation of worker morale to productivity. The Harvard University professors who did the study concluded that factors such as informal group relationships and special attention focused on workers have more influence on productivity than do physical or other objective conditions.

hazard insurance The insurance covering physical damage to property.

H bond A current-income savings bond issued by the U.S. government to the general public. The government discontinued issuing these bonds in 1980.

head teller The bank teller whose responsibilities include supervising other tellers and maintaining sufficient but not excessive cash on hand at all times. Other functions of a head teller vary among banks.

health maintenance organization (HMO) A prepaid group medical service organization emphasizing preventive health care. It is defined in the Health Maintenance Organization Act of 1973 as "an organized system for the delivery of comprehensive health maintenance and treatment services to voluntary enrolled members for a prenegotiated, fixed periodic payment." Subject to meeting certain standards and conditions specified in the act and associated regulations, HMOs must be offered to participants in group health plans as an alternative choice for coverage.

hedge A transaction undertaken to reduce risk. In futures markets, a hedge is the purchase or sale of a futures contract to offset an undesired short or long position. Usually a hedge involves equal and opposite positions in the cash market and the futures market at the same time (that is, a long position in one market and a short position in the other). Other hedging instruments include options, interest rate swaps, currency swaps, FRAs, and forwards.

hedge clause The fine print at the top of a tombstone advertisement that states that new issues of stock cannot be bought unless an investor is first given a copy of the prospectus.

hedge ratio The proportion of underlying securities or options needed to hedge a written option. The hedge ratio is determined by the delta. *See also* delta; delta hedging.

hedging Taking action to neutralize risk. Investors, dealers, and bankers hedge in various markets, including the stock, option, foreign exchange, and commodity markets. Hedging entails controlling the risk of one transaction by engaging in an offsetting transaction. For example, a bank can hedge a large holding of a foreign currency by selling the same amount of the currency for future delivery at a fixed price.

heir A person who inherits real property. An heir of the body is an heir in the direct line of the decedent. A son, for example, is the heir of the body of his father or mother. *Distinguish from* next of kin *and* distributee. *See also* collateral heir; direct heir.

heir of the body *See* heir.

heirs-at-law The persons who inherit the real property of a person who dies without leaving a valid will to dispose of his or her property.

hereditament Any kind of property that can be inherited. If the property is visible and tangible, it is a corporeal hereditament. If not, it is an incorporeal hereditament, for example, a right to rent or a promise to pay money.

HH bonds Current-income savings bonds issued to the general public by the U.S. government. Amounts of HH bonds available to individual investors are limited.

high balance (1) *See* high credit. (2) *See* over-limit account.

high credit The highest outstanding balance a cardholder account has ever had. *Also called* high balance.

highest and best use The legal use that produces the highest net income to land, which when capitalized gives the land its highest value.

high-level language A programming language in which one instruction is translated into many machine-language instructions.

high-ratio loan A mortgage loan in an amount approaching the appraised value or sales price of the collateral securing it.

high-risk A classification given to a merchant who has had a fraud transaction occur during the current month. The term is displayed on the authorizing member's screen when the merchant requests an authorization.

hit To accept a price bid from a dealer.

HMO *See* health maintenance organization.

hold The restriction of payment on part or all of the funds in an account.

holder A person who is in possession of an instrument and who is entitled to receive payment of the instrument.

holder in due course Under the Uniform Commercial Code, a party who accepts an instrument in good faith, for value, and without notice that it has been dishonored, it is overdue, or there is any claim against it.

holder-in-due-course doctrine The doctrine that a borrower may not withhold payments on a loan because of dissatisfaction with the merchandise, if the note holder is a holder in due course (that is, if the note was purchased in good faith from an earlier note holder). This doctrine has appeared as a provision of the Uniform Commercial Code adopted by most states. However, subsequent legislation has severely limited application of this provision when consumer paper is involved.

holder-in-due-course rule A Federal Trade Commission rule that requires sellers to ensure that consumers retain the right to assert claims and defenses against whoever holds the debt instrument used in purchasing goods or services.

holder of record A person who, according to a corporation's records, is the owner of its securities. The term is often used with reference to dividend payments, which are made to holders of record on a specified date.

holder-of-record date The date that identifies stock owners who will receive a dividend payment. *See also* ex-dividend, for stocks traded within 4 days of the holder-of-record date.

holding company A company that owns stock in other corporations and influences the management decisions of those companies in which it owns stock. *See also* parent company.

holding company (one-bank or multibank) A corporation or bank that owns or controls one or more banks. *See also* multibank holding company; one-bank holding company.

holding period yield The calculated yield received on a security while it was owned, which recognizes purchase and sale prices plus interest or dividends received.

hold statement A monthly statement of a depositor that the bank has been requested not to mail. The statement may be sent to a branch for the depositor to pick up or held in safekeeping.

hologram A three-dimensional image, created by a technology using lasers and precision optical equipment, that appears on credit cards and makes them difficult to counterfeit.

holographic will A will entirely in the testator's handwriting.

home banking A variety of arrangements enabling a customer to obtain current information about his or her bank accounts by telephone or computer link (cathode ray tube and keyboard) with a bank. Home banking is viewed by some as a simplified and more convenient way for consumers to pay their bills than by checks. Presently, home banking services are largely experimental and are combined with other services, such as ordering merchandise from catalogs and obtaining such information as news reports and current financial figures.

home debit A check presented to a bank for payment that is drawn on the same bank.

home equity line (HEL) A line of credit secured by a person's home that usually allows a lien to be placed on the home and allows for future advances to the consumer up to the amount of the line. This type of loan became popular after the Tax Reform Act of 1986, which phased out the deduction for most other types of interest payments. This type of loan was also the subject of the Home Equity Loan Consumer Protection Act of 1988, which requires new disclosures concerning these types of loans. *See also* equity line.

Home Equity Loan Consumer Protection Act of 1988 A federal law that regulates home equity lines of credit loans. It requires that certain disclosures be given with the application and prohibits a creditor's unilateral modification of the terms of the loan unless the consumer defaults or there is a change in circumstances affecting the consumer's ability to repay the loan.

home improvement loan A loan made for home remodeling, repairs, renovations, or improvements.

Home Mortgage Disclosure Act of 1975 A federal law requiring certain depository institutions to disclose the amount and location of their home mortgage activities to the public and to government officials. This act is governed by Regulation C of the Federal Reserve System and administered by the applicable regulatory agency.

home office protection rule Formerly, a clause in state banking laws that restricted banks from establishing branches in a community in which the home office of another bank was located. It was designed to protect the community bank from outside competition.

homeowners association An association of owners that meets periodically and acts to protect or enhance the owners' interests with respect to the condominium or subdivision in which they live.

homeowner's policy An insurance policy that provides coverage for home contents and personal liability

protection, in addition to the coverages provided by standard hazard insurance policies.

homestead The land and buildings on it occupied by the owner as a home for himself or herself and family, if any, and in most states protected to some extent by statute against the claims of creditors.

homestead estate The rights of the head of a family or household to real estate owned and occupied as a home, which are exempt from seizure by creditors.

homestead right The right granted by state statute protecting certain property belonging to a debtor from the claims of creditors.

horizontal combination The joining together of businesses that produce the same products or products that are highly substitutable.

horizontal integration The expansion of a firm by acquiring other firms or divisions engaged in the same stage of production of the same product.

hospital and health care revenue bond A bond usually secured by first repayment priority from a hospital's revenues. Proceeds of the issue are used for the hospital's buildings and equipment.

hot card A card being used on an account on which excessive purchasing is occurring. Excessive purchasing on an account is usually indicative of a lost or stolen card or purchasing that is otherwise unauthorized.

hot card list *See* restricted card list.

hot money Large quantities of liquid funds that are subject to rapid transfer from one bank, currency, or country to another in response to perceived risks or opportunities.

house check *See* on-us check.

household equipment draft The sales draft that evidences the purchase of a large piece of equipment. *Also called* equipment dealer draft.

housing code A local regulation that may restrict the number of people legally permitted in a dwelling or provide minimum standards for maintenance, sanitation facilities, ventilation, heating, and lighting.

HUD *See* Department of Housing and Urban Development (HUD).

HUD public housing notes and bonds Notes and bonds issued by local communities to fund public housing or urban renewal. The U.S. Department of Housing and Urban Development (HUD) guarantees approved securities for payment of interest and repayment of principal.

hull insurance Marine insurance that covers losses related to hulls (the means of transportation), as opposed to cargo or freight.

human resource accounting A system of accounting that deals primarily with the cost-benefit ratio of human resource decisions.

human resources management The planning, organization, and control of employees and how they are treated in an organization. *Also called* personnel management.

humped yield curve A yield curve in which rates on medium-term maturities are higher than rates on either short- or long-term maturities.

hurdle rate The minimum rate of return that will justify undertaking a project.

hybrid financial instruments Financial instruments, such as certificates of deposit whose interest is determined by the price of gold, that cross the boundaries existing among banking, securities, and futures markets.

hypothecate To pledge property as security for a debt, without transferring title.

hypothecated account An account that has been pledged or assigned as collateral for a loan.

hypothecation Originally, a pledge to secure an obligation without delivery of title or possession; now, generally, any pledge to secure an obligation, such as the hypothecation of securities for a loan.

hypothecation agreement An agreement in which the owner of an asset or security consents to its use as collateral for a loan to a third party.

IBANCO A nonstock membership corporation responsible for administering and promoting its bank card program throughout the world.

ICERC *See* Interagency Country Exposure Review Committee.

identification The process of recognizing, by using unique machine-readable names, those users or resources that have been previously described to an electronic data-processing system.

identifier A code that uniquely identifies the party to a funds transfer and may include specification of the type of identifier code that is being supplied. *See also* identifier code; identifier code type.

identifier code A code that uniquely identifies a party to a bank. *See also* identifier.

identifier code type A code that specifies the type of identifier code being used to identify a party to a bank. *See also* identifier.

identifying number A number provided by the Internal Revenue Service for tax purposes. In the case of an individual, it is his or her Social Security number.

ILSA *See* International Lending Supervision Act of 1983.

image An exact duplicate array of data stored in, or in transit to, a different medium.

image transmission *See* facsimile transmission.

immediate beneficiary A beneficiary of a trust who is entitled to receive immediate benefits from the trust property, whether or not those benefits are limited to income. *Compare with* secondary beneficiary, ultimate beneficiary. *Also called* present *or* primary beneficiary.

immediately available funds *See* cleared funds.

immediate-or-cancel order A market or limited-price order that will be wholly or partially executed when received, with the unexecuted portion to be treated as canceled.

immunization The process of establishing and maintaining equal durations for assets and liabilities to reduce interest-rate risk. *See also* duration.

immunized portfolio *See* immunization.

impaired claim In bankruptcy, a claim that the debtor does not intend to pay in full.

impaired class In bankruptcy, a class of creditors that will not receive the full amount due them.

imperfect competition A market in which a producer is able to exert influence over the price at which its product is sold. Such a situation is likely to arise when markets are characterized by few producers, by producers that have slightly differentiated products, or by buyers who are not aware of all the alternatives.

implementation period The time during which necessary actions are taken either to install a new system or to change an existing system.

implicit interest (1) Interest that is implied in a contract but is not explicitly paid or received. This interest rate equates the present value of the payments on a note with the face of the note. *See also* imputed interest. (2) Nonprice competition such as merchandise premiums, longer banking hours, and free checking used to attract depositors.

implicit rent The rental value of owner-occupied property.

implied contract A contractual agreement that can be assumed by the nature of the actions of the parties but is not evidenced by an express written agreement.

implied duties of a trustee The responsibilities expected of a trustee in addition to the specified duties mentioned in the trust agreement or in federal or state laws.

implied trust A trust created by operation of law or by judicial construction. *Distinguish from* express trust, which is created by express language, orally or in writing.

implied warranty A guarantee not specifically made by a seller but implied by law or custom. This guarantee assumes that the seller has title to a product and that the product or service is usable for the purpose for which it was bought.

import quotas Restrictions (aggregate quantitative limits) imposed by a country on the import of specific goods or services, generally established to protect domestic producers of a good from a surge of imports, dumping, or subsidized competition. Import quotas may also be imposed for national security reasons.

impound To seize an item and hold it in legal custody. Impounded items can be cash or other assets.

imprest funds (1) Funds loaned or advanced to a customer. (2) Funds such as petty cash that are established by a business and periodically replenished.

imprinter A device supplied to each merchant that is affiliated with a bank card plan to produce an image of the embossed characters of bank cards on all copies of sales drafts and credit slips.

imprinter fee The amount a bank charges a merchant for use of a bank-owned imprinter.

imprinter plate *See* merchant plate.

imputed income Income received in some form other than money, usually stated in terms of goods or services. Imputed income includes wages paid in kind, rental value of owner-occu-

pied homes, food and fuel produced and consumed on farms, and interest payments by financial intermediaries, which do not explicitly enter the national accounts.

imputed interest (1) An estimate of the fair market interest rate earned or charged on a loan that does not carry an explicit rate, or whose stated rate is significantly different from the market rate. (2) Interest income that is not charged on a loan, but which the Internal Revenue Service estimates for taxation. *See also* implicit interest.

inactive account A cardholder or other account in which there has never been any activity or one in which activity has not occurred for a specified period. *See also* dormant account.

inactive stock A stock issue that is not often traded.

inactive trust A trust in which the trustee has no duty except to hold title to the property.

inadvertent error An error that results in consumer compliance violations but that, in some instances, will not result in exposure to civil liability. Such errors include mechanical, electronic, or clerical errors that a creditor demonstrates were not intentional and that occurred notwithstanding the maintenance of procedures reasonably taken to avoid any such errors.

in and out The purchase and sale of the same security within a short period to take advantage of fluctuations in price.

incentive bonus A cash payment, usually made at the end of the calendar year, that varies in size according to an employee's performance.

Incentives Inducements, either financial or nonfinancial, to reward goal achievement.

incentive stock option A bonus or profit-sharing arrangement designed to attract or retain key employees that allows key employees to purchase stock in the business at less than market price. The number of shares that an employee may purchase is often tied to specific performance objectives.

incidents of ownership The rights of the insured or his or her estate to the economic benefits of an insurance policy, which make the proceeds of the policy subject to estate tax.

inclusion ratio For generation-skipping tax purposes, a ratio that is used to determine the portion of a trust or property transferred in a direct skip subject to generation-skipping tax.

income (1) The returns from property, such as rent, interest, dividends, profits, and royalties. (2) The money return or other material benefits received for land or labor. (3) The amount by which revenues exceed related expenses for an accounting period. *See also* contractual income; earned income; fixed income; real income.

income account A general ledger account in which various sources of revenue are recorded. This account is closed out (the balance is transferred) to retained earnings at the end of an accounting period.

income approach to value One of the methods used in estimating property value for incomeproducing real estate. It is based on the premise that a property's earning power is the critical element that determines value. There are many techniques and methods used to convert a property's income into value, including direct capitalization and discounted cash flow analysis.

income beneficiary A party entitled to income from a trust.

income bond (1) A debt obligation in which the promise to pay interest is conditional on the earnings of the obligor. (2) Bonds that are issued only to replace older bonds on which a corporation has defaulted. Both the principal amount and interest rate on income bonds are greater than on the bonds they replace. Interest is paid only if earned, but unpaid interest accrues to be paid when and if possible. *Also called* adjustment bond.

income elasticity of demand The percentage change in demand for a product or service divided by the percentage change in income from all customers.

income funds Mutual funds that invest in securities with a high current yield. Capital gains are not an expected feature of income funds.

income in respect of a decedent (IRD) Income items and deductible obligations that would have been receivable or payable by the decedent had he or she lived. These items or obligations are received or paid by the decedent's estate or successors to the property. They have the same tax consequences to the estate or successors and retain the same character they would have had in the hands of the decedent.

income property Real property capable of producing an income. It refers generally to all forms of nonresidential properties such as apartment buildings, office buildings, shopping centers, and warehouses.

income shares *See* dual-purpose fund.

income statement A financial statement that shows a summary of a firm's or individual's income and expenses for a specific period. *Also called* profit and loss statement, operating statement, *and* earnings statement.

income stocks Stocks bought for their high current yield rather than for the possibility of capital gains. Generally, income stocks are stocks of companies whose relatively stable operations and satisfactory financial condition permit the payment of relatively large and stable dividends over the year. Income stocks are often contrasted with growth stocks, which the investor buys because he or she expects to realize capital gains rather than income.

income tax The tax levied by a government on the earnings of a legal entity, including a person or corporation. The tax rate is usually expressed as a percentage of income and varies according to the level and type of taxed income.

income velocity of money The number of times during a given period that the same dollar or other monetary unit becomes another person's income. The income velocity of money equals the gross national product divided by currency plus demand deposits.

incoming interchange Sales drafts received by a cardholder bank.

incompetent person A person who is legally incapable of managing his or her affairs because of mental (not physical) deficiency.

incontestable clause The stipulation usually found in an insurance contract stating that, after a specific time from

the inception of the contract, the issuer may not contest its validity.

incorporate The legal act of forming a corporation.

incorporation by reference The reference in one document to the contents of another document in such a manner that the material referred to is made a part of the former document as if it were set forth in full.

incorporeal hereditament *See* hereditament.

incoterms An international standard for the interpretation of trading terms, such as CIF (cost, insurance, freight) and F.O.B. (free on board), established by the International Chamber of Commerce.

incremental cost The cost associated with an additional unit of input or the production of an additional unit of output.

incur To sustain or become liable for, usually with reference to a cost, expense, loss, or debt.

indefeasible Incapable of being annulled or rendered void, as an indefeasible title to property.

indemnify To agree to compensate or reimburse an individual or other legal entity in the event of a potential loss.

indemnity Protection or exemption from loss or damage.

indemnity agreement An agreement exempting the customer from liability. An indemnity agreement is usually completed for nonreceipt of a cashier's check.

indemnity bond A written instrument under seal by which the signer, usually together with his or her surety or bondsman, guarantees to protect another against loss. An indemnity bond in which the obligation (assumed by the surety) is not a fixed amount is known as an open penalty form of indemnity bond.

indenture (1) In trust, an agreement between two or more legal entities that stipulates reciprocal rights and duties. (2) In investments, a contract underlying a bond issue. The contract is signed by the issuing corporation and by the trustee acting for the bondholders. The contract sets forth the rights and responsibilities of the corporation, trustee, and bondholders, and the terms of the security issue. (3) A mutual agreement in writing between or among two or more parties in which usually each party has a counterpart or duplicate. It was originally so called because the parts were indented by a notched cut or line so that the two parts could be fitted together.

independent bank A bank that is not controlled by a holding company or other outside interest.

independent executor An executor of a will who, after filing his or her inventory, does not make further accounting to the probate court. An independent executor is recognized by statute in only a few states.

index arbitrage An application of program trading in which securities traders try to profit from differences in the cost of futures contracts on stock indexes and the cost of stocks on those indexes. *See also* portfolio insurance; program trading.

indexation policy A government policy aimed at reducing the real income transfers associated with inflation. Indexation involves adjusting wages, taxes, and long-term contracts for inflation.

index bond *See* purchasing power bond. *Also called* indexed bond.

index fund A mutual fund that invests in stocks that reflect the composition of one of the leading market indicators, such as Standard & Poor's 500 Index. The intention is to mirror market performance.

index rate A rate on which variable rate loans and mortgages are based. The rate is usually published in newspapers periodically, such as the prime rate or U.S. Treasury bill or note rates. The index is adjusted as rates rise or fall. Adjustments may be made in accordance with the terms of the note and state law and can be daily, weekly, monthly, and so on.

indirect claim A deposit or other financial claim issued by a financial intermediary. Unlike a bond or other direct financial claim on a nonfinancial corporation, an indirect claim does not finance a specific borrower. *Compare with* direct claim.

indirect compensation Any payments in addition to base salary or guaranteed year-end bonuses. Employee-benefit plans are forms of indirect compensation.

indirect liability The liability of the endorser or guarantor of an instrument. Although the endorser is indirectly liable and is not responsible for the interest or installment payments, this person becomes directly liable if the maker defaults.

indirect loan (credit) A loan purchased from the person who arranged the loan to the consumer, such as a retailer. Consumer loans are purchased from retailers by sales finance companies, commercial banks, or other lenders. *Compare with* direct financing. *See also* dealer financing.

indirect tax Any tax that can be shifted to another through price increases.

indirect wages *See* indirect compensation.

individual account identification Personal or individual account identification numbers as assigned by a financial institution or its agent when the card is issued.

individual account identifier That portion of the primary account number that identifies the specific account within the issuer's file to which a transaction is applied.

individual investor Any member of the public with money to invest. The individual investor usually trades in smaller lots than the institutional investor.

individual retirement account (IRA) A tax-deferred account that allows a customer to deposit a stipulated amount and to earn interest. The tax on the account is deferred until retirement, when it presumably will be taxable at a lower rate. Withdrawal is not permitted, without penalty, until the individual reaches age 59 1/2. Depositors meeting certain criteria are also able to defer tax on the original deposit (called the contribution) in the year in which it is made. The ability to defer tax on the contribution, however, was sharply curtailed by the Tax Reform Act of 1986.

industrial bank A type of finance company, chartered under some state laws, that makes loans and accepts savings deposits.

industrial bond A bond issued by any corporation other than a railroad or utility.

industrial development bond A bond issued to support the economic development of a community. Funds raised by the bond are used to construct facilities for lease to a corporation that will bring jobs to the community. Repayment is based on the corporation's lease payments.

industrial property Buildings used for producing, distributing, and changing the form of raw materials; assembling components and parts; or packaging, warehousing, and transporting finished products.

industrial relations The art of improving relations between management and employees. Typically, this is a function in organizations that have unions.

inelastic demand A measure of the relationship between changes in the price for a product or service and changes in the quantity demanded. The demand for a firm's product is inelastic if the percentage change in quantity is less than the percentage change in price (both expressed in absolute values). Under such circumstances, a relatively large price increase will cause a comparatively small decline in the quantity of a product purchased, raising the total revenue received by the firm. *See also* elastic demand.

infant A person not of legal age, which at common law was 21 years but which in some states has been changed by statute. *Also called* minor.

infirmity Any omission in detail whose effect is to invalidate a transfer of title. Infirmities include lack of endorsement, conflict between written and numerical amounts, and absence of signature.

inflation A continuing increase in the general level of prices in an economy, which results from increases in total spending relative to the supply of goods on the market. Inflation is also associated with increases in wages and production costs, and a decrease in purchasing power.

informal account A bank account that is opened without detailed legal documentation.

informal market Any place where trades occur, usually over a telephone or other communications device. All transactions not conducted on organized exchanges are conducted in an informal market. *Compare with* organized market.

information track One of the areas in the magnetic stripe on a credit card within which information is encoded. *See also* track.

inherent risk The risk of a particular item containing an error in the first place, before considering the influence of internal control and audit.

inheritance tax A tax on the transfer of the estate of a decedent's property. The inheritance tax is generally imposed by the state and is paid by the individual beneficiaries. *Distinguish from* estate tax, which is a tax on the estate as a whole.

inheritance tax return The return that an executor or administrator is required to make to the state, on the basis of which the inheritance tax due the state is calculated and paid. An inheritance tax return should be distinguished from the federal estate tax return.

initial issue Credit cards sent out at the inception of a credit card plan.

injunction The order of a court that instructs a defendant to refrain from performing an act injurious to the plaintiff.

in loco parentis Literally, in the place of a parent. This phrase refers to a person who takes the place of a child's parent, usually someone who is not a legally appointed guardian.

in-plant banking A banking service that provides a company's employees with facilities for banking transactions on the company's premises.

input (1) (Noun) Data to be transferred from an external storage medium into the internal storage of a computer (2) (Noun) The routines that direct input into a computer. (3) (Noun) The device or collective set of devices necessary for input. (4) (Verb) To enter information into a computer.

input-output analysis Economic analysis that uses advanced mathematical techniques to show the relationship between various industries within an economy by determining input and output levels for each industry.

input sequence number (ISN) A consecutive sequence number that allows for input message control between the sending bank and the wire service.

inquiry An audit technique that entails seeking answers and gaining insight into audit matters.

inquiry balance The balance of an account that will be relayed to the borrower or depositor, after proper identification, by phone, in person, or through an ATM or CBCT.

in shape for sale A term describing the condition in which a security will make a good delivery.

insider Under Regulation O, an executive officer, director, principal shareholder, or person with related interests.

insider trading Purchases or sales of a company's stock by officers, directors, or principal owners. This concept has broadened to include trading by anyone with inside knowledge of a company. *Also called* inside trading.

insolvency The inability to pay one's debts on maturity; having a negative net worth.

insolvency clause A clause included in credit-insurance contracts stipulating that claims may be filed with the insurance company only if the customer becomes insolvent.

insolvent The state of being unable to pay one's debt obligations when they become due. *See also* insolvency.

inspection certificate A certificate issued by an independent third party when outside inspection is required under a merchandise contract.

installment buying A means of purchasing consumer goods by making small, periodic payments in the future for goods received in the present.

installment contract A contract to repay a loan, with interest, in equal periodic payments. *Also called* installment sales paper *and* installment paper.

installment credit A loan, extended by financial institutions or retail firms, to be repaid along with an interest charge in fixed periodic payments or, if a variable rate of interest is charged, to be repaid in amounts that vary with the interest charged. *Also called* installment lending, consumer credit, *or* personal loan.

installment lending *See* installment credit.

installment loan A loan repaid in equal periodic payments. *See also* personal loan; installment credit.

installment note A note, usually used in consumer and personal credit transactions, in which the principal is paid in specified installments, together with interest on the unpaid balance, until the note is paid in full.

installment paper *See* installment contract.

installment payments (1) Payments on an installment loan. (2) Equal periodic payments of income, such as monthly or quarterly payments to trust beneficiaries.

installment plan A method of selling in which a purchase is made and paid for in a series of small payments.

installment sales financing Financing that involves the purchase of, or advance of funds against, a dealer's installment sales contracts.

installment sales paper *See* installment contract.

instant cash A term sometimes used to describe cash advances, especially cash drawn from an automated teller machine. *Also called* instant money.

Institute of Internal Auditors (IIA) An international organization devoted to the interests of the internal auditing profession.

institutional house A brokerage firm that specializes in serving large investors (for example, pension funds or insurance companies) rather than individual investors. *Also called* institutional brokerage firm.

institutional investor A firm that specializes in investments for its own account or the accounts of others. Examples include banks, trusts, investment companies, insurance companies, and nonprofit organizations.

institutional lender In mortgage lending, a financial institution that invests in mortgages either directly or through the purchase of mortgages or mortgage-backed securities in the secondary mortgage market.

institutional market That part of the financial market made up of corporations, financial institutions, and other large investors that need large quantities of cash or have large amounts of cash to invest. This is contrasted to the retail market of individual investors.

Institutional Network System (Instinet) A computerized, privately owned trading network that allows its fee-paying members to deal privately with each other without paying brokerage commissions. An offer to buy or sell a given amount of an issue is held in the computer until a contra party searches for and locates the offer. The two parties are put in contact via computer and close the trade themselves. These trades are recorded on the consolidated tape.

institutional trust accounts Trusts established by large investing bodies, such as insurance companies, pension plans, and profit-sharing funds of corporations.

instructing bank In a funds transfer, the bank that instructs the sender to execute the transaction. *Also called* ordering bank.

instructing bank name and address A data element in funds transfers that identifies the instructing bank by name and address.

instructing party In a funds transfer, the party instructing the sender to execute the transaction. *Also called* ordering party *and* originator.

instruction (1) A set of characters that defines an operation and, as a unit, causes the computer to perform the operation on the indicated quantities. (2) The operation or command to be executed by a computer, together with associated computer addresses. (3) A communication or part of a communication that contains the authorization and required details for a funds transfer.

instruction date In a funds transfer, the date on which the sender initiated the instruction.

instrument (1) Any device in telecommunications that originates or receives signals. (2) A document in which some contractual relationship is expressed or by which some right is conferred.

instrumentalities A term often applied to agencies of the federal government, whose obligations are not the direct obligation of the federal government.

insufficient funds A banking term indicating that the maker's account balance does not contain sufficient funds to cover a check or checks. It is commonly abbreviated NSF. *See also* nonsufficient funds; NSF.

insurable interest An interest in some person or property such that the person possessing the interest is entitled to obtain life or property insurance on the person or property.

Insurance A contract in which, for a fee (premium), one party agrees to pay a sum to another party if the latter suffers a particular loss. The party who undertakes the risk is the insurer. The party who wishes to be protected from loss is the insured party. *See also* the following entries: broad form personal theft insurance; credit insurance; credit disability insurance; credit life insurance; D&O insurance; hazard insurance; hull insurance; key man insurance; liability insurance; life insurance; limited payment life insurance; marine insurance; mercantile open-stock burglary insurance; money and securities insurance; non-filing insurance; open cargo insurance; ordinary life insurance; personal liability insurance; product liability insurance; property damage liability insurance; residual value insurance; term life insurance; unemployment insurance; universal life insurance; upset insurance; whole life insurance; workmen's compensation insurance.

Insurance binder The written evidence that an insurance company or its agent has agreed to provide temporary hazard or title insurance coverage. An insurance binder is valid only for a specified time, after which it must be replaced by a permanent policy.

Insurance company An institution that primarily sells insurance but, by investing surplus funds in real estate and other loans, also acts as an important holder of mortgages in the secondary mortgage market.

Insurance trust A living trust whose principal will be the proceeds of a life insurance policy. An insurance trust is used by individuals and corporations. For example, a corporation may use the proceeds of such a trust to buy the stockholdings of a deceased stockholder. *See also* funded insurance trust; unfunded insurance trust; stock-purchase trust.

Insured bank A bank that is insured by the Federal Deposit Insurance Corporation. National banks and members of the Federal Reserve System must be insured.

Insured closing letter A document from a title insurance company that insures a lender against the failure of the company's agent to perform his or her duties in conformity with the lender's instructions.

Insured deposits Deposits in banks that are guaranteed by the Federal Deposit Insurance Corporation against losses due to bank failures.

Insured loan A loan insured by the Federal Housing Administration or a private mortgage insurance company.

Insured party *See* insurance.

Insured pension plans Retirement and other employee-benefit plans for which the source of the benefits is life insurance paid wholly or partially by the employer.

Insurer *See* insurance.

Intangible assets Assets with no physical existence that have a long life. Their value is derived from the rights and privileges that are incident to ownership. Examples include patents, trademarks, copyrights, franchises, and goodwill. *See also* goodwill; intangible property.

Intangible property Property that cannot be perceived by the senses, such as a legally enforceable right. The right possessed by the holder of a promissory note or a bond is intangible property. *Compare with* tangible property.

intangible tax A state tax on bank deposits, bonds, stocks, and notes.

intangible value The value of a company's intangible assets.

integrated company A company that, within one organization, has a business substantially balanced between the component parts of its particular industry. Thus an integrated oil company may own crude oil facilities, refineries, and marketing operations.

integrated document A document that serves more than one purpose. For instance, a single document incorporating both loan note provisions and Truth in Lending disclosures would be an integrated note and disclosure form.

integration The sharing of data among computer systems and subsystems.

interactive The ability to enter data and receive a rapid response from the system, based on the data entered.

Interagency Country Exposure Review Committee (ICERC) A committee made up of representatives from the Federal Reserve Board, the Office of the Comptroller of the Currency, and the Federal Deposit Insurance Corporation. Pursuant to the International Lending Supervision Act of 1983, ICERC identified four uniform categories for classifying assets with transfer risk problems. The classification categories include Substandard, Value Impaired, and Loss. The fourth category (nonclassified assets) is Other Transfer Risk Problems. An allocated transfer risk reserve (ATRR) is required against Value Impaired assets; an asset classified as Loss can no longer be carried as an asset. *See also* allocated transfer risk reserve (ATRR); International

Lending Supervision Act of 1983 (ILSA); transfer risk.

interbank bid rate The rate at which a bank purchases, or makes a bona fide offer to purchase, U.S. dollars from another financial institution in exchange for another currency.

interbank funds transfer An electronic transfer of funds through an account balance at the Federal Reserve or an account balance at a correspondent bank.

interbank loan The credit extended from one bank to another.

interbranch Any action or function occurring between or among branches of banks.

interchange (1) Mutual acceptance and exchange of data messages between financial institutions. (2) The exchange of debit and credit transaction data between merchant banks and cardholder banks, based on an agreement between the participants. *See also* incoming interchange; outgoing interchange.

interchange authorization limit An amount at or below which an authorizing member may authorize transactions for the issuer, and over which the issuer must authorize transactions.

interchange fee A charge levied and collected by either the merchant bank or card-issuing bank for the processing of interchange transactions. *Also called* handling charge.

interchange group The members of an interchange system.

interchange register A listing of all transactions that are exchanged between a merchant bank and a cardholder bank.

interdepository transfer A depository service that allows a participant to deliver a securities position to a participant in another depository.

interdistrict settlement A means of processing the transfer of government securities between member banks in different Federal Reserve districts. This means of settlement relies on one end-of-day net settlement for each institution.

interest (1) The amount paid by a borrower to a lender in exchange for the use of the lender's money for a certain period. Interest is paid on loans or on debt securities (for example, bonds or notes) either at regular intervals or as part of a lump-sum payment when the issue matures. (2) A share, right, or title in property. (3) A charge levied by the bank on a cardholder account according to the terms of a cardholder agreement. (4) The amount paid by a bank on savings deposits. *See also* accrued interest; add-on interest; compound interest; effective interest rate; effective rate of interest; explicit interest; implicit interest; nominal interest rate; real rate of interest; simple interest.

interest earned but not collected *See* accrued interest.

interest on the unpaid balance The interest charged at an agreed rate, calculated on the balance remaining on the obligation.

interest penalty A fee or additional charge made when the terms of a financial contract are altered.

interest rate arbitrage The movement of funds from one money market center to another through the foreign exchange market, to obtain higher interest rates.

interest rate cap An optionlike feature for which the buyer pays a fee

or premium to obtain protection against a rise in a particular interest rate above a certain level. For example, an interest rate cap may cover a specified principal amount of a loan over a designated time period such as a calendar quarter. If the covered interest rate rises above the rate ceiling, the seller of the rate cap pays the purchaser an amount of money equal to the average rate differential times the principal amount times one-quarter. *Also called* cap. *Compare with* interest rate floor.

interest rate ceilings (1) The maximum interest rates that depository institutions under Regulation Q and other regulations and statutes were permitted to pay customers for funds deposited with them. Thrifts could pay 1/4 percent interest more than banks. Interest rate ceilings are no longer in effect. The Depository Institutions Deregulation Committee phased out Regulation Q effective March 31, 1986. (2) Sometimes used in reference to state laws that limit interest rates on loans.

interest rate exposure The extent to which an institution will experience a gain or loss if interest rates change.

interest rate floor An optionlike feature for which the buyer pays a fee or premium to obtain protection against a decline in a particular interest rate below a certain level. The seller of the floor reimburses the purchaser based on the difference between the floor rate and the interest rate, if lower. *Also called* floor. *Compare with* interest rate cap.

interest rate futures A class of financial futures. Interest rate futures involve a contract that gives the investor the right to buy a fixed-income, short-term security at a certain price at a given future date. The contract locks in a certain rate of interest on funds to be invested at a future date.

interest rate implicit in the lease The discount rate that, when applied to the minimum lease payments (which include the guaranteed residual value) and the unguaranteed residual value, causes the aggregate present value to be equal to the fair value of the leased property minus any investment tax credit retained by the lessor. This discount rate is used in classifying the lease.

interest rate mismatch The risk/ opportunity banks face that a shift in interest rates will reduce/increase interest income. The mismatch arises out of the repricing schedule of assets and liabilities. The banks' traditional interest rate mismatch, lending long-term and borrowing in short-term markets, exposes them, for example, to the risk that rates will rise: as interest rates rise, low-yielding short-term liabilities will be replaced and repriced more rapidly than assets. Some money center banks manage their interest rate mismatches actively in the hopes of taking advantage of anticipated interest rate changes. *See also* duration; gap; gap management.

interest rate risk (1) For investments, the risk of capital loss as the market value of a security or other asset (or liability) changes in response to interest rate movements. (2) The risk attributable to a change in interest rates, for example, funding of long-term, fixed-rate assets with short-term (or floating-rate) liabilities, in a rising-rate environment.

interest rate swap A transaction in which two counterparties exchange interest payment streams of differing character based on an underlying notional principal amount. The three main types are coupon swaps (fixed

rate to floating rate in the same currency), basis swaps (one floating-rate index to another floating-rate index in the same currency), and cross-currency interest rate swaps (fixed rate in one currency to floating rate in another).

interest-sensitive asset A short-term asset on which the interest received changes with market conditions. A variable rate loan is an example of an interest-sensitive asset. *Also called* rate-sensitive asset *or* sensitive asset.

interest sensitivity, interest sensitive *See* rate sensitivity; rate sensitive.

interest subvention *See* subvention.

interest swap A technique that is used (generally by a floating-rate borrower) to reduce the risk of widely fluctuating interest rates. It is an agreement (separate from the loan agreement) between the borrower and a bank in which the borrower agrees to pay a fixed rate of interest and in return receive a floating rate of interest. The combination of the floating rate paid on the loan and the difference between the fixed and floating rate in the swap fixes the total interest cost to the borrower over the specified time period.

interface The tie-in between two data-processing systems; a common boundary where automatic data-processing systems or parts of a single system meet and interact. It is often the vital link needed in the installation and conversion of many systems.

interim bond *See* temporary bond.

interim closing Any closing of the books of account that does not occur at the end of a fiscal year, for example, preparation of interim (generally quarterly) financial statements.

interim dividend A dividend declared during a firm's fiscal year, before that year's income is determined.

interim financing Financing of real estate for a short term, usually between two events, such as the purchase of property and the date that the permanent mortgage loan will be closed. Construction financing and gap financing are examples of interim financing.

interlace To assign successive storage locations (for example, on a magnetic drum), usually to reduce access time.

interlock To arrange the control of machines or devices so that they operate interdependently to ensure their proper coordination.

interlocking directorates The condition that exists when a person serves on the board of directors of two or more companies at one time. This practice is illegal if the companies are natural competitors, engage in interstate commerce, and have combined capital, surplus, and undivided profits of $1 million or more.

Intermarket Trading System An electronic communications network that links the seven U.S. stock exchanges and NASDAQ, enabling securities traders to obtain the best bids and offers nationwide. It was established in 1978, after the Securities Acts Amendments of 1975 called for the creation of an efficient, competitive national market system for trading securities.

intermediary (swap market) A counterparty who enters into a swap in order to earn fees or trading profits. Most intermediaries, or swap dealers, are major U.S. money center banks, major U.S. and U.K. investment and merchant banks, and major Japanese securities companies.

intermediary bank In funds transfers, a bank between the receiving bank and the beneficiary's bank through which a transfer must pass, if specified by the sending bank. In such cases, this is the receiving bank's credit party.

intermediary bank name and address A data element in funds transfers that identifies the intermediary bank by name and address.

intermediate network facility Any message-processing entity positioned between the acquirer and the issuer.

intermediate-term debt Debt maturing in more than 1 year but less than 5 to 7 years.

intermediation The transfer of funds from an ultimate lender, through a financial institution, to the ultimate borrower. A bank intermediates credit when it obtains money from a depositor and lends it to a borrowing customer. *Compare with* disintermediation.

internal bond A bond issued by a country payable in its own currency. *Distinguish from* an external bond, which is a bond issued by one country and sold in another country and payable in the currency of that other country.

internal controls questionnaire A device designed to evaluate the internal control environment of an entity (or specific function) through a series of questions concerning the existence of predetermined controls. An affirmative response indicates the existence of a control technique, whereas a negative response indicates the lack of a respective control.

internal control system A system of objectives and controls designed to provide for the safeguarding of assets and the reliability of financial records.

internal financing Paying for capital outlays from internal sources, without borrowing. Firms can finance many outlays from retained earnings and depreciation, assuming they have the liquidity to do so.

internal rate of return (IRR) The rate of return on an investment. It is calculated by finding the discount rate that equates the present value of future net cash flows to the cost of the original investment.

internal security audit A security audit conducted by personnel responsible to the management of a bank or the department being audited.

International Bank for Reconstruction and Development (IBRD) An organization that provides loans for economic development to member countries when private funds are unavailable. It was founded at the economic conference held at Bretton Woods in 1944 and began operations in 1946. *Also called* World Bank.

international banking facility (IBF) A functional unit located within a bank in the United States that allows U.S.-chartered depository institutions, U.S. offices of Edge Act corporations, and U.S. agencies and branches of foreign banks to conduct a banking business with foreign residents in a regulatory environment broadly similar to that of the Eurocurrency market, without having to use an offshore facility. Essentially, banks are permitted to establish a segregated set of asset and liability accounts in their domestic office, in order to participate in the Eurodollar market without incurring the expense of maintaining an overseas branch. An international banking facility may take Eurodollar deposits from, and make Eurodollar loans to, only nonresident, nonbank entities for non-U.S. operations, free of Federal Reserve regulations on reserve requirements and interest rate ceilings. Facilities are also exempt from the insurance coverage and assessments imposed by the Federal Deposit Insurance Corporation.

International Chamber of Commerce An organization of businesses, with members from 80 countries, that meets periodically to resolve international business disputes and to establish mutually agreed rules of international commerce.

International Lending Supervision Act of 1983 (ILSA) Legislation enacted to strengthen the bank regulatory framework, particularly with respect to international lending. It required bank regulators to evaluate country exposure and transfer risk; this led to the establishment by the Interagency Country Exposure Review Committee (ICERC) of uniform categories for transfer risk. It mandated that banks record a special reserve (called the allocated transfer risk reserve or ATRR) when so required by ICERC. It also set forth requirements for accounting for fees on restructured loans and disclosure of material foreign country exposures (detailed disclosure requirements were established by bank regulators and the SEC). In addition, ILSA put statutory power behind the federal banking agencies' authority to establish minimum capital standards for banks (including banks with no foreign loan exposure). *See also* allocated transfer risk reserve (ATRR); capital adequacy; Interagency Country Exposure Review Committee (ICERC); transfer risk.

International liquidity Liquidity that can be transferred between countries.

International Monetary Fund (IMF) Founded at the economic conference at Bretton Woods in 1944, this United Nations agency was established to promote international monetary cooperation; to maintain orderly economic development; and to assist in establishing exchange rates for foreign currencies. Member countries contribute an amount of gold or U.S. dollars and some of their own currency based on quotas as subscriptions to establish a general fund. Member countries can borrow from the fund to offset trade deficits.

International Money Market (IMM) An organized market for futures trading.

International Organization for Standardization (ISO) The central body for the formation and dissemination of industry standards for all national standards bodies. The American National Standards Institute (ANSI) is the U.S. member of ISO.

International Record Carrier A commercial organization offering regulated or tariffed telecommunication services for the transmission of data between countries.

International Securities Identification Number (ISIN) A 12-digit code that uniquely identifies the country of issue and the specific issue, devised by the International Organization for Standardization to facilitate international securities trading.

interproduct competition (direct) Competition that arises when a firm offers products from different product classes to the same market, for example, a brokerage firm that offers both securities and high-interest certificates of deposit to the same market.

interproduct competition (indirect) Competition that arises when a firm offers products from different product classes to a market with limited purchasing power.

interrogatory A question put in writing.

in terrorem clause A provision of a will or trust agreement intended to frighten a possible beneficiary into doing or refraining from doing something at the peril of forfeiting his or her possible benefits. An example is the provision in a will that would disinherit any named or potential beneficiary who contested the will.

interstate banking The establishment of a banking presence in another market across state lines for the purpose of taking deposits.

interstate commerce Transportation of products and securities across state lines for sale.

Interstate Land Sales Full Disclosure Act Legislation that discourages fraud, misrepresentation, and deceit in the sale of subdivision lots over interstate boundaries.

interval sampling A method of sampling in which every nth item is selected, beginning with a starting point chosen either judgmentally or randomly. The interval is determined by dividing the total population by the sample size. *Also called* systematic sampling.

inter vivos Literally, between living people.

inter vivos trust A living personal trust that becomes operative during the maker's lifetime. *Also called* living trust. *Distinguish from* trust under will *or* testamentary trust.

intestacy The condition resulting from a person's dying without leaving a valid will.

intestate (1) (Adj.)Without having made and left a valid will. (2) (Adj.) Not devised or bequeathed; not disposed of by will. (3) (Noun)A person who dies leaving property but no will. A court in the state where the dead person lived will appoint a personal representative to distribute the property according to the state's law. *Compare with* testate.

intestate succession The descent and distribution of property of a person who dies without leaving a valid will.

in-the-box A security on which good delivery has been made.

in-the-money An option is in-the-money if it has current value (for example, if the price at which a call option can be exercised is below the current price of the asset covered by the option).

intracity clearing A fast, efficient method of clearing securities on a same-day settlement basis. With this method, banks can use securities received the same day in outgoing transfers with the New York network.

intraday overdraft *See* daylight overdraft.

intraproduct competition (direct) Competition that arises when two firms offer products from the same product class to the same market, such as when one bank's VISA card and another bank's MasterCard are both offered to a nationwide market.

intrinsic value (1) The worth inherent in an object, as distinguished from its value for which it can be exchanged at a particular time. (2) The net benefit to be derived from exercising an option contract immediately. It is the difference between the price of the underlying instrument and the option's exercise price. An option generally sells for at least its intrinsic value.

inventory (1) (Noun) The materials owned and held by a business, such as raw materials, intermediate products and parts, work-in-progress, and finished goods. These materials may be intended for either internal consumption or sale. (2) (Noun) A detailed list of items owned and held by a business and their corresponding values. (3) (Noun) An account, schedule, or catalog made by an executor or administrator of all goods, chattels, and sometimes the real property of a deceased person. (4) (Verb) To take an inventory.

inventory financing The wholesale financing by a bank of a dealer's inventory while using it as security for the loan. Inventory financing includes floor planning and warehouse financing. *See also* floor planning; warehouse financing.

inventory turnover A measure of the rate of usage for a company's stock of goods. The ratio is calculated by dividing cost of goods sold by the average value of inventory. It can also be calculated by using sales in place of cost of goods sold.

inverted market A futures market in which contracts for delivery in the nearer months are selling at premiums to contracts for delivery in the more distant months.

invest To purchase a security or other asset. To invest is to accept risk by placing funds at another's disposal for income or gain. It is the opposite of divest.

investigator The security personnel involved in investigating fraudulent accounts.

investment (1) The purchase of capital assets by a business. (2) Assets acquired in order to earn income in the form of interest, dividends, or capital gains.

investment account Securities held primarily to (1) generate interest income, (2) provide a liquidity reserve of securities with current market yields, (3) use temporarily idle cash balances in securities that could be pledged as collateral against public and certain other deposits and liabilities, and (4) meet purchase requirements of various regulatory agencies.

investment adviser Any person who, for compensation, engages in the business of advising others, either directly or through publications or writings, as to the value of securities or as to the advisability of investing in, purchasing, or selling securities. *Also called* investment counsel.

Investment Advisers Act of 1940 A federal law regulating investment advisers, which requires registration of all types of investment advisers and prohibits fraudulent activity on the part of advisers. *See also* investment adviser.

investment analyst A person who studies and compares assets, usually for brokerage houses or investment institutions.

investment bank A type of banking firm that assists corporations in raising capital. *See also* investment banker; underwriter.

investment banker An agent for an issuer of corporate securities. Responsibilities of the investment banker include determining the type and terms of a new security issue and whether it should enjoy a public or private placement; the assembly of a syndicate to market the security; and the maintenance of an orderly and fair trading market in the early days of a new issue.

investment banking The marketing of new security issues, usually through an investment banker or underwriter. Entire stock or bond issues are purchased from the issuing corporation and subsequently either sold to investors or distributed to dealers.

investment company A company engaged primarily in investing in securities of other companies. Examples include mutual funds, face amount certificate companies, unit investment trusts, and closed-end management companies.

Investment Company Act of 1940 A federal law regulating investment companies with large pools of assets that sell securities to the public. To protect investors, money market funds and other mutual funds are regulated under this act. *See also* investment company.

investment-grade securities High-quality securities eligible for investment by banks, including U.S. Treasury and government agency bonds, notes, and bills; state and municipal bonds of the four highest ratings; and corporate bonds. Generally, investment grade is a rating at or above Baa (Moody's Investors Service) or BBB (Standard & Poor's).

investment letter A document signed by investors who buy a private placement of securities directly from the issuer. The document states that the securities are being bought for investment and not for immediate resale to the public. Privately placed securities are called letter or restricted bonds (or stock). *Also called* letter of intent. *See also* private placement.

investment management service A service offered by a trust department that includes management of an investment account but not custody of the securities. The trust department recommends investment policy and renders periodic reviews.

investment manager A person or company who manages the investments of institutions or individuals for a fee.

investment portfolio Various assets held by a bank, person, business, institution, or government agency.

investment powers The powers of a fiduciary to manage investments given to the fiduciary by an owner of property or securities.

investment risk A term used to describe potential declines in the principal value of fixed-income assets. Investment risk encompasses interest rate risk, maturity risk, and opportunity-cost risk.

investment securities (1) Investments purchased for a portfolio and not for resale to customers. (2) High-quality or investment-grade securities. *See also* investment-grade securities.

investment trust An organization that invests its capital in securities. The capital is obtained through the sales of its own stock. The income from its investments and capital gains is used to defray its operating and selling expenses, and the balance is available for distribution to its stockholders. There are two kinds of investment trusts: closed-end and open-end. Capitalization of closed-end investment trusts remains constant, and its shares are traded on the open market.

Mutual funds and mutual investment funds (open-end investment trusts) issue additional shares as demand increases. *See also* real estate investment trust; unit investment trust.

investor (1) A person or institution that accepts risks by placing funds at the disposal of another party for an expected gain or income. (2) One who purchases securities or other assets.

invisible trade International transactions in intangible items, such as insurance, interest, dividends, travel, and transportation.

invoice A commercial bill for goods sold or services rendered.

invoice price The total billing price for deliveries of futures contracts.

involuntary alienation The transfer of title or ownership of property against the will or without the exercise of the will of the owner, such as a sale of property for taxes.

involuntary bankruptcy A bankruptcy proceeding in which the creditors place a person or entity into bankruptcy.

IRR *See* internal rate of return.

irredeemable bond A bond that bears no maturity date. Such bonds are valued for their income stream only. *See also* consol.

irregularities The intentional misrepresentation of financial statements or embezzlement of assets.

irrevocable letter of credit A letter of credit that cannot be changed or canceled without the consent of all parties to the credit. *Compare with* revocable letter of credit.

irrevocable trust A trust that by its terms (a) cannot be revoked by the settlor or (b) can be terminated by the settlor only with the consent of someone who has an adverse interest in the trust. This is someone whose interest would be in not terminating the trust, such as a beneficiary.

ISDA The International Swap Dealers Association. It is the trade association for the swap industry, which among other things promotes the standardization of terminology, contracts (agreements), and practices.

ISO issuer identification number *See* issuer identification number.

issue (1) (Noun) Those securities of a company that are sold to the public. (2) (Verb) To sell or distribute a company's stocks or bonds to the public. (3) (Noun) The daily issuance of credit cards on new accounts. (4) (Noun) All people who have descended from a common ancestor. Issue is a broader term than children. *Also called* descendant.

issued-and-outstanding The portion of bonds, stocks, and so on that a board of directors has authorized for sale, the corporation has sold, and the public currently owns. This term excludes securities that have been repurchased from the public and are either held in the corporation's treasury or have been retired. For common stock, this term refers to the number used to calculate earnings per share.

issued capital (stock) In finance, that part of a corporation's authorized capital stock that either is issued and held by the public or has been issued to the public and subsequently reacquired by the corporation.

issue price The price at which a new issue of securities is placed on sale by investment bankers who market the issue.

issuer (1) The corporation, person, or government whose note, bond, stock certificate, or other financial instrument is offered for sale. (2) A member of an interchange system who issues cards (for example, a bank that belongs to MasterCard International and issues MasterCard cards). Within a transaction interchange network, the institution issues and verifies identification and authentication information on a customer.

issuer identification For credit cards, the major industry identifier and the issuer identifier.

issuer identification number The identification number of the issuer as set forth in American National Standard Specifications for Credit Cards, ANSI X4.131983, and Embossed Credit Cards Specifications, Numbering System, and Registration Procedures, ISO 2894-1974.

issuer identifier That portion of a primary account number (PAN) that, when combined with the majority industry identifier, identifies the card issuer and/or primary processing endpoint.

item advance A technique in grouping records that permits successive operation on different stored records.

itemized statement A recap of account activity during a designated period.

item number A sequential number assigned to the computer input program to identify the position of a specific item within a batch.

Items of tax preference For purposes of the alternative minimum tax, those exemptions and deductions that are excluded in determining taxable income for regular income tax purposes, but that are included in determining taxable income against which the alternative minimum tax is calculated. Items of tax preference are sometimes referred to as ITPs or TPIs (tax preference items).

job evaluation The process of systematically studying the relationships among all jobs in a firm to establish their relative values. Criteria such as required physical skills or mental effort, responsibility or accountability, and working conditions are used to establish the ranking. *Also called* position evaluation.

job evaluation committee A management group that meets to determine the ranking of all jobs in a bank.

joint account (1) An account carrying the names of two or more people. (2) Any investment, charge, bank account, or other account that lists two or more people who share equally in the rights and liabilities of the account.

joint and several account (with right of survivorship) A jointly held account that can be drawn against using a check or withdrawal slip having the signature of either owner. On the death of either owner, the survivor maintains the right to the account's funds, subject to tax laws.

joint and several guarantee An endorsement or guarantee that causes an entire liability to be enforceable against any or all of the obligors.

joint and survivorship A phrase usually applied to annuities under which both husband and wife are joint beneficiaries during their lifetime and, after the death of either, the survivor becomes the sole beneficiary, subject to tax laws.

joint applicant *See* joint account.

joint bond A bond that is the obligation of more than one company.

joint liability A liability shared by two or more people. In the event of legal proceedings, people jointly liable must be acted against as a group.

joint ownership The common ownership of real or personal property by two or more people. The people involved are either joint tenants or tenants in common.

joint purchase An estate planning technique in which an older-generation family member purchases a life estate and a younger-generation family member purchases a remainder interest in an asset from a third party. The relative amount each person pays is usually determined in accordance with the 10 percent tables. At the death of the life tenant, the asset passes to the remainderman free of transfer tax. The life tenant may also be able to amortize the life estate for federal income tax purposes.

joint tenancy Ownership of a piece of property shared equally by two or more people, each having full right of usage. If one owner dies, the survivor(s) take(s) full ownership. *Distinguish from* tenancy in common *and* tenancy by the entirety.

joint tenant by the entireties Joint tenancy by husband and wife.

joint tenants with right of survivorship The same as joint tenancy, which assumes the right of survivorship. The right of survivorship provides that, in the event of the death of one owner, the remaining tenant(s) immediately become(s) owner(s) of the property, subject to tax laws.

joint venture A commercial undertaking by two or more people organized to accomplish a single purpose. A joint venture differs from a partnership, because its existence continues only as long as its specific purpose continues.

journal A book in which original entries concerning transactions are recorded before the entries are transferred to the appropriate ledger accounts.

journal entry The bookkeeping treatment of a business transaction.

journal tape The tape containing the record of all the transactions in the terminal, processor, and so on.

judgment (1) A sum due for payment or collection as the result of a court order. (2) The decision or sentence of a court of law. (3) (Money judgment) The award of payment of a sum of money. *Distinguish from* decree *and* award.

judgmental forecasting A prediction of future trends based on informed human judgment rather than solely on quantitative data. The term applies to forecasting of any kind--economic, sales, costs. *Also called* qualitative forecasting.

judgmental sampling A nonstatistical method of selecting a sample based on the auditor's judgment of what constitutes a representative sample.

judgmental system of evaluating applicants As used in the Equal Cred-

it Opportunity Act, any system for evaluating the creditworthiness of an applicant other than a demonstrably and statistically sound, empirically derived credit system. The judgmental system allows the use of any pertinent elements that have a demonstrable relationship to a determination of creditworthiness.

judgment creditor The individual who has obtained legal judgment against a debtor.

judgment debt A debt for which the court has awarded a judgment.

judgment debtor The debtor against whom a creditor has obtained legal judgment.

judicial accounting An account of proceedings prepared for submission to a court having jurisdiction.

judicial settlement The settlement of an account according to the order, judgment, or decree of a proper court, the effect of which in many states is determined by statute.

judiciary-supervised personal trust A trust relationship that requires judiciary review and approval of a trustee's actions. Examples include estate management and settlement, or acting as guardian for a minor or an incompetent person.

jumbo A security in a large denomination.

junior A security or other financial instrument or lien whose claim on the issuer's income or assets is subordinate to (ranks lower than) the claim of another instrument or lien. For instance, common stock is junior to preferred stock.

junior equity Common stock. The claims of common stockholders are subordinate or in a "junior" position to those of preferred stockholders if a corporation is liquidated.

junior mortgage A lien that is subordinate to the claims of the holder of a prior, senior, lien.

junior security A security issue whose claims are subordinate to those of some other issue if a corporation is liquidated.

junk bond A form of bond that, because of its very low credit rating or no credit rating at all, is considered a high-risk investment and consequently carries a high interest rate. Junk bonds have become increasingly popular in recent years in financing corporate transactions such as leveraged buyouts.

jurat (1) A person under oath. (2) A memorandum added to an affidavit stating when, before whom, and, in some jurisdictions, where an oath was taken.

jurisdiction The legal right, power, or authority to hear and determine a cause, such as the jurisdiction of a court.

justified price The price that an informed and prudent purchaser would pay.

Kansas City Board of Trade (KCBT) A marketplace for trading futures in wheat and futures contracts and options based on the Value Line Stock Index.

Keogh plan A retirement plan for self-employed people and their employees, to which yearly tax deductible contributions up to a specified limit can be made if the plan meets certain requirements of the Internal Revenue Code.

key One or more characters within an item of data that are used to identify the data or to control its use. *See also* cryptographic key.

key account A merchant that is particularly important to a card plan, in terms of volume, prestige, or both.

key currency A strong currency that is used as a peg for satellite currencies. Nations in a trading block frequently peg their currencies to that of the strongest nation in the block.

key indicator Information extracted from various mediums tracked over time to provide auditors and line management with timely information concerning unusual trends or occurrences that warrant further attention.

key man insurance Insurance for people considered crucial to the effective operation of a business. Creditors sometimes require such insurance when lending if they feel that the death of these people would hurt the business's ability to meet its debt obligations.

Keynesian A term used to describe the economic theories of John Maynard Keynes. A key feature of those theories is the assumption that fiscal policies are important determinants of short-term economic activity.

kickback A payment made for the referral of business or customers. The payment is distinct from a commission or finder's fee because the person whose business is being referred does not know that a kickback is being offered and accepted. The Real Estate Settlement Procedures Act prohibits certain kickbacks made by title companies, attorneys, or insurance companies to real estate brokers for referring customers.

kicker *See* equity participation.

kick-out clause A clause that allows a trustee to terminate the trust and distribute its remaining assets because the cost of maintaining the trust becomes impractical.

kiddie tax A tax on the unearned income of a minor child who has not reached the age of 14 years before the close of the taxable year and who has at least one living parent. All unearned income over $1,000 will be taxed to the child at the parent's marginal tax rate.

kin Persons of the same blood or members of the same family.

kind Used in the phrase "distribution in kind" to indicate distribution of the property itself and not the cash value of the property.

kindred Persons related by blood.

kiting Attempting to draw against uncollected or nonexistent funds for fraudulent purposes. For example, a depositor issues a check, overdrawing an account at one bank or drawing against uncollected funds at that bank, and deposits into that account another check, similarly drawn against insufficient or uncollected funds.

labor organization *Sometimes called* a union.

labor relations The policies, programs, and processes that management uses in relating to employees in a union environment.

laches Failure to do a thing at the proper time, such as undue delay in asserting a right or asking for a privilege. (From the French "lache" meaning laxness or negligence.)

laddered maturities Equal spacing of maturities of securities in a portfolio, so that over time the shortening of the maturities provides a steady flow of liquid assets into the liquidity account. Funds from maturing issues are reinvested at the long end of the ladder.

Laffer curve A graph that compares the effect of a change in tax rates to the accompanying changes in tax receipts.

lagged reserve requirements A system that requires depository institutions to hold reserves in one period against deposits outstanding in an earlier period. From the late 1960s through the early 1980s, the Federal Reserve followed a system of lagged reserve requirements. At other times, it has imposed reserve requirements on a largely contemporaneous basis.

lagging indicator (1) An economic data series that consistently moves with overall economic activity but turns up or down later than the general economy. (2) In stock markets, a series that turns up or down later than average stock prices. Chartists interpret a turn in a lagging indicator as confirming that the market is likely to continue moving in its current direction.

laissez faire A French expression meaning, literally, allow (them) to do. It connotes a policy of nonintervention by government in economic affairs.

land contract An installment contract for the purchase of land, providing for a deed upon payment of the last installment.

land court A court that exercises jurisdiction over issues related to, and interest in, real property.

land trust An unincorporated association for holding real property, in which title is put in the name of one or more trustees for the benefit of the association's members, whose interests are evidenced by land trust certificates.

lapse (Noun) The falling of a gift into the residuary estate because the donee dies during the testator's lifetime. Such a gift is known as a lapsed legacy or lapsed devise.

lapsed devise *See* lapse.

lapsed legacy *See* lapse.

large blocks A large number of shares bought or sold in one trade. The New York Stock Exchange defines a large block as a trade of 10,000 shares or more. The daily volume of shares traded in large blocks is considered to measure institutional activity in the stock market.

last In over-the-counter tables, the column showing the last price of the day offered for a stock or bond.

last in, first out (LIFO) A method of inventory valuation that assumes that the most recent purchases are used first in determining the cost of goods sold. As such, ending inventory is valued assuming the earliest purchases remain in ending inventory. *Compare with* first in, first out (FIFO).

last trading day The final day under an exchange rule during which trades may be made in futures contracts for delivery in a particular month. Futures contracts outstanding at the end of the last trading day must be settled by delivery of underlying securities or by agreement for monetary settlement if the former is impossible.

last will and testament The will last executed by a person. Because all former wills ordinarily are revoked by the last one, the term emphasizes that the will in question is the latest and, therefore, the effective will of the maker. It is a legally enforceable declaration of a person's wishes in writing regarding matters to be attended to after, but not operative until, his or her death. A last will and testament usually but not always relates to property and is revocable (or amendable by means of a codicil) up to the time of the person's death or loss of mental capacity to make a valid will. Originally, "will" related to real property and "testament" to personal property. But today, will applies equally to real and personal property.

late charge (1) The fee charged for delinquent payment on an installment loan or line of credit, usually calculated as a percentage of the loan balance or payment. (2) A penalty assessed against individual cardholder accounts for failure to make minimum payments. Late charges are usually imposed 15 days after the due date.

late notice A notice mailed to a borrower when the required payment has not been made. Late notices are mailed between 5 and 15 days after the missed payment.

late posting payment A payment received and credited after the billing date.

laundered money Funds sent through numerous accounts or depositories one after another in an attempt to conceal the source of the money. *See also* money laundering.

lawful reserve *See* legal reserves.

law of comparative advantage A principle stating that a country with higher real costs of production for all exportable goods and services will nevertheless benefit from importing those in which it has the greatest comparative disadvantage and exporting those in which it has the least comparative disadvantage.

law of diminishing returns A principle stating that incremental additions of one factor of production to a fixed factor of production will ultimately decrease the additional output received from the added factor.

laws of descent Laws governing the descent of real property from ancestor to heir, to be distinguished from laws, rules, or statutes of distribution governing the disposition of personal property. *Sometimes called* canons of descent.

laws of distribution *See* statutes of distribution.

layered trusts Independent trusts, each one of which is created for the benefit of only one generation of beneficiaries, to avoid application of the generation-skipping tax.

LBO *See* leveraged buyout.

LDC Less(er) developed country.

LDC loan swaps The exchange by one lender of some or all of its exposure to a particular borrower in an LDC with a second lender for its exposure to a borrower in the same or a different LDC. In some transactions, loans are sold for cash or swapped for equity. *See also* loan swap.

lead bank (1) The bank managing a loan syndication. (2) The largest or dominant bank in a multibank holding company.

leading edge (1) The right edge of a check, used as the reference edge. (2) The forefront of new developments.

leading indicator (1) An economic data series that consistently moves with overall economic activity, but turns up or down sooner than the general economy. (2) In stock markets, a series that turns up or down sooner than average stock prices. Analysts feel a turn in a leading indicator helps predict trends in the stock market.

lead manager The institution managing an underwriting syndicate for an issue of securities.

learning curve The graphic representation of a person's efficiency at grasping a particular task, as measured over time. Typically it takes an "S" shape, growing slowly, then rapidly, and then more slowly.

lease A contract in which one party grants to another party the right to use or occupy property owned by the former. The granting party is the lessor; the party using the property is the lessee.

leaseback (1) The process of selling an asset to an outside investor and simultaneously contracting to use it for a fee. (2) The sale of property to a party that leases it to the vendor for a period of years at a rental that will give a return and amortize the investment. *See also* sale and leaseback.

leased fee The interest held by a lessor.

lease financing A specialized area of finance dealing with renting property owned by a lender, financing the leases of a company engaged in rentals, and financing the purchase of an item to be leased out by a borrower.

leasehold Land held under a lease.

leasehold interest A property interest of a tenant or lessee.

leasehold mortgage A loan to a lessee secured by his or her leasehold interest.

lease service charge *See* earned income.

leasing asset An asset rented rather than owned by a person or business.

ledger A collection or book of accounts. A business may have both a general ledger and subsidiary ledgers. *See also* stock ledger.

ledger balance A bank's record of the balance in a customer's account. A ledger balance is the balance that appears on a bank statement and differs from the available or collected balance by the amount of uncollected funds. The ledger balance is used for customer information and for creation of the bank's general ledger.

ledger journal An accounting record that functions as both journal and ledger.

left-hand side (1) The asset side of a balance sheet. (2) The debit side of a double-entry bookkeeping system. (3) The rate at which a bank offers a foreign currency.

legacy A gift of personal property by will. A legacy is the same as a bequest. The decedent is called the testator (testatrix), and the recipient of the legacy is the legatee.

legal capital (1) That portion of the paid-in capital of a corporation that comprises the par or stated value of its stock. (2) That portion of a corporation's net assets with restricted withdrawal under corporation law.

legal charity One that comes within the legal definition of a charity.

legal common trust fund A common trust fund invested wholly in property that is legal for the investment of trust funds in the state in which the common trust is administered. The term is employed most often in or with respect to common trust funds in states that have a statutory or court-approved list of authorized investments for trustees, where the terms of the trust do not provide otherwise.

legal description A method of geographically identifying a piece of land that a court of law will accept.

legal entity A thing, other than a person, that exists, and can sue, be sued, and be otherwise dealt with as if it were a natural person. In this sense, a corporation, state, or city is a legal entity.

legal investment An investment that conforms to the requirements of the statutes. It is a term used principally with reference to investments by trustees and other fiduciaries and by savings banks. Legal investment is often abbreviated to "legal." *Distinguish from* authorized investment. *See also* legal list.

legal lending limit The maximum amount of money a bank can lend on an unsecured basis to any one borrower or combination of borrowers who are financially related. The limit is set by statute and is generally expressed as a percentage of capital stock and surplus, although differences exist for national and state-chartered banks.

legal list (1) The legally authorized investments for savings banks and trust funds in states with statutes restricting such investments. (2) A list prepared by the superintendent of banks in such states, showing securities that are believed to meet statutory requirements.

legal name An individual's personal name, consisting of first and last names, used as identification when the person enters into certain transactions. The name must be currently in use for financial purposes and must be used without fraudulent intent.

legal opinion The statement of counsel (usually by a law firm that specializes in the approval of public borrowings) concerning the legality of a bond issue. The issuer must obtain this statement before a municipal issue can be floated. Issuers of municipal bonds usually print the legal opinion on the back of each certificate. If separate from the certificate, the legal opinion should be safeguarded as carefully as the instrument itself, because the legal opinion is essential in a resale of the security.

legal ownership An estate or interest in property that is enforceable in a court of law. *Distinguish from* equitable ownership.

legal rate of interest The maximum rate of interest that may be charged on a loan. This interest rate is established by the laws of the state having jurisdiction over the transaction. Interest rates charged in excess of this ceiling are considered usurious. *Also called* usury rate.

legal reserves That portion of both its demand and time deposits that a depository institution must by law maintain in a form prescribed by law.

legals *See* legal investment.

legal tender The authorized currency, backed by the government, that must be accepted in payment of all public and private debts.

legal title Title to property recognized by and enforceable in a court of law. *Distinguish from* equitable title.

legal transfer delivery The delivery, along with securities being sold, of certain legal documents needed because the endorsement does not match the name on the face of the certificate.

legatee A person receiving a gift of personal property by will who is not a blood relative or next of kin. *See also* will.

lender of last resort A term often used to describe the Federal Reserve System.

lender's agreement The signed agreement between a bank and the Farmers Home Administration or other guarantor describing bank loan servicing and other responsibilities.

lender's liability A legal phrase used to describe the liability of a lender for not dealing fairly with a borrower. It is usually used to describe lawsuits filed by borrowers against lenders for wrongfully demanding payment on a loan, or refusing to advance funds on a committed loan.

lending limit The maximum amount of credit a lending officer has authority to extend to a borrower without first obtaining approval from someone higher in the organization. This limit is typically based on each lending offificer's experience and position within the organization. *Also called* lending authority.

lessee (1) The party (tenant) who holds the exclusive right of possession under a valid lease. (2) A party who leases property or services from another.

lessor (1) A party who leases property to a tenant. (2) A party who leases property or services to another.

lessor markup The amount by which the capitalized cost exceeds the asset cost of the leased property. *Also called* pack.

letter bonds *See* letter stock.

letter of administration A certificate of authority to settle a particular estate issued to an administrator by the appointing court. *Distinguish from* letter testamentary.

letter of attorney A written document that describes the authority of an agent who is known as an attorney-in-fact. *See also* power of attorney.

letter of conservatorship A certificate of authority issued by the court to a person or corporate fiduciary to serve as conservator of a person's property.

letter of credit An engagement by a bank or other person made at the request of a customer that the issuer will honor drafts or other demands for payment upon compliance with the conditions specified in the credit. The credit may be revocable or irrevocable. The engagement may be either an agreement to honor or a statement that the bank or other person is authorized to honor. Under a direct-pay letter of credit, the bank pays off all maturing obligations and obtains reimbursement from the borrower. *See also* commercial letter of credit; confirmed letter of credit;

deferred payment letter of credit; evergreen letter of credit; irrevocable letter of credit; performance letter of credit; red clause letter of credit; reimbursement letter of credit; revocable letter of credit; revolving letter of credit; sight letter of credit; standby letter of credit; transferable letter of credit; traveler's letter of credit; unconfirmed letter of credit.

letter of dispute A letter signed by the customer detailing the nature of the dispute. *See also* Fair Credit Billing Act of 1974.

letter of intent *See* investment letter.

letter of lien A document signed by the buyer of goods stating that the seller will retain possession of the goods until they have been paid for.

letter of transmittal (1) A detailed legal document sent to holders of securities by the maker of a tender offer, asking that the holder sell his or her stock. *See also* tender offer. (2) A letter notifying the recipient that a particular document is being sent by the writer of the letter to the recipient.

letter stock A special issue of common stock that a corporation is legally permitted to sell, without SEC registration, to a small group of investors. The buyer must sign a letter of intent stating that the purchase of stock is for investment and will not be sold. Letter bonds can also be issued. *Also called* restricted stock.

letter testamentary A certificate of authority to settle a particular estate issued by the appointing court to the executor named in the will. *Distinguish from* letter of administration.

level payment amortization An amortization plan in which mortgage payments are constant, but the amounts accruing to principal and interest vary with each payment.

level payment mortgage A mortgage that requires fixed, periodic loan repayments during the term of the loan, providing for amortization of the loan over its original term. Part of each payment is credited to the interest, and the balance is used to reduce the principal. *Also called* a fixed payment mortgage. *See also* amortization schedule.

level playing field A situation in which commercial banks are allowed to offer the same types of services and compete in the same manner as nonbank thrift institutions and other financial conglomerates. *Often called* regulator equity.

level-yield amortization A method of computing amortization (for example, of interest payments) that applies a constant rate to the declining (unpaid) principal balance. *Compare with* straight-line amortization.

leverage The issuance of senior securities or the use of borrowed money to increase the return possible on equity capital. The issuance of preferred stock, which has a fixed maximum dividend, leverages a firm's common stock. Options and futures also provide leverage. For an example of how an investor uses leverage, *see* margin account. *Also called* trading on the equity.

leveraged buyout (LBO) (1) Corporate acquisition through stock purchases financed by the issuance of debt (which may include junk bonds). (2) More generally, an LBO may be used to effect a change in ownership or a reconstitution of a company's capital structure, maximizing financial leverage; few or none of the borrowed funds are retained by the company

itself. LBOs are generally among those transactions called highly leveraged transactions (financings).

leveraged lease A tax-oriented lease involving at least three parties in which the lessor usually funds 20 percent to 50 percent of the investment and leverages the remainder with nonrecourse debt. The lessor's net investment declines during the early years and rises during the later years of the lease.

leverage ratios Relationships among balance sheet values that measure the extent to which owners rather than creditors finance a business.

liabilities repriced before assets (LRBA) A measure of the gap between the maturities of liabilities and assets that takes into account the possible repricing of certain types of assets and liabilities before maturity. LRBA is used in the management of bank funds. *See also* gap.

liability (1) An amount owed. (2) A source of financing, such as a deposit in a bank. (3) A legal obligation to make good some loss or damage that results from an action or transaction. *See also* current liabilities; limited liability; unlimited liability.

liability for endorsement A contingent liability arising from the endorsement of an obligation owed by another person and continuing until the original debtor has met or has failed to meet the obligation. If the original debtor defaults, the contingent liability becomes a direct liability of the endorser.

liability insurance Insurance that protects against claims made by others for injuries received through use of the insured party's products or facilities.

liability management The management and control of liabilities to optimize a bank's earnings without excessive risk or liquidity exposure.

LIBID (London interbank bid rate) The rate that a bank is willing to pay for funds in the international interbank market.

LIBOR (London interbank offered rate) The interest rate offered by banks in London for Eurodollar deposits.

library (1) An area of a disk that may contain source programs, object or load programs, and procedures. (2) The room in which tapes are stored. *See also* program library.

license and permit bond A bond guaranteeing proper compliance with statutory requirements and municipal ordinances. Government bodies generally require this bond of people such as pawnbrokers, plumbers, and electricians.

licensee A bank to which a licensing authority--such as VISA, U.S.A. Inc., or MasterCard International Inc.--has granted the right to issue bank cards and operate a bank card plan.

lien A legal claim or attachment filed on record against property, as security for the payment of an obligation. A lien is the guaranteed right of a lender or investor to specific property in case of default.

life beneficiary The beneficiary of a trust, usually for the term of the beneficiary's life but sometimes for the term of another person's life.

life cap The maximum amount by which the interest rate on an adjustable rate mortgage may be raised during the lifetime of the loan. *See also* annual cap; rate cap.

life estate Either an estate for the life of the life tenant alone or an estate for the life of some other person. If the estate is for the life of a person other than the life tenant, it is called an estate pur auter vie.

life expectancy The length of time a person of a given age may be expected to live according to the statistical tables that have been worked out by or for life insurance and other companies.

life insurance Insurance that protects against a loss of income resulting from the insured party's death. Life insurance usually stipulates a specific sum to be paid to a beneficiary when the insured party dies. *See also* credit life insurance.

life insurance trust *See* insurance trust.

life interest The estate or interest that a person has in property that will endure only during his or her own or someone else's lifetime.

lifeline account An account required by some state legislatures that provides at least minimal banking services such as checking and savings to low-income consumers at prices that they can afford.

life tenant A person who owns an estate in real property for the term of his or her own life or another person's life, or for an indefinite period, limited by a lifetime.

LIFFE The London International Financial Futures Exchange.

LIFO *See* last in, first out.

lifting a leg In the futures market, an arbitrageur will simultaneously buy cash securities and sell futures contracts (long arbitrage), or sell the cash market and buy the futures (short arbitrage). If an arbitrageur chooses to close out one position but not the other, he or she "lifts a leg."

LIMEAN The mean of LIBID and LIBOR.

limit *See* credit limit.

limit control (1) The component of a bank card operation that monitors cardholder balances relative to credit limits and takes appropriate action when credit limits are exceeded. (2) The process of monitoring balances and taking appropriate action when credit limits are exceeded. *Also called* credit review.

limited branching Restricted branching by banks in some states, usually by number or by distance from the head office.

limited check A draft that is not valid if greater than a specified amount or if presented for payment after a specified date. Payroll departments most often issue limited checks for control purposes.

limited guardianship In some states, a guardianship that allows a partially disabled or incompetent person to delegate limited powers and authority to a limited guardian.

limited liability Liability that is limited to a stated maximum amount. The term is generally used to refer to the position of stockholders who are liable only to the extent of their investment in the business.

limited open-end indenture A mortgage arrangement that sets a limit on the amount of mortgage bonds that may be issued in the future under the same indenture and with the same priority lien on corporate assets.

limited open-end mortgage *See* limited open-end indenture.

limited partnership A partnership in which certain partners are designated general partners, and some are designated limited partners. Liabilities of limited partners are limited if certain legal requirements are met. Limited partners are quite common in real estate investment.

limited payment life insurance Life insurance in which an insured party pays a premium for a specified number of years. The insurer then pays a fixed sum to a beneficiary when the insured party dies.

limited power of appointment A power, in some way limited, of the donee (the person who has received the power) to pass on an interest in property; for example, the time within which the donee must exercise the power. Limited power of appointment is the opposite of general power of appointment. All powers that are not general are special or limited powers. *Also called* special power of appointment.

limited-purpose trust company A trust company, state-chartered and regulated, that is permitted to perform specified trust functions. The major securities depositories were incorporated in this fashion, so that banks could legally deposit trust assets with them and could participate in book-entry settlement.

limited recourse *See* partial recourse agreement.

limited recourse agreement An indirect lending arrangement in which a dealer sells or discounts installment contracts to a bank and is liable for a limited time, a limited amount, or both if default occurs.

limited reduction plan An amortization plan that provides for only a limited reduction of the principal before the loan matures.

limited repurchase *See* partial recourse agreement.

limited-service bank *See* nonbank bank.

limited tax bond A bond that is secured by the pledge of a special tax, a group of taxes, or a specified portion of real estate tax. It is limited as to rate of interest or amount of issue.

limited-tax GO bond A general obligation (GO) bond issued by a municipality whose taxing power is restricted. A limited-tax GO bond is a less desirable security than an unlimited GO bond issued by the same municipality.

limit order An order that places a limit or condition on the time for executing an order or the price at which it is bought or sold. If the condition is not satisfied, the order is not executed. *Also called* limited order.

lineal descendant A person in the direct line of descent, such as a child or grandchild. *Distinguish from* collateral heir.

line and staff organization A form of business organization. The line part of an organization delivers the product or service to the customer; the staff provides support to the line.

linear programming A mathematical technique used to solve problems involving the selection of the optimal set of variables, with certain specific constraints placed on the solution set. This kind of programming involves the construction of a mathematical model for a particular "real-world" situation.

line functions Functions that contribute directly to a bank's objectives, such as accepting and processing deposits, making loans, and investing.

line management The managers and management of line functions.

line of credit (1) An expression by a bank of the maximum amount it is willing to lend to a particular customer over a future period. (2) The amount of money as expressed in the bank's determination. This amount may be borrowed without submitting a new loan application. *See also* revolving line of credit; nonrevolving line of credit.

line printer A piece of peripheral computer equipment that prints an entire line of characters as a unit at a very high speed. *Compare with* serial printer.

lines of authority The manner in which authority is delegated from top management through an organization.

linkage (1) Identification of a hedging instrument (for example, a futures contract) with the item being hedged (for example, a loan or deposit). (2) In programming, coding that connects two separately coded routines.

liquid (1) The state of having enough cash or marketable assets to meet needed expenditures. (2) The state of being readily convertible into cash, without substantial loss of principal.

liquid assets Assets of short maturity that can be sold quickly and without significant loss.

liquidate The process of converting an asset into cash. *See also* liquidation.

liquidated claim A claim of debt in which the amount due is fixed by law, or has been ascertained and agreed to by the parties involved, and no bona fide dispute regarding the amount exists between those parties.

liquidating dividend (1) A distribution of assets, as distinguished from a distribution of earnings. The term is generally used in connection with the dissolution of a corporation. (2) Payments of a going concern resulting from the disposition of wasting assets, such as mining property or timber. *See also* wasting assets.

liquidation (1) The conversion of an asset to cash. (2) The complex procedure in which a corporation's assets are sold, and the net proceeds after all expenses are passed along to creditors, bondholders, and shareholders. (Trade creditors are paid first, then bondholders, and finally shareholders.) Payments are made in accordance with the laws and contracts protecting each class of creditor. (3) Any transaction that offsets or closes out a long or short position. *Also called* evening up *or* offset.

liquidation cost per installment The primary costs involved in the payment of each installment on a loan, including a teller's time and bookkeeping and collection expenses.

liquidation cost per loan The cost involved in removing a loan from the active file and canceling and returning a note.

liquidation value (1) The net proceeds that could be obtained in dismantling a business, that is, selling all assets and paying all liabilities. Liquidation value, which generally occurs under forced circumstances (that is, a distress sale), will generally be less than the value that could be obtained from the sale of assets in the normal course of business. *Compare with* going-concern concept. (2) The price realized from the sale of an investment portfolio.

liquid cushion The protection provided by holdings in cash or securities (such as short-term marketable government bonds) that are readily convertible into cash.

liquidity (1) The ability of a bank or business to meet its current obligations. (2) The quality that makes an asset quickly and readily convertible into cash.

liquidity account A memorandum account that is maintained for managing assets, including all liquid assets held by a bank. Liquid assets in this context are usually considered to be highgrade, readily marketable assets with maturities of less than 1 year.

liquidity diversification *See* laddered maturities.

liquidity needs A bank's estimate of the amount of funds necessary to cover estimated withdrawals or payments of funds and to meet the legitimate credit needs of customers.

liquidity preference hypothesis An adaptation of the expectations hypothesis to allow for a liquidity premium. It assumes that the yield curve reflects the net present value of all expected interest rates that will prevail in the future, as modified by a willingness to pay a liquidity premium for relatively short maturities. Under this hypothesis, the yield curve points in the direction that rates are expected to move (for example, a rising yield curve indicates that the market expects rates to rise), but with an upward bias because of liquidity preference. *Compare with* expectations hypothesis.

liquidity premium A premium placed on very short-term assets because of their very liquid nature. Although these assets usually yield less than comparable assets with longer maturities, investors are willing to buy them because they are so liquid.

liquidity ratios Relationships between current assets and current liabilities that indicate a bank's or a business borrower's ability to meet its current liabilities. *See also* acid test ratio; current ratio.

liquidity risk The risk of loss because of inadequate liquidity. Sometimes when a bank is in serious difficulty, it may be unable to acquire needed funds in the market at any reasonable price.

listed securities Bonds or stocks that have been accepted for trading on an organized securities exchange. Unlisted securities are normally traded over the counter. However, some exchanges permit trading of certain unlisted securities with the consent of the Securities and Exchange Commission.

listed stock A firm's stock that has been accepted for trading by a stock exchange.

listing Meeting the necessary requirements and being accepted for trading securities on a stock exchange.

litigation A lawsuit or legal controversy.

lives in being Lives in existence at a given time. *See also* rule against perpetuities.

living trust A trust that becomes operative during the lifetime of the settlor, as opposed to a trust under will. *Also*

called trust inter vivos *or* voluntary trust.

living will A document that allows a person to state in advance his or her wishes regarding the use or removal of life-sustaining or death-delaying procedures in the event of a terminal illness or injury.

Lloyd's of London The oldest insurance company in existence.

load (1) (Noun) A commission paid by a buyer for shares of an open-end mutual investment fund. (2) (Verb) To enter data or programs into storage, for example, to load master files. (3) (Verb) To prepare an input-output device for operation, for example, to load paper into a printer.

load fund A mutual fund that sells its shares through an agent that acts as a middleman and charges a sales commission. (No-load funds sell directly to the investor and charge no fee or a small fee.)

loading up Under bankruptcy law, the process in which a debtor obtains credit immediately before filing a bankruptcy proceeding.

loan A business contract in which a borrower agrees to pay interest for the use of a lender's funds. Loans are classified according to the lender or borrower involved, whether or not collateral is required, the time to maturity, conditions of repayment, and other variables. *See also* character loan; downstream loan.

loan administrator An employee who handles loan transactions. The loan officer usually computes relevant interest charges, accepts collateral, and performs other loan-related functions.

loan application A form that a potential borrower uses to request a loan. The form asks for information required by law and necessary for the bank to make a lending decision.

loan commitment A binding pledge by a lender to a borrower to make a loan, usually at a stated rate within a given time for a given purpose, subject to the borrower's compliance with stated conditions.

loan contract The written agreement, between a borrower and lender of funds, that sets forth the terms and conditions of the loan.

loan department The department of a bank that processes loan transactions.

loan forgiveness The act of relieving a borrower from the obligation to repay a loan.

loan guarantee certificate A certificate issued by a guarantor advising a lending institution what percentage of a particular loan is guaranteed. *Also called* loan guaranty certificate.

loan guarantee fee A nonrefundable fee that a guarantor charges a bank for its guarantee.

loan loss provision An expense account that is charged to establish or increase the reserve for possible loan losses. On the bank's income statement, this expense is subtracted from net interest income to derive "net income after provision for loan losses." The amount in the reserve appears on the bank's statement of condition, or balance sheet, as an offset to the loans account. When a loan is charged off, the amount of the loss is a credit to the loans account and a debit to the reserve account. *Also called* provision for loan losses *and* provision for possible credit losses.

loan loss ratio *See* loss ratio.

loan loss reserve A statement of condition, or balance sheet, account set up by a bank based on its expectations about future loan losses. As losses occur, they are charged against this reserve. That is, the loan account is credited and the reserve account is debited. The reserve is established by a debit to an expense account called the loan loss provision, with a corresponding credit to the loan loss reserve. *Also called* allowance for loan losses *and* reserve for possible credit losses.

loan maturity The date when a note becomes due and payable.

loan note guarantee A signed commitment setting forth the terms of a guarantor's guarantee to a bank.

loan note guarantee report of loss A bank's report of a loan default to the guarantor.

loan participation *See* participation.

loan policy A written statement of the guidelines and standards that a lender follows in determining whether a loan applicant will qualify for the credit requested.

loan production office (LPO) An office of a bank that arranges for loans but does not accept deposits. Depending on the location of the office relative to the bank's home office and the prevailing regulations, the loans may or may not be approved or disbursed at the LPO.

loan sale The sale, transfer, or assignment of a loan or a loan participation to a third party with or without the knowledge of the borrower. Generally accepted accounting principles and regulatory accounting principles set forth specific criteria for when a sale of a loan may be recorded as a sale, as opposed to a collateralized borrowing. Recourse is one of the primary factors taken into consideration. Legal documentation, as well as economic substance, may differ for various types of transactions referred to as sales.

loan schedule A list of the due dates, amounts of payments, balances after payments, and other information relevant to a specific loan.

loan shark A person or firm that lends money to a poor credit risk at an excessively high or illegal rate of interest.

loan submission A package consisting of papers and documents required for the approval of a loan.

loan swap The exchange by one lender of all or part of a particular loan with a second lender for all or part of a loan to the same or a different borrower. Under generally accepted accounting principles (GAAP), if the loans swapped are deemed to be substantially-the-same (as defined in GAAP), there is generally no gain or loss recognized. If the loans swapped are not substantially-the-same, the fair values of the loans are considered in determining the amount of gain or loss to be recognized. *See also* fair value; LDC loan swaps; substantially-the-same.

loan syndication A group of banks that join together to make a loan too large for one bank to make.

loan-to-value ratio The ratio between the amount of a loan and the appraised value of the security for that loan, expressed as a percentage of the appraised value.

lobby depository A receptacle on a bank's premises that allows customers to make deposits without teller assistance.

local *See* floor trader.

local item A deposited check drawn on another bank within the same city or geographic area.

local system A computer system not connected to any other computer facility.

local transaction date The month and day on which a transaction takes place.

lockbox A banking service provided for the rapid collection of a customer's receivables and rapid credit to the customer's account. The service includes collecting the mail from the company's post office box; sorting, totaling, and recording the payments; processing the items; and making the necessary bank deposit.

locked-in trade An executed trade, the terms of which have been agreed to by both parties. A locked-in trade is guaranteed by the clearing corporation to settle, unless both parties agree to cancel the trade.

locked market A market in which the bid price equals the asked price.

lockup certificates of deposit Certificates of deposit sold with the understanding that they will not be traded.

log A record of everything pertinent to a machine run, including an identification of the machine run; record of any alteration of switch settings; identification of input and output tapes; copy of mutual key-ins; identification of all machine errors and failures; and record of all actions taken.

logging The procedure of recording on a storage device the occurrence of particular types of transactions or system activities.

logical flowchart A detailed solution of work order in terms of the logic or built-in operations and characteristics of a specific machine. Concise symbolic notation is used to represent the information and describe the input, output, and arithmetic and logical operations involved.

log-normal distribution A normal probability distribution of a variable expressed in logarithmic form. This distribution is often used for prices of assets or commodities because it implies that the price can rise to infinity but cannot fall below zero. *See also* normal distribution.

long (1) Owning more than one has contracted to sell. (2) A market position established when a person has bought a futures contract but not yet closed out the position through an offsetting sale. To "go long" is to establish a long position, for example, to buy a futures contract.

long coupon A bond, bearer or registered, with an initial interest payment period longer than the normal interest payment interval for the bond. For example, a bond that pays interest semiannually is said to have a "long coupon" if the first interest payment is scheduled more than 6 months from the dated date of the bond.

long hedge A hedge effected by purchasing a futures contract. This hedge locks in a yield on funds to be received at a future date. Processors or exporters may use a long hedge as protection against an increase in the cash price of a commodity.

long position (1) An investor, dealer, or market maker with a long position in a particular security owns the securities. The term is generally used when the owner has taken or is prepared to take steps to change the position. For instance, the owner may be willing to sell, be actively buying, or may have written put options against part of the holdings. (2) The term can also mean that the securities are in transit during a trade settlement.

long-term capital gains Profits earned on the sale of assets held for more than a minimum period prescribed by law, which is changed from time to time. At times, tax laws permit the profits on these assets to be taxed at a lower rate than other income. *Also called* long-term gains.

long-term debt (1) Generally, debt maturing in 5 to 7 or more years. *Also called* long-term financing. (2) In accounting, generally refers to debt that matures after 1 year.

long-term investment (1) A security purchased with the expectation and intent of holding it for a long period. (2) A security or other investment maturing in more than 1 year.

loro account *See* due to account.

loss (1) Any item of expense, as in the expression "profit and loss." (2) Any sudden, unexpected, involuntary expense or unrecoverable cost. (3) The excess (deficit) of the value of an asset given up (liability extinguished) over the value received (paid). (4) The amount charged off to bad debts or fraud.

loss carryback The offsetting of a current year's taxable loss against previous years' taxable income.

loss carryforward Taxable losses from previous years deducted from taxable income in the current and subsequent years, to reduce taxes. *Also called* tax credit, tax loss credit, carryforward, *and* loss carryover.

loss carryover *See* loss carryforward.

loss exposure *See* exposure.

loss ratio The ratio of bad debts or losses to loans made. The ratio is sometimes computed by substituting the average loans outstanding for loans made.

lost card A bank card reported to the credit card issuer as lost or misplaced by the cardholder of record.

lost instrument bond A bond that indemnifies the issuer of a document from consequences that may arise if a person other than the recognized owner possesses the document.

lost in transit (1) Any item lost in the clearing process. (2) Any item lost in the process of transfer. (3) An item lost between a credit card processing center and either the clearing house or the local office handling the item.

lost securities *See* Rule 17f-1.

lower of cost or market (LCM or LOCOM) A conservative valuation method applied in financial accounting, commonly to inventory, marketable equity securities, and certain other financial instruments. The asset is carried on the books at the lower of original cost or current market value.

LPO *See* loan production office.

lump-sum distribution For pension plans, the distribution of a person's benefits in one payment rather than equal installments over a specified period or the person's lifetime. The Internal Revenue Code imposes certain requirements in order for the distribution to qualify for special tax treatment.

lump-sum method An investor using this method to buy additional shares in a mutual fund pays the total amount all at once. This method may reduce the sales charge to the investor.

luxury goods or services In bankruptcy, goods or services, not required for the support or maintenance of the debtor or a dependent, totaling more than $500 and purchased within 40 days of filing bankruptcy.

Macaulay's duration The first formulation, in 1938, of the principle of duration. It is fully consistent only on the assumption of a flat yield curve, which remains flat as yield levels change. For simple applications of duration analysis, however, Macaulay's duration is an adequate approximation of true duration. *See also* duration.

machine language (1) A set of symbols, characters, or signs, and the rules for combining them, that convey instructions or data to a computer. (2) Data expressed in code that a computer or a peripheral machine can read directly, use, or write without further processing. (3) A language that a computer uses directly.

machine pay A way to post checking account activity by entering checks and deposits into the journal only on the first run.

machine readable Documents containing data in a form that a machine can process without the need for further translation, for example, data on punch cards, magnetic tape, punch paper tapes, OCR, or MICR.

machine word *See* computer word.

macroeconomics The study of economic aggregates such as national income, employment, and output.

macro-prudential policy Activities of central banks and other national authorities designed to promote the safety and soundness of the overall banking system as well as the orderly growth and efficiency of the financial system. In part, macro-prudential activities such as the lender-of-last-resort role and deposit insurance are intended to ensure the resiliency of the overall system so as to withstand major shocks to confidence.

magnetic card A card with a magnetic surface that can store data by selectively magnetizing portions of the flat surface.

magnetic disk *See* disk.

magnetic drum A magnetically coated, rotating cylindrical drum used to store information.

magnetic encoding The encoding of data on ferromagnetic material by introducing electronic impulses to that material.

magnetic ink An ink containing particles of a magnetic substance that can be detected by magnetic sensors.

magnetic ink character recognition (MICR) Magnetic codes on the bottom of a check that allow a machine to read the check. MICR encoding can include the amount of the check, the account number, the bank's number, and the serial number of the check.

magnetic ink character recognition (MICR) characters Characters used to print or encode information on documents so they can be processed by machine.

magnetic stripe A stripe of magnetic tape affixed to the back of bank debit or credit cards, containing important identifying data such as an account number.

mail deposit A deposit received by a bank from a depositor through the mail instead of over the counter.

mail float The float that occurs while a check is in the mail from the payer to the payee, or from the payee to his or her bank. *See also* postal float.

mailing holder *See* card mailer.

mail order (MO) A written direction received by mail from a cardholder wishing to have a purchase amount charged to his or her account. Special authorization procedures usually govern mail orders.

mail teller The employee responsible for processing mail deposits.

mail transfer The transfer of bank funds from one location to another, the instructions for which are transmitted by mail. Here, the funds transfer is defined by the instruction method.

mainframe The central processing unit of a large computer system.

main location The location of a merchant's head office.

main storage The central storage for any computer system where all logical, arithmetic, and control operations occur under program control.

maintenance Any activity intended to keep hardware or software in satisfactory working condition, including tests, measurements, replacements, adjustments, and repairs.

maintenance charge A service charge assessed against an account to cover the cost of preparing statements and other routine records. *Also called* activity fee.

maintenance costs *See* liquidation cost per loan; liquidation cost per installment.

maintenance margin A sum, usually smaller than but part of the original margin, that must be maintained on deposit at all times. If a customer's equity in any futures position drops to or under the maintenance margin, the broker must issue a margin call asking for the amount of money required to restore the customer's equity in the account to the original margin.

major industry identifier The first digit of the primary account number, signifying the major industry issuing a plastic money card.

majority-owned subsidiary A subsidiary with more than 50 percent of the outstanding voting capital stock owned by the parent company or by another majorityowned subsidiary of the parent company.

make a market *See* market maker.

maker The one who subscribes to and therefore makes him- or herself liable for a legal obligation, such as the maker of a promissory note.

making a market The process of being prepared both to buy and to sell certain securities, at quoted bid and offering prices. A dealer is making a market when he or she continues to quote bid and offering prices over a certain period.

Maloney Act A 1938 amendment to the Securities Exchange Act of 1934 that regulates associations of brokers and dealers.

managed float *See* dirty float.

management (1) The planning, organizing, directing, and controlling of a bank, function, or firm to accomplish its stated objectives. (2) The use of people and resources to accomplish specific objectives. (3) Those people responsible for directing any enterprise. *See also* centralized management.

management accounting A broad field of accounting concerned with the development and use of economic information within an organization for planning, decision making, and control. Management accounting includes cost accounting. *Compare with* financial accounting.

management by exception The process of managing by responding only to unfavorable variances between actual and projected performance. By responding only to unfavorable variances, management effectively focuses on those areas with problems.

management by objectives (MBO) Management through setting, planning, and achieving goals. In an MBO system, performance is measured against goals.

management consultant An outside person hired by an organization to investigate and make recommendations on action to take in a particular area of the organization's affairs.

management information system (MIS) A computer-based system capable of integrating data from various sources to provide management with information necessary to the decision-making process.

management override A situation that occurs when senior management or members of senior management with sufficient real or apparent authority cause subordinates to override established control procedures.

management science The application of scientific principles or techniques to any aspect of management.

manager A person who plans, organizes, and controls functions and people necessary to an organization, an operation, a transaction, or a relationship.

managing agency account An agency account for which the agent has managerial duties and responsibilities appropriate to the property and conforming with the terms of the agency. *Distinguish from* safekeeping account *and* custody account.

managing agent (1) An agent who assumes an active role in administering another's property. (2) The head agent in a group or syndicate.

managing underwriter The syndicate organizer. *Also called* syndicate manager principal underwriter *or* lead underwriter.

mandatory Obligatory, such as a power of a trustee that the trustee must exercise. Mandatory power is the same as a direction.

manual *See* organization manual; policy manual; procedure manual.

manual input (1) Data entered manually into a computer system using an input device. (2) Any data that must be entered manually into any piece of equipment, for example, a teller or accounting machine.

margin (lending) (1) The purchase of a security paid for in part by a loan

from a broker. (2) That part of the purchase price not covered by the loan. (3) The excess of the value of collateral over the value of the loan made against it. (4) The amount of cash or Treasury bills that must be deposited with a broker for each futures contract as a guarantee of fulfillment of the contract. *Also called* security deposit.

margin account An investor's credit account with a broker or dealer, which permits the investor to pay only part of the purchase price and borrow the rest from the broker. The part paid initially--the margin--is a percentage of the total price. This percentage is called the margin requirement. Regulations G, T, and U of the Federal Reserve Board govern the credit permitted on margin accounts.

marginal cost The additional cost attributable to production of one more unit of product.

marginal revenue The incremental revenue resulting from the sale of an additional unit of output.

marginal risk A borrowing customer who is considered to be a borderline safe customer.

marginal tax rate The tax rate that applies to the last dollar of taxable income.

marginal utility The additional usefulness of any added unit of a product or service.

margin call A demand for additional collateral because of an adverse change in price.

margin loan A loan by a broker to a customer who uses the funds to buy securities on margin (on credit).

margin of safety The balance of income remaining after payment of fixed charges (or preferred dividends), expressed as a percentage of gross revenues (net sales). This calculation is used to approximate the percentage by which gross revenues can decline or operating expenses can increase before the continued payment of debt service is endangered.

margin requirement (1) The minimum amount a customer must provide to purchase securities on margin (on credit). The Federal Reserve System sets requirements for stock margins. (2) The minimum initial deposit with a futures exchange that is required of all holders of futures contracts. Changes in the value of such contracts are credited (or charged) to those deposits each day.

marine insurance Insurance that protects against hazards involved in ocean trade (ocean marine insurance) or other transportation (inland insurance).

marital deduction The portion of a decedent's estate that may be given to the surviving spouse without becoming subject to the federal estate tax levied against the estate. This term came into general use under the Internal Revenue Act of 1954.

marital rights The rights that a husband and wife have in each other's property.

marital status The state of being unmarried, married, or separated, as defined by applicable state law. The term unmarried includes people who are single, divorced, or widowed.

Maritime Administration An arm of the U.S. Department of Commerce that issues notes, bonds, and other obligations secured by mortgages on ships and directly guaranteed by the federal government.

marketability The ease with which an asset can be sold. Marketability differs from liquidity, because liquidity also involves minimal loss as well as ease of sale.

marketable title A title that a reasonably prudent person, knowing all the facts, regards and accepts as good.

market analysis The research that measures the extent and characteristics of a given market. *Also called* market research *and* marketing research.

market data approach *See* sales comparison approach to value.

market discipline The refusal to entrust funds to a financial institution because of negative reaction concerning the way in which the institution has been managed.

market if touched An order that automatically becomes a market order if the stipulated price of the security, commodity, or futures contract is reached.

marketing The conveying of goods, services, or ideas--all of which may be called "products"--from producers to consumers through various business activities concerned with meeting the needs and wants of consumers. The activities revolve around the conception and enhancement of products, and the pricing, promotion, and distribution of those products.

marketing concept A business philosophy that maintains that the company's profit goals are best met by understanding and meeting the needs and wants of its target market within an organized and efficient framework.

marketing mix The combination of four marketing activities--product development, pricing, promotion, and distribution--aimed at creating demand among the target markets.

marketing plan A plan developed to accomplish a marketing objective. A marketing plan consists of an assessment of the current situation, identification of specific objectives, identification of a target market, definition of specific marketing strategies and tactics, and provision for measurement and evaluation of results.

marketing profile A resource providing information about a market's characteristics. Bank management uses a marketing profile to assess future problems, opportunities, and potential growth and changes in a market.

marketing research *See* market analysis; market research.

market liquidity risk The possibility that a financial instrument cannot be sold quickly and at full market value.

market maker A firm that establishes a position in a security, that is, maintains an inventory and acts as a dealer of that security. A market maker stands ready to buy or sell that security for its own account.

market order A trade order in which the buyer or seller does not specify an exact price per share but agrees to trade immediately at the best price available in the market at that time.

market penetration The share of any market held by a firm. For example, a bank's penetration of the consumer market might be stated as a percentage calculated by dividing the number of trade area households having any type of account with the bank by the total number of households in the trade area. *See also* market share.

market potential The amount of a commodity or service that could be sold in a specific market during a specific time.

market price (1) The price at which the amount demanded and the amount offered for sale are equal. (2) The current price of a security. (3) The price at which the last order was executed.

market rates Rates of interest resulting from the demand for and supply of funds in the money market.

market research The systematic collection, review, and analysis of data related to marketing existing or new goods or services.

market risk The possibility of a decline in the price of a specific security or other asset. Market risk refers to the loss that a holder of an investment may have to assume at the time of its sale.

market segmentation (1) Categorizing the general population into heterogeneous groups in order to design optimal marketing strategies for each. (2) The extent to which a market is not fully arbitraged, so that rates on comparable maturities with comparable risks differ from one market segment to another.

market share One seller's portion of the total sales of a product, usually measured as a percentage. *See also* market penetration.

market targeting Developing a marketing mix to satisfy the needs of a potentially profitable market with relatively homogeneous needs.

market value (1) The highest price that a property will bring in the market with neither party acting under duress and both knowing all possible uses of the property. (2) The current value of a security. This may mean the value of the last recorded sale on the present date; the value at market close of the prior business day; or the closing value at the date of the report in which the market value is shown, depending on use.

marking to market The process of recalculating the exposure in a trading position in securities, option contracts, or futures contracts. In exchange-traded contracts, the exchange clearing house marks members' positions to market each day using closing market prices. Members must maintain a certain minimum level of margin at the exchange clearing house and must post additional margin if the marking-to-market process reduces margin below the minimum. *See also* margin.

Massachusetts rule A term frequently applied to a rule for the investment of trust funds enunciated by the Supreme Judicial Court of Massachusetts in 1830. The Massachusetts rule is now commonly referred to as the prudent-investor rule. *See also* prudent-investor rule for trust investment.

Massachusetts trust An unincorporated organization created for profit under a written instrument or declaration of trust. Under a Massachusetts trust, compensated trustees manage the property held in trust for the benefit of people whose legal interests are represented by transferable trust certificates. *Also called* business trust.

mass market The entire, unsegmented market of buyers of a product.

mass storage device A type of memory device that can retain and communicate vast amounts of data, often in the trillion-bit range.

master control An application-oriented routine, usually applied to the highest level of a subroutine hierarchy.

master data Data that are altered infrequently and supply other basic data for processing.

master file (1) A file composed of records having similar characteristics or containing data that are relatively permanent. A cardholder master file would contain such information as account numbers, names, addresses, credit limits, expiration dates, and the number of cards issued. (2) The updated record of the closing balance in each account at a bank, produced by combining the previous day's file with the tape for the current day's transactions.

master limited partnership A form of limited partnership primarily used as an investment vehicle for a large number of investors. Interests in master limited partnerships are usually listed and traded on national or regional stock exchanges. In many large business transactions, they may enjoy tax advantages over corporations.

master trust An arrangement designating the custodianship and accounting for all employee-benefit assets of a corporation or a controlled group of corporations to a single trustee. A master trust facilitates the uniform administration of the assets of multiple plans and multiple investment managers.

matched book A portfolio of assets and liabilities with equal maturities. Although the term applies to whatever group of assets and liabilities is being discussed, a matched book is mostly used in managing money

market assets and liabilities.
Compare with unmatched book.

match fund (Verb) To fund a loan or
other assets by issuing a liability with
the same (matched) maturity or duration.

materiality In accounting, the dividing
line between significant and insignificant.

mathematical model The mathematical characterization of a process,
object, or concept as a variable in an
equation to determine how each
would behave in various situations.

matrix In mathematics, a two-dimen-
sional, rectangular array of quantities.

maturity The date on which the principal of a bond or note becomes due
and payable.

maturity date The date on which a
loan, debt security, or other financial
instrument is due and payable.

maturity imbalance A mismatch
between maturities of assets and
liabilities.

maturity tickler A reminder file maintained by a bank to ensure that notes
will be presented for payment as they
fall due. In this file, all items are
classified by due dates.

maximum net debit position A limit
on the amount of uncovered payment
that a participant may release over a
payment system.

May Day rule A May 1, 1975, ruling
of the Securities and Exchange
Commission that ended the NYSE
system of fixed brokerage commissions.

McFadden Act Legislation enacted in
1927 that specifically guarantees the

rights of states to control the branching of banks, including national
banks, within individual state borders.

mean The "average" of all observations.

mechanic's lien A lien filed against
real property as a result of nonpayment for work performed or materials
delivered. State statutes governing
the filing of such liens and their priority status vary widely.

medium The material on which data
are recorded. It usually applies to
paper tape, punch cards, and magnetic tape rather than disks, drums, or
core devices.

medium-term debt Generally, debt
maturing in 1 to 5 years. However,
definitions for this term vary.

meeting bond interest and principal
Making payments of interest and
principal on bond issues when they
are due.

megabyte One million bytes.

**Member Appraisal Institute (MAI)
Award** The highest professional desig-
nation awarded by the American
Institute of Real Estate Appraisers.

member bank (1) An institution that
belongs to the Federal Reserve
System. (2) A bank that is one of the
banks in a multibank holding company.

memo entry A miscellaneous change
to an individual cardholder account
record. *Also called* memo adjustment.

memorandum account A record of
financial transactions, maintained by a
bank, that is not included among its
assets and liabilities.

memory (1) The capacity of a computer to process and store data. This capacity is expressed in thousands of bytes. (2) A computer's storage space. *Also called* storage. (3) Any device into which a unit of data can be copied and kept.

memory capacity The maximum number of storage locations in a computer's memory.

menu A list of choices on a computer display station, one of which the operator may select to perform an operation.

mercantile open-stock burglary insurance Insurance that protects against merchandise losses by theft, occurring after hours and involving forcible entry.

merchandise balance *See* retail balance.

merchant A person, firm, or corporation that is contractually affiliated with a bank card plan in order to accept bank cards in payment for goods or services.

merchant accounting The recording by a bank of the number and dollar value of all sales drafts and credit slips submitted by each merchant.

merchant affiliate An affiliate that receives paper from a merchant.

merchant agreement A written agreement between a merchant and a bank containing their respective rights, duties, and warranties with respect to accepting bank card transactions and related matters.

merchant application A request form completed when a merchant signs up with a bank card plan. The application contains basic data about the merchant, such as type of business, number of locations, and bank references.

merchant assessment *See* merchant discount.

merchant bank (1) A European form of an investment bank. (2) A bank that has entered into a merchant agreement with a merchant to accept deposits generated by bank card transactions.

merchant base The total number of merchants that have signed merchant agreements with a bank card plan. A merchant base may be expressed as the number of agreements or number of merchant locations.

merchant call report A form used by bank card sales personnel to record the results of each merchant sales or service call.

merchant chargeback A transaction being challenged by a cardholder bank against a merchant bank. The transaction being challenged comes to the merchant bank through interchange. *Also called* "incoming" chargeback.

merchant collusion The situation in which a merchant has cooperated with a person using a fraudulent bank card to defraud a bank credit card plan. *See also* merchant fraud.

merchant depository account A demand deposit account established by a merchant with a bank for payment of sales drafts submitted to the bank for collection under the card plan.

merchant deposit transmittal (MDT) *See* merchant summary slip.

merchant directory A consolidated listing of all merchants participating in a bank card plan.

merchant discount Compensation received by a bank from a merchant for processing and accepting the credit risk on credit card sales. *Also called* merchant assessment.

merchant file A computer record of information on all merchants serviced by a processing center.

merchant fraud The process by which a merchant submits, and receives payment for, sales drafts imprinted with a lost, stolen, revoked, or counterfeit credit card while knowing that the bank card is invalid. *See also* merchant collusion.

merchant identification card An embossed card supplied to each merchant to be used in imprinting the merchant summary slip that is included in the sales draft envelope. Minimum embossed data include merchant account number, name, location, and checking account number. *Also called* merchant plastic. *See also* deposit envelope.

merchant member A merchant affiliated with a bank card plan.

merchant membership fee The amount charged to merchants for the privilege of being affiliated with a bank card plan.

merchant number A series or group of digits that numerically identifies each merchant with a merchant bank for account and billing purposes.

merchant operating guide A document that the bank provides to each merchant location, describing the basic operating procedures merchants must use in handling bank card transactions and deposits.

merchant-oriented data entry (MODE) A Chicago-based point-of-sale system.

merchant outlet A merchant location.

merchant penetration The total number of merchant outlets affiliated with a bank card plan, expressed as a percentage of total merchant outlets in the market area served by the plan.

merchant plastic *See* merchant identification card.

merchant plate A plate attached to a credit card imprinter that records the information necessary to identify the merchant who made the sales charged on the credit card. *Also called* imprinter plate *or* station plate.

merchant rebate The retroactive downward adjustment of merchant discounts, paid by merchants whose volume or average ticket size exceeds a predetermined amount during a stipulated period. *Also called* merchant volume discount.

merchant solicitation The process of calling on merchants to seek their affiliation with a bank card plan.

merchant statement In bank card usage, a summary statement of the merchant's account with the bank for accounting and billing purposes, produced and mailed at specified intervals, usually monthly.

merchant summary slip A multipart form used to total daily merchant sales, imprinted with the merchant identification card and submitted to the bank together with sales drafts. *Also called* batch header ticket, sales summary slip, *or* merchant deposit transmittal.

merchant volume The total amount of transactions at a bank's merchant outlet(s).

merge (1) To combine items into one sequenced file or document from two or more similarly sequenced files or documents without changing the order of the items. (2) To combine two or more formerly independent firms under a single ownership.

merger The combination of two or more enterprises. If the enterprises are of the corporate type, the merger involves the exchange of securities, the issuance of new securities, or both.

merit rating The assessment of an employee's performance made to justify an increase in compensation.

message (1) A set of data elements used to support the exchange of information between financial institutions. No communications (header/trailer, protocol, or character code) implications are assumed or identified. (2) A communication containing one or more transactions or related information.

message amount A data element in funds transfers that is the sum of the transaction amounts of a message.

message authentication The technique used between the sender and the receiver to validate the source and part or all of the text of a message. The resulting code from this process can be either an authenticator, message authentication code (MAC), or test based on the technique used.

message authentication code (MAC) A code in a message between the sender and the receiver used to validate the source and part or all of the text of the message. The code is the result of an agreed calculation between the sender and the receiver.

message cryptographic check digits (MCCD) The set of digits used to authenticate and protect the integrity of information sent over open communication lines.

message status indicators Information, supplied by the sending bank or wire service, that defines special circumstances pertaining to the transmission of a particular message (for example, suspected or possible duplication).

message type A code that designates the type and function (class of business) of a message.

message type code A data element in funds transfers. A message type code defines the purpose of the message at the most general level (for example, customer transfer, administrative message, or system message).

metes and bounds A system of surveying used to describe real estate. "Metes" means measurements and "bounds" refers to the boundaries of the tract of land described.

mezzanine loan An unsecured loan with a maturity of at least 5 years. The loan carries a detachable warrant or similar feature to permit the lender to share in any future success of the business. Mezzanine loans come in both junior and senior varieties and are dependent on cash flow for repayment. Such loans have been popularized recently as a result of the increase in leveraged buyouts.

MICR clear band *See* clear band.

MICR encoder Any equipment that applies MICR E13B font characters to a check.

MICR encoding *See* magnetic ink character recognition (MICR).

microcomputer A small but complete computer system, including software and hardware. A microcomputer is the smallest kind of computer in which the central processing unit is a microprocessor.

microeconomics The study of the economics of individuals, businesses, and industries.

microfiche A sheet of microfilm capable of containing microimages in a grid pattern.

microfilm A high-resolution film used to record images too small to be read without magnification.

microprocessor A computer processor that is completely contained on a single integrated circuit.

microsecond One-millionth of a second.

Midwest Securities Trust Company (MSTC) A regional depository, founded in 1973, serving the security exchanges for Chicago.

mineral rights The right or title to all or certain specified minerals in a given tract of land.

minicomputer A computer that is smaller, slower, and less costly than a large mainframe computer. It is generally used for a specific applications system.

minimum balance The amount of money that a depositor must have on deposit in a specific account to qualify for special services or to waive a service charge.

minimum lease payments The payments that the lessee is required to make in connection with the leased property. These payments include rent and any guarantee by the lessee of the residual value at the expiration of the lease, as well as any payment the lessee must make or can be required to make upon failure to renew or extend the lease.

minimum payment The smallest monthly payment an open-end credit account holder can make and remain in compliance with the terms and conditions of the agreement.

minimum property standards The minimum acceptable building standards for properties covered by Federal Housing Administration mortgage insurance, established by FHA regulations.

minor A person under legal age, that is, under the age at which he or she is accorded full civil rights. *Also called* infant.

minority (1) The state of being under legal age, which is 18 years in most states but 21 in some states. (2) Sometimes used in the United States to describe non-Caucasian races.

minority interest The portion of a subsidiary's net worth that relates to shares not owned by the controlling company or other members of the consolidated group of companies.

minority stockholders A group with common corporate interests but holdings too small to influence significantly the actions of the corporation under regular voting procedures. *See also* cumulative voting system.

mirror swap A reverse swap written with the original counterparty.

miscellaneous charges Any charges, other than advice charges, that are germane to a transfer.

misencoded card A valid card on which erroneous information (for example, name, account number, or expiration date) has been encoded or otherwise inadvertently applied.

misencoded payment A payment erroneously entered so that the encoded amount does not agree with the written amount.

mismatch A condition in which maturities of assets are longer than maturities of liabilities, or vice versa. *See also* gap.

misposting An error that causes a monetary transaction to be posted to the wrong account.

missent item An item sent in error to the wrong bank.

missing payment A payment that has been made but not posted to the appropriate account.

missing sales slip A condition where the number of sales drafts posted to an account during the billing process does not agree with the physical count of sales drafts accompanying the monthly statement.

missing securities *See* Rule 17f-1.

missort A check or other instrument incorrectly routed.

mixed deposit A deposit including both checks and cash.

mixed property Property that has some of the attributes of both real and personal property, such as fixtures and keys to a house.

MMDA *See* money market deposit account.

mobilization system A cash management system designed to transfer funds collected in the field into a concentration bank. The purpose of a mobilization system is to move funds efficiently from where they are collected to where they are needed for investment, loan paydown, or compensation.

model *See* mathematical model.

modem A device that allows computers to communicate with each other over telephone lines.

modified pass-through security A pass-through security whose principal and interest payments have been restructured to more adequately suit the needs of investors or issuers. *See also* collateralized mortgage obligation; participation certificate.

modular (1) The standardization of devices or major assemblies to permit the combining or intercoupling of two or more units of a computer. (2) The feature of being able to add more units to a computer.

module (1) A component that can be fitted as a unit into a larger unit or system. (2) A unit of measurement used for planning and standardizing. (3) A hardware or software package used to perform a specific function, such as a security module.

modulus ten check digit (MOD 10) The formula for calculating a check digit for an account number or any group of digits where a check digit is required. The term is derived from the fact that the result of the check digit calculation is subtracted from the next higher multiple of 10 to arrive at the final result, which is the check digit.

monetarism The body of theory related to the quantity theory of money. The basic precept of monetarism is that the quantity of and changes in the money supply have an important influence on a nation's economy. In its crudest form, monetarism contends that if the money supply (defined in one way or another) is increased at a fixed and stable rate, optimal behavior of the economy will result.

monetary aggregates Definitions of money. Because all measures of money are arbitrary, the Federal Reserve defines money in several ways (M1, M2, M3, L) and uses one or more of these definitions of monetary aggregates in conducting monetary policy.

monetary base Those assets that depository institutions can use to meet their legal reserve requirements. The monetary base consists of deposits (reserves) held by depository institutions at Federal Reserve banks plus Federal Reserve currency and U.S. Treasury currency and coins outstanding.

monetary instrument A term defined by the Bank Secrecy Act as currency or the equivalent, such as cashier's checks, traveler's checks, and so on. Transactions involving the deposit or withdrawal of these items in excess of $10,000 trigger the need for a currency transaction report.

monetary policy The management by a central bank of a nation's money supply to ensure the availability of credit in quantities and at interest rates consistent with specific economic objectives.

monetary transaction (1) Any transaction posted to an account that has a dollar value. (2) Any transaction involving money.

monetary unit sampling (MUS) The generic term for dollar unit sampling.

money (1) Legal tender; the coin and currency declared by a government as the accepted medium of exchange. (2) Anything that serves the function of money (that is, a medium of exchange, a standard of value, or a store of value). *See also* cheap money; fiat money.

money and securities insurance Insurance that protects against the loss of money and securities because of robbery.

money center A city with an active money market and financial community, such as New York, Chicago, or San Francisco.

money center bank A major bank located in a money center (a city that has a major money market capability), such as New York, Chicago, or San Francisco. Money center banks often serve as correspondents to regional respondent banks, offering such services as piggyback participation in a depository or master trust services.

money expansion multiplier Under a fractional reserve banking system such as the one in the United States, financial institutions can expand their deposit liabilities by more than the amount of any addition to their reserve base. The money expansion multiplier is the ratio by which deposits expand when the reserve base is increased (or by which they contract when the reserve base is decreased).

money factor The factor used to compute the payments on a consumer lease. This factor is used because a lease does not have interest, and the computation of an annual percentage rate is not necessary.

money illusion The tendency to ignore changes in the value of money through inflation or deflation. Thus during an inflationary period, people tend to continue to enter into and to price contracts as though money were as valuable as before the inflation. Over time, though, the money illusion disappears and the expected rate of inflation comes to be considered in the pricing of contracts.

money laundering The term given to the process in which money from illegal activities is transferred into legal investments or converted into other assets. *See also* laundered money.

Money Laundering Control Act of 1986 Legislation that established the federal crime of money laundering and other related crimes and provides for the punishment of those crimes.

money market The market in which short-term debt securities are bought and sold. As a loose network of parties willing to buy or sell financial securities and credit instruments, it is an unorganized market, located wherever investors trade. The instruments traded are short-term, typically 90 days or less, and involve high-quality credit. Participants in this market include banks and other financial institutions, the U.S. Treasury and other governments, the managers of money market funds, and numerous specialized dealers.

money market certificate (MMC) A certificate whose rate of interest is tied to rates on short-term Treasury securities. Banks issued these certificates during the phase-out of ceilings on interest rates.

money market deposit account (MMDA) A type of savings account created in late 1982 that is federally insured, provides easy access to the funds on deposit, and pays an interest rate competitive with money market funds.

money market fund A mutual fund that buys high-quality, short-term notes, acceptances, or certificates of deposit (usually 60 days or less) of many corporations or governments. The fund thereby diversifies to minimize default risk. The fund sells shares to investors, who receive regular payments of interest. The percentage of interest varies from period to period, based on the interest earned and the expenses paid by the fund during the period. An investor can sell his or her shares back to the fund at any time, usually receiving the exact amount of the original investment plus any accrued, unpaid interest to date. However, should the fund suffer a major loss, the shareholder has no guarantee that his or her investment will be fully repaid.

money market instruments Private and government obligations with a maturity of 1 year or less, including U.S. Treasury bills, bankers' acceptances, commercial paper, finance paper, short-term tax-exempts, CDs, and Eurodollar deposits.

money market loan A short-term loan to major commercial borrowers at a favorable rate.

money market rates (1) Interest rates on various money market instruments. The rates reflect general economic factors and the relative liquidity, security, size, and term of investment. (2) Loan rates set by reference to market rates, for example, LIBOR plus 1 percent or CD plus 1 percent.

money market securities Short-term, high-quality, and generally accepted senior securities whose market prices, expressed on a yield basis, relate more closely to the prevailing interest rate for money than to the risks in a company's operations or in general business conditions.

money multiplier The relationship between the monetary base and the money supply.

moneyness The extent to which an asset can be used as or substituted for money; the degree to which an asset meets the various arbitrary definitions of money.

money order An order issued by a post office, bank, or telegraph office for payment of a specified sum of money, usually at another office. Two types of money orders exist. The first type is a product marketed by firms under the strict security rules of a franchise agreement with various outlets. The second type is sold by individual institutions as a convenience to their customers. Both types are imprinted by checkwriting equipment that produces amounts that cannot be easily altered.

money rate of return *See* nominal return.

money stock *See* money supply.

money supply There are four basic measures of our nation's money supply: M1--the sum of currency, demand deposits, traveler's checks, and other checkable deposits; M2--M1 plus overnight repurchase agreements (RPs) and Eurodollars, money market mutual fund (MMMF) balances (general purpose and broker-dealer), money market deposit accounts, and savings and small time deposits; M3--M2 plus large time deposits, term RPs, term Eurodollars, and institution-only MMMF balances; L--M3 plus other liquid assets.

monopoly The exclusive control by one seller over a particular product or service, evidenced by an ability to control supply, dictate prices, or otherwise curb competition.

monopsony The exclusive control by one buyer over a product or service, evidenced by an ability to control demand, dictate prices, or otherwise curb competition.

Monte Carlo method The solution of a problem by trial and error using repeated calculations.

monthly payment loan A consumer or mortgage loan requiring a payment each month.

monthly service charge *See* service charge.

monthly statement An account summary mailed monthly to a customer (for example, a cardholder) reflecting pertinent items such as previous balance, new transactions, finance charges for the billing period, new balance, and minimum payment required.

Moody's Investors Service, Inc. A major investment advisory service. This service publishes financial manuals that analyze many thousands of corporations that sell securities to the public. It also continuously rates the investment quality of the debt instruments issued by these corporations and by governments. These bond ratings are announced regularly and greatly influence investors' decisions.

moral suasion Public or private actions of Federal Reserve bank officials (such as letters, telephone calls, press releases) designed to influence commercial banks and thereby achieve monetary control.

moratorium A legally authorized delay in the payment of a debt or some legal action.

Morris Plan bank A type of financial institution that was first established in

1910 by Arthur J. Morris to make small and medium-sized unsecured loans to consumers who could convince two others to cosign the loan with them. Because most banks at that time only made loans to businesses, Morris Plan banks were one of the earliest institutions that provided consumer credit.

mortality rate The number of people from a large group (usually 100,000) who, experience shows, will live to reach each age up to the death of the last survivor. By inference, the mortality rate establishes the life expectancy for the average person of each age.

mortality tables A statistical analysis of death rates, based on actuarial forecasts, that estimates the percentage of deaths that will occur at each age each year. Mortality tables are used to determine insurance premiums.

mortgage An instrument in which the borrower (the mortgagor) gives the lender (the mortgagee) a lien on property (commonly real property) as security for the payment of an obligation. The borrower continues to use the property and, when the obligation is fully extinguished, the lien is removed. If the subject matter of the lien is personal property other than securities (such as machinery, tools, or equipment), the mortgage is called a chattel mortgage. *See also* chattel mortgage; closed-end mortgage; commercial mortgage; conventional mortgage; development mortgage; direct reduction mortgage; equity participation mortgage; graduated payment mortgage; level payment mortgage; package mortgage; price level adjusted mortage; purchase-money mortgage; quick-pay mortgage; renegotiable rate mortgage; residential mortgage; reverse annuity mortgage; second mortgage; shared appreciation

mortgage; term mortgage; Veterans Administration mortgage; wraparound mortgage.

mortgage assumption An assignment of an existing mortgage in which the assignee personally assumes liability for the unpaid debt.

mortgage-backed bonds Bonds traded mainly in the United States that pay interest semiannually and repay principal either periodically or at maturity, and where the underlying collateral is a pool of mortgages. *See also* collateralized mortgage obligation; pay-through bond.

mortgage-backed certificate A certificate backed by a pool of mortgages.

mortgage-backed securities Securities representing an undivided interest in a pool of mortgages or trust deeds with similar characteristics. Payments on the underlying mortgages are used to make payments to the security holders. Mortgage-backed securities, such as those issued by the Federal National Mortgage Association, are secured by conventional mortgages and guaranteed as to interest and principal.

mortgage banker A firm or person that originates and generally sells mortgages to institutional or other investors. The mortgage banker then generally continues to collect payments on the mortgages for the mortgage holder.

mortgage banking (1) The packaging of mortgage loans secured by real property for sale to an investor, with servicing retained by the seller for the life of the loan in exchange for a fee. Servicing rights can also be sold with the loans or separately. (2) The origination, sale, and servicing of mortgage loans by a person or business.

mortgage banking company A company specializing in making, selling, and servicing real estate loans.

mortgage bond A bond backed by a first mortgage on some part of the issuer's real property.

mortgage broker A firm or person who brings a borrower and lender together for a commission. A mortgage broker does not service a mortgage.

mortgage company *See* mortgage banking company.

mortgage constant The ratio of annual payments to principal on a mortgage. A mortgage constant is the total interest and principal paid annually, expressed as a percentage of the original mortgage.

mortgage discount The difference between the principal of a mortgage and its selling price.

mortgagee The one to whom a mortgage is given; the lender.

mortgagee clause A special clause normally attached to a fire insurance policy covering mortgaged properties and giving the lender claim to payments due to property loss.

mortgage equity capitalization In income-producing property valuation, a method of capitalizing the net income remaining after mortgage payments, including the present worth of the property after sale and satisfaction of the mortgage.

mortgage insurance The insurance of a mortgage so that, if there is a default, the insurance company or other insurer will take all or part of the loss. Private mortgage insurance companies insure primarily the top portion (20 percent or 25 percent) of

the mortgage, while the Federal Housing Administration insures 100 percent of the mortgage.

mortgage insurance company (MIC) A private firm that insures a portion of the total mortgage debt in return for a fee. The purpose of mortgage insurance is to permit a low down payment on a conventional mortgage loan.

mortgage insurance premium (MIP) The amount paid by a mortgagor for mortgage insurance--either to the Federal Housing Administration or to a private mortgage insurance company (MIC).

mortgage kicker A benefit given to the lender beyond conventional interest payments as an incentive to grant a loan on income property. A mortgage kicker is typically an interest in equity or annual income.

mortgage loan A loan used to finance construction or purchase of single-family houses, condominiums, cooperatives, homes, and business properties. A mortgage loan is collateralized by real property, such as farms, private residences, commercial land, and buildings.

mortgage pattern (1) A method of rating risks on a mortgage according to the real estate security, borrower's credit, and terms of the mortgage. (2) The arrangement of payments and other terms established by a mortgage contract.

mortgage policy A policy that insures title in the borrower and the priority of the lender's lien.

mortgage portfolio (1) The total mortgage loans held by the original lender or an investor. (2) The mortgage loans serviced by a mortgage banker.

mortgage risk The risk of principal or anticipated loss of interest on a mortgage loan.

mortgagor The person who gives the mortgage; the borrower.

most-favored-lender doctrine Under the National Banking Act, the ability of national banks to charge the maximum rate of interest allowed to any other state lender located in the same state.

motivation research The marketing research that studies the reasons for consumer purchases.

multibank holding company Any company that (a) owns either directly or indirectly, controls, or otherwise has the power to vote at least 25 percent of the voting stock in each of two or more banks or other bank holding companies; (b) controls the election of a majority of directors in each of two or more banks; or (c) places 25 percent or more of the voting shares in each of two or more banks in trust for the benefit of its shareholders or member banks of the holding company.

multicurrency clause A clause that permits a borrower in the Eurobond market to make payments in a different currency from time to time or to borrow in a different currency on rollover at maturity.

multicurrency loan A loan involving several currencies.

multidrop connection A type of connection in which more than one terminal is connected to the same communications line.

multiemployer plan Under the Employee Retirement Income Security Act, a pension plan maintained pursuant to one or more collective bargaining agreements to which more than one employer is required to contribute.

multilocation merchant A merchant with stores at more than one location.

multinational corporation (MNC) A business that has production facilities or other fixed assets in at least one foreign country and makes its major management decisions in a global context.

multiple banking *See* full-service banking.

multiple capital structure company A company having more than one class of outstanding securities.

multiple-component facility A facility under which several different options for drawing funds are available to the borrower. These may include issuing notes, drawing on short-term or medium-term credits, or swinglines. *See also* note issuance facility (NIF); swingline.

multiple payee checking *See* automatic bill payment.

multiplier The ratio by which changes in investment spending, government spending, exports, or imports cause a chain reaction that results in greater changes in total national income. *See also* money multiplier.

multiprogramming A technique for simultaneously handling numerous routines or programs, interspersing them by means of an interweaving process.

multitasking *See* concurrent processing.

municipal bond A bond issued by a state or local government, its agencies or authorities, or a U.S. possession or territory. Such bonds are often called "tax-exempts," because interest paid on most of these issues is exempt from federal, state, and local income taxes. Municipal bonds are not registered with the Securities and Exchange Commission but must have a legal opinion printed on or attached to the certificate. The legal opinion, prepared by a qualified bond counsel, states that the municipality has a legal right to issue debt securities. The bond trustee authenticates each bond, receives funds to pay interest and repay principal, and safeguards the rights of the bondholders under the indenture. The commercial side of a bank may serve as underwriter and dealer for municipal bonds through its bond trading group.

municipal note A short-term, tax-exempt debt security issued by a state or local government. *See also* bond anticipation note; project note; revenue anticipation note; tax anticipation note.

municipals Securities issued by a municipality. *See also* municipal bond; municipal note.

Municipal Securities Rulemaking Board (MSRB) An independent, self-regulatory organization that sets the rules for investment bankers, brokers, and dealers active in the municipals market. Being governments, the issuers are not subject to MSRB regulations, but the MSRB and the Securities and Exchange Commission cooperate in various ways.

mutual fund A registered investment trust company. A mutual fund is an "open-end" investment company whose primary activity is investing, usually in a diversified portfolio of securities. The stockholder in a mutual fund buys shares from, or sells them back to, the mutual fund in a direct sale, not through a stock

exchange. "Open-end" means that the fund's capitalization increases whenever it sells new shares to the public and decreases when the shares are redeemed.

mutual fund group An investment company with more than one fund.

mutual investment fund *See* mutual fund.

mutual mortgage insurance fund One of four Federal Housing Administration (FHA) insurance funds into which all mortgage insurance premiums and other specified FHA revenues are paid and from which insured losses are met.

mutual savings bank A specialized savings institution that is owned by the depositors and managed for them by a self-perpetuating board of trustees. A mutual savings bank has no capital stock and therefore no stockholders. The profits, after deductions for necessary business expenses, accrue to the benefit of the depositors in dividends or reserved surplus for their greater security. *See also* savings bank.

mutual wills Wills made by two or more people (usually, but not necessarily, husband and wife), containing similar or identical provisions in favor of each other or the same beneficiary.

naive forecast A forecast made from projections of past trends. It is a technical term, not meant as a derogatory term.

naked option An option written by someone who does not own the covering securities.

naked position An unhedged position.

naked trust *See* passive trust.

named-schedule bond A fidelity bond that, by listing their names on an attached schedule, covers several employees of a firm.

name of receiver The descriptive name of an institution or party to receive reclaimed securities.

nanosecond One-billionth of a second. *Also called* millimicrosecond.

national association All national banks must use the word "national," the initials N.B.A. (national banking association), or N.A. (national association) in their title. *See also* national bank.

National Association of Bank Auditors and Comptrollers (NABAC) *See* Bank Administration Institute.

National Association of Securities Dealers Automated Quotation (NASDAQ) system An automated price quotation service for over-the-counter securities.

National Association of Securities Dealers, Inc. (NASD) The prime regulator of the market in securities not listed on an exchange. Members of NASD include securities dealers, brokers, and industry-affiliated organizations, most of whom are either members or affiliates of national exchanges. The NASD governs its members concerning trading policy and procedures, recordkeeping and reporting requirements, and customer relations.

national bank A commercial bank operating under a federal charter, supervised by the Office of the Comptroller of the Currency. The word

"national," or the initials N.B.A. (national banking association) or N.A. (national association) must appear in the bank's corporate title. A national bank must belong to the Federal Reserve System and to the Federal Deposit Insurance Corporation.

national bank examiner An employee of the Office of the Comptroller of the Currency whose function is to examine or audit banks periodically. The purpose of such an examination is to determine the strength of a bank's financial position and the security of its deposits and to verify that the bank maintains procedures that are consistent with federal laws and regulations.

national banking association *See* national association; national bank.

National Bank Surveillance System (NBSS) A computer system for collecting and monitoring data maintained by the Office of the Comptroller of the Currency and used to detect significant changes in the condition of a specific bank or the national banking system as a whole.

National Credit Union Administration (NCUA) The federal regulatory agency for federally chartered and federally insured credit unions. The NCUA administers the National Credit Union Share Insurance Fund.

national debt *See* federal debt.

National Flood Insurance Act A federal law establishing a program, administered by the Federal Insurance Administration, to provide flood insurance to homeowners whose houses are located in specially designated flood areas.

National Flood Insurance Program A national program offered to local communities to enable them to participate in a national flood insurance program.

National Institutional Delivery System (NIDS) A joint industry service to simplify the process of comparing and settling broker-to-institution trades. Trade recording and confirmations are centralized through NIDS, regardless of the regional depository to which the broker or institution belongs.

National Quotations Bureau (NQB) A bureau that maintains lists of national market makers in specific securities. To find an over-the-counter market maker, a trader may refer to the NQB pink (equity securities) or yellow (debt securities) sheets.

natural guardian The parent of a minor; originally the father, but now either the father or the mother. Natural guardianship relates only to the person of a minor.

nearby contract A futures contract that is nearing maturity.

nearbys The nearest active trading month of a financial futures market.

near money Noncash assets that can be rapidly converted into cash and therefore can substitute for money in some respects. Near money generally designates very short-term U.S. securities and various kinds of savings accounts.

negative amortization An increase in the unpaid balance of a loan, which occurs when unpaid interest is added to the loan principal. For example, in the initial years of a graduated payment mortgage, the borrower pays an interest rate below the coupon rate of interest and pays no amortization. The difference between the coupon rate of interest and the interest paid is added to the loan balance, which has not declined because no amortization has been paid. Consequently, the borrower has a larger loan at the end of the period than at the beginning.

negative authorization An authorization system in which canceled, revoked, or suspended accounts on which there will be no authorizations are filed or otherwise loaded into a system.

negative authorization list A list of accounts requiring exception authorization handling, that is, accounts on which routine authorization will not be made.

negative carry (1) A situation that exists when the income from an asset is less than the cost of the funds that were borrowed to hold the asset. (2) The cost incurred in excess of income when borrowing to finance the holding of securities.

negative confirmation The auditing system by which a bank statement or letter is sent to a customer. The customer replies only if he or she does not agree with the balance or other facts in the statement or letter. *Compare with* positive confirmation.

negative factor or value Under the Equal Credit Opportunity Act, a factor, value, or weight that is less favorable to a group of applicants than the creditor's experience warrants or that is less favorable than the factor, value, or weight assigned to a class of applicants that is not similarly classified.

negative file (1) A record containing all accounts on which charge privileges have been revoked. (2) A list of card identifiers corresponding to cards for which transactions may not be authorized.

negative gap A maturity mismatch in which interest-sensitive liabilities exceed interest-sensitive assets.

negative pledge clause (1) A covenant in an indenture stating that the corporation will not pledge any of its assets unless the notes or debentures outstanding under the particular indenture are at least equally secured by such a pledge. (2) A clause in a loan agreement in which an individual borrower agrees not to further pledge his or her assets. *Also called* covenant of equal coverage.

negotiability The extent to which a financial instrument can be transferred by endorsement.

negotiable Transferable by endorsement. Title to a negotiable instrument can be transferred by delivery, without the need for further certification. Negotiable instruments must be safeguarded as if they were cash. Bearer securities are automatically negotiable by nature, whereas registered securities can be rendered negotiable only by completing a power of assignment.

negotiable certificate of deposit (CD) A transferable receipt issued by a commercial bank in return for a customer's deposit of funds. The bank agrees to pay the amount deposited plus interest to the bearer on a specified future date. Negotiable CDs are typically issued in large denominations.

negotiable instrument A written instrument (such as a check, promissory note, draft, or bill of exchange) payable to order or to the bearer. A negotiable instrument is transferred by endorsement and delivery or by delivery alone. It must meet all the requirements of Uniform Commercial Code (UCC) Article 3.

negotiable order of withdrawal (NOW) account An account that provides the payable-on-demand feature of a checking account and that also pays interest. It is a plan for transferring funds in which a savings account withdrawal ticket becomes a negotiable instrument that closely resembles a check, to effect a transfer to a third party (other than the drawer and drawee). In effect, a NOW account is an interest-bearing checking account.

negotiated plan A pension, profit-sharing, or other employee-benefit plan for which a group of employees has bargained with an employer, usually through a union as the bargaining agent.

negotiation (1) Dealings between parties with the goal of reaching agreement as to the amount, price, quantity, quality, or other terms under discussion. (2) The transfer of negotiable instruments.

negotiation credit A draft drawn under a letter of credit that is freely negotiable at any bank, including the issuing bank. These drafts can be in foreign exchange or U.S. dollars.

net The amount that remains after certain deductions are made.

net asset value (NAV) (1) The market value of all securities plus other assets, minus liabilities, divided by the number of shares outstanding. Net asset value is used to compute the price of a share in an open-end investment company (a mutual fund). (2) In mutual fund listings, the current value of the fund's holdings. It is the basis for the amount received when an investment is redeemed. This amount also serves as a bid price.

net capital inflow (outflow) The net movement of capital investment funds into (or out of) a country.

net change (1) The difference between an account or value at two different times. (2) The difference between the last closing price reported for one trading day and that reported for the preceding trading day.

net charge-off The gross amount charged to the allowance (reserve) for possible credit losses, less recoveries received, during a specified period.

net debt Gross debt of an entity minus sinking-fund accumulations and all self-supporting debt.

net earnings *See* net income.

net estate All of a person's property after deducting debts, taxes, and other expenses or liabilities. *Compare with* gross estate.

net income The excess of total revenues over total expenses.

net interest cost The average rate of interest over the life of a bond that an issuer must pay to borrow funds.

net interest margin The difference between interest income, adjusted to a tax-equivalent basis, and interest expense.

net investment For direct financing leases, the difference between gross investment and unearned income.

net operating income (NOI) The amount remaining after deducting operating expenses from operating income earned. It generally refers to net income before deducting interest expense and income taxes.

net position The value representing the amount due to or from a financial institution for transactions exchanged and processed during the day.

net present value (NPV) The present value of an asset's net expected future cash flows, discounted at the marginal cost of capital to the firm, minus the cost of the investment.

net profit (or loss) *See* net income.

net profit margin Net income after taxes divided by total sales.

net rentable area Usually applied to apartments or office buildings, the net square footage of a building rentable to tenants, excluding stairwells, elevator space, maintenance areas, halls, and other public areas.

net sale (1) The sum received from the sale of a security, less commissions, fees, taxes, and allowances for the individual transactions. (2) Gross sales receipts less shortages, allowances for prompt payment, returns, discounts, warranty costs, and uncollectible accounts.

net settlement (1) The batch settlement processing of several customers' trades simultaneously by calculating a balance of purchases and sales and arriving at one lump sum of cash or quantity of securities either due to or from the customer. (2) The net settlement of CHIPS in which the day's payments among CHIPS participants are netted and settled in a process that culminates with settlement transfers over the Fedwire.

network In teleprocessing, a number of communication lines connecting a computer with remote terminals. A network can also involve two or more interconnected computers.

net worth Assets minus liabilities of a business. This is the owners' equity. *Also called* shareholders' equity.

net worth certificates An accounting entry on a savings institution's financial statement that the regulatory authorities allow the institution to include as part of net worth. The regulatory authorities have used net worth certificates to keep savings institutions solvent.

net writers Options market makers and traders who have written or sold more options than they have purchased.

net yield That part of gross yield, including discount points, that remains after deducting all costs.

new balance The balance owed after payments and credits are deducted from the previous balance and new purchases, cash advances, other debits, and finance charges are added.

new issue The initial offering of a security for sale to the public.

new money The additional amount of money produced by a new issue in excess of the amount necessary to redeem maturing or refunded issues.

New York Clearing House Association (NYCHA) The clearing association for New York City banks.

New York Futures Exchange (NYFE) A subsidiary of the New York Stock Exchange (NYSE) used for trading in futures on individual stocks. The exchange also trades stock index futures and options contracts based on the NYSE composite index.

New York Stock Exchange (NYSE) The largest and oldest stock exchange in the United States. Only listed securities are traded on the NYSE.

New York Stock Exchange (NYSE) averages A very broad indicator of general market prices, consisting of stocks listed on the NYSE.

New York Stock Exchange (NYSE) composite index A weighted average of the prices for all NYSE common stocks, indicating trends or conditions in the stock market.

New York Stock Exchange (NYSE) composite transactions A listing of the activity for the New York, Midwestern, Pacific, Philadelphia, Boston, and Cincinnati stock exchanges.

New York Stock Exchange (NYSE) volume The total number of shares traded (in a period, generally a single day) on the NYSE.

next day funds Funds immediately available for another transaction the next business day and, subject to settlement, available the next business day for same day funds transfers or withdrawals in cash. *Also called* clearing house funds.

next-day settlement Payment for a securities trade that is made in the depository environment on the day following trade date. Not all securities are eligible for next-day settlement. Instead, they must be settled the regular way on the fifth day following trade date.

next friend Although not regularly appointed a guardian, one who acts for the benefit of any person who for some legal reason cannot appear for himor herself.

next of kin The person or people in the nearest degree of blood relationship to the decedent. Next of kin usually refers to people who are entitled by law to the property of someone who has died without leaving a valid will. Next of kin does not include the surviving spouse, however, except where specifically provided by statute. *Distinguish from* heir.

N.G. An expression used to designate a check as "not good" because of insufficient funds.

niche strategy A marketing strategy of packaging financial services to capture the business of a specific group or segment of bank customers.

NIF *See* note issuance facility.

night depository A service offered to merchants wishing to deposit receipts after regular banking hours. A merchant can drop a pouch of money into an opening outside the bank, down a chute to the night depository vault.

ninety-day savings account An account paying interest usually equal to that paid on 90-day deposits in savings certificates. The account is a passbook account and subject to substantial interest penalties if funds are withdrawn before the end of the 90-day period. If funds remain on deposit after 90 days, the pledge is automatically renewed for an additional period.

NINOW The traditional demand deposit account; a noninterest-bearing NOW account.

no-book transaction A transaction that is processed but not entered into a customer's passbook, for which a temporary receipt is issued.

no-load fund A mutual fund with no sales charge for executing transactions. The offer price for a no-load fund is the same as the figure for net asset value (the price at which the fund will buy back its shares).

nominal interest rate (1) An interest rate actually paid without any adjustment for inflation. Nominal interest

rates include a real rate of interest plus an inflation premium equal to the expected rate of inflation. (2) A stated rate of interest. *Compare with* effective interest rate; real rate of interest.

nominal price A price quotation on futures for a period in which no actual trading occurred.

nominal return The monetary rate of return on an investment, unadjusted for any change in the level of price (inflation). *Compare with* the real return, which is adjusted for inflation.

nominal yield *See* nominal return.

nomination The naming or proposing of a person for an office, position, or duty, distinguished from appointment. Thus the testator nominates but the court appoints the executor under a will.

nominee (1) A person named for an office, position, or duty. (2) In trust business, usually the person, firm, or corporation in whose name registered securities are held.

nonaccrual asset An asset, usually a loan, on which the accrual of interest has been discontinued. Loans, other than consumer loans, are placed in nonaccrual status if reasonable doubt exists as to timely collectibility or if payment of principal and interest is contractually past due 90 days or more and the loan is not well secured and in the process of collection. Consumer loans will not usually be placed in a nonaccrual status until they are 120 days past due or are assigned to a legal collection status. Interest income on nonaccrual loans is recognized only in the period realized. Loans are returned to accrual status when the collectibility of both principal and interest on a timely basis is reasonably assured and all delinquent principal and interest are brought current or the loan becomes well secured and in the process of collection.

nonbank bank A financial institution owned by a nonbanking company (for example, a retailing firm, insurance company, or brokerage firm) that avoids being defined as a bank holding company for regulatory purposes by limiting the activity of its bank to only one of the two functions that define a commercial bank (that is, it both accepts demand deposits and makes commercial loans). Such banks can take deposits and extend credit to consumers and thus compete with commercial banks while their parent companies engage in activities forbidden to bank holding companies (such as underwriting corporate securities, underwriting insurance, offering mutual funds, and so on). *Also called* limited-service bank.

nonborrowed base The monetary base minus discount window borrowings by depository institutions.

nonborrowed reserve path In conducting monetary policy, the Federal Reserve uses discount window borrowings as an operating target (that is, it tries to hold discount window borrowings at a predetermined level on a daily or weekly basis). To hold borrowings at that level, the Federal Reserve supplies more or fewer nonborrowed reserves. As a guide, it first estimates how much change will be needed in the level of nonborrowed reserves; that estimated change becomes the nonborrowed reserve path. *See also* discount window.

nonborrowed reserves Total reserves of depository institutions minus borrowings from Federal Reserve banks.

noncallable bond A bond that, under the terms of the issue, cannot be called by the obligor (the corporation) for redemption or conversion.

noncash item Any instrument that a bank declines to accept as a cash item and therefore handles as a collection item. The bank will not credit the customer's account until settlement for the item occurs.

noncash transaction Under generally accepted accounting principles (GAAP), for purposes of preparing a statement of cash flow, a noncash transaction results in no cash inflow (outflow) in the period in which it occurs (for example, conversion of debt to equity).

non compos mentis Meaning literally "not of sound mind." This term includes all forms of mental unsoundness.

noncontributory pension plan A plan entirely funded by the employer. No contributions by the employee are permitted.

nondiscretionary account *See* directed trust account.

nondiscretionary investment agency A relationship in which the trust department serves as agent (does not take title to trust assets) and the principal retains control of decisions on investments. The agent recommends investments and provides a review of the results.

nonearning asset An asset that does not produce income, such as vault cash, required reserves, or a nonaccrual loan. *Compare with* earning assets.

nonexempt employee Under the Fair Labor Standards Act, an employee who must receive additional compensation for overtime hours worked.

nonfiling insurance Insurance purchased by a lender to protect against any loss that might result if the lender did not properly file or record a lien on the collateral.

noninterest income Income a bank derives from sources other than interest (for example, fees and service charges, trading income, investment securities gains, and other income).

nonlegal investment An investment that does not conform to the requirements of certain statutes. This term refers principally to trust investments. *Distinguish from* unauthorized investment.

nonlegals Securities that do not conform to the statutory requirements of some states concerning investments for savings banks and trust funds. *See also* legal list.

nonmember bank A state-chartered bank that is not a member of the Federal Reserve System.

nonmonetary transaction Any transaction posted to an account that does not have a dollar value affecting the account balance. Nonmonetary transactions include changes to cardholder master file records, such as name changes, address changes, and changes of credit limit.

nonnotification plan An indirect lending arrangement in which a dealer does not inform a customer that his or her installment sales contract has been sold to a bank. The customer continues to make payments to the dealer.

non-par The description of a check that will not be paid at face value.

Charges payable to the bank on which it is drawn will be deducted.

non-par bank An institution that is not a member of the Federal Reserve System and deducts an exchange or settlement charge from the face amount of checks drawn on it.

non-par check A check that cannot be collected at its face value when presented by another bank. Non-par banks deduct an exchange charge from the face of checks.

non-par item *See* non-par check.

nonperforming asset An asset, such as a loan, that is not currently accruing interest or on which interest is not being paid. *See also* nonaccrual asset.

nonperforming loan A loan that is not currently accruing interest or on which interest is not being paid.

nonrate gap The ratio of noninterest-bearing liabilities plus shareholders' equity less nonearning assets to earning assets.

nonrecourse agreement A type of retail dealer financing in which a dealer has no liability for the paper sold to a bank in case of default, except for the warranty, the genuineness of the paper, the terms of the sale, and the title.

nonrecourse paper An instrument in which the assignor or endorser assumes no liability for payment of the primary obligation. An example would be a conditional sales contract endorsed by a dealer to a finance company specifying that the dealer has no liability for payments not met by the original debtor.

nonrecurring charges or income Those expenses or receipts charged against or credited to a company's income statement that are extraordinary and not likely to recur.

nonrevolving line of credit A specified maximum line of credit on which a borrower may draw for a limited period. In contrast to a revolving line of credit, a nonrevolving line may be drawn on only once. *Compare with* revolving line of credit.

nonsampling error An error in the sample due to factors other than sampling fluctuations.

nonskip person For generation-skipping tax purposes, any person or trust that is not a skip person. For example, the child of a transferor is a nonskip person.

nonsufficient funds An expression indicating that a check or item drawn against an account exceeds the amount of collected funds in the account. *See also* insufficient funds; NSF.

no par value A security to which the issuer has not assigned a specific dollar value.

no-par-value capital stock Capital stock that has no par or nominal value but may have a legal or stated value.

no passbook savings A savings account for which no passbook is maintained but for which a periodic statement is sent to the depositor.

no protest A designation made by a bank to instruct another collecting bank not to protest a specific item if nonpayment occurs.

normal distribution A bellshaped curve depicting a symmetric probability distribution of a continuous random variable. The distribution is defined by the mean and standard deviation, such that approximately two-thirds of all observations will fall within one standard deviation above and below the mean, about 95 percent will fall within two standard deviations above and below the mean, and so on. *Also called* normal probability distribution.

normal yield curve The yield curve that is generally expected. At present, the term is usually applied to a rising yield curve (with higher interest rates on longer maturities) because in recent decades a rising yield curve has been more common than a declining yield curve. In earlier decades, however, a declining yield curve was more common and, therefore, considered normal.

normative economics Economic arguments and statements that are not based on statistics or facts, but involve value judgments and opinions.

nostro account A term meaning "our account with you" that designates an account maintained by a bank with a foreign correspondent. *See also* due from account. *Compare with* vostro account.

notarial acknowledgment (1) The acknowledgment of the due execution of a legal instrument before a notary public. (2) The statement of a notary public as to the fact and date of the acknowledgment, with the notary public's signature, seal of office, and date of expiration of commission to serve as notary public.

notarial certificate The certificate of a notary public as to the due acknowledgment of an instrument.

notarization (1) Authentication of documents and signatures by a notary public. (2) A method of applying additional security to a key using the identities of the originator and the ultimate recipient.

notary public A public officer who takes acknowledgment of or otherwise attests or certifies deeds and other writings or copies of them, usually under his or her official seal, to make them authentic. A notary public also takes affidavits, depositions, and protests of negotiable instruments.

notation In systems, the act, process, or method of representing facts or quantities by a set of marks, signs, figures, or characters.

note (1) A written promise to pay a specified amount, either on demand or at a future date. (2) Currency. (3) A medium-term (1- to 5- or 10-year maturity) security. *See also* bank note; Federal Reserve note; Federal Reserve bank note; promissory note; United States note.

note issuance facility (NIF) A medium-term arrangement enabling borrowers to issue short-term paper, typically of 3 or 6 months maturity, in their own names. Usually a group of underwriting banks guarantees the availability of funds to the borrower by purchasing any unsold notes at each rollover date, or by providing a standby credit. Facilities produced by competing banks are called, variously, revolving underwriting facilities (RUFs), note purchase facilities, and Euro-note facilities.

note notice A form containing the details of a note that a bank's loan department sends as a reminder to the maker of the note several days before it becomes due.

note option An option to retain for a while any funds received for the U.S. Treasury in a bank's tax and loan account. If a bank chooses the "note option," it must pay interest to the Treasury. *Compare with* remittance option.

note payable An amount owed by a business to a bank or other lender in the form of a short-term loan. A note payable entails a written promissory note given by the borrower to the lender.

note receivable The amount owed to a business on a promissory note from a customer or other debtor.

notice day A day on which notices of intent to deliver, pertaining to a specified delivery month, may be issued.

notice of dishonor An oral or written notification to those liable for payment of a negotiable instrument stating that it was not paid when presented at the proper time.

notice of guaranteed delivery An alternative form sent to an investor with the letter of transmittal announcing a tender offer. If the investor decides to tender his or her shares but cannot arrange physical delivery of the certificates during the short time allowed by the offer, the investor may still accept the offer and execute the notice guaranteeing delivery.

notice of protest A declaration made and witnessed by a notary public stating that a check, bill of exchange, or note has been presented and payment refused.

notice to creditors A written notice posted in public places or newspapers asking creditors of an estate to present their claims for what the executor or administrator owes them. A notice to creditors is usually also a notice to debtors to pay what they owe the estate.

notification plan The act of pledging accounts receivable as loan security and notifying the customers maintaining the accounts receivable of such action. The payments on the account are then usually sent directly to the party making the loan.

notional principal A hypothetical amount on which swap payments are based. The notional principal in an interest rate swap is never paid or received. It is essentially a reference amount for purposes of computing interest flows. Notional principal is also used in caps, floors, and FRAs.

novation Substitution of a new debt for an old debt in accordance with an agreement between the borrower and lender.

NOW account *See* negotiable order of withdrawal (NOW) account.

NSF Not sufficient funds. *See also* insufficient funds; nonsufficient funds; N.G.

nuncupative will An oral will made by a person on his or her deathbed or by one who is conscious of the possibility of meeting death in the near future, such as by a person in active military service. It is declared in the presence of at least two witnesses and later reduced to writing by someone other than the testator and offered for probate in the manner prescribed by statute.

NYCHA *See* New York Clearing House Association.

objective indicators A group of statistical indicators intended to forecast changes in exchange rates.

obligation (1) The responsibility to perform some act or pay a sum of money when due. (2) Any kind of indebtedness.

obligee One to whom an obligation is owed, for example, a bondholder.

obligor One who has an obligation to discharge, for example, a corporation that issues bonds.

observation The techniques by which the auditor gathers audit evidence through what he or she sees or observes.

occupancy expense Expense relating to the use of property. Occupancy expenses include rent, heat, and upkeep.

odd-days interest Interest earned in closed-end credit transactions, which accrues with respect to days that are not part of a regular payment schedule. "Odd days" generally arise in connection with dealer paper (retail installment sales contracts assigned to the bank) when the period before the first payment is either longer or shorter than the intervals between the remainder of the payments.

odd lot Less than a round lot--generally, any number of shares of stock less than 100. *See also* round lot.

odd-lot dealer In securities trading, a member of the exchange who stands ready to buy or sell odd lots (a trading unit smaller than the normal round-lot transaction). Brokers who wish to buy or sell an odd lot for a customer must execute the order with an odd-lot dealer.

OECD *See* Organization for Economic Cooperation and Development.

off-balance-sheet activities Banks' business, often fee-based, that does not generally involve booking assets and taking deposits. Examples are trading of swaps, options, foreign exchange forwards, standby commitments, and letters of credit.

off-balance-sheet financing Credit obligations such as loan commitments and standby letters of credit that arise in the normal course of banking business but are not reflected in the bank's statement of condition.

offer (1) A statement of willingness to buy at a stated price. (2) The price at which a person is willing to sell a security.

offering circular A circular offering tax-exempt municipals. Municipal governments do not have to issue a prospectus, as do corporations.

offering price (1) The price at which a new security is first offered to the public. (2) In mutual fund listings, the asking price.

off-host An operating mode in which the terminals do not have access to a positive file at a card-issuing bank. On-line/off-host implies connection to negative files stored in the front-end processor of the card-issuing bank. *Compare with* on-host.

Office of the Comptroller of the Currency (OCC) The office within the U.S. Treasury Department that has responsibility for the overall supervision and examination of national banks.

Office of Thrift Supervision (OTS) A new arm of the Department of the Treasury created under the Financial Institutions Reform, Recovery and Enforcement Act of 1989 to regulate federally chartered savings and loan associations.

official check A term sometimes used for a cashier's check. *See also* cashier's check.

off-line equipment Peripheral equipment that does not communicate directly with the central processing unit of a computer.

off-line processing The advent of personal computers (PCs) in banking enables users to use the intelligence of the PC to do off-line processing on the PC before or after connecting to a mainframe computer for on-line processing. An example is preparing a number of funds transfer payment orders off-line on the PC, then transmitting the payment orders to a mainframe computer at a bank for further processing.

offset (1) Either of two equal entries on both sides of an account. *See also* evening up; liquidation. (2) The bank's legal right to seize any funds that a guarantor or debtor may have on deposit, to cover a loan in default. (3) The number, stored on a bank card, that is subtracted from the keyed-in personal identification number to obtain the true personal identification number.

offshore banking unit A banking unit that conducts business in other countries but is not allowed to do business in the country where it is located.

off-the-run issue A security issue of governments or agencies that is not routinely quoted by brokers and dealers.

of record As shown by the record. This term is usually used in such entries as "attorney of record," showing that the one named is the recognized representative of the party at interest.

oil drafts Sales drafts used by oil companies.

old and new balance proof A method used to verify the correct pickup of old balances and to establish the net amount of increase or decrease to ledger controls.

oligopoly An industry having few sellers. Because each seller must consider the actions of other sellers before determining price and output, oligopolies tend to restrict competition and set higher prices.

omnibus accounting A method of accounting used in broker-to-broker transactions in which individual accounts are not separately identified. In contrast, banks must identify subaccounts (individual customers) during all phases of processing securities.

Omnibus Drug Initiative Act of 1988 A federal law that modifies the reporting and recordkeeping procedures of financial institutions. Amendments relate specifically to verification of identification in customer check purchases of $3,000 or more; cash transactions of less than $10,000 in specific geographic areas; customer records when customers are in violation of the law; and offshore deposits of $110,000 or more.

on account On credit. On account describes a sale or purchase for which payment occurs after the merchandise is received.

one-bank holding company A company that owns 25 percent or more of the voting stock of one commercial bank. *See also* Bank Holding Company Act.

one-man picture A bid and ask quotation from only one dealer.

one-way (one-sided) market A market in which firm quotes are available on only one side, either bid or asked.

on-host An operating mode in which the terminals have access to a positive file at a card-issuing bank. On-line/on-host implies connection to positive files stored in the bank's files. *Compare with* off-host.

on-line data reduction The processing of data as received by a computing system or generated by a source.

on-line equipment Peripheral equipment that communicates directly with the central processing unit of a computer.

on-line operations The performance of functions that are a part of the main processing operation.

on-line processing (1) The operation of terminals, files, and other auxiliary equipment under direct and absolute control of the central processor, to eliminate human intervention at any stage between initial input and final output. (2) An operation performed by auxiliary computer equipment while connected to the computer, such as magnetic tape feeding data directly to the central processing unit.

on-line storage Storage controlled by the central processing unit.

on margin On credit. The purchaser deposits with a broker a percentage of the total value of securities bought and borrows the remaining funds needed from the broker. Federal Reserve Regulations G, T, and U determine minimum margin requirements.

on-the-spot loan The extension of funds on a preapproved credit line or credit card.

on-us check A check deposited or otherwise negotiated at the bank on which it is drawn. *Also called* house check.

open book As used in Euromarkets, a negative gap. *Also called* unmatched book *or* short book. *See also* negative gap.

open-book account A retail charge account that is a seller's accounting record of unsecured sales of merchandise.

open cargo insurance Insurance that protects against loss of cargo during shipment.

open contract A contract bought or sold without the transaction being completed by subsequent sale or purchase or by making or taking actual delivery of the financial instrument.

open-end credit The extension of credit, through bank credit cards or personal lines of credit, that allows customers to continue to add purchases or cash advances to their credit accounts. *Compare with* closed-end credit.

open-ended Open to change.

open-end fund A mutual fund that sells new shares to all new investors and redeems shares at the market price when investors wish to sell. Thus the assets of the fund increase and decrease as investors move money into and out of the fund. *Compare with* closed-end fund.

open-end investment company *See* mutal fund.

open-end investment trust An investment trust in which the trustee, by the terms of the trust, is authorized to invest in shares of stock other than those in the trust at the time of the inception of the trust or of the participation in the trust.

open-end mortgage A corporate trust indenture under which bonds, in addition to the original issue, may be authenticated and delivered by the trustee from time to time. *Compare with* closed mortgage.

open-end mortgage bonds Bonds issued under an indenture that allows additional bonds to be issued in the future under the same indenture.

opening price (or range) The price (or range) recorded at the time designated as the official opening by the exchange.

open interest The total number of open contracts (unliquidated purchases and sales) in an options or futures market. Publication of this figure helps investors evaluate market pressures.

open-market operations The purchase and sale of U.S. obligations, municipal obligations, other money market instruments, and foreign exchange by the Federal Reserve. These operations influence the growth of the nation's money supply and are the principal means by which monetary policy is implemented.

open mortgage loan A past-due mortgage loan that a mortgagee holds, without requiring refinancing or an extension agreement.

open order An order placed to buy or sell a stock or other security at a fixed price.

open-rate method A method for a dealer's sale of commercial paper. The issuer receives a down payment from the dealer when the "paper" is delivered to the dealer, and the balance when the notes are sold.

open repo A repurchase agreement that is automatically renewed until one of the parties terminates it.

open-to-buy *See* available credit.

operand That which is operated upon.

operating capital The funds available for financing the day-to-day activities of a business.

operating company *See* parent company.

operating expense (1) Annual expenses of an income property before allowances for income-tax, depreciation, and mortgage payments. (2) An expense incurred as a result of a firm's normal operations. *See also* direct expense.

operating income (loss) *See* net operating income; operating profit.

operating instruments *See* operational targets.

operating lease (1) A lease that is not a direct financing lease or sales-type lease. (2) A lease that the lessee can cancel. The lease may or may not be for the useful life of the asset being leased. *Compare with* financial lease.

operating leverage The relative significance of fixed costs in a firm's operations.

operating losses The losses incurred as a result of a firm's normal operations.

operating profit Earnings from a firm's normal business operations. This figure generally excludes revenue from loan interest, investments, and so on, except where these activities are part of the firm's regular business operations. *Also called* operating income.

operating ratio (1) The ratio of operating expense to operating profit. (2) Any balance sheet or earnings ratio computed by averaging ratios of individual banks.

operating risk Potential losses that are derived from the normal operations of the bank.

operating statement *See* income statement.

operating system Software that controls the execution of computer programs and may provide scheduling, debugging, input and output control, accounting, compilation, storage assignment, and data management.

operational auditing A method of auditing whose objective is to ensure that specific operational functions are performed both effectively and efficiently.

operational targets The immediate focus of Federal Reserve monetary policy. Operational targets are generally bank reserves or the federal funds rate. The Fed tries to affect its operational targets in order to accomplish its ultimate objective of creating monetary conditions conducive to a smoothly functioning, noninflationary economy. *See also* monetary policy.

operations Those functions that handle the physical needs of a bank and its customers. Examples include funds transfer, recordkeeping, and building maintenance.

operations analysis *See* operations research.

operations management The managers and management of the operations functions in a bank. *See also* operations.

operations manager (1) The person responsible for an operations function in a bank. (2) The person responsible for the operational phases of a bank card plan, including accounting, sales draft auditing, and statement preparation.

operations research (OR) The use of mathematical methods of analysis to solve operational problems within an organization. The objective of this research is to provide management with a more logical basis for making sound predictions and decisions.

opinion survey A type of research that involves determining the personal evaluations, attitudes, or preferences of a selected group of interviewed subjects.

opportunity cost The benefits that were forgone by choosing one alternative over another.

optical character recognition (OCR) The electronic reading of numeric or alphabetical characters from printed documents. *Also called* optical scanning.

optical scanning *See* optical character recognition (OCR).

optimum output The production level that results in the lowest marginal and average unit cost.

option The right to buy or sell a security or commodity at a specified price during a specified period. The holder of an option has the right, but not the

obligation, to buy (call option) or sell (put option) a security or commodity at a specified price during a specified period. The writer of an option is obligated to sell (call option) or purchase (put option) the instrument only if the holder chooses to exercise the option. *See also* foreign exchange option.

optional payment bond A bond that gives the holder the choice of receiving payment of interest, principal, or both in the currency of one or more foreign countries, as well as in domestic funds.

options book The aggregation of all written and purchased options held by a market participant.

Options Clearing Corporation (OCC) The corporation that provides clearing facilities for all option trades on U.S. securities exchanges. Its Intermarket Clearing Corporation assures clearing operations at the New York Futures Exchange.

option to purchase The right to purchase real property within a specified time, on stated terms, in return for a certain price.

ordering bank *See* instructing bank.

ordering party *See* instructing party; originator.

orderly market (1) A market in which heavy buy or sell orders can be executed without large price changes. (2) A market in which the specialist for the security equalizes any imbalance of orders (that is, more purchases than sales or more sales than purchases).

order of distribution An order by a probate or other court having jurisdiction over an estate, directing the distribution of estate property to those entitled to receive it.

ordinary court *See* probate court.

ordinary income The income received from a person's or firm's normal business activities. Ordinary income is distinguished from capital gains for the purpose of taxation.

ordinary life insurance Insurance in which the insured party pays an annual premium during life. The insurer then pays the total amount due the beneficiary on the insured party's death.

OREO *See* other real estate owned.

Organization for Economic Cooperation and Development. (OECD) An organization whose members include Australia, Austria, Belgium, Canada, Denmark, Finland, France, West Germany, Greece, Iceland, Ireland, Italy, Japan, Luxembourg, the Netherlands, New Zealand, Norway, Portugal, Spain, Sweden, Switzerland, Turkey, the United Kingdom, and the United States. Yugoslavia takes part in certain work of the OECD and is included in certain statistics relating to OECD countries.

organization manual A written statement that defines the responsibilities and functions of the people, divisions, and departments of an organization, specifying the formal relationships between them.

organization tax A duty levied on a corporation at the time it secures a state charter.

organized market A market having a tangible, fixed location, for example, a stock or futures exchange. *Compare with* informal market.

original asset (1) Stocks, bonds, or other property placed in a trust at the time of its creation. (2) An estate at the time of appointment of the executor or administrator.

original investment (1) The initial amount paid for a security or other asset. (2) A trust investment received (a) by the trustee of a testamentary trust as part of the decedent's estate, or (b) by the trustee of an inter vivos trust from the settlor.

original issue discount An amount of imputed interest that must be recognized and reported on an accrual basis for federal income tax purposes with respect to sales of property in which payments of principal are deferred and the parties have failed to provide for adequate interest and/or payments of interest at regular intervals.

original issue discount (OID) bond A bond issued without coupons and sold at initial offering at a discount from face value.

original margin The margin needed to cover a specific new position in futures contracts.

original maturity The term to maturity at the time of a security's issuance.

originate To make or create, as to originate a loan.

originating bank A bank that receives paperless entries from businesses participating in an automated clearing house (ACH) system and that forwards those entries to the ACH.

origination fee (1) The amount charged for services performed by a company handling the initial application and processing of a loan. (2) The fee charged for preparation and submission of a proposed mortgage loan. (3) *See* cash advance fee.

originator The initiator of instructions to transfer funds to a beneficiary to satisfy an obligation. Other parties to the transfer are involved in moving the funds from the originator's bank account to the beneficiary's bank account.

originator identifier A data element (code) in funds transfers that uniquely identifies the originator. It may include specification of the type of identifier code that is being supplied.

originator's bank The bank acting for the originator of a funds transfer.

originator's reference The originator's transaction reference that identifies the original transaction in a transfer.

originator-to-beneficiary information A data element in funds transfers that involves information to be conveyed from the originator to the beneficiary. *Also called* details of payment.

orphan's court *See* probate court.

orphan's exclusion A deduction from the gross estate for amounts that pass to a child of the decedent, if the child is under 21 years of age at the decedent's death and there is no surviving spouse of the decedent and no known surviving parent of the child.

OTC market *See* over-the-counter market.

other real estate (ORE) *See* other real estate owned.

other real estate owned (OREO) The real estate acquired by a bank through foreclosure of a mortgage, through a deed issued in lieu of fore-closure, or in settlement of any other obligation to the bank. *Also called* other real estate (ORE) *and* owned real estate. *Sometimes called* real estate owned (REO).

our account (1) A "due from" account, a nostro account (our account with you). (2) When used in funds transfer messages, "our account" refers to the account that is "due to" the sending bank.

outgoing interchange Transactions deposited with a merchant (acquiring) bank and sent to a cardholder (issuing) bank.

out-of-area card *See* foreign card.

out-of-plan card A bank card issued by another bank or to a transaction originating with a merchant affiliated with another bank or bank card association. *Also called* foreign card *or* out-of-area card.

out-of-the-money An option contract is out-of-the-money when there is no benefit to be derived from exercising the option immediately. A call option is out-of-the-money when the price of the underlying instrument is below the option's exercise price. A put option is out-of-the-money when the price of the underlying instrument is above the option's exercise price.

output (1) (Noun) The data transferred from the internal to the secondary or external storage of a computer or to any device outside the computer; the routines or devices necessary to accomplish such a transfer. (2) (Verb) To transfer data from the internal storage of a computer onto external storage media.

output-oriented base An organizational design based on product, customer, or geographic groupings.

output sequence number (OSN) A consecutive sequence number that allows for output message control between the service and the receiving bank.

outright sale A method for sale of commercial paper through a dealer. The issuer sells its note outright to a dealer and immediately receives face value less the dealer's charges.

outside financing The process of raising funds for business expansion through the sale of securities rather than the use of retained earnings.

outstanding (1) Any uncollected or unpaid funds, such as accounts receivable or notes payable. (2) Any securities, such as stocks or bonds, that have been issued and not yet paid or bought back. (3) The total amount of a loan portfolio.

outstanding check A check written by a depositor that has not yet been presented for payment to or paid by the depositor's bank.

over and short account The general ledger account that records all differences among different sets of records of a bank's daily business. *Also called* difference account.

overbought The price level of a security or market that has risen sharply because of vigorous buying that may have left prices higher than they will be later.

overcapitalized The state of a corporation that has too much invested capital in relation to its expected earnings or its income-producing assets.

overdraft (1) The amount by which a debit or charge against an account exceeds the balance of the trust account. (2) A negative balance in a depositor's account that results from

paying checks for an amount larger than the depositor's collected balance. (3) A check that overdraws an account. Banks are not legally obligated to pay an overdraft.

overdraft banking A service offered to demand deposit customers in which a line of credit is associated with the customer's account. Checks drawn on insufficient funds are paid from this line of credit rather than returned to the presenter.

overflow The condition that arises when the result of an arithmetic operation exceeds the capacity of the storage space allotted in a digital computer. *Compare with* underflow.

overhead Business costs not related to specific units of product. The term includes all indirect labor costs and indirect material expenses.

overlapping debt That portion of the debt of other government units for which residents of a particular municipality are responsible.

overlay An amount included in a tax levy on general property, to cover abatements and taxes that will probably not be collected.

over-limit account An account in which the outstanding balance exceeds the authorized credit limit.

overline The portion of any loan that exceeds a bank's legal lending limit.

overnight delivery risk The risk that funds for an instrument in transit overnight will be paid out before they are collected, when settlement for one side of a transaction occurs before settlement on the other side.

oversold The price level of a security or market that has fallen sharply because of vigorous selling that may have left prices lower than they will be later.

oversubscription privilege A stockholder's right to buy a proportionate share of any securities not taken in the initial offering, which gave the stockholder a right to buy a proportionate share of a new stock issue.

overt act An act done openly in pursuing an avowed interest or design, as opposed to a threat without any act taken to carry it out.

over-the-counter (OTC) market A decentralized market for trading securities by negotiation, in which one buyer and one seller negotiate an acceptable price through their agents. The OTC market is a nationwide network of brokers and dealers who buy and sell securities that generally are not listed on any national exchange.

over-the-window delivery The direct delivery of a security made to the receiving window of a bank, brokerage house, or securities depository.

overtime The daily hours of work, exceeding the number established by contract or law, for which wage earners normally receive extra pay.

overwrite To record new data over previously stored data. The old data are automatically erased as the new data are entered.

owned real estate *See* other real estate owned.

ownership The right to services and benefits provided by an asset. Ownership is usually evidenced by the possession of legal title or by a beneficial interest in the title.

ownership certificate A form required by the government that discloses the real owner of stocks registered in the

name of a nominee. Such a form must also accompany coupons presented for collection on bonds belonging to nonresident aliens or on partially tax-free corporate bonds issued before January 1, 1934.

owner's policy A policy that insures the title to a purchase of real property.

pack (1) (Verb) To compress numeric data in a storage medium to allow two digits to be stored in a single position or byte. (2) (Noun) *See* lessor markup.

package mortgage A mortgage that includes personal property, such as kitchen appliances.

packet A group of bits switched and transmitted as a unit, including data and control elements.

paid-in capital The sum received by a corporation for its stock. The statutes of some corporations require a minimum amount of paid-in capital to commence operations.

paid-in surplus The contributions of capital received by a corporation that are not credited to capital stock. Paid-in surplus results from the sale of Treasury stock at a price greater than its purchase price; issuance of par value stock at a price greater than par value; issuance of non-par stock at a price greater than stated value; forfeited payments made on subscribed stock; and contributions by stockholders and people outside the corporation.

PAN-PIN pair An account number and its corresponding secret code.

paper (1) *See* commercial paper. (2) Original, photocopied, or facsimile sales drafts, credit vouchers, cash advance drafts, and other obligations arising from the use of a card and bearing either the imprint or another reproduction of embossed information contained on such a card. (3) (Jargon) Investment securities.

paper gain or loss The unrealized gains or losses on any instrument in a portfolio, based on comparing current market quotations and the original costs. Until the instrument is sold, any gain or loss is solely on paper.

paper profit or loss *See* paper gain or loss.

paper profits The difference between an investor's cost for a security holding that has not yet been sold and its current market value.

paper tape Long, narrow strips of paper used to enter and store data in the form of punched holes or otherwise.

par (1) The principal amount of the mortgage. (2) The face value of stocks and bonds. (3) The basic declared value of a currency. *See also* par value.

parallel simulation A process in which a separate set of application programs that mirror the functions performed by the actual programs are developed and run against real data. The results of the simulation are compared with actual production; any discrepancies are evaluated and resolved.

parastatal A government-owned corporation.

par bond *See* current coupon bond.

parent company A company that owns a controlling interest in an unconsolidated subsidiary company.

parity (1) Equality between the declared or market values of two nations' currencies. (2) The relationship between production cost and sale prices during an earlier period, used to evaluate current cost-price relationships.

parity bit A check bit appended for control purposes to an array of binary digits to make the sum of all the binary digits always odd or always even.

parity check A checking of a summation in which the binary digits in a character or word are added and the sum checked against a single previously computed parity digit. This check tests whether the necessary number of ones and zeros are encoded in the computer to represent a number or word correctly.

parity digit *See* parity bit.

parol evidence Oral and extrinsic evidence, as contrasted to written or documentary evidence. It comes from the French "parole," meaning word or spoken utterance.

partial call The redemption of a portion of a bond issue before maturity, which does not completely eliminate the debt.

partially amortized mortgage A mortgage that partially amortizes principal by providing for principal repayment down to a given amount, with a lump-sum repayment of the remaining principal at maturity.

partially secured loan A loan with collateral worth less than the face value of the loan.

partial payment (1) In loan collection, the receipt of a payment that is less than the full payment due. (2) A cardholder payment that covers less than the minimum payment amount required to keep the account current.

partial recourse agreement An agreement between a bank and a dealer who sells retail contracts to the bank in which the dealer agrees that he or she will be liable for a limited period of time or for a limited amount if the borrower defaults. A similar agreement may be made for repurchase plan. *See also* limited recourse agreement; nonrecourse agreement; recourse plan; repurchase plan.

participating bank A bank that does not handle the processing for its own bank card plan and, by agreement, participates with the processing bank in its cardholder portfolio.

participating bond A bond that shares in the earnings of the issuer under specified conditions, in addition to the specified interest return.

participating preferred stock Preferred stock that allows its holders to participate in extra dividends (that is, in addition to the fixed amount the holder is entitled to) during years in which the common stock dividend exceeds that of preferred stock. This raises the dividend to equal that of common stock.

participation An interest in a loan. A participation is the acquisition by a third party from the lender of an interest in a loan. The acquisition of this interest may occur concurrently or subsequent to the making of the loan. The participation may be disclosed to the borrower or it may occur without the borrower's knowledge or consent. The lender is the "lead," and the third party acquiring the interest in the loan is the participant. The relationship is frequently formalized by an agreement in writing known as a participation certificate. The participant generally acquires an undivided interest in the loan and is dependent on the lead bank for protection of its interests in the loan. Generally accepted accounting principles (GAAP) distinguish between a participation and a syndication, which results in different accounting treatment for the recognition of fee income.

participation certificate (PC) A modified pass-through security, issued and guaranteed by the Federal Home Loan Mortgage Corporation, that represents an undivided interest in a pool of conventional residential mortgages.

participation loan A loan in which more than one lender participates, although only one of the lenders services the loan. The buyer buys only a portion of the principal balance of the loan; the seller retains the unsold portion. *See also* participation.

participation mortgage *See* participation loan.

participative management A philosophy of management that believes that employees need to participate actively in the running of the business in order to feel commitment and ownership.

partition Division, apportionment, and allocation of property between two or more people who are entitled to fractional interests in the whole property. A partition is frequently used in connection with a parcel of real property that must be sold to satisfy interests of the parties owning unallocated shares in such property.

partnership An association of two or more persons for the conduct of an enterprise other than in corporate form. The rights, duties, and responsibilities of the people so associated may be covered by a partnership agreement; if not, they are determined by law. *See also* limited partnership.

partnership agreement A written agreement between business partners that outlines the provisions of their business arrangements. *Also called* articles of partnership.

partnership freeze A method of restricting (freezing) the growth in value for federal estate tax purposes of a higher-bracket taxpayer's business or investment interests that are not in corporate form. The higher-bracket taxpayer receives a limited but preferential interest in a partnership holding the business or investment interests, while the future appreciation in the assets passes to the other partners, who are usually taxpayers in lower tax brackets. *See also* recapitalization.

part-service benefit The credit toward a pension provided by an employer for all or part of a participant's years of service with the company before the adoption of a pension plan. *Also called* past service benefit.

par value (1) The nominal or face value of a stock or bond certificate, expressed as a specific amount marked on the face of the security. Par value is not related to market value, which is the amount a buyer is willing to pay for an item. (2) An amount expressed in gold or U.S. dollars declared by a country to be the basic value of its currency, according to the requirements of the International Monetary Fund. *Also called* par.

pascal An advanced computer programming language.

pass A complete cycle of reading, processing, and writing on a computer (that is, a machine run).

passbook A book given to bank depositors that records deposits, withdrawals, and interest earnings. If they are used at all, passbooks are generally required when a customer makes a withdrawal.

passbook loan A loan secured by the borrower's savings account. The borrower leaves the passbook to the account and a withdrawal agreement (giving the lender the right to withdraw the pledged funds) with the lender as security. The use of passbook loans has been rare in recent years.

passbook savings A savings account that uses a passbook in which the bank records transactions.

passive income (1) Income derived from investments. (2) Income from limited partnerships or any other business in which a taxpayer does not materially participate. Under the 1986 Tax Reform Act, a taxpayer may not deduct losses from such passive activities to the extent that such passive losses exceed passive income. Special rules apply to rental activity. The deduction for excess passive losses will be phased out in annual steps and completely phased out in 1991.

passive income generator (PIG) An investment in a limited partnership or other business in which a taxpayer does not materially participate and, therefore, that produces passive income.

passive losses Losses from limited partnerships or any other business in which the taxpayer does not materially participate. Under the 1986 Tax Reform Act, passive losses may not be deducted to the extent that such losses exceed passive income. Special rules apply to rental activity. The deduction for excess passive losses will be phased out in annual steps and completely phased out in 1991.

passive trust A trust for which the trustee has no active duties to perform. *Also called* a bare, dry, *or* naked trust. *Compare with* active trust.

"pass the dividend" The decision of a company's board of directors not to declare a dividend. Directors are reluctant to "pass (forgo) the dividend" because it damages the stock's standing for many years.

pass-through account An account held at a member bank by nonmember banks or other depository institutions that are required by the Federal Reserve to hold reserve accounts. Those requirements may be met by holding deposits in a bank that holds an equivalent amount on deposit at a Federal Reserve bank.

pass-through certificate *See* pass-through security.

pass-through security A security that represents an undivided interest in a pool of mortgages. Principal and interest payments from the mortgagors are passed through to security holders as received. Because mortgagors may prepay their mortgages, the pass-through payments to security holders may fluctuate. *See also* modified pass-through security.

password A protected word or set of characters that identifies or authenticates a user or a specific resource.

past-due account A loan account on which the payment has not been made in accordance with the terms of the agreement or note.

past-due payments Payments that have become due but have not been made according to the terms of the agreement or note. *See also* default; delinquent account.

past service benefit *See* part-service benefit.

pay (Verb) For payment orders, to settle an account with the ultimate payee or beneficiary using legal tender.

payable date The date established by a board of directors for payment of a dividend to the stockholders of record, usually 15 to 20 days after the record date.

payable-through draft *See* treasurer's draft.

payback period The time required for the return on an investment to equal the initial outlay. The payback period provides a rule of thumb for evaluating the feasibility of a proposed investment. This method of evaluation is often inadequate, however, because it ignores the timing (that is, the present value) of the returns.

pay-by-phone A service enabling customers to instruct their financial institution by telephone to initiate one or more payments from their accounts.

pay date The date on which funds will be available to the beneficiary for withdrawal in cash. Often abbreviated as PDate.

paydown (1) The net reduction in debt when the amount of a new securities issue is less than that of a maturing issue. (2) A partial payment on a debt.

payee The person named in an instrument as the recipient of the sum shown. Thus the payee is the party that receives the payment of an instrument.

payee line The line on a check for entering the name of the party to whom the check is being paid.

paying agent An agent who receives funds from an obligor to pay maturing bonds and coupons, or from a corporation to pay dividends.

paying teller A bank employee responsible for paying funds to depositors.

payment A transfer of funds in any form between two parties.

payment coupon The section of a billing statement containing payment information that the customer should return with the payment.

payment date *See* entry date.

payment document Any paper document used to transfer funds from one party to another.

payment due date The date on which payment must reach the appropriate processing center to keep an account in a current status.

payment-in-kind paper *See* PIK (payment-in-kind) paper.

payment method A code that specifies how a payment will be made to a party in a funds transfer.

payment order An instruction to a bank at which the sender has an account, authorizing in some manner the bank to debit this account and to transfer the funds to another party for its own account or another's account. The receiving bank has to ensure in some way, for example by a test, that the instructions are authorized before making payment.

payment record (1) A customer's repayment record for installment loans and other credit transactions. (2) The extent to which a borrower has made payments of principal and interest at the prescribed times.

payment service A service that moves messages among subscribers and also effects settlement for those messages constituting funds transfer transactions.

payments mechanism Any device, instrument, or system that can transfer money, including cash, checks, credit cards, electronic funds transfer (EFT) devices, automated tellers, and point-of-sale terminals.

payment system A communication system permitting the exchange of information necessary to carry out transfers of funds.

payor The party that delivers funds or initiates a funds transfer to pay a beneficiary party for goods received or services rendered.

payout ratio The percentage of earnings paid out as dividends. *Also called* dividend payout ratio.

payroll A record showing the wages and/or salary earned by or paid to employees during a specific period.

payroll deduction plan A method of deducting predetermined amounts of pay to cover such items as hospital insurance or other benefits.

payroll records The documentation, authorization, computation, distribution, and payment of wages and salaries to employees.

pay-through bank An intermediary bank through which a funds transfer is carried out.

pay-through bond A mortgage-backed debt obligation of the issuer. Interest and amortization are paid periodically, as well as prepayments of principal that occur.

pay-through information Information pertaining to a transfer channeled through an intermediary bank.

pay to The designated payee to whom the paying bank should provide the specified funds.

pay-up The additional cash cost of swapping into a higher-priced security.

peak The phase of the business cycle at which economic activity is at its highest level.

pecuniary bequest A bequest of property--often made in connection with the establishment of a marital deduction trust--that is expressed in terms of a specific dollar amount rather than a proportion of the assets involved. *Distinguish from* fractional share bequest.

pecuniary legacy A gift of money by will. *See also* pecuniary bequest.

peer group In the National Bank Surveillance System, the 20 groups into which statistics for national banks are classified, based on asset size and other characteristics. Each bank is then compared with the other banks in its group.

peg An exchange rate level maintained by a government. The rate may be set (pegged) at, above, or below par.

pegged exchange rate An exchange rate that is supported at a fixed rate against another currency. *See also* fixed exchange rate.

pendente lite During the continuance of a suit at law or in equity.

penetration A successful unauthorized access to an electronic data-processing system.

penetration pricing The use of a low initial price to capture a large share of a market as early as possible.

Pennsylvania rule A rule that requires extraordinary dividends received in trust to be credited to income if declared from earnings of the corporation during the life of the trust, or to principal if declared from earnings accumulated before commencement of the trust.

penny stock A stock that typically trades over-the-counter at less than $1.00 a share. Penny stock prices are very volatile because they are issued by firms with erratic earnings.

pension plan An arrangement evidenced by a written agreement providing for the accumulation of funds from a corporation or its employees or both to be used for monthly or other periodic payments to employees of the corporation after their retirement.

pension trust A trust established by an employer (commonly a corporation) to provide benefits for incapacitated, retired, or superannuated employees, with or without contributions by the employees.

P/E ratio *See* price-earnings ratio.

per capita (by the head) A term used in the distribution of property; distribution to persons as individuals (per capita) and not as members of a family (per stirpes). For example, "I give my estate in equal shares to my son A and to my grandsons C, D, and E (the sons of my deceased son B) per capita." C, D, and E take as individuals (not as the sons of B); each takes the same share as A, namely, one-fourth of the estate.

percentage growth (1) The difference between an item at two different times, expressed as a percentage of the earlier figure. (2) The increase in sales from 1 year to the next, as reflected in an annual earnings report. This percentage is determined by finding the difference between 2 years sales figures and then dividing the difference by the previous year's sales.

percentage lease A lease providing for payment of rent based on a percentage of the gross sales over a fixed amount.

per diem Literally, "by day." An allowance or charge that is computed for each day.

perfect competition A market in which a producer has no influence over the price at which its product is sold, for example, a wheat or corn farmer. Such markets are usually characterized by a large number of producers supplying an identical product.

perfected lien A security interest in an asset that has been properly documented and filed with the appropriate legal authority to protect the claim of the creditor.

perfecting title Correcting the defects in a chain of title so that the owner has a perfect title.

performance (1) The fulfillment of a promise, contract, or other obligation according to its terms. (2) The quality and quantity of an employee's work.

performance appraisal *See* performance evaluation.

performance bond A bond issued by a surety company to guarantee that the insured will perform the work in accordance with the plans and specifications and within the contract price. A performance bond is frequently used to insure the performance of a general contractor on a construction project.

performance evaluation The process by which an assessment is made of an employee's performance and ability.

performance letter of credit *See* standby letter of credit.

performance standard (1) A method of controlling the use of industrial land by enforcing standards of operation. (2) A level of quality and output used to evaluate the work of individuals.

periodic rate An amount of finance charge, expressed as a percentage, that is applied to an appropriate balance at specified intervals, usually monthly, provided there is a balance that is subject to a finance charge.

periodic statement The billing summary produced and mailed at specified intervals, usually monthly.

period of digestion The period immediately following the issuance of a large or new security during which issues are sold to relatively permanent investors.

peripheral An auxiliary machine controlled by the central processing unit of a computer.

peripheral equipment Auxiliary machines that supplement the central computer.

perk A fringe benefit, such as an automobile, that is generally only available to a select group of employees. It is short for perquisite.

permanent loan A long-term mortgage, usually for more than 10 years.

perpetual bond A bond with no maturity date; a consol. A perpetual bond pays fixed amounts of interest forever. *See also* consol.

perpetuity Duration without limitation as to time. *See also* rule against perpetuities.

person A natural person or a corporation, government subdivision, agency, trust, estate, partnership, cooperative, or association.

personal banker A program where a bank employee is assigned to provide personalized customer service to a valued customer. Personal bankers are professionals who understand the unique financial needs of each customer and have the authority to handle their nonroutine banking transactions.

personal effects Goods of a personal character, such as clothes and jewelry.

personal financial statement Statement of an individual's personal financial resources and obligations, comparable to a balance sheet for a business.

personal identification number (PIN) A number or word, selected by a cardholder or randomly assigned by the card issuer, to provide personal security in accessing a financial service terminal and to prevent use of a bank card by unauthorized parties. *See also* true personal identification number.

personalized sales draft A sales draft that has been specially printed for a merchant to provide stronger identification than a standard form.

personal liability insurance Insurance against possible assessment of personal liability for damages (for example, the type of insurance that protects a homeowner from liability if the mailman breaks a leg on the homeowner's property).

personal line of credit *See* overdraft banking; check credit.

personal loan A loan obtained by an individual for personal (as opposed to business or investment) purposes. A personal loan may or may not be secured. *Also called* consumer loan *and* consumer credit.

personal property Any property that is not designated by law as real property. Personal property is property that is subject to ownership and is not fixed or immovable. Personal property may be tangible or intangible; tangible personal property consists of physical objects, whereas intangible personal property consists of human rights.

personal representative (1) A party appointed by a court to carry out the terms of a will. This court appointment occurs if no executor was named in the will or if the named executor cannot serve. If the decedent left property but no will, the personal representative distributes the property according to the laws of the state in which the decedent lived. *Also called* representative. (2) A person who acts or speaks for another person under his or her authority. (3) A general term applicable to both the executor and administrator.

personal selling One-on-one contact between a seller's representative and a potential buyer for the purpose of arousing interest and convincing the buyer to purchase products. Personal selling lays the groundwork for long-term relationships between buyer and seller.

personal trust An account in which an individual's assets are placed in custody to be used by a beneficiary of the trust.

personal trust account The trust account of an individual, typically one with a high net worth. Examples include accounts supervised by a court, such as estates and guardianships; personal trusts established during the lifetime of the creator or after the creator's death; and personal trust agencies.

personal trust agency An agent for a personal trust account. The agent does not assume legal title to the trust assets but may register securities in a nominee name for convenience. The customer or his or her investment adviser makes the decisions on investments. The agent may provide safe-keeping and custody and serve as escrow agent. It also collects income and principal payments and is responsible for buying, selling, receiving, and delivering securities on orders from the customer.

personalty Personal property. *Compare with* realty.

personnel management *See* human resources management.

personnel security The procedures established to ensure that only persons with the required authority and appropriate clearances have access to sensitive information.

per stirpes (by the branch) A term used in the distribution of property; distribution to persons as members of a family (per stirpes) and not as indi-

viduals (per capita). Two or more children of the same parent take per stirpes when together they take what the parent, if living, would take. For example, "I give my estate to my son A and to my grandsons C, D, and E (the sons of my deceased son B). My grandsons are to take per stirpes." C, D, and E take as the sons of B (not as individuals), each receiving one-sixth of the estate (one-third of the one-half to which B would be entitled if living), while A receives one-half of the estate. Taking per stirpes is also known as taking by right of representation.

pertinent element of creditworthiness In relation to a judgmental system of evaluating applicants, any information about applicants that a creditor obtains and considers that has a demonstrable relationship to credit-worthiness.

petition A written request to a court or judge for the granting of some remedy or relief.

petitioning on creditors' bond A bond providing that, if a petition in bankruptcy filed by creditors is dismissed, the bonding company will pay the debtor all expenses, costs, and damages.

petty cash A small cash fund that organizations use for incidental expenses. As the cash is used, the fund is replenished to the original level.

Philadelphia Depository Trust Company (PHILADEP) The securities depository used by members and affiliates of the Philadelphia Stock Exchange.

Phillips curve A graph that depicts the trade-off relationship between inflation (or wage growth) and unemployment for any economy.

PHLX The Philadelphia Stock Exchange.

photo card A bank credit card containing a picture of the cardholder.

physical delivery of securities The transfer of actual certificates from seller to buyer, following the sale of securities. *Compare with* book entry; book-entry securities.

physical depletion The exhaustion of a natural resource, such as a mineral or gas, by its actual extraction.

physical security (1) The use of locks, guards, badges, and administrative measures to control access to a computer and related equipment. (2) The measures required for protecting the structures that house a computer, related equipment, and their contents from damage by accident, fire, and environmental hazards. (3) Protection of a bank, its personnel, and its customers.

pickup An increase in yield because of a swap into a higher-yielding security.

pick up card An instruction directing an authorizer or a merchant to take possession of a bank card from a cardholder and return it to the issuing bank.

pick-up tax An estate tax imposed by many states equal to the excess of the state death tax credit available for federal estate tax purposes over the state inheritance tax imposed on a decedent's estate. Some states with no separate inheritance tax impose only a pick-up tax equal to the available state death tax credit. Because the pick-up tax "soaks up" the state death tax credit, it is sometimes called a "sponge tax."

picosecond One-trillionth of a second.

piercing the corporate veil An action in which shareholders become personally liable for corporate debts. This usually arises when a corporate entity has been used to perpetrate a fraud or commit an injustice.

piggyback bank A bank that, by retaining a depository participant bank as agent, indirectly has access to depository services.

piggyback item An item missing from its assigned pocket in a sorter and sorted "free" to an unidentified pocket, as when one document attaches itself to or overlaps another during processing.

PIK (payment-in-kind) paper Bonds or preferred stock that pay interest or dividends in additional securities (more paper) rather than in cash. PIK paper is essentially non-investment-grade paper subordinate to everything on the balance sheet except common stock.

PIN (personal identification number) *See* personal identification number.

PIN assignment The process of establishing the relationship between authentication and identification data for a customer.

PIN issuance The act of conveying PIN information to a customer.

pink sheets A daily publication that lists over-the-counter stocks, showing names of market makers and stock prices. A similar publication that lists bonds is called the yellow sheets.

PIN verification The verification of a customer's authenticity by an issuer.

pip The smallest possible change in the quoted price for a currency. For example, if one currency is quoted in terms of another at 1.0234, an increase to 1.0235 would be one pip.

placement (1) An interest-bearing deposit with another (typically foreign) bank. (2) *See* private placement.

plain-vanilla swap A swap with a simple structure, for example, a U.S. dollar interest rate swap in which one party makes floating-rate payments based on the 6-month LIBOR and receives fixed-rate funds expressed as a spread over the rate on U.S. Treasury securities. The maturity is usually 5 to 7 years and the deal size is typically at least $50 to $100 million.

PLAM *See* price level adjusted mortgage.

plan manager (1) The individual responsible for all bank credit card activities. (2) The person responsible for managing a benefit plan.

planned unit development (PUD) A comprehensive development plan for a tract of land, providing for residential and commercial uses and for supporting services such as schools and recreational facilities.

plastic bond A nickname for a bond in which the principal and interest payments are backed by credit card receivables. *See also* securitization.

plat A map, usually recorded as part of the public record, representing a piece of land subdivided into lots with streets, boundaries, easements, and dimensions.

platform That portion of a bank's lobby where officers, new-accounts personnel, and so on are located.

pledge (1) (Verb) To transfer property to a trustee or creditor as security on a debt. (2) (Noun) The bailment

of goods by a pledgor (bailor) to a creditor (bailee or pledgee) as security for some debt or engagement.

pledged assets Collateral. Property, securities, or other valuables that back a bond or note issue or a loan are considered pledged assets.

pledgee *See* bailee.

pledging requirement A requirement that banks provide collateral against deposits of local, state, and federal government units to insure them against financial loss in the event of failure. The depositor typically specifies the pledging ratio and type of collateral. Most depositors often include Treasury and municipal obligations.

pledgor *See* bailor.

plus Government securities are quoted for sale in thirty-seconds of a percent. To fine tune such a quote to sixty-fourths, a plus is used. Thus a quote of 11+ is a quote of 11/32 + 1/64, or 23/64. The quote does not include the handle (the whole number that precedes the quoted fraction). *See also* handle.

pocket money Coin and currency.

point (1) A unit of measure related to the pricing of a fee on a loan. One point is 1 percent of the subject loan. (2) In "basis point," 1/100 of 1 percent. (3) In currency trading, a pip. *See also* basis point; pip.

point of sale (POS) (1) The location in a merchant establishment where a sale is consummated by payment for goods or services received. (2) A terminal used to transfer funds from a bank account to pay for purchases.

point-of-sale (POS) system A system that permits bank customers to transfer funds from their bank accounts and execute other financial transactions at a retail point of sale.

point-of-sale (POS) terminal A device placed in a merchant location that is connected to a bank's system by telephone lines and is designed to authorize, record, and forward electronically payment for each sale as it occurs.

poison pill An antitakeover strategy designed to make the purchase of a company's stock by a corporate raider prohibitively expensive. Specifically, the corporation effects provisions in its articles or bylaws of incorporation that allow for the issuance of new stock to existing stockholders at a reduced price in the event of a potentially hostile takeover. *See also* corporate raider.

policy manual A written statement of decisions that management has made and expects employees to follow in conducting the business of the organization.

political uncertainty An unknown future political action taken by a government that may change the status of the borrower.

pollution control bond A class of municipal bonds. The proceeds from these bonds are used to fund the construction of facilities for controlling air and water pollution. Pollution control bonds are similar to industrial revenue bonds.

pooled income fund A fund to which several donors transfer property while retaining an income interest and giving the remainder to a single charity.

pooled mortgages A group of mortgages packaged together to serve as collateral for a security. Pooling mortgages provides diversification and

thus lessens risk to the security holder.

pooling of interest An accounting method used in business combinations (for example, mergers) that combines the balance sheets of the merged firms. This method is intended to present as a single interest two or more common stockholder interests that were previously independent. No acquisition is recognized, and the former bases of accounting are retained. Generally accepted accounting principles set forth the conditions under which the pooling of interest method should be used. *Compare with* purchase accounting.

pool rate A rate of interest that a bank uses to transfer funds between departments. A branch that typically supplies funds when it generates deposits is credited the pool rate, while a loan center that uses funds is charged the pool rate.

poor merchant description An error in the printout of a merchant's name and location on a descriptive statement; a poor description, *not* the description of a poor merchant.

population The aggregate of items from which the auditor intends to draw the sample.

port A computer socket into which a terminal or other peripheral equipment can be plugged.

portability A pension plan feature that allows participants to change employers without changing the source from which benefits (for both past and future accruals) are to be paid.

portfolio The assets owned by one organization or person and managed as a collective whole toward specific investment goals. Trust departments manage customers' portfolios, buying and selling as the portfolio manager deems appropriate.

portfolio insurance An application of program trading that attempts to minimize falling prices by using stock index futures to hedge stock portfolios. *See also* index arbitrage; program trading.

position (1) A bank's net balance of purchases and sales in a foreign currency at any given time, especially at the end of a business day. (2) An interest in a market, either long or short, in the form of open contracts.

position description A statement of the purpose and major responsibilities or duties of a job.

position evaluation *See* job evaluation.

position-schedule bond A fidelity bond that covers any employee of a firm who occupies the position named in the schedule attached to the bond.

positive authorization An authorization procedure covering every account on file in a computer system. Each account is accessed and checked to determine its status before an authorization is granted or declined.

positive carry (1) A condition in which the yield on a security or other asset is greater than the interest on funds borrowed to finance the security. (2) The amount by which the yield on an asset exceeds the cost of the funds borrowed to carry it.

positive confirmation The auditing system under which customers contacted during a bank audit must reply to a letter of inquiry regarding balances, loans, and so forth. *Compare with* negative confirmation. *See also* direct verification.

positive file A list of card identifiers corresponding to cards that have been issued. A positive file contains at a minimum the current balance for each active cardholder account. Depending on the specific system, the file may also contain cardholder privileges, personal identification numbers, card security numbers, and so on.

positive gap A maturity mismatch in which interest-sensitive assets exceed interest-sensitive liabilities.

post To transfer to a ledger changes on accounts recorded in journals or other posting mediums.

postal float The time delay between the mailing of a check or invoice and its subsequent receipt. *Also called* mail float.

post-dated check A check bearing a future date.

posthumous child A child born after the father's death. *Distinguish from* after-born child.

posting (1) The process of making entries in accounts. (2) The process of recording debits and credits to individual cardholder accounts to reflect merchandise sales, instant cash, cash advances, adjustments, payments, and any other charges or credits.

posting date A date when a transaction is charged or credited to a cardholder account. *See also* entry date.

post-purchase feelings The last stage of the buying process, in which the customer tends to doubt the correctness of his or her choice. A customer's attitudes toward a firm and its products are based on the customer's experience in consuming the product. When these feelings are negative, they may also be called buyer's remorse or post-purchase anxiety.

pour-over The transfer of property from one estate or trust to another when a certain event occurs as provided in the instrument. *See also* spillover trust.

power (1) A common term used in a trust department for a stock power, bond power, or power of assignment. A power involves a form that, when properly signed and executed, allows ownership of securities to transfer from seller to buyer. The form may be printed on the back of a certificate or may be a separate document. To be valid, the power must meet all terms for good delivery or legal transfer delivery. (2) Authority or right to do or to refrain from doing a particular act, such as a trustee's power of sale or power to withhold income.

power in trust A power that the donee (the trustee) must exercise in favor of the beneficiary of the trust.

power of alienation The power to assign, transfer, or otherwise dispose of property.

power of appointment A right given to a person to dispose of property that he or she does not fully own. A power of appointment may be general or special. Under a general power, the donee may exercise the right as he or she sees fit. A special power of appointment defines for whom the donee may exercise the power. For example, a wife who is given the power to appoint among her children has a special power of appointment.

power of assignment *See* assignments; power.

power of attorney A document, sometimes witnessed and acknowledged, authorizing the person named to act as agent (attorney-in-fact) for the person signing the document. If the attorney-in-fact is authorized to act for the principal in all matters, he or she has a general power of attorney; if the attorney-in-fact has authority to do only certain specified things, he or she has a special power of attorney. If the authority granted in the power of attorney survives the disability of the principal, the attorney-in-fact has a durable power of attorney. *See also* bond power; letter of attorney; stock power.

power of retention The power expressed or implied in a will or trust agreement permitting the trustee to retain certain or all of the investments comprising the trust property at inception, even though they may not be suitable for new investments made by the trustee.

power of sale The power expressed or implied in a will or trust agreement permitting the trustee to sell investments comprising the trust.

preaudit The preliminary work performed by an internal audit team designed to determine the risks, objectives, and scopes related to the audit to be performed.

preauthorization order (PO) An agreement that permits a cardholder to effect a transaction, after signing an authorization with a merchant for purchases to be made from the merchant at one or more future dates, without the cardholder having to sign the resulting sales drafts or slips.

preauthorized electronic funds transfer An electronic funds transfer authorized in advance to recur at substantially regular intervals. In wholesale funds transfers, this is also called repetitive funds transfers.

preauthorized payments Payments made automatically from a demand deposit account on the basis of preauthorization by the account holder. A typical application is the preauthorization of an insurance company to debit an account for insurance premiums. In wholesale funds transfers, only portions of the transfers are preauthorized. Usually the date and amounts vary.

precatory words Expressions in a will requesting, but not directing, that a thing be done or not done.

precision A measure of the degree of accuracy of the most likely error.

preemptive right A prior right or privilege, such as the right of a stockholder to be offered the privilege of buying additional shares before the stock is offered to others. *See also* rights.

pre-examination The analysis and review that a bank examiner undertakes in advance of the examination to establish objectives, determine the scope of the examination, and identify the bank's key activities. The examiner coordinates data and personnel needs with the bank during this phase, which may begin up to 60 days before the actual examination.

prefect's court *See* probate court.

preference In bankruptcy, the term used to describe a transfer of property to another, usually a creditor, which results in the creditor receiving more than it would have otherwise obtained in the bankruptcy proceeding. A bankruptcy court can look back 90 days against any transfer; if the transferee is an insider, the court can look at any transfer within 1 year. If a preference resulted, the court can order the property or value returned to the estate for distribution to all creditors.

preference stock A class of stock that has senior rights over some other class of stock. The legal description of the individual issue specifies its rights.

preferred dividend coverage The extent to which income is adequate to pay preferred dividends. Preferred dividend coverage is calculated as net income after taxes and interest divided by annual preferred dividends payable.

preferred provider organization A group of physicians or other health care providers that contract directly with an organization to provide health care for its members. Such organizations typically provide services at reduced costs.

preferred stock One of the two major types of equity securities. (Common stock is the other type.) Preferred stock receives dividends before common stock, and the dividend rate for most preferred stock is fixed at the time of issuance. If a corporation is liquidated, preferred stockholders are given preference to the company assets ahead of common stockholders. Unlike common stock, preferred stock does not usually entail voting rights. *See also* callable preferred stock; called preferred stock; convertible preferred stock; cumulative preferred stock; participating preferred stock; prior preferred stock; protected preferred stock; stock.

prelegal section The component of a loan collection operation that is responsible for the effort to collect accounts that are in an advanced stage of delinquency before legal action is taken.

preliminary title report The results of a title search by a title company before issuing a title binder or commitment to insure the title.

premailer A notification sent to inactive cardholders before the reissue date asking if they would like to receive a new card.

premium (1) The amount by which the market price exceeds the face or par value of a bond. *Compare with* discount. (2) The amount payable to the holder of a callable bond by the issuer if and when the bond is called. (3) The payment made for an insurance policy. (4) A gift given to consumers to motivate them to desired behavior, for example, a cash bonus given to a depositor.

premium bond A bond selling above par, because it was issued when interest rates were higher than current market rates.

premium on an option The fee paid by the purchaser of an option to the option's writer. The writer may keep the premium, even if the option is never exercised.

premium on securities The amount by which a security (a bond or a share of stock) is bought or sold for more than its face or par value, as opposed to a discount on securities.

prepaid expenses A classification of expenditure made to benefit future periods. Such items are classified as current assets and constitute a part of a firm's working capital. Prepaid expenses include prepaid rent, certain taxes, royalties, and unexpired insurance premiums.

prepaid finance charge Under Regulation Z, any finance charge paid separately in cash or by check before or at consummation of a transaction,

or withheld from the proceeds of the credit at any time.

prepayment (1) Any amount paid to reduce the principal of a loan before the due date or in excess of the stipulated amortization. (2) An arrangement between a customer and the designated department in which the customer can prepay his or her payments for a specified period without the account becoming past due.

prepayment fee *See* prepayment penalty.

prepayment penalty A charge for the privilege of repaying an obligation before the agreed maturity date. Prepayment penalties are often charged on loans extended at an interest rate considered favorable to the lender in the long, rather than the short, run.

prepayment privilege (1) The right of a borrower to repay a debt before maturity. (2) An optional clause in a mortgage that gives the mortgagor the right to pay all or part of a debt before its maturity.

prepurchase activity In marketing, the first stage in the buying process, during which a person becomes sensitive to cues that he or she believes will help satisfy a need. During this period, a customer is most open to and aware of promotions.

present beneficiary *See* immediate beneficiary.

presenting bank The bank that forwards an item to another bank for payment.

present interest An unrestricted right to the immediate use, possession, or enjoyment of property or the income from property, such as a life estate or the right to receive income for a term of years.

presentment A demand for acceptance or payment made by the holder of a negotiable instrument on the maker of a note or the drawee of a check or draft.

present value The value today of a single payment or stream of payments to be received over a specified future period, discounted at an appropriate rate of interest. *Also called* time value of money.

preservation-of-consumer-claims-and-defenses rule *See* holder-in-due-course rule.

presumption of death A principle of common law, later incorporated in many state statutes, to the effect that a presumption of death arises from a person's continuous and unexplained absence from home or place of residence without any intelligence from or concerning him or her for a certain period, usually 7 years.

pretermitted child A child to whom the parent's will leaves no share of his or her estate without affirmative provision in the will showing an intention to omit. A pretermitted child is frequently an after-born child, a posthumous child, a child erroneously believed to be dead, or a child unintentionally omitted.

pretermitted heir An heir not included in the descent or devolution of the parent's estate.

previous balance (1) The balance last posted in an account. (2) The balance for a cardholder account as of the last billing period.

previous balance method The method used for calculating finance charges

on accounts that have not been converted to the average daily balance. The finance charges are calculated after subtracting payments and credits posted during the billing period from the previous balance.

price-earnings (P/E) ratio The relationship of the current stock price to the earnings over the past year, calculated by dividing the current stock price by the earnings per share.

price flat The usual method of pricing a fee for a repurchase agreement. The repurchase price is set to include interest and costs of the transaction.

price level adjusted mortgage (PLAM) A fixed-rate mortgage designed to enable more people, especially young families, to afford a home. The monthly payments are tied to changes in the rate of inflation rather than to interest rates. Monthly payments are initially lower than for conventional fixed-rate mortgages but are much larger in later years, when the borrower's income is expected to be higher. During the life of the loan, the mortgage principal grows at the rate of inflation, whereas housing values frequently grow faster than inflation, thus allowing some buildup of equity. The fixed interest rate is also lower than conventional rates because inflation is factored out of money market rates to determine the PLAM rate.

price risk The risk of loss of capital because of a rise in interest rates. Price risk varies directly with the term to maturity.

pricing strategy A technique for assessing fees, service charges, interest rates, and other pricing elements with the objective of making the product acceptable to the target market and generating a profit.

primary account number (PAN) The embossed and/or encoded number on a bank card, consisting of the major industry identifier, the issuer identifier, the individual account identifier, and the check digit. The primary account number identifies the card issuer to which the transaction will be routed and the account to which the transaction will be applied, unless specific instructions with the transaction message indicate otherwise.

primary beneficiary *See* immediate beneficiary.

primary capital The term includes common stockholders' equity, minority interest in equity of consolidated subsidiaries, perpetual preferred stock, perpetual debt securities, mandatory convertible securities (including mandatory stock purchase contracts), and the allowance for possible credit (loan) losses. Primary and secondary capital add up to total capital under the old capital adequacy framework. In the new risk-based capital framework, the components of capital are defined differently. They are referred to as Tier One and Tier Two capital. *See also* capital adequacy.

primary data Information obtained from original sources for a specific study, such as a survey of corporate accounts to determine their degree of satisfaction with a bank's performance.

primary distribution The original (first) sale of an issuer's securities.

primary earnings per share An earnings-per-share calculation based on the number of outstanding shares of common stock and common-stock equivalents.

primary market The market in which the issuer sells newly issued securities to the investor. Middlemen who aid in this initial sale of a company's

securities include underwriters, brokers, and dealers. *Compare with* secondary market.

primary mortgage market The market in which lenders originate mortgages by making direct loans to individual mortgagors.

primary offering A new issue of securities.

primary reserves Bank reserves that provide immediate liquidity but do not generate income. Primary reserves consist chiefly of cash assets, cash in vault, reserves at the Federal Reserve bank, balances due from banks, and cash items in the process of collection. *Compare with* secondary reserves.

prime merchant category A classification of merchants that are shown by historical data to be good producers of credit card volume and most likely to become affiliated with a bank card plan.

prime rate A benchmark that a bank establishes from time to time and uses in computing an appropriate rate of interest for a particular loan contract. The benchmark is generally based on numerous considerations, including the bank's supply of funds, cost of funds, administrative costs, and the competition from other suppliers of credit. Factors used in setting the prime rate and the circumstances in which it applies vary from bank to bank. This benchmark, however, is only one factor among several that banks use in pricing loans. For any specific loan, the interest rate actually charged may be above or below a bank's benchmark rate. The actual rate will be determined on the basis of several variables, including perceived risks, nature of collateral, length and size of loan, competition, and the overall relationship with the customer.

primogeniture The status of being the first born or eldest.

principal (1) A party who appoints another to act on his or her behalf, for example, as an agent or attorney-in-fact. (2) The actual amount of a deposit, loan, or investment, exclusive of interest charges. (3) The primary borrower on a loan, as opposed to the guarantor. (4) The original amount of an estate or fund together with accretions, which may include income. (5) The individual with primary ownership or management control of a business.

principal balance The outstanding balance of a mortgage or other loan, exclusive of interest and any other charges.

principal beneficiary (1) The beneficiary who is ultimately to receive the principal of an estate. (2) The beneficiary who is the settlor's primary concern. *Also called* ultimate beneficiary.

principal, interest, taxes, and insurance (PITI) The components that commonly are included in a monthly mortgage payment. The tax and insurance portions may or may not be required as part of the monthly payment, depending on bank policy, and they may be adjusted to reflect changes in taxes or insurance costs.

principal transfer agent A corporate agent responsible for the original issuance of securities and for the transfer of a security from one owner to another. If an issuer appoints co-transfer agents in other cities to speed issuance of new certificates, a principal transfer agent remains responsible for the centralized maintenance of ownership records.

prior estate A previously existing interest in a property, that is, the former owner's interest.

priority (1) A sender's request to expedite transmission of a message through a wire service. (2) The actual transmission of a priority message through a wire service.

prior lien A lien recorded before other liens and paid before other liens if liquidation occurs.

prior preferred stock Stock that has senior rights to dividends over junior issues of preferred stock and common stock.

prior redemption privilege A privilege frequently extended by a debtor to the holders of called bonds permitting them to redeem their holdings before the call date or maturity date. There are chiefly three types of offers with prior redemption: (a) with interest in full to the call date; (b) with interest in full to the call date, less a bank discount (usually 1/2 percent per year) based on the period from the date of collection to the date of call; and (c) with interest to the date of collection only.

privacy The right of individuals and organizations to control the collection, storage, and dissemination of information about themselves.

privacy protection The establishment of appropriate administrative, technical, and physical safeguards to ensure the security and confidentiality of records containing data about a person. This protection attempts to prevent any anticipated threats or hazards that could result in substantial harm, embarrassment, inconvenience, or unfairness to the person about whom such records are maintained.

private company A company whose shares are not publicly traded (that is, not listed on an exchange). It may be referred to as a closely held corporation because it is generally owned by a small number of investors.

private enterprise (1) An economic system typified by private ownership and control of business. (2) A business that is not publicly owned or controlled.

private foundations In general, all charitable foundations except those deriving substantial support from the public. Private foundations fall into two categories: (a) private operating foundations, whose assets and income are substantially used to carry on their exempt function, such as museums; or (b) private nonoperating foundations, which include most family foundations.

private label card A bank card that can be used only in a specific merchant's stores.

private mortgage insurance (PMI) Insurance written by a private company protecting the mortgage lender against loss from a default on a mortgage. Companies in this industry are called mortgage insurance companies (MICs).

private placement The sale of an entire issue to a small group of investors. Registration of the issue with the Securities and Exchange Commission is not necessary. The buyers must sign an investment letter stating that the investment is not for the purpose of immediate resale. For large private placements, typical buyers are insurance companies, pension funds, or mutual funds. *Compare with* public offering.

private trust (1) A trust created for a designated beneficiary. *Distinguish from* charitable trust. (2) A trust

created under a declaration of trust or under a trust agreement, such as a living trust or an insurance trust, to be distinguished from a trust coming under the immediate supervision of a court. *See also* court trust.

privilege tax A duty, levied by a U.S. state government on a foreign corporation, based on the amount of the company's stock owned by residents of the state or on the value of the company's assets within the state.

privity A relationship between people participating or sharing in the same rights to property.

probability (1) The belief that a future condition or event will develop or occur. (2) A measurement of the likelihood that an event will occur in the future.

probability proportional to size (PPS) The method of sample selection in which the probability of selecting an item is proportional to its relative size.

probate (1) (Verb) To present a will to the court to establish its validity and/or to appoint the executor or administrator. It is the first step in the settlement of an estate. Most states require at least two subscribing witnesses to probate a will. (2) (Noun) The act of proving before a court that a will is valid.

probate court The court that has jurisdiction over wills and intestacies and sometimes over guardianships and adoptions. *Also called* court of probate, surrogate's court, ordinary court, orphan's court, *and* prefect's court.

probate in solemn form The probate of a will in a formal proceeding after notice to the interested parties, as opposed to probate in common form, which is an informal proceeding without such notice.

probate of will Formal proof before the proper officer or court that the instrument offered is the decedent's last will.

problem bank list A current list of banks, maintained by the Federal Deposit Insurance Corporation, that require financial assistance.

problem definition The art of logically explaining a problem to a programmer, using flowcharts and logic diagrams, so as to present all requirements involved in the computer run.

procedure manual A written statement of how tasks are to be accomplished within an organization.

procedure-oriented language (1) A source language oriented to the description of procedures for machine computing. (2) A programming language designed for the convenient expression of procedures used to solve a wide class of problems.

processing (1) The preparation of an application for consideration. (2) Doing necessary work on any task or project. (3) Putting a program through a computer run.

processing center (1) An affiliate's location(s) for the operations of its bank card program. (2) A central location providing identical processing services (for example, authorization or interchange) for more than one affiliate.

processing date The date on which a transaction is processed by a merchant (acquiring) bank.

processing float The time required to process an invoice for payment or to process a payment received for deposit.

processing priority The level of urgency requested for the processing of a funds transfer.

processing priority code A code that specifies the processing priority requested for a funds transfer. This term is designated as a data element in funds transfers but solely for future reference, because none of the networks can currently accommodate or respond to this code.

processing unit The parts of a computer that (1) perform the processing and control functions for the system, (2) perform operations on data, and (3) control output.

processor In software, a computer program that includes the compiling, assembling, translating, and related functions for a specific programming language.

product In marketing, any good, service, place, idea, or other entity that is offered to a market for sale or acceptance. A tangible good that has physical and psychological characteristics that make it desirable to the consumer.

product class For a market or market segments, a category of similar products (for example, all consumer savings instruments, as opposed to one instrument).

product development The process of taking ideas for new or enhanced products and developing them into actual goods and services that can be sold profitably. The basic steps in this process include (1) idea generation, (2) screening to weed out ideas that are not viable or likely to succeed, (3) a business analysis to forecast sales and profitability, (4) development of a sample, (5) market testing to determine consumer acceptance, and (6) introduction or commercialization of the new product.

product dividend A dividend of a product of a firm, declared by its directors in place of a cash dividend. *See also* property dividend.

production credit association (PCA) A local farm credit cooperative association chartered by the Farm Credit Administration to make secured non-real estate loans to members.

production routine A routine that produces the results of a problem or program as designed, in contrast with those routines designed to provide support or housekeeping or to compile, assemble, and translate.

product item A specific version of a product (for example, a 1-year certificate of deposit).

product liability insurance Insurance that protects an entrepreneur against claims that a product has caused injuries.

product life cycle The typical path of four stages taken by a new product or service: introduction, growth, maturity, and decline.

product line For an individual firm, a group of product items that are closely related, such as the full line of savings services: statement savings, short- and long-term certificates, and so on.

product mix The composite of products that an organization offers for sale.

product strategy Activity taken with regard to a product line to enhance the product's appeal to the target market. Product strategies include expanding or contracting the product mix, or adding new features and benefits to existing products.

profit The excess of revenues over costs incurred in earning the revenues.

profitability ratios Ratios that indicate how efficiently a business is managed. *See also* profit-margin-on-sales ratio; profit-on-net-worth ratio; return on assets; return on equity.

profit and loss account An account used by a business to summarize revenues and expenses.

profit and loss statement *See* income statement.

profit center A unit in a bank that generates income. In a profit-planning system, that unit budgets both income and expenses. *Compare with* cost center.

profit margin The difference between the cost of a product or service and its selling price, usually expressed as a percentage of the selling price.

profit-margin-on-sales ratio A ratio used to analyze levels and trends of profitability. It is calculated as net profit after taxes divided by sales.

profit-on-net-worth ratio A profitability ratio indicating how well invested funds are used. It is calculated as net profit after taxes divided by net worth.

profit planning The systematic analysis of earnings and expenses for each unit within a firm to ensure that the firm's efforts are directed toward the most profitable use of available resources.

profit-sharing bond A bond that both participates in the issuing company's profits and receives a guaranteed interest rate.

profit-sharing plan An arrangement by which employees, in addition to their wages, receive a share of the net profits of a business.

profit-sharing trust A trust established by an employer to share the profits of the enterprise with the employees. A profit-sharing trust is a form of employee-benefit plan, often administered by a trust department.

pro forma statement (1) A financial statement that assumes future events in order to project conditions of the company as a result of those events. For example, a pro forma statement may assume future sales to project anticipated income. (2) Presentation of data as if certain events had taken place or different accounting procedures had been applied.

program (1) (Noun) A sequence of instructions to a computer, written in a special form the computer can interpret. A program tells the system where to get input, how to process it, and where to put the results. (2) (Noun) A set of instructions that tells which operations are to be done and how to do them. (3) (Verb) To write a sequence of instructions for a computer.

program check A method for determining that programs and machine functions are correct, usually accomplished by running a sample program or by using mathematical or logical checks.

program generator A program designed to enable a computer to write additional programs automatically.

program library The location where the central processing unit stores programs. *Also called* library.

programming *See* linear programming.

programming flowchart A flowchart representing the sequence of operations in a program.

programming language The communication system used in the set of instructions that direct the computer to perform specific functions.

program product A licensed program for which a monthly charge is made. A program product performs functions related to the processing of user data.

program trading The use of computer programs to enter into the simultaneous trading of both a stock and a stock index future to profit on changes in the spreads created between the two. *See also* index arbitrage; portfolio insurance.

progressive tax A duty levied at an increasing rate as the tax base increases in size.

progress payments Partial advances made by a lender at specified stages of completion of a building being financed under a construction loan. *See also* advance.

prohibited basis The Equal Credit Opportunity Act provides that consumer credit cannot be denied on a prohibited basis. Prohibited bases include race, color, religion, national origin, sex, marital status, age (provided that the applicant has the capacity to enter into a binding contract), the fact that all or part of the applicant's income derives from a public assistance program, or the fact that the applicant has in good faith exercised any right under the Consumer Credit Protection Act.

project note A municipal note, with a maturity ranging from 3 to 12 months, that provides short-term financing for federally assisted public housing and urban renewal projects. The Department of Housing and Urban Development may guarantee these notes as to principal and interest.

promissory note A written promise made by one person, the maker, to pay a certain sum of money to another person, the payee, or to his or her order, on demand or at a determinable future date.

promotion mix Elements used to inform a target market about a particular offering. These include advertising, sales promotion, and publicity. Some writers include personal selling as part of the promotion mix.

promotion strategy A plan for communicating to a target market the need-satisfying benefits of a product or service available for purchase. A promotion strategy uses the promotion mix elements in a targeted way to communicate the end result of the firm's product, pricing, and distribution strategies.

prompt A computer directive, usually on a cathode ray tube, that tells the operator what to do next.

proof Any process that tests the accuracy of a function or operation. *Also called* balancing.

proof department The central unit of a bank where the sorting, distributing, and verifying of all bank transactions occur.

proof machine Equipment that records the dollar amount for each sorted group of items being proved and that balances the total to the original input amount. This machine

usually sorts the items, too. *Also called* transit machine.

property Assets subject to ownership. Essentially, real property is fixed or immovable, while personal property is movable.

property damage liability insurance Automobile insurance that pays for damage to another car or property not belonging to the insured party.

property dividend A dividend, declared by a corporation in place of cash dividends, that shareholders receive as actual property of the issuer. A property dividend is not the same as a product dividend.

property report As required under the Interstate Land Sales Full Disclosure Act, a report that provides information important to lot buyers in advance of sale.

proportional tax A duty levied at a constant rate regardless of the size of the tax base.

proprietary debit card A bank card designed for the exclusive benefit of customers of the issuing institution.

proprietorship A business entity owned and operated by a single individual. The owner is fully liable for all debts incurred by the business.

proprietorship certificate A document that is filed with a bank as evidence of private, individual ownership of a business.

prorate (1) To divide proportionately, according to the share, interest, or liability of each party. (2) To assign or redistribute, according to some formula, a portion of a cost to a department, operation, period of time, and so on.

prospectus An official document that must be given to buyers of new issues registered with the Securities and Exchange Commission (SEC). A prospectus is an abstract of the lengthy registration statement that the issuer files with the SEC. It describes the issuer's products and business, the industries in which it competes, its physical facilities, and its management background. It also presents historical financial statements and describes the issue and intended use of the funds to be received. The SEC neither approves nor disapproves the prospectus.

protected check A check prepared in such a way as to prevent alterations. For example, when a check's paper is protected, any erasure to the check removes color, thus showing that an alteration has been attempted.

protected preferred stock Preferred stock that has its dividends guaranteed, in case the corporation does not earn a profit during a certain year. A special fund established from previous corporate earnings pays the dividends when they are due.

protection ring One level of privileged modes in an electronic data-processing system that gives access rights to authorized users, programs, and processes.

protective tariff *See* tariff.

protest (1) (Noun) An affidavit stating that a check or draft was presented for payment and payment was refused. A protest states whether a notice of dishonor has been given to the secondary parties. (2) (Verb) To submit such an affidavit.

prove (1) To verify or to subject an item to a satisfactory test. (2) To verify the accuracy of calculations performed by a person or department.

(3) To check that the dollar total of the items in the subparts of a list equals the dollar total of the subparts. *Also called* proof (both a verb and a noun).

provision for loan losses A charge against current earnings based on such factors as the bank's actual loan loss experience, management's expectations of potential loan losses, as well as anticipated economic conditions. The charge is made to build up a bank's allowance for possible credit (loan) losses. *See also* allowance for loan losses. *Also called* loan loss provision.

provision for possible credit (loan) losses *See* provision for loan losses.

proxy (1) A person empowered by another to act as his or her agent in voting shares of stock. (2) The instrument evidencing the authority of the agent to vote.

proxy statement A statement required under Securities and Exchange Commission regulations whenever a proxy is solicited from stockholders of a corporation.

prudent-expert rule *See* prudent-investor rule for trust investment.

prudent-investor rule for trust investment A rule stating that, in investing, all that can be required of a trustee is that the trustee conduct him or herself faithfully, exercise sound discretion, and observe how persons of prudence, discretion, and intelligence manage their own affairs not in regard to speculation, but in regard to the permanent disposition of their funds, considering the probable income as well as the probable safety of the capital to be invested. The Employee Retirement Income Security Act of 1974 (ERISA) set forth a federal prudent-investor rule for those persons or institutions dealing with pension plan assets. The act added to the prudent-investor rule the requirement that trustees adhere to the investment standards of a person knowledgeable and experienced in investments. Thus the prudent-investor rule became the prudent-expert rule under ERISA. The term "prudent-investor rule" was called the "prudent-man rule" and was originally stated in 1830 by the Supreme Judicial Court of Massachusetts in *Harvard v. Amory*, 9 Pick. 446 (1830).

public administrator In many states, a county officer who settles the estates of people who die intestate when there is no member of the family, creditor, or other person having a prior right of administration who is able or willing to administer the estate.

public assistance program Any federal, state, or local government program that provides a supplement to income because of either entitlement or need.

public debt (1) The debt of the federal government alone. (2) The total debt of the federal government and all local governments.

public file The Community Reinvestment Act (CRA) requires a bank to maintain a CRA file that is readily available to the public. The file contains the records of the bank's CRA statements as well as any correspondence from the public that has reference to its CRA statements or activities, and any responses to the comments the bank wishes to make. A complete file must be maintained at the bank's head office. If the bank operates in more than one community, data relating to that community must be available at a designated branch in that community.

public funds Accounts established for any government agency or authority.

public housing bond Debt securities issued by state or local governments to support the housing needs of the public. Funds raised by the sale of these bonds are used to make loans to developers, home buyers, and lending institutions that service home buyers. The Department of Housing and Urban Development may guarantee some of these bonds.

publicly owned corporation (1) A company owned by some unspecified number of people who have purchased shares of its capital stock. (2) A company whose shares are traded on the open market.

public offering An issue of securities offered to the general public that must be registered with the Securities and Exchange Commission. *Compare with* private placement.

public official bond A fidelity bond that protects against losses due to dishonesty or mishandling of public funds by a public official.

public trust *See* charitable trust.

public utility A privately owned corporation that provides public services, such as electricity, gas, telephone, or water.

public utility revenue bond A municipal revenue bond issued to raise funds to create or improve electricity, gas, water, and sewer services.

public warehouse financing A method of financing inventories. The inventory is placed in a warehouse located away from the borrower's premises, under the control of the lender's agent. As the inventory is sold, the inventory is released and the funds are transferred to the lender. *See also* warehouse financing.

pull order A method used to keep a bank card from being mailed at reissue. A pull order is typically used when an account is in a past-due or over-limit status at the time of reissue.

pull statement A process in which a cardholder's statement is segregated during regular mailing procedures and routed to the bank's department requesting the statement.

punch card (1) A heavy, stiff paper of constant size and shape, suitable for punching data handled mechanically by a computer. (2) A card that may be punched with holes to represent letters, digits, or characters. *Also called* punched card.

punched tape A tape with a pattern of holes to represent data.

purchase (Noun) Any and every method of acquiring property except by descent.

purchase accounting An accounting method used in business combinations that treats the transaction as the acquisition of one company by another. Purchased goodwill is recorded by the acquiring company as the difference between the cost of the acquired company and the fair values of tangible and identifiable intangible assets less liabilities. Generally accepted accounting principles set forth the conditions under which the purchase method should be used. *Compare with* pooling of interest.

purchase and sale (P&S) statement A statement provided by a broker showing changes in a customer's net ledger balance, after offsetting a previously established position.

purchase decision In the buying process, the culmination of prepurchase activity, in which a consumer assesses information gathered to reduce the risk associated with a decision about a product and makes the purchase.

purchased funds Short-term funds that are rate sensitive, such as federal funds, commercial paper, and large denominated time deposits.

purchase funds The sum set aside by a company's managers to reacquire its own securities. Purchase funds differ from sinking funds only in that sums are set aside fully at the managers' discretion.

purchase-money bond A bond in which the proceeds fund construction of major projects, such as a bridge or toll road. The bond trustee holds title to the completed facility until the debt is retired.

purchase-money mortgage A mortgage given by a purchaser of real property to the seller in partial payment of the purchase price.

purchasing power bond A bond with principal, and perhaps interest, tied to an inflation index. Thus the nominal value of a purchasing power bond increases as the price level rises. *Also called* index *or* indexed bond.

purchasing power uncertainties The probability that market prices or exchange rates may change, thus altering the value of investments.

pure competition A market composed of many sellers and buyers of identical goods and services, all of whom have full knowledge of relevant information.

purge To remove extraneous or stale data or records from a file. *Also called* delete.

purpose statement The signed affidavit required by the Federal Reserve's Regulation U, in which the borrower must indicate the planned use for any loan secured by stock.

put *See* put option.

put bond A bond with a put option. It can be redeemed at a stated price during a stated period of time.

put option An option providing the holder with the right, but not the obligation, to sell a specified financial instrument at or before a specified time at a specified price.

pyramid debt The borrowing of funds in rapid succession without first repaying previous debt, usually to meet obligations on earlier loans. Such a practice will rapidly erode a borrower's financial position.

pyramided reserves A term describing bank reserve patterns before the Federal Reserve System was established. Large quantities of reserves flowed into New York and other chief financial centers. Small banks placed some of their reserves in larger banks that, in turn, placed reserves in larger banks.

qualified disclaimer A disclaimer made under Section 2518 of the Internal Revenue Code. If a qualified disclaimer is made, the property subject to the disclaimer is treated as never having been transferred to the disclaimant for federal estate tax purposes. Basically, to be a qualified

disclaimer, the disclaimer must be made in writing within 9 months of the creation of the interest, the disclaimant cannot have accepted any benefit from the property, and the property must then pass without direction of the disclaimant to either the spouse of the decedent whose property is being disclaimed or to someone other than the disclaimant.

qualified domestic relations order (QDRO) An order issued by court in a divorce, legal separation, or separate maintenance proceeding that relates to child support, alimony, or the division of marital property. In general, a qualified domestic relations order is required for the assignment of an employee's benefits under either a qualified or nonqualified retirement plan in a divorce.

qualified endorsement An endorsement containing the words "without recourse" or similar language intended to limit the endorser's liability if the debtor fails to honor the instrument.

qualified plan or trust An employer's trust or plan that qualifies under the Internal Revenue Code of 1986 for the exclusive benefit of his or her employees or their beneficiaries in such manner and form as to entitle the payments made by the employer to the plan or trust to the deductions and income tax benefits set forth in that code.

qualified residence interest Interest paid on indebtedness that is secured by a perfected security interest on the taxpayer's principal residence or a second residence owned by a taxpayer (total debt not to exceed $1 million). Such interest is fully deductible for federal income tax purposes.

qualified stock option A privilege granted to an employee of a corporation in which he or she may purchase at a special price a limited number of shares of the corporation's capital stock, under conditions set forth in the Internal Revenue Code.

qualified sub-Chapter S trust A trust that is an eligible shareholder in a sub-Chapter S corporation because there is only one income beneficiary, all income is distributed to the beneficiary currently, and no principal is distributable during the income beneficiary's life to anyone other than the income beneficiary.

qualified terminable interest property (QTIP) A terminable interest that will qualify for the marital deduction if the donor or executor makes an appropriate election. In order to be QTI property, the surviving spouse must be entitled to all of the income of the property during the spouse's life, and no person, including the spouse, may have the right to appoint the property to anyone else during the spouse's life. The major benefit of a QTIP marital trust to a grantor is that at the surviving spouse's death, the remaining trust property is not subject to a general power of appointment in the spouse, but instead passes to beneficiaries selected by the grantor.

qualifying distribution As applied to a private foundation, any amount paid out to accomplish a legitimate eleemosynary purpose (and for incident administrative expenses) or to acquire an asset to directly carry out such a purpose.

qualitative forecasting See judgmental forecasting.

quality (of a bond) The degree of risk to an investor.

quality assurance program Procedures established by the internal audit department to self-regulate adherence to established policies and procedures.

quality circle A productivity-generating technique in which employees involved in a common task "brainstorm" and recommend ways to improve efficiency and increase production in their areas of responsibility.

quality control The policies and procedures used to determine and to maintain a desired level of quality in operations or products.

quality rating (bond) A rating assigned to securities by investment advisory services to measure the degree of risk to an investor.

quantity theory A theory based on the tenet that $MV = PT$ (the quantity of money multiplied by its velocity equals the price level multiplied by the number of transactions), or some variant of that tenet. The key assumption is that changes in the quantity of money primarily influence prices, because velocity is assumed to be constant and the number of transactions is determined by other factors.

quarterlies Interim financial reports on the financial condition of a publicly held company, released each quarter of the fiscal year. See also 10-Q report.

quasi contract An obligation, similar in character to that of a contract, that arises not from an agreement between the parties but from some relationship between them or from a voluntary act by one or more of the parties. For example, the management of the affairs of another or of a common property without authority would be a quasi contract.

quasi-public company A corporation operated privately but for a purpose that promotes the general interest.

query To extract from a file records based on a requested criterion (for example, records listing all of the customers in a file whose balance is greater than $1,000).

queue A waiting line or list of items in a system waiting for service (for example, tasks to be performed).

quick assets Those assets of a business, exclusive of inventories, that could be converted into cash within a short period, usually less than 1 year.

quick deposit box *See* lobby depository.

quick-pay mortgage A mortgage with an original maturity of 15 years or less.

quick ratio *See* acid test ratio.

quiet enjoyment A covenant in a warranty deed that gives the right of possession without disturbance caused by defects in title.

quitclaim deed A form of conveyance of real property in which the grantor conveys and the grantee receives only the title that was vested in the grantor, but without warranty of title by the grantor.

quota (1) A stated maximum quantity of imports that one country will allow from another. (2) The quantitative limit assigned to each member of the International Monetary Fund for its use of the Fund's reserves. This limit also determines the voting power and the subscription of that member.

quotation A firm offer to buy or sell a given security in a given market at a given time.

quotation board A large display board, usually found in a brokerage office, that posts daily prices for selected securities.

quote An offer by a dealer to buy or sell at a stated price.

rabbi trust A form of employee-benefit plan in which an employer establishes a trust to provide nonqualified deferred compensation to certain key employees. The trust usually contains restrictions on revocation and is subject to claims of general creditors of the employer. Employer contributions are not taxable as income to the employee at the time of contribution. Any income earned prior to distribution to the employee is taxed to the employer. The name "rabbi" originated because the first plan of this type reviewed by the I.R.S. concerned a trust established for a rabbi.

rack (1) A piece of equipment used for sorting and classifying. (2) The bank department where items involved in commercial operations are sorted, distributed, and proved.

raised check A check on which the dollar amount has been fraudulently increased.

random access memory (RAM) The area in a computer where data are kept when called up from the computer's mass storage.

random numbers A sequence of digits such that when the digits are grouped into numbers, no pattern in successive numbers can be detected and each number has an equal chance of occurring.

random personal identification number (PIN) A PIN selected from all possibilities over a range, and defined by the character set and length of the PIN.

random processing The treatment of data in an arbitrary sequence, by the input against which the data will be processed, without respect to the data's location in external storage.

random sample A group of units selected in such a way that all units under consideration have an equal probability of being chosen.

random selection A sample selection technique that chooses each sample item randomly using a random number table or a random number generator.

range A cell or a rectangular group of cells within an electronic spreadsheet.

ratable distribution The proportionate distribution of an estate according to a percentage. For example, if all the legacies cannot be fully paid and each of them is reduced by the same percentage, there is ratable distribution.

rate (1) A proportionate relationship. (2) The speed at which a flow occurs. *See also* error rate; exchange rate.

rate cap The maximum rate that may be charged on a variable rate loan or mortgage. The cap may be set by the loan documents or by law. *See also* annual cap; life cap.

rate floor The lowest rate allowed on a variable rate loan or mortgage. The floor is designated in the loan documents.

rate of exchange *See* exchange rate.

rate of return (1) The yield obtainable on a security, based on its purchase price or current market price. The rate of return may be the amortized yield to maturity on a bond or the current income return. (2) The income earned on any investment, expressed as a percentage of that investment.

rate risk *See* interest rate exposure.

rate sensitivity, rate sensitive The exposure of assets or liabilities to changes in interest rates. Rate-sensitivity analysis involves comparing assets and liabilities to determine the net exposure. Such comparisons may be made for several different ranges of maturity, thus measuring 90-day sensitivity, 1-year sensitivity, and so on. An array of comparisons for several different maturities is called a rate-sensitivity profile. *See also* assets repriced before liabilities; liabilities repriced before assets; gap; gapping.

rate structure The charges made to customers for their use of bank funds, specified in terms of annual percentage rates.

rating (1) The value of a particular security, relative to the value of other securities. Several investment advisory services provide such ratings. (2) A person's financial or credit standing.

rating agencies *See* Moody's Investors Service, Inc.; Standard & Poor's.

rating scale The range of values against which a particular quality is compared. Bonds are usually rated on a scale from AAA to D. Employment applicants are often rated on several characteristics.

ratio analysis A technique for analyzing a financial statement that examines the relationships among certain key values reported in the statement. Examples of key values include the current ratio, debt ratio, leverage ratios, liquidity ratios, profitability ratios, profit-margin-on-sales ratio, profit-on-net-worth ratio, sales-to-inventory ratio, sales-to-net-worth ratio, and sales-to-total-assets ratio.

rational expectations theory A relatively modern economic theory of how economic agents react to economic stimuli. This model assumes that economic agents include current government economic policies and present and past events in their economic decision-making process concerning future events.

ratios The comparison of various figures found on a firm's financial statements, for purposes of analysis. *See also* leverage ratios; liquidity ratios; operating ratio; profitability ratios.

raw data Data that have not yet been processed or are not yet in machine-readable form.

read (1) To acquire or to interpret data from a storage device, a data medium, or any other source. (2) To introduce data into a component of an automatic data-processing machine. (3) To copy, usually from one form of storage to another, particularly from external or secondary to internal storage. (4) To accept or to copy data from input devices or a memory register. (5) To transcribe data from an input device to internal or auxiliary storage.

reader card A card placed behind a sales draft to enable the keypunch information to be read.

reader/printer Equipment used by the retrieval section of a bank to locate and photograph data contained on microfilm.

reader/sorter Any automated equipment that reads a MICR E13B font.

read-in To pick up data from a source external to the computer and transmit the data to internal storage.

read only memory (ROM) A permanent set of computer instructions that an operator can read but not change.

read-out To pick up data contained in internal storage and transmit the data to a storage external to the computer.

read-write head A part of a disk drive that reads data from or writes data onto a disk or magnetic tape.

reaging (1) Extending the term of a delinquent loan; bringing the account up to date and adding the missed payments to the end of the loan, thereby extending the maturity. (2) A device that stores data not alterable by computer instructions.

real bills approach (to liquidity management) An approach that maintains that commercial loans should be made on a short-term, self-liquidating basis.

real effective exchange rate An exchange rate that is both adjusted for inflation differentials between countries (real) and weighted for the volume of trade with different countries (effective).

real estate The right, title, or interest that a person has in real property, as distinguished from the property itself.

real estate agent A person licensed by the state who, for compensation, lists, sells, leases, or rents real property through a contractual arrangement with, and under the direction of, a real estate broker. An agent cannot work independently of a broker. *See also* real estate broker.

real estate broker A person licensed by the state to conduct a brokerage business, that is, to bring together interested parties for the purpose of transacting a real estate deal. A broker may represent the seller or buyer, or upon full disclosure, both parties at the same time. Whichever party the broker represents, the broker also has a fiduciary relationship with the contra party and an obligation to fully disclose all relevant facts about the property. The broker's fee usually takes the form of a commission (often a percentage of the selling price).

real estate investment trust (REIT) An organization, usually corporate, established to accumulate funds for investment in real estate holdings, or to extend credit to others engaged in construction. Funds for investment are usually accumulated by selling shares of ownership in the trust.

real estate mortgage and investment conduit *See* REMIC.

real estate owned (REO) (1) All real estate directly owned by a bank, usually excluding real estate taken to satisfy a debt. (2) *See* other real estate owned.

Real Estate Settlement Procedures Act (RESPA) A federal law requiring lenders to provide home mortgage borrowers with information about known or estimated settlement costs. This act also establishes guidelines for escrow account balances and the disclosure of settlement costs. It is administered by the Department of Housing and Urban Development.

real gross national product The nation's output of goods and services adjusted to allow for inflation using 1982 prices as a basis for comparison.

real income Nominal income adjusted for inflation, that is, income expressed in terms of the amount of goods and services it will buy.

real interest rate *See* real rate of interest.

realize (1) To convert into cash or a receivable item through sale. (2) To convert into services through use. (3) To exchange for property that may be classified as or converted into a current asset.

realized profit or loss A profit or loss that results from selling or disposing of an asset, as distinguished from a paper profit or loss that results from holding rather than selling an asset.

realized value Under the Consumer Leasing Act, a term that includes (1) the price received by the lessor for the leased property, (2) the highest offer, or (3) the fair market value at the end of the lease term.

real market The market in which sizable trades can be executed. Quoted rates may not stand up in this market, if substantial buy or sell orders come in.

real property (1) Land, buildings, and other kinds of property that legally are classified as real property, as opposed to personal property. Real property includes buildings, minerals, and other products of the soil, including the air space above land. *See also* real estate. (2) The right, title, or interest that a person has in the ownership of real estate. In some states, this term is synonymous with real estate.

real property transaction An extension of credit in connection with which a security interest is or will be retained or acquired in real property.

real rate of interest The rate of interest adjusted to allow for inflation. The nominal interest rate less the expected rate of inflation is the real rate of interest. *Also called* real interest rate. *See also* nominal interest rate.

real rate of return The rate of return adjusted to allow for inflation. *Also called* real return. *See also* rate of return.

real time (1) The actual time during which processing occurs. (2) The actual time during which a computation should be performed so that the results can be used to guide a physical process. (3) An application in which response to input is fast enough to affect subsequent input, such as a process control system or a computer-assisted training (CAT) program. (4) (Adj.) On-line.

realtor A collective membership mark, which is owned by the National Association of Realtors and may be used only by a real estate professional who is a member of the association and who subscribes to its strict code of ethics.

realty A brief term for real property, and also for the business of buying and selling real property. *Compare with* personalty.

rebate (1) The return of some portion of interest that was previously collected, because a loan is repaid before its maturity date. (2) The return of part of a payment, representing some deduction from the full amount previously paid.

recap *See* recapitulation.

recapitalization (1) Any major change in a corporation's outstanding stock or paid-in surplus. (2) A reorganization of the equity structure of a close-ly held corporation, usually resulting in the creation of a new class of preferred stock. Taxpayers in the higher brackets exchange their common stock for this new preferred stock. They thereby "freeze" the value of their interest in the corporation for federal estate taxes and transfer the future appreciation of the company to the common stockholders in the lower tax brackets.

recapitulation The process of assembling subtotals taken from batch proof sheets and proof machines, to provide totals for final bank settlement. *Also called* recap.

recasting A collection technique, usually reserved for extreme situations, in which the past-due payments are added to the current unpaid balance and the total is recalculated for payment over an extended term.

receipt (1) A written acknowledgment that money or something else of value has been received. (2) A dated, legally validated acknowledgment of payment for a debt. The creditor forwards or gives the receipt to the debtor.

receipts acceleration The acceleration of the collection process for cash receipts.

receivables The accounts that are owed to a firm.

receivables turnover The ratio of net sales to average net receivables calculated to evaluate the quality of a firm's accounts receivable. The resulting figure indicates the average length of time that the firm's receivables remain outstanding.

receiver (1) An agent appointed by a bankruptcy court to manage a corporation during reorganization. (2) A court-appointed officer who receives the rents, issues, and profits of land or a business; manages a personal estate; or performs other duties under the court's guidance during the pendency of a suit. (3) The bank to which a payment order is addressed. *See also* receiving bank. (4) The person, institution, or other entity responsible for and authorized to receive a message. *Also called* recipient.

receiver information Miscellaneous information pertaining to a transfer and intended for the receiving bank.

receiver's correspondent bank A bank that acts as a reimbursement bank on the receiver's side in a transfer of funds.

receivership A form of bankruptcy in which a business is operated, during its reorganization, by a court-appointed trustee. The trustee (receiver) attempts to settle the financial difficulties of the company, while creditors can exercise their rights only to the extent permitted by the terms of the receivership.

receiving bank (1) A bank that receives any item. (2) A bank that receives paperless entries from an automated clearing house (ACH) after an originating bank has entered them in the ACH system. (3) The bank to which the message is delivered. *Also called* receiver.

receiving party The party, either the customer or the agent bank, named in a trade confirmation to receive the securities.

recession A period in which most economic activity slows. As a specific phase of the business cycle, a recession begins when economic activity begins to decline and ends when economic activity begins to increase.

recipient *See* receiver.

reciprocal account *See* due from account.

reciprocal buying The purchase of items from vendors who are one's customers.

reciprocal statutes Similar statutes in two or more states, providing mutual provisions or reciprocal treatment within the states affected concerning the subjects treated in the statutes. An example of reciprocal statutes would be similar provisions regarding corporation or inheritance taxes in two or more states.

reciprocal trust A trust created by one person in return for the creation by the beneficiary of a similar trust for that person.

reciprocity A mutual exchange of courtesies between two states or institutions; specifically, recognition by each state or institution of the validity of licenses or privileges granted by the other to its citizens or members.

reclamation (1) Money due to or owed by a bank because of an error made in listing the amount of a check on a clearing house balance. (2) In securities trades, the process of rejecting a delivery and recovering payment.

recognizance Acknowledgment of a former debt upon the record.

reconcilement A process of comparing and balancing one accounting record against another. It normally entails reconciling a general ledger account to a subsidiary ledger.

record A collection of related items of data, treated as a unit. For example, one line of an invoice may form a record, and a complete set of such records may form a file.

recordation (1) A recording that a lien has been created against certain property that is described in a mortgage. Such an entry is usually made in the appropriate public record of the county or other jurisdiction in which the particular property is located. (2) The registering of any official document.

record change A change of information contained in the master file.

record date *See* holder-of-record date.

recording The filing of a legal instrument in a county's public records.

recourse A general legal term meaning that the purchaser of a financial asset from an original creditor has a claim on the original creditor in case the debtor defaults. Specific arrangements to provide recourse arise in a variety of innovative transactions, including various types of securitized assets. Such arrangements can take many forms, including an explicit guarantee that credit losses will be reimbursed or the assets replaced by assets of similar quality; an agreement to repurchase assets before maturity; or more indirectly, indemnification by a third-party guarantor for any losses that occur. *See also* recourse plan.

recourse plan The right to collect from a maker, seller, assignor, or endorser of an instrument or installment credit obligation if the first party liable fails to meet the obligation. For example, should the consumer default, the retail dealer accepts full responsibility for the paper. *See also* full recourse; nonrecourse agreement; partial recourse agreement; repurchase plan.

recovery *See* salvage.

red clause letter of credit A letter of credit that provides for advances of payment to the beneficiary or to an agent before the presentation of documents, to enable him or her to accumulate goods or to arrange for goods to be shipped.

redeem (1) To buy back foreclosed property within a prescribed period. *See also* redemption period. (2) To repay the principal amount of a debt security, plus any accrued interest, at the date of maturity.

redemption (1) A statutory or contractual right to repurchase or repossess pledged, sold, or mortgaged property within the time allowed by and according to statutory or contractual conditions. (2) The right of a party under a disability to redeem or recover property taken from him or her, under color of right during the period of his or her disability. (3) Repayment of principal and interest to retire a security.

redemption notice A notice issued when a firm or municipality wishes to redeem outstanding debt securities.

redemption period The time in which a mortgagor, by paying the amount owed on a foreclosed mortgage, may buy back property. The specific time is subject to state law.

redemption price The price at which a bond may be redeemed before maturity, at the issuer's option.

red flag A warning that something may not be right when reviewing a credit application; for example, a 25-year-old applicant who states he has been on the job for 15 years, or a salary that is not in line with the type of work.

"red" futures contract month A month more than a year away, for which futures contracts are traded. The designation is used to distinguish between the same month in two different years, one with contracts maturing in the current year and the other (the "red" month) with contracts maturing a year later.

red herring A short, preliminary prospectus, available to potential investors in a new issue before the final prospectus is published. A red herring includes information about the company and industry, and financial statements, but it does not indicate the offering price or related information, which is determined just before the issue is offered for sale. A red herring is so named because the front cover of the preliminary prospectus bears notices printed in red, announcing that it is not the final, official prospectus.

rediscount To sell or discount a negotiable instrument a second time. Rediscount often refers to discounted instruments that banks subsequently sell to the Federal Reserve bank.

rediscount rate A synonym for discount rate.

redlining A practice in which certain areas of a community are eliminated from eligibility for mortgages or other loans, either intentionally or unintentionally, allegedly because the area is considered a poor investment risk. In effect, a red line is drawn around the eliminated area on a map. This practice is illegal.

reduced rate loans Loans that have been renegotiated, for economic or other reasons related to the debtor's financial difficulties, to rates below those that a bank would be willing to accept for new loans with comparable risk.

reel A spool of tape, generally magnetic tape.

referee A person appointed in court proceedings for the judicial settlement of a trustee's accounts, in order to conduct hearings with the interested parties and to report his or her findings to the court.

reference In a funds transfer environment, a transaction identifier that is normally included as part of the information supplied with the transaction itself and that can subsequently be used to distinguish the transaction identified from all other transactions (for example, in nostro account reconciliation).

Reference Book A book published by the Dun & Bradstreet Corporation, containing the names and credit ratings of commercial and industrial enterprises.

reference for the account owner The reference that identifies the transaction to the account owner bank.

reference for the beneficiary A data element in a funds transfer that is a reference enabling the beneficiary to identify the transfer. *Also called related reference.*

reference group One or more persons whose attitudes, opinions, and behavior influence the actions of others.

reference number (1) A numeric or other symbolic means of identifying a particular transaction. (2) A number assigned to each monetary transaction in a descriptive billing system. Each reference number is printed on the monthly statement to aid in retrieving the document, should the cardholder question the transaction.

reference rate A rate identified (for example, in an interest rate swap, cap, or future rate agreement) as the rate on which interest or other contractual payments will be based. Generally, the reference rate is a floating rate such as LIBOR or the prime rate.

referral (1) The directing of a potential customer from one area of the bank (for example, commercial lending) to another (for example, the employee-benefit trust department). (2) The directing of a client to the bank by a lawyer, accountant, or other professional.

refinance (1) To retire existing securities by selling new issues. (2) To retire existing loans or notes by changing their terms or by making new loans or notes. Refinancing provides an opportunity to take advantage of a fall in interest rates or to extend the maturity of an obligation. *See also* troubled debt restructuring.

refinancing The retirement of existing securities, or the repayment of a debt from the proceeds of new borrowings. *See also* troubled debt restructuring.

refreshing *See* buffering.

refunding The issuance of new debt securities to replace an older issue. *See also* refinancing.

refunding bond A bond used to retire other indebtedness. A drop in interest rates may make it worthwhile for a company to call in and replace one issue with another low-interest issue.

refund slip *See* credit slip.

regional bank A medium to large bank located outside the major money centers. *See also* money center bank.

regional banking The establishment of a banking presence in nearby states by merger, acquisition, or a new charter. Regional banking occurs when reciprocal laws are passed allowing bank holding companies in one state to acquire or establish a bank in another.

regional check processing center (RCPC) A Federal Reserve processing center, located outside Federal Reserve cities and designed for efficient processing of checks.

regional compact Groups of states whose laws mutually permit bank holding companies in the other states to acquire banks within their geographic boundaries. Regional compacts have led to the creation of superregional banks that are able to compete head on with major money center banks.

register (1) (Verb) To record and maintain a record of the ownership of a security. (2) (Verb) To file a statement with the Securities and Exchange Commission before issuing new securities. (3) (Noun) A device for temporary storage of one or more words to ease arithmetic, logical, or data transfer operations.

register check A draft used in some parts of the country instead of cashier's checks, money orders, or bank drafts.

registered as to principal A term applied to a coupon bond, for which the owner's name is registered on the bond and on the books of the company. Such bonds are not negotiable and cannot be sold without an assignment.

registered bond A bond whose negotiability is withdrawn by a writing on it that specifies to whom it belongs and by a registry to that effect at a specified office.

registered bond as to interest only A bond that has a bearer certificate; however, the issuer records the owner's name and address so that interest checks can be sent automatically when due.

registered bond as to principal only A bond whose owner's name is inscribed on the certificate and recorded on the issuer's books. Interest coupons are detached from the bond and presented for payment when interest is due.

registered form An instrument, such as a bond, that is issued in the name of, and payable only to, the owner.

registered representative (registered rep.) A person employed by and soliciting business for a brokerage or broker-dealer firm. The term "registered" means that the individual is licensed by the exchange and the Securities and Exchange Commission. *See also* stockbroker.

register of wills In some states, the title of the officer who receives wills offered for probate and who grants letters testamentary and letters of administration.

registrar (1) With stock, the agent that affixes its signature to each stock certificate issued, to prevent overissuance. (2) With bonds, the agent that maintains the record of ownership for registered bonds. *See also* transfer agent.

registration The evidence of ownership, as indicated on a registered bond or certificate of stock.

registration date The month, day, and year that a particular certificate is registered in the owner's or holder's name.

registration statement A statement that sets forth certain facts as prescribed by statute and by rules and regulations that implement the statute. With certain exceptions, a registration statement must be filed with the Securities and Exchange Commission before a public offering of new securities is made.

regression analysis A mathematical technique that describes how one random variable tends to move in response to the movement of another random variable.

regressive tax A duty levied at a decreasing rate as the tax base increases in size.

regular-way settlement A settlement procedure, used for most types of securities, that normally allows 5 business days for the settlement period.

regulation *See* Federal Reserve regulations.

Regulation 9 A regulation issued by the Comptroller of the Currency establishing standards for national banks in their use of fiduciary powers and collective investment funds. The full title of the regulation is Regulation 9-Fiduciary Powers of National Banks and Collective Investment Funds.

Regulation A The Federal Reserve regulation that governs borrowing by depository institutions at the Federal Reserve discount window. Credit extended is usually in the form of an advance on the bank's promissory note secured by U.S. government and federal agency securities, eligible commercial, agricultural, or construction paper, or bankers' acceptances. The credit cannot be extended for speculative purposes, and paper offered as collateral must be acceptable for discount or purchase under criteria specified in the regulation. *See also* adjustment credit; emergency credit; extended credit.

Regulation AA The Federal Reserve regulation that deals with consumer complaints, prohibits unfair or deceptive practices involving cosigners, and prohibits unfair late charges.

Regulation B The Federal Reserve regulation that prohibits creditors from discriminating on certain specified grounds against credit applicants, establishes guidelines for gathering and evaluating credit information, and requires written notification when credit is denied.

Regulation BB The Federal Reserve regulation that implements the Community Reinvestment Act and is designed to encourage state member banks and BHCs to help meet the credit needs of their communities. The OCC, FDIC, and FHLBB have identical rules.

Regulation C The Federal Reserve regulation that requires depository institutions making federally related mortgage loans to make annual public disclosure of the amount and locations of certain residential loans. This is done to implement the provisions of the Home Mortgage Disclosure Act of 1975, and it applies to most commercial banks, savings and loan associations, building and loan associations, homestead associations, and credit unions that make federally related mortgage loans.

Regulation CC The Federal Reserve regulation that covers the availability of funds deposited by customers, disclosures of a bank's policy on availability, and standards that must be used in endorsing checks.

Regulation D The Federal Reserve regulation that imposes uniform reserve requirements on all depository institutions against deposits and Eurocurrency liabilities. Regulation D defines such deposits and requires reports of deposits to the Federal Reserve.

Regulation E The Federal Reserve regulation that establishes the rights, liabilities, and responsibilities of parties in electronic funds transfers and that protects consumers using electronic funds transfer systems.

Regulation F The Federal Reserve regulation that requires state-chartered member banks that have 500 or more stockholders and at least $1 million in assets, or whose securities are registered on a national securities exchange, to register and file financial statements with the Federal Reserve Board of Governors. The OCC, FDIC, and FHLBB have similar securities regulations.

Regulation G One of four Federal Reserve regulations concerning credit extended to finance securities transactions. Regulation G governs credit secured by margin securities extended or arranged by parties other than banks, brokers, and dealers. *See also* Regulations T, U, and X.

Regulation H The Federal Reserve regulation that defines the membership requirements for state-chartered banks; describes membership privileges and conditions imposed on these banks; explains financial reporting requirements; and sets out procedures for requesting approval to establish branches and for requesting voluntary withdrawal from membership.

Regulation I The Federal Reserve regulation that requires each bank joining the Federal Reserve System to subscribe to the stock of its district

Reserve bank in an amount equal to 6 percent of the member bank's capital and surplus. Half the total must be paid on approval. The remainder is subject to call by the Board of Governors of the Federal Reserve System. Ownership of Federal Reserve stock must be adjusted with changes in the member bank's capitalization.

Regulation J The Federal Reserve regulation that establishes procedures, duties, and responsibilities for the collection of checks and other cash and noncash items, in the handling of returned checks, and in funds transfers by Federal Reserve banks.

Regulation K The Federal Reserve regulation that governs the organization, capitalization, and operations of domestic corporations involved in international banking or finance. Regulation K also governs certain operations of foreign banking organizations in the United States.

Regulation L The Federal Reserve regulation implementing the Management Interlocks Act that seeks to avoid restraints on competition among depository organizations by restricting the interlocking relationships that a management official may have with depository organizations.

Regulation M The Federal Reserve regulation that implements the consumer leasing provisions of the Truth in Lending Act.

Regulation N The Federal Reserve regulation that is internal to the Federal Reserve System. Regulation N governs relationships and transactions among Federal Reserve banks and foreign banks, bankers, and governments. It also describes the role of the Federal Reserve Board of Governors in these relationships and transactions.

Regulation O The Federal Reserve regulation that restricts the amount of credit member banks may extend to their own executive officers, directors, and principal shareholders. Regulation O also prohibits banks that maintain correspondent account relationships with other banks from extending credit on preferential terms to each other's executive officers. Similar rules apply to state nonmember banks.

Regulation P The Federal Reserve regulation that sets minimum standards for security devices and procedures that state-chartered member banks must establish to discourage robberies, burglaries, and larcenies and to assist in identifying and apprehending people who commit such acts.

Regulation Q The Federal Reserve regulation, phased out in 1986, that established maximum interest rates payable by member banks on savings and time deposits.

Regulation R The Federal Reserve regulation that tries to prevent interlocking relationships between securities dealers and member banks, in order to avoid potential conflicts of interest, collusion, or undue influence on member banks' investment policies or investment advice to customers.

Regulation S The Federal Reserve regulation that establishes the rates and conditions for reimbursement to financial institutions for providing records to a government authority, as authorized under the Right to Financial Privacy Act of 1978.

Regulation S-X Securities and Exchange Commission Regulation S-X, Article 9, contains substantially all the requirements for bank holding company financial statements, related footnotes, and supplemental schedules required to be filed with the SEC and included in annual reports to shareholders.

Regulation T The Federal Reserve regulation that governs extension of credit by securities brokers and dealers, including all members of national securities exchanges.

Regulation U The Federal Reserve regulation that governs extension of credit by banks for purchasing and carrying margin securities.

Regulation V The Federal Reserve regulation that assists in financing contractors, subcontractors, and others working for national defense.

Regulation W The Federal Reserve regulation that prescribed minimum down payments, maximum maturities, and other terms applicable to extensions of consumer credit. Such action was authorized by executive order during World War II, by congressional legislation in 1947-48, and again during the Korean conflict. With the repeal of authorizing legislation in 1952, Regulation W was revoked.

Regulation X (1) A Federal Reserve regulation that extends the provisions of Regulations G, T, and U (governing extensions of credit for purchasing or carrying securities in the United States) to certain borrowers and types of credit extensions not specifically covered by those regulations. (2) A Department of Housing and Urban Development (HUD) regulation that implements the Real Estate Settlement Procedures Act (RESPA).

Regulation Y The Federal Reserve regulation that relates to the bank and nonbank expansion of bank holding companies and to the divestiture of impermissible nonbank interests of BHCs, pursuant to the provisions of the Bank Holding Company Act.

Regulation Z The Federal Reserve regulation that prescribes uniform methods of computing the cost of credit, disclosure of credit terms, and procedures for resolving billing errors on certain credit accounts, pursuant to the provisions of the Truth in Lending Act.

regulator Any of the major regulatory authorities that oversee the operation of financial institutions in the United States. For banks, this would include the Office of the Comptroller of the Currency, the Federal Reserve Board, the Federal Deposit Insurance Corporation, and the 50 state banking divisions.

regulatory tax A duty levied on occupations and products primarily to regulate them rather than to raise revenue.

reimbursement An arrangement by which a correspondent bank is repaid for payments made to other parties, according to another bank's instructions.

reimbursement arrangement An arrangement in which a foreign correspondent bank is reimbursed for payments made according to the instructions of the bank issuing credit.

reimbursement bank A bank used where there is no account relationship between the ordering and paying bankers. A reimbursement bank provides the cover (that is, replenishes the account) for the transaction.

reimbursement letter of credit A letter of credit where a correspondent bank is authorized to effect reimbursement to the bank that pays the beneficiary of the credit. A reimbursing bank is usually engaged as an intermediary when the bank issuing the credit does not have an account relationship with the bank paying the beneficiary.

reimbursement method A data element in funds transfers that has instructions specifying how the receiver is to obtain reimbursement for the payment requested by the sender. If previously agreed, these instructions may specify a debit party other than the sender.

reimbursement party The party that is the source of funds to the receiver of a funds transfer instruction.

reinvestment rate (1) The interest rate at which funds from a maturing asset, or an asset that is sold, can be reinvested. (2) The interest rate at which interest payments received on an investment can be reinvested.

reinvestment risk The chance that a security's coupons will be reinvested at yields different from the security's stated yield to maturity.

reissue The process in which a new card is issued to a cardholder account on which the bank card has expired or will expire.

reissue month The month when customers' new cards are sent out to replace cards that are expiring.

REIT *See* real estate investment trust.

related reference *See* reference for the beneficiary.

relationship banking (1) A selective marketing strategy that focuses on attracting, maintaining, and improving relations with individual bank customers. Relationship banking strives to satisfy clients' total financial services needs. (2) A program offering a package of banking services to a customer. Frequently, customers are

offered lower costs based on the number or type of accounts they have.

relationship pricing Setting prices that provide an incentive for consumers to use multiple products.

release (1) An action by a person having or claiming to have some right, title, or interest in real or personal property, or some claim, right, or cause of action against another person, by which all such rights or claims of rights are forgiven, barred, and extinguished. A release may be oral but usually is evidenced by a written document signed by the person releasing the rights. (2) The act of passing checks from one bank department to another, for further processing. (3) The act of surrendering collateral to a borrower on repayment of a loan. (4) The act of giving a bill of lading to a drawee on payment or acceptance of a draft.

release deed *See* satisfaction of mortgage.

release of liability An agreement in which a lender terminates a mortgagor's personal obligation for the payment of a debt. *See also* satisfaction of mortgage.

release of lien An instrument discharging secured property from a lien. *See also* satisfaction of mortgage.

release time and date The time and date that a sender authorizes a wire service to forward the message to the receiver.

remainder A future estate or interest in property that will become an estate or interest in possession on the termination of the prior estate or interest created at the same time and by the same instrument. For example, A conveys Blackacre to B for life and on

B's death to C in fee simple. C's interest is a remainder. The term "remainder over" is sometimes used in such phrases as "To A for life, with remainder over to B," calling attention to the fact that there is a prior estate or interest. *Distinguish from* reversion.

remainder beneficiary The beneficiary of a trust who is entitled to the principal outright, after the interest of the prior beneficiary has been terminated.

remainder interest A future interest that will become an interest in possession after the termination of a prior interest created at the same time and by the same instrument as the future interest. For example, H leaves his estate in trust with income to be paid to W, and on her death the trust is to terminate and the property is to be delivered to C. C has a remainder interest.

remainderman A beneficiary entitled to receive the principal of an estate after the prior estate has expired. For example, a man's estate may leave the income from a trust to his widow. When she dies, the principal will pass to their son, the remainderman. Originally, the term applied, and in most states still does apply, to real property only.

REMIC (real estate mortgage and investment conduit) A type of collateralized mortgage obligation (CMO) similar to passthrough certificates authorized by the Tax Reform Act of 1986. REMICs divide cash flows into two different classes--regular and residual. Investors in each class receive payments of distinct priorities and timing. The regular-class instruments are classed as debt; residual-class instruments are classed as assets.

reminder letter The first in a series of collection letters, sent by a creditor to a debtor, when the latter has neglected to make a payment on time.

remittance coupons A book of coupons that a creditor provides to the debtor of an installment loan. The debtor then remits a coupon with each payment.

remittance document An instrument, usually card or paper, accompanied by a payment that may be cash, a check, money order, or electronic transfer of funds. *Also called* turnaround document.

remittance letter The transit letter accompanying a list of checks sent for collection from one bank to another, when the sending bank does not maintain an account with the receiving bank. The receiving bank then pays for the checks by remitting a bank draft to the sending bank.

remittance option An option to remit immediately to the U.S. Treasury any funds received for the Treasury in a bank's tax and loan account. *Compare with* note option.

remittance payment A payment sent by mail to a processing center.

remitter The source of funds in a payment order.

remitter advice method A data element in funds transfers that is a code specifying the method to be used (for example, telephone, letter, or wire) to notify the remitter that the account has been credited or that funds are available.

remote batch processing The method of inputting data for the computer to process through a remote terminal rather than at the computer center, where normal batch processing occurs.

remote electronic banking Electronic funds transfer systems that bank customers use to conduct business at a location other than a bank office, for example, a point-of-sale terminal or customer-bank communication terminal.

remote job entry (RJE) The submission of job control statements and data to a computer from a remote terminal, causing the jobs to be scheduled and executed as though encountered in the computer's own input stream.

remoteness of vesting *See* rule against perpetuities.

remote service unit An automated teller machine placed in a location other than a banking facility.

remote terminal An input and output device that is not at the immediate site of the computer.

renegotiable rate mortgage A mortgage with a short term, but amortized over a long period. At the end of the term, the lender agrees to refinance at a rate determined by an index of interest rates. The borrower may or may not have the option of paying the loan in full at the end of the term.

renounce (1) The act in which a person or trust institution named under a will as executor or trustee declines to accept appointment. (2) The act of a surviving spouse under the decedent's state law declining to take the provision made for him or her under the other's will and taking his or her share of the estate as if the other had died without a will. (3) Any action in which the beneficiary of any interest in real or personal property refuses to accept such an interest.

rent The price paid for the use of real (or personal) property.

renunciation In the trust business, an act, in accordance with prescribed procedures, by which a person or trust institution named as a fiduciary declines to accept the appointment.

reopen To sell more of an outstanding issue of U.S. Treasury securities, instead of offering a new issue.

reorganization A major change in the financial structure and operation of a corporation having financial difficulties. Reorganization (as used in Chapter 11 of the Bankruptcy Code) requires a court to change management and appoint trustees, for the purpose of reorganizing operations, to return the corporation to a profitable status.

repatriation of funds The return of funds held by a party in one country to that party's own country.

repetitive filings Under bankruptcy law, the term used to describe the practice of filing, dismissing, and refiling bankruptcy petitions to keep creditors at bay.

replacement cost Used in the cost approach of the appraisal process. Replacement cost is the cost of construction at current prices for an equivalent substitute improvement using modern materials and design standards. It would not necessarily be an exact duplicate because it would not include any obsolescence or deficiencies. *See also* reproduction cost.

replacement value The cost of replacing a lost or ruined asset.

replenishment deposit A payment that increases the balance of the originator's account serviced by the receiver (for example, the result of a bank transfer for its own account).

repo *See* repurchase agreement.

reporting days (Federal Reserve) Depository institutions with $42.1 million or less in total deposits (in 1989) report deposits to the Federal Reserve and calculate required reserves quarterly. Larger depository institutions report deposits weekly and maintain reserves with Federal Reserve banks on 2-week periods that end on Wednesdays. Depository institutions with reservable liabilities under $3.4 million (in 1989) are exempt from reserve requirements altogether. The specific figures given for 1989 are indexed and adjusted annually by the Federal Reserve.

report program generator (RPG) A processing program that can generate object programs that produce reports from existing sets of data.

repossession In bank operations, the act of taking physical possession of the security on a defaulted loan.

representative (1) A general term designating either an executor or an administrator. (2) The person who acts or speaks for another under his or her authority.

representative money Money (usually paper) that is convertible into full-bodied money. A silver certificate that could be exchanged for silver bullion would be an example.

representative office An office located outside a bank's normal geographic area or country that does not conduct normal banking business, like accepting deposits or making loans. It normally has only a few employees who attempt to develop business that can be channeled to the home office or who facilitate business

that originates at the home office. *Also called* rep office. *See also* loan production office.

representative selection Selection of a sample with the objective of being representative or typical of the population from which it was selected.

reproduction cost A term used in the cost approach of the appraisal process. Reproduction cost is the cost of construction at current prices of an exact duplicate of the existing structure, including all the deficiencies and obsolescence of the structure. *See also* replacement cost.

repudiation The intentional and willful default on a debt, generally referring to the act of a government or part of a government.

repurchase agreement A sale of securities with a simultaneous agreement to buy back the same securities at a stated price on a stated date. A repurchase agreement is the most common form of overnight investment for corporate funds. Normally in minimum amounts of $1 million, a repurchase agreement is supported 100 percent by securities from the bank's (or broker's) inventory. Most commonly, the collateral is Treasury bills. Regional and subregional banks will occasionally offer repurchase agreements in amounts of $500,000 or even $100,000 minimums. *Also called* repo *or* RP. *See also* repurchase plan. *Compare with* reverse repurchase agreement.

repurchase plan An agreement between a lender and a dealer in which the dealer agrees to repurchase the collateral in the event of the buyer's default, providing the lender returns the collateral to the dealer's place of business. The agreement usually provides that the collateral must not be damaged, or, if it is, the amount to be repaid may be reduced by the amount necessary to repair the damage. In a repurchase plan, the lender must return the collateral, as opposed to a recourse agreement, where the dealer must pay the lender even if the collateral cannot be found.

request for conditional commitment to guarantee loan A bank's request to the Farmers Home Administration or another guarantor, to indicate the guarantor's willingness to guarantee a loan on the terms that the bank spells out in its application for a guaranteed loan.

request for contract of guarantee A bank's request to a guarantor to issue a guarantee on the bank's loan, as presented in its application for a guaranteed loan.

res Literally, thing. In the phrase "trust res," it is the same as trust property.

rescheduling Renegotiation of the terms of an existing debt. *Also called* restructuring. *See also* troubled debt restructuring.

rescission Cancellation of a contract without penalty. Under the Truth in Lending Act, the ability of a consumer to terminate a credit transaction unilaterally, that is, without the creditor's consent.

research and development (R&D) The efforts to find and develop new materials, products, processes, and uses for present materials.

reservable deposits Deposits at depository institutions that are subject to the legal reserve requirements imposed by the Federal Reserve System. Transaction account balances up to $41.5 million are subject to a 3 percent reserve; above $41.5 million, the required reserve is 12 percent.

Eurocurrency liabilities have a 3 percent reserve requirement, as do nonpersonal time deposits with original maturities of less than 1 1/2 years. Nonpersonal time deposits with original maturities of more than 1 1/2 years have a 0 percent requirement. These ratios for reserve requirements can be changed from time to time.

reserve account An account, held at a Federal Reserve bank, that a depository institution uses to meet legal reserve requirements.

reserve checking/overdraft checking A combination of a checking account and a preauthorized personal loan. *Also called* cash reserve, check credit, *and* personal line of credit. *See also* overdraft banking.

reserve computation period The period for which the amount of required reserves is calculated. Depository institutions compute their required reserves on the basis of average deposits over a 2-week computation period ending on Mondays. These institutions then maintain reserves against those deposits over a 2-week period ending 2 days later, on Wednesdays.

reserve deficiency The amount by which reserves held by a depository institution fall short of legal requirements.

reserve for loan losses *See* allowance for loan losses.

reserve maintenance period The period during which required reserves, calculated for a slightly different period, must be maintained. Depository institutions, subject to contemporaneous reserve requirements, maintain required reserve balances for a 2-week period ending on Wednesdays. The required reserve balances are computed for a 2-week period ending 2 days earlier, on Mondays.

reserve ratio The ratio of reserves required by law to the deposits against which they must be held.

reserve requirements Those funds that a financial institution is required by law to set aside, generally in the form of cash or balances at a Federal Reserve bank.

reserves (1) A portion of the profits allocated to various reserve accounts for estimated losses. If an actual loss is incurred, it is charged against the reserve rather than to income. The creation of a reserve is the result of an accounting entry and does not, in and of itself, set aside cash or other funds. *See also* allowance for loan losses. (2) Cash on hand or deposited with the Federal Reserve, used by depository institutions to meet legal reserve requirements. (3) Funds in cash or quickly convertible into cash, if necessary, to meet current needs. *See also* primary reserves; pyramided reserves; secondary reserves.

residence (1) The place where a person resides, either temporarily or permanently. *See also* domicile. (2) As used in Regulation Z, any real property in which the customer lives or expects to live. This term is important in real estate transactions. When an interest to secure an obligation is taken in a customer's principal residence, notice of the right of rescission must be given to the customer. *See also* dwelling.

residential mortgage A loan extended using a residence as collateral. The collateral is usually a single-family owner-occupied home or a two- to four-family multiple-dwelling unit.

residential real property Improved real property used or intended to be used for residential purposes, including single-family homes, dwellings for two to four families, and individual units of condominiums and cooperatives.

residual cost (or value) (1) The difference between the cost of a particular asset and any amortized account or portion of an account. *See also* book value. (2) In a lease, the value of the property at the end of the lease (for example, the balance remaining due on an automobile lease at the end of the lease term).

residual value insurance Used in lieu of a lessee's guarantee to protect the lessor's investment in the residual value of leased property. Usually the lessor is the named insured and pays a premium for this insurance at the inception of the lease.

residuary clause The provision in a will or trust agreement that disposes of the decedent's property remaining in the estate after taxes, debts, expenses, and charges are paid, and all other gifts in the will or trust agreement are satisfied.

residuary devise A gift, by will, of the real property remaining after all specific devises are made.

residuary devisee *See* residuary estate.

residuary estate The property that remains after all other gifts in the will have been satisfied. Those who take the residuary estate are known as residuary legatees (as to personal property) and residuary devisees (as to real property).

residuary legatee A person who receives the remainder of a testator's personal property after all other legacies are satisfied. *See also* residuary estate.

residuary trust A trust composed of the testator's property remaining in the estate after taxes, debts, expenses, and charges are paid, and all other gifts under the will are satisfied.

residue In the expression "rest, residue, and remainder," that portion of a decedent's estate remaining after the payment of all debts, expenses, and charges and the satisfaction of all legacies and devises.

resolution A formal document expressing the intention of a corporation's board of directors.

Resolution Funding Corporation (RefCorp) A federally chartered corporation established to raise funds for the Resolution Trust Corporation's use in liquidating failed FSLIC institutions and rescuing those that are salvageable. *Also called* REFCO.

Resolution Trust Corporation (RTC) A federal agency created by the Financial Institutions Reform, Recovery and Enforcement Act of 1989 (commonly known as FIRREA) to oversee the liquidation of assets of insolvent savings and loan associations.

Resolution Trust Corporation Oversight Board A policy-making board that will govern the actions of the Resolution Trust Corporation, composed of the secretary of the Treasury, the secretary of Housing and Urban Development, the chairman of the Federal Reserve, and two independent members appointed by the president and confirmed by the Senate.

resources The assets owned by a bank. Resources generally include cash on hand and due from others, investments, loans, buildings, furniture, and fixtures.

respondent bank A bank that regularly buys the services of a correspondent bank for stipulated activities, such as trade clearing or indirect depository participation. *Also called* downstream correspondent.

respondentia In ancient Greece, an agreement applying to loans secured by cargo on shipping vessels. In the event the ship was lost, the loan was canceled. *See also* bottomry.

response time The length of time required to complete an electronic transaction. Response time is the time that elapses between generating an inquiry to, and receiving a response from, a computer.

responsibility accounting A system in which individuals are responsible for expenditures under their control. Costs thus are identified with individuals, rather than products or procedures.

restraint of trade Actions taken by a firm or group of firms to restrict competition, effect a monopoly, or artificially maintain prices in a particular market or markets.

restraint on alienation of property A limitation on a person's right to transfer title to property or property rights.

restricted account A cardholder record to which a status code has been posted, indicating that the cardholder may not use his or her account.

restricted card list A listing of cardholder accounts, in either alphabetical or numerical sequence, on which transactions are restricted and not to be completed by merchants without authorization. *Also called* cancellation bulletin, hot card list, warning bulletin, warning list, *or* card recovery bulletin.

restricted stock *See* letter stock.

restrictive endorsement An endorsement that restricts the negotiability of the instrument, for example, for deposit only.

restructured loan A loan on which the interest rate has been lowered or the maturity has been lengthened to make it easier for the borrower to make payments. The alternative to restructuring in most cases is an outright default. *See also* troubled debt restructuring.

restructuring *See* troubled debt restructuring.

resulting trust A trust that results in law from things people do, regardless of whether they actually intend to create a trust. For example, a resulting trust occurs when a person disposes of property under circumstances that imply that he or she does not intend that the person taking or holding the property shall have the beneficial interest in it. *Distinguish from* constructive trust *and* express trust.

retail balance On a cardholder's account, that portion of a total balance reflecting the purchase of goods or services, as opposed to cash advances. *Sometimes called* merchandise balance.

retail banking Banking services offered to consumers and small businesses. The "full-service" commercial bank offers both retail and "wholesale" banking services, dealing with both consumers and businesses of all sizes.

retail credit (1) Charge accounts, credit cards, or installment loans extended to consumers by merchants. (2) Loans extended directly to consumers by banks such as personal loans, auto loans, and so on.

retail credit bureau A center of local consumer credit information. Its primary function is to furnish reports on consumers desiring to obtain money.

retail lending Loans to individuals, including home mortgages and consumer installment loans. *Also called* consumer lending.

retail paper Another name for dealer paper. *See also* dealer paper.

retainage The amount of a contractor's bill that is withheld until the job has been completed.

retained earnings Earnings, not distributed to stockholders, that have not been transferred to the surplus account. Retained earnings are a part of the company's net worth.

retention rate *See* buy rate.

retention ratio The component of a firm's capital generation rate, equal to one minus the payout ratio.

retire *See* redeem.

retirement (1) The withdrawal of a security from circulation, usually through redemption. (2) The removal of a fixed asset from service, at the end of its productive life or on its sale.

retirement plan trust A trust established to enable employees on retirement to receive a pension from funds created out of payments made by the employees, their employer, or both.

retrieval system A device that provides for the visual display or printout of stored data on hard copy.

return items Checks, drafts, or notes that have been dishonored by the drawee bank or maker and have been returned to the presenting party.

return on assets (ROA) A profitability ratio. Return on assets is net income divided by average total assets. Return on assets indicates how efficiently assets are employed.

return on equity (ROE) A profitability ratio. Return on equity is net income divided by average total equity. Return on equity indicates how efficiently equity capital is invested.

return on investment (ROI) The rate of profit earned relative to the value of average capital investment. The return on investment is usually expressed as a percentage for purposes of comparability with the return on other investments.

revaluation An increase in the official value of a nation's currency relative to gold or other currencies. A revaluation occurs when a government reduces the amount of its currency it will offer in exchange for a certain quantity of another currency or gold.

revenue The income from any property or service. *See also* marginal revenue.

revenue anticipation note (RAN) Short-term municipal notes sold in anticipation of the receipt of revenues, and payable from the proceeds of those revenues. Tax anticipation notes are the most common.

revenue bond A bond issued to finance a specific revenueor income-producing project, with interest and principal repaid out of that income.

revenues (1) The income of government, mainly received from taxes. (2) The total income received from all sources by a company. (3) A term used variously to refer to the total income of a business or government, income generated only from the sale of goods, or income generated only from sources other than sales.

revenue stamp An adhesive stamp, issued by the federal or state government, that must be purchased and affixed, in amounts provided by law, to documents or instruments representing original issues, sales, and transfers of stocks and bonds; deeds of conveyance; and certain types of foreign insurance policies. *Also called* documentary stamp.

revenue tariff *See* tariff.

reverse *See* reverse repurchase agreement.

reverse annuity mortgage (RAM) A credit instrument that enables homeowners to live on the equity in their house without selling it. The owner takes out a mortgage under the terms of which the lender pays the owner a fixed sum monthly for a stated period of time, using the mortgage-free property as collateral. At the end of the term, the borrower must repay the lender to avoid having to sell or refinance the property. *Also called* reverse mortgage.

reverse conversion An arbitrage trade in options involving the sale of the underlying instrument and the establishment of a synthetic long position in options on the underlying instrument (the purchase of a call and sale of a put). *See also* arbitrage; conversion; synthetic positions.

reverse money transfer A debit transfer in which the credit party is the sender. *Also called* charge wire *and* direct debit.

reverse mortgage *See* reverse annuity mortgage.

reverse repurchase agreement A purchase of securities with a simultaneous agreement to sell back the same securities at a stated price on a stated date. Compare with a repurchase agreement, which is a sale of securities with an agreement to buy the same securities back at a stated price on a stated date. A reverse repurchase agreement is a repurchase agreement originated by the lender, rather than the borrower. *Also called* reverse, reverse repo, *or* security resale agreement.

reverse stock split An action in which the issuer replaces outstanding, very low-priced stock with a reduced number of shares. This action causes a proportionate increase in the market price per share. This action may also make the stock more attractive to those investors who avoid low-priced shares in the belief that they are speculative.

reverse swap One form of activity in the secondary swap market. A reverse swap offsets the interest rate or currency exposure on an existing swap. It can be written with the original counterparty or with a new counterparty.

reversible encryption DEA transformation of clear text so that the encrypted text can be decrypted back to the original clear text.

reversion The interest in an estate remaining in the grantor after a particular interest, less than the whole estate, has been granted by the owner to another person. Reversion should be distinguished from remainder: the

reversion remains in the grantor, the remainder goes to a grantee.

reverter The interest that the grantor retains in property for which he or she has conveyed an interest less than the whole to another party. If the grantor makes the conveyance subject to a condition that may or may not be broken sometime in the future, he or she retains a possibility of reverter.

review The degree of work performed by a public accounting firm in conjunction with the issuance of financial statements of a nonpublic entity that is greater in scope than a compilation but less in scope than an audit and does not provide a basis for the expression of an opinion on the financial statements. However, the accountant's report would generally state that, based on his or her review, the accountant is not aware of any material modifications that should be made to the financial statements for them to conform to generally accepted accounting principles.

revocable letter of credit A letter of credit that may be canceled at any time by the issuing bank. *Compare with* irrevocable letter of credit.

revocable trust A trust agreement that can be altered or terminated by the person establishing the trust. The agreement may provide for the management of property by an individual or company, for the beneficiary of the trust. *Compare with* irrevocable trust.

revocable trust with consent or approval A trust in which the maker reserves the right to end the trust and reclaim the trust property, but only with the consent of one or more other people. For example, A creates for his son B a trust that may be revoked by A with C's consent (in this case, C may be B's mother). *Distinguish from* irrevocable trust.

revocation The act of annulling or making inoperative a will or trust instrument.

revolver A revolving line of credit. *See also* revolving line of credit.

revolving letter of credit A letter of credit that covers a series of commercial transactions by allowing for automatic reinstatement of amounts available under the credit.

revolving line of credit A specified maximum line of credit on which a borrower may draw for a limited period. The balance may fluctuate from zero up to the maximum amount. *Compare with* nonrevolving line of credit.

revolving underwriting facility (RUF) *See* note issuance facility.

rider A document that modifies the protection offered under an insurance policy.

right (1) The privilege, attaching to a share of stock, to subscribe to other securities in a fixed ratio. (2) That which is reserved by a grantor, as the right of amendment or revocation, as opposed to the power granted to the trustee.

right-hand side The rate at which a bank will buy foreign currencies.

right of anticipation The privilege given a mortgagor or term borrower, by a provision in the debt instrument, to pay all or any portion of the outstanding balance of the obligation before its due date, without penalty.

right of election The right of a surviving spouse, under the decedent's estate law, to take his or her intestate

share in preference to the provision made in the decedent's will.

right of offset (setoff) (1) The common-law right of a lender to use the balances in any of the customer's accounts as payment for a loan in the event of default. Bankruptcy proceedings may affect the enforceability of this right. (2) Generally accepted accounting principles set forth specific criteria for when assets and liabilities may be setoff (netted) on the balance sheet.

right of rescission Under Regulation Z and the Truth in Lending Act, the right of a borrower to rescind certain transactions in which a lien is being placed on his or her home within 3 days after signing the mortgage documents. During this 3-day period, the creditor is not to disburse the proceeds.

right of survivorship In a joint tenancy or tenancy by the entirety, the right of the surviving tenant to take ownership of the property on the death of the other tenant, subject to tax laws.

rights The privilege of buying shares of new stock at a price somewhat lower than the subscription price. A corporation gives stock rights to its present stockholders, to retain their present percentage of ownership of its stock shares outstanding. Rights are sometimes traded on the securities markets.

rights offering An offering, to existing stockholders, of the right to buy additional shares of stock. The rights may be exercised (used to buy stock) or sold to someone else, who can then exercise the rights.

Right to Financial Privacy Act A law that regulates how federal agencies may obtain records from financial institutions. It provides for notice to the customer before records may be obtained, but it contains many exemptions, including grand jury subpoenas.

rising yield curve A yield curve in which rates on long-term maturities are higher than rates on shorter maturities. The opposite effect (that is, when short-term rates are higher than long-term rates) is called an inverse (inverted) yield curve.

risk The degree of possibility that a loss will be sustained in a loan or investment, or other transaction. In payment systems, risk includes a number of possibilities such as operations risk, fraud risk, credit risk, and settlement risk, as well as the risk that a computer or facilities outage can result in loss.

risk-adjusted capital A measure of capital adequacy that attempts to recognize the amount of risk reflected in a bank's asset portfolio.

risk analysis (1) An examination of the sources of risk in a loan or investment, and their separate and combined effects. (2) A systematic review of an electronic data processing system's assets and vulnerabilities to estimate an expected loss from certain events based on the probability of those events occurring.

risk assessment A process for identifying exposure to risk in order to develop a cost-effective strategy for controlling it.

risk assets As used by security analysts, all assets of a bank except cash due from banks and U.S. government land agency obligations.

risk-based capital An international agreement concerning the capital adequacy standard of international

banking institutions. It has been adopted in the United States through standards issued by the Office of the Comptroller of the Currency, the Federal Reserve Board, and the Federal Deposit Insurance Corporation. Risk-based capital defines the measurement of capital risk, adjusts assets to reflect an appropriate level of credit risk, and includes off-balance-sheet transactions in determining appropriate levels of capital. *See also* capital adequacy.

risk capital (1) Equity capital. If a business fails, the stockholders' claims are subordinate to the bondholders' claims. (2) Funds invested in an enterprise with a high risk for stockholders. *Also called* venture capital. *Distinguish from* risk-based capital.

risk categories (1) The classification of lending risks for purposes of risk analysis. (2) In risk-based capital, the categories into which on- and off-balance sheet exposures are grouped. The risk-based capital guidelines, as issued by U.S. regulators in 1989, set forth four major risk categories, with risk weightings ranging from 0 to 100 percent.

risk diversification Investment in diversified types of assets to reduce risk exposure.

risk evaluation The measurement of the probable frequency and severity of financial loss inherent in each exposure to risk.

risk feature An item affecting mortgage risk.

risk-free rate The rate of interest on a risk-free asset (a U.S. Treasury security). The risk premium on any security can be estimated by comparing its yield with that of a risk-free security of comparable maturity.

risk identification The development of an inventory of resources, the dangers that could affect them, and the possible ensuing adverse effects of those dangers.

risk pooling Investing in financial assets with different risk/return characteristics.

risk rating (1) The analysis of mortgage risk to estimate, in precise relative terms, the soundness of individual transactions. (2) A function performed at many banks in which the loan review department establishes ratings for each credit based on the risk involved. (3) For risk-based capital, *see* risk categories.

risk/return trade-off A trade-off signifying that more risk generally means more return, and vice versa. In most markets, an investor may obtain a greater return on an investment if the investor is willing to take greater risk of default.

role playing A method of training in which employees act out all the parts in a particular situation in order to gain experience and comfort with newly learned behavior.

roll-out The sale of corporate assets to investors in a limited partnership.

rollover (1) The process of refinancing a maturing security by issuing another security, refinancing a loan by borrowing, or reinvesting the proceeds from the sale of a security or from a maturing security in another security. (2) The process of extending a maturing contract for forward delivery of a commodity or foreign currency. (3) The carrying forward each month of a portion of an outstanding balance on a cardholder account. (4) The repeated investment of the proceeds of short-term securities on maturity.

(5) The extension of a maturing certificate of deposit to a new maturity date, or the conversion of a deferred fund to another vehicle (for example, the rollover of an IRA). *See also* tax-free rollover.

roll-up The incorporation of existing limited partnerships into a master limited partnership.

rotating internship A method of training in which trainees in various parts of an organization are interchanged.

round lot The usual unit of trading in a security, or a multiple thereof. A round lot of stock is generally 100 shares. For bonds, $1,000 par value is typical. *See also* odd lot.

round turn A procedure by which a person's long or short position is offset by an opposite transaction or by accepting or making delivery of the actual financial instrument.

routine An ordered set of instructions for a computer that may have some general or frequent use.

routing number *See* transit number.

routing transit number *See* transit number.

royalty (1) The compensation for using property or knowledge, usually an agreed portion of the income arising from such use. (2) A payment reserved by the grantor of a patent, lease of a mine, oil property, or similar right, and payable proportionately to the use made of the right or output by the grantee. (3) Agreements in which an author, musician, or inventor receives a certain payment on each copy of his or her work that is sold.

royalty interest in mineral leases and rights *See* working interest.

rubricated account Any account that has been earmarked for a specific purpose.

RUF (revolving underwriting facility) *See* note issuance facility.

rule A regulation. A rule is a specific guide to one action rather than a series of actions, such as "always count cash twice before giving it to a customer."

Rule 17f-1 A regulation of the Securities and Exchange Commission that deals with loss, counterfeiting, and theft of securities other than government securities. This rule established the Securities Information Center, Inc. (SIC) as a central agency to cope with these serious problems. Financial institutions must report most incidents to SIC and usually to the transfer agent. Thefts and counterfeits are also reported to the police. The rule also requires financial institutions to inquire whether securities that come into their possession have been reported as missing, lost, counterfeit, or stolen.

Rule 387 The New York Stock Exchange rule governing extension of delivery-versus-payment (DVP) privileges by its member brokers. Brokers can extend DVP privileges only to customers who use an electronic confirmation and institutional delivery system, which speeds settlement.

rule against accumulations The limitation imposed by common law or statute on the accumulation of income by a trustee.

rule against perpetuities A rule of common law that makes void any estate or interest in property so limited that it will not take effect or vest within a period measured by a life or lives in being at the time of the

creation of the estate, plus 21 years and the period of gestation. *Sometimes called* rule against remoteness of vesting.

rule in Shelley's case A rule of law that nullifies a remainder interest in heirs of the grantee. For example, A conveys Blackacre to B for life, remainder to heirs of B. Under this rule, B's heirs received nothing and B took a fee simple absolute interest in Blackacre. This rule has been abolished by statute or judicial decision in many states.

rule of 78s A method of calculating the rebate on an installment loan if the borrower pays in full before maturity. With this method, the rebate is calculated as a fraction. The numerator of the fraction is the sum of the remaining number of months to maturity. The denominator is the sum of the months of the original term. This fraction is then multiplied by the original finance charge and other rebatable amounts, such as dealer reserve, life, and disability insurance, to determine the amount of the rebate. With the advent of simple interest loans, this method has been largely eliminated.

rule of exceptions The principle by which a manager focuses on tasks that deviate from the normal routine and delegates routine operations to subordinates.

run (1) A list of bid and asked quotes from a dealer. (2) A single, continuous performance of a computer program or routine.

runaway A cardholder account that has exceeded the excess purchases limitation and may have exceeded its credit limit, on which charges continue to be received or there is otherwise an indication of unauthorized use.

run book A book of instructions for the operator on the running of each program or job.

runner An employee who is the messenger responsible for delivering items among various banking offices.

safe deposit box A metal container owned by a bank, kept in the vault, and rented to customers for their use. The bank usually charges the customer an annual fee for use of a safe deposit box. The safe deposit box has two keys. One is held by the customer and the other by the bank, and both are needed to open the box. *See also* dual control.

safe deposit vault An area within a bank's vaults where customers can rent space in which to store their valuables.

safekeeping A service provided by a bank in which customers' valuables, including those too large for safe deposit boxes, are protected in the bank's vaults for a fee. The provision of safe deposit boxes and the custody of securities are two important forms of safekeeping. Safe deposit services do not provide the client with a receipt for specific assets; in other forms of safekeeping, a definitive receipt is given.

safekeeping account An agency account in which the agent receives, safeguards, and delivers the property in the account on demand by the principal or on his or her order. The principal is given a specific, itemized receipt for the property. *Distinguish from* custody account *and* managing agency account.

salary A specified payment for services, usually paid weekly, biweekly, or monthly. A salary is distinguished from a wage, which is generally paid per hour of services.

salary administration The process of determining individual salaries and the policies and procedures for salaries.

salary compression (1) The effect caused when low salaries at upper levels of management reduce the opportunity for salary increases for junior officers or employees. (2) The situation that exists when the market value of a job exceeds the salary being paid internally by the organization.

sale The transfer of ownership of property from one party to another for compensation.

sale and leaseback The sale of an asset and the simultaneous agreement to lease it back from the purchaser.

sale of remainder interest An estate-planning technique in which an older-generation family member sells a remainder interest in an asset he or she owns to a younger-generation family member while retaining the life estate. The cost of the remainder interest is determined in accordance with the ten percent tables. At the death of the life tenant, the asset passes to the remainderman free of transfer tax. Unlike a joint purchase, the life tenant may not amortize the life estate for federal income tax purposes.

sale on approval A sale in which title to the property remains with the seller until the buyer manifests his or her intention to buy.

sale or return A clause in a sales contract that stipulates that, although ownership of the goods sold will pass to the buyer immediately on delivery, the buyer may return the goods if they are unsatisfactory.

sale-repurchase agreement A repurchase agreement.

sales audit A verification of proper preparation and acceptability of bank card sales drafts, credit slips, merchant summaries, and cash advances.

sales authorization The process of having a merchant obtain a bank's approval for sales in excess of preestablished floor limits. Sales authorization may also be required for reasons other than the amount of the sale.

sales comparison approach to value One of the methods used in estimating property value. In this method, the subject is compared with similar properties (termed comparable sales) that have recently sold. When properties are systematically compared, value differences are determined to estimate the worth of the subject property. *Also called* the direct sales comparison *or* market data approach.

sales draft An instrument, arising from the use of a bank card, that evidences an obligation on the part of the cardholder to pay money to the card issuer. *Also called* sales slip *and* ticket.

sales draft clearing In interchange arrangements, the exchange of bank card items between merchant banks and cardholder banks.

sales draft envelope *See* deposit envelope.

sales finance company A company that buys installment contracts from dealers who sell durable consumer goods. Frequently, a subsidiary of a manufacturing firm (a "captive"

finance company) finances the purchase of that firm's products.

sales manager (1) The person responsible for managing a sales force. (2) The person responsible for soliciting and servicing credit card merchants.

sales slip *See* sales draft.

sales summary slip *See* merchant summary slip.

sales-to-inventory ratio A turnover ratio (sales divided by inventory) that approximates how many times per year a firm sells the equivalent of a complete inventory.

sales-to-net-worth ratio A turnover ratio (sales divided by net worth) that determines the owner's investment in the business to generate sales.

sales-to-total-assets ratio A turnover ratio (sales divided by total assets) that indicates whether a business is generating an acceptable volume of sales, given its investment in assets.

Sallie Mae *See* Student Loan Marketing Association.

salvage An attempt to obtain repayment for some portion of a loan that a bank has already written off the books.

same day funds Funds that are available today for transfer or withdrawal in cash, subject to settlement of the transaction through a payment mechanism. *Also called* available funds.

sample A collection of elements drawn from a larger group of elements and studied to determine characteristics of the group as a whole. A truly representative sample helps the statistician determine accurately the properties of the entire group. Sampling is also an important part of the auditing process.

sample evaluation The process of drawing conclusions concerning the population based on the sample results.

sampling error Difference between a population value and the sample estimate, due to the fact that only a sample of values is observed.

sampling risk The probability of obtaining an error-free sample if the population actually contains errors equal to the upper error limit.

SAN-1 The first optional subsidiary account identification number held in addition to the primary account number (PAN).

SAN-2 The second optional subsidiary account identification number held in addition to the primary account number (PAN) and SAN-1.

satisfaction of mortgage A recordable instrument given by the lender to evidence repayment in full of mortgage debt. *Sometimes called* a release deed *or* discharge of mortgage. *See also* release of lien.

satisfactory account A term used in credit references, indicating that the terms of the account have been met as agreed.

savings account An interest-bearing account that a depositor may use to accumulate a fund gradually from earnings or income.

savings and loan association A state or federally chartered financial institution that accepts savings and checkable deposits from the public and invests them primarily in mortgage loans. A savings and loan association

may be either a mutual or a capital stock institution and may also make loans to businesses and consumers.

Savings Association Insurance Fund (SAIF) As mandated by the Financial Institutions Reform, Recovery and Enforcement Act of 1989, the fund under the control of the FDIC that receives deposit insurance assessments from savings associations. *See also* Deposit Insurance Fund (DIF) *and* Federal Deposit Insurance Corporation assessment.

savings bank An institution that primarily accepts interest-bearing time and checkable deposits for investment in mortages and high-grade securities. A savings bank may also make loans to businesses and consumers. *See* mutual savings bank *and* stock savings bank for specific types of savings banks.

savings bond A security issued by the U.S. Treasury Department. This bond is nonnegotiable and is bought from, or sold back to, the federal government at a set price. Its principal attraction is its relative lack of risk from price changes, because it is not subject to market fluctuations.

savings certificate A fixed-maturity time deposit, offered in smaller denominations, primarily to individuals. The interest rate paid on a savings certificate usually exceeds the rate paid on a regular savings account, but a penalty is paid if funds are withdrawn before maturity.

savings club An account in which the customer makes stated deposits at specified intervals, to meet a specific goal.

savings deposit An interest-paying account used to safekeep and accumulate funds.

scalp To trade for small gains. It typically involves establishing and liquidating a position quickly, usually within the same day.

scalper A speculator in futures contracts who buys and sells actively on very small movements in price.

scarcity A condition that exists when the demand for a particular good or service exceeds the supply at current prices. In one sense, all "goods" by definition are scarce, thereby necessitating the pricing mechanism to allocate them efficiently.

scenic check A type of check that portrays a scene or colorful pattern.

schedule of charges A schedule showing the rates charged for handling various transactions.

schedule of distribution A list showing the distributive shares of an estate.

scrip Evidence of a fractional part of a bond or a share of stock.

scrip agent An agent who issues shares or cash as requested by an investor surrendering scrip (fractional shares of stock).

scrip dividend A dividend payable in the future.

seal An impression, device, sign, or mark, recognized by statute or judicial decision as having the legal effect of a common-law seal. The common-law doctrine of contracts under seal has been abolished in most states.

seasonal loan A short-term loan to be repaid from earnings at the end of a given business season.

seasonal variation A deviation from the average level of regular economic or business activity, due to periodic changes in climate, holidays, vacations, and so on.

seasoned securities Securities that have been on the market long enough to be held by permanent investors. Seasoned securities include any securities with a well-recognized reputation that are generally accepted by the investing public.

SEC *See* Securities and Exchange Commission.

secondary beneficiary A beneficiary whose interest in a trust is postponed or subordinate to that of the immediate (primary) beneficiary. *Compare with* immediate beneficiary.

secondary capital Limited life preferred stock and long-term debt. Primary and secondary capital add up to total capital under the old capital adequacy framework. In the new risk-based capital framework, the components of capital are defined differently, and are referred to as Tier One and Tier Two capital. *See also* capital adequacy.

secondary data Information originally compiled for another purpose that can be used in analyzing a firm's current competitive and economic environment.

secondary financing Financing real estate by using loans that are subordinate to the first mortgage.

secondary market A market for the resale of securities, such as the dealer market or a stock exchange, where ownership is transferred from one owner to another. The first sale of any security is in the primary market; all subsequent sales are in the secondary market.

secondary market commitment A written agreement between a mortgage lender and an investor in which the investor states the terms, rates, and conditions for the purchase of loans or mortgage-backed securities from the mortgage lender.

secondary mortgage market Transactions involving the sale and purchase of existing mortgages. Mortgage loans originate in the primary mortgage market; the sale of those loans occurs in the secondary mortgage market. Purchases by the Federal National Mortgage Association (Fannie Mae) and the Federal Home Loan Mortgage Corporation (Freddie Mac) are part of the secondary mortgage market.

secondary offering An offering to sell a sizable quantity of securities that have been previously owned. Advertisements for secondary offerings appear only as a matter of record.

secondary reserves Funds invested in high-quality, short-term assets that can be quickly converted to cash without major loss. *Also called* liquidity account. *Compare with* primary reserves.

second mortgage A real estate mortgage subordinate to a first mortgage.

sector A major part of the economy (for example, the business or financial sector).

sector fund A specialized mutual fund that invests only in a particular industry, for example, oil, technology, or utilities. *Also called* market fund.

secular trust An irrevocable trust created by executive-level employees to protect their retirement benefits from limitations imposed under the Tax Reform Act of 1986 and adverse changes in corporate control. Income from the trust is taxable on a current, not a deferred, basis; however, the

funds are beyond the reach of management and company creditors.

secured account An account against which collateral or other security is held.

secured creditor A person whose claim against another person is protected by collateral that he or she holds, to ensure the settlement of the claim.

secured demand loan A demand loan for which the lender holds collateral as security. The value of the collateral should at least equal that of the loan.

secured liability An obligation that is guaranteed by the pledge of some asset or collateral. In the event of default or inability to liquidate the liability, title of the pledged asset may pass to the creditor.

secured loan A loan against which a tangible asset has been pledged in case of default on the loan.

Securities Act of 1933 A congressional act that sets forth registration requirements for the issuance of securities in a public offering. While banks are among those entities exempted from the registration requirements, bank holding companies are not. Further, the banking regulators (for example, the Office of the Comptroller of the Currency) have issued registration requirements that apply to banks; these requirements are similar to those of the SEC.

Securities Acts Amendments of 1975 Legislation that revised the securities acts of the 1930s to further protect investors. The law reformed both the method and the manner by which self-regulatory organizations operate, including the SEC's oversight authority; created a federal mechanism for the regulation of municipal securities and brokers, dealers, and banks engaged in the municipal securities business; and granted the SEC broad, discretionary authority to oversee the development of a national market system, including the regulation of clearing agencies, securities depositories, and transfer agents.

Securities and Exchange Commission (SEC) The federal agency that regulates the public sale of securities and related disclosures. The SEC monitors issuers, underwriters, exchanges, and over-the-counter dealers.

securities depository A physical location or organization where securities certificates are deposited and transferred by bookkeeping entry. *Also called* clearing agency.

Securities Exchange Act of 1934 A congressional act that established the Securities and Exchange Commission. It imposes ongoing disclosure requirements for entities whose securities are publicly traded (for example, proxy statements, annual reports).

Securities Information Center, Inc. (SIC) The entity designated to operate the data base for the Lost and Stolen Securities Program. *See also* Rule 17f-1.

Securities Investor Protection Corporation (SIPC) A nonprofit membership organization created by the Securities Investor Protection Act of 1970 to provide financial protection to customers of failing brokers or dealers who are members.

securities theft and counterfeiting *See* Rule 17f-1.

securities trading The buying or selling of securities through the recognized primary and secondary markets.

securitization The process of converting receivables (for example, loans) into securities. It is accomplished by originating loans, combining them into pools with similar features, and selling securities that are secured by the principal and interest payments from the original loans. The types of loans used in this process include automobile receivables, credit card receivables, residential mortgages, and others. *See also* pass-through security.

security (1) A written document showing ownership of equity in a corporation (stock) or showing evidence of indebtedness (bond, note, or certificate). (2) The property or asset that is given, deposited, or pledged to ensure the fulfillment of an obligation.

security agreement An agreement that creates or provides for a security interest. An agreement granting a creditor a security interest in personal property, which is normally perfected either by the creditor taking possession of the collateral or by filing financing statements in the proper public records.

security audit An examination of electronic data processing security procedures and measures to evaluate their adequacy and compliance with established policy.

security data A set of characters on a bank card that controls its use and limits fund withdrawals at off-line terminals. The security data may also contain an enciphered form of the cardholder personal identification number.

security department (1) The department responsible for physical security. (2) The component of a credit card operation that investigates, apprehends, and prosecutes people who perpetrate fraud against a bank.

security deposit *See* margin (lending).

security instrument A mortgage or trust deed evidencing the pledge of real estate as security for the repayment of a mortgage note.

security interest (1) Under Federal Reserve Regulation Z, any interest in property that secures performance of a consumer credit obligation and is recognized by state or federal law. (2) A form of interest in property providing that property may be sold on default to satisfy the obligation for which the security interest is given. (3) An agreement in personal property or fixtures that secures payment or performance of an obligation.

security operating system An operating system that controls hardware and software functions, to provide the level of protection from penetration or physical damage appropriate to the value of the data and resources managed by the system.

security record Any set of records kept on the custody of securities.

security ticket *See* fanfold.

segregation One of several subaccounts of a participant's securities account, which a depository will record by book entry at the participant's request. Securities assigned to the participant's segregation account are those owned by others for whom the participant acts as agent.

seignorage The amount by which the face value of new coins exceeds the cost of their metal content. Seignorage is profit to the government that produces the coins.

selection check A process of checking, usually automatically, to verify that the correct register or other device has been selected in the performance of an instruction.

self-directed individual retirement account An individual retirement account for which the customer directs the investment of the funds, usually in stocks, bonds, and mutual funds.

self-employed retirement plan *See* Keogh plan.

self-liquidating bond A bond serviced from the earnings of a municipally owned enterprise, usually a utility. The earnings must cover the debt service with a reasonable margin of protection if the bonds are to be regarded as entirely self-liquidating.

self-liquidating loan A loan that will be liquidated from the proceeds of the activity financed by the loan. For example, a loan made to a farmer for purchasing seeds is a self-liquidating loan.

self-regulatory organizations (SROs) Associations of businesses whose members establish and enforce their own formal rules of conduct. Government commissions may also regulate such organizations. Examples of SROs include the stock exchanges and the National Association of Securities Dealers.

self-supporting debt A debt incurred for an enterprise requiring no tax support other than the specific tax earmarked for that enterprise.

sellers market A market in which the demand for goods and services at current prices exceeds supply. Sellers have a great influence on the prices charged in such a market, and prices usually rise as a result.

seller's option The settlement date agreed to by buyer and seller.

seller take-back A real estate loan in which the seller provides all or part of the financing and takes either a first or second mortgage on the property.

selling as agent Selling securities for an issuer in the capacity of an agent, not an underwriter. In this case, title to the securities--and, hence, marketing risk--remains with the issuer. The commission or fee received by the agent is based only on sales effort.

selling below the market A description of a security currently quoted at a price less than that of similar securities of comparable quality and acceptance.

selling fee (commercial paper) The fee that a dealer charges for marketing commercial paper for the issuer.

selling rate The exchange rate used by the seller of a currency.

selling syndicate A group of dealers that each buys portions of a new issue from the underwriters. The syndicate sells the issue to the investing public in the primary market, thus supplementing the selling efforts of the underwriters.

sell-out If the buyer in a securities transaction fails to accept delivery, the seller may resort to a "sell-out." This means that, after a certain time and with notification, the seller is free to sell to another party at the best available price and bill the buyer for any loss.

sell short To sell stock or another asset that one does not own, in the belief that the price will fall. The asset can then be purchased at a price lower than the sale price, thus producing a profit.

sender (1) The originator of a message to a wire service. (2) One who transfers funds from himself or herself to another.

sender net debit cap A maximum ceiling on the aggregate net debit position (that is, the value of all sends in excess of all receives) that a sender could incur on an individual network at any time (for example, CHIPS). A cross-system sender net debit cap would establish a ceiling for the aggregate net debit position across more than one network at any time (for example, CHIPS and Fedwire).

sender's correspondent bank A bank that acts as a reimbursement bank on the sender's side in a transfer of funds.

sending bank (1) A bank that inputs a message to a wire service. (2) A bank that forwards checks for collection directly to the Federal Reserve or another bank.

senior debt Debt that is paid ahead of other (junior) debt if liquidation occurs.

senior equity Preferred stock that ranks before junior equity (common stock) if the issuing company's assets are liquidated and distributed.

senior lien A lien that ranks above other liens and is paid ahead of them if liquidation occurs.

Senior Real Estate Analyst (SREA) The highest designation of a member of the Society of Real Estate Appraisers. The major designations from the society are Senior Residential Appraiser (SRA), Senior Real Property Appraiser (SRPA), and Senior Real Estate Analyst (SREA).

senior security Any stock or bond that ranks above common stock in claims against the issuing corporation's assets. If liquidation occurs, a firm repays its creditors in order of ranking seniority.

separate property The property that one person owns free from any rights or control of others, for example, the property that a married woman owns independently of her husband.

separate trading of registered interest and principal of securities (STRIPS) *See* STRIPS.

separator An encoded character on a bank card's magnetic stripe that indicates a break in information or the end of a field. *Previously called* field separator.

sequential file A file whose records are organized on the basis of their successive physical positions, such as their positions on magnetic tape.

sequential processing Handling data in chronological sequence.

sequestered account An account that has been impounded under due process of law, thereby making its disbursement subject to court order.

serial bonds Bonds of the same issue maturing at fixed intervals, over a period of years rather than all at one time.

serial printer A device that prints characters one at a time. *Compare with* line printer.

series bonds An issue of bonds with a single maturity, which are issued on successive dates. Series bonds differ from serial bonds, which are issued simultaneously and mature on different dates.

series of options Options of the same class (kind), which have the same strike (exercise) price and expire on the same date.

service A vehicle for conveying messages between sending and receiving banks (for example, CHIPS, Fedwire, S.W.I.F.T., and telex). *Also called* wire service.

service award Any recognition given to an employee for length of service.

service charge (1) An extra fee added to the price of some special service, such as the extension of credit. (2) A charge assessed by a depository for processing transactions and maintaining accounts. The total charge may be a fixed amount plus a variable charge that depends on the level of activity.

service company A company that will originate installment loans or equity loans for a lender. In addition to developing the business, it may also handle collections, foreclosures, repossessions, and so on, and may provide credit insurance against loss to the lender.

service organization An organization formed when one or more mutual organizations such as a federal credit union purchase stock in a new organization. The new organization, or service organization, can be operated on a for-profit basis and permits the mutual organization to diversify outside its traditional business.

services In international trade, intangible items exchanged abroad. Services include such items as transportation, travel, and insurance for shipments that result in the transfer of exchange from one country to another.

servicing (1) Making timely payments of principal and interest. (2) The collection of mortgage payments. Additional servicing responsibilities include the securing of escrow funds, payment of property taxes and insurance from escrow funds, follow-up on delinquencies, and the accounting for and remitting of principal and interest payments to investors.

servicing agreement A written agreement between the mortgage originator and investor defining the rights and obligations of each party.

servicing costs *See* liquidation cost per installment; liquidation cost per loan.

servient estate An estate limited by the right of the owner of another parcel of land to use it for a special purpose.

setback (1) The distance from a lot line that--by law, regulation, or deed restriction--must not be covered by any structure. (2) The distance between a lot line and a building line.

settle *See* settlement.

settlement (1) The winding up and distribution of an estate by an executor or administrator, to be distinguished from the administration of an estate by a trustee or guardian. (2) A property arrangement frequently involving a trust. (3) A transfer of funds to complete one or more prior transactions that were made subject to final settlement. Settlement is the point at which underlying claims and obligations are satisfied. (4) The conclusion of a transaction: completing all necessary documentation, making the necessary payments, and, where appropriate, transferring title.

settlement check A memorandum that the manager of a clearing house

association issues to settle the results of a clearing house exchange between member banks. The local Federal Reserve bank adjusts the accounts of clearing house banks daily.

settlement clerk A clerk in a bank's proof department who assembles daily totals for the department on a settlement sheet that becomes a subsidiary record to the bank's general ledger.

settlement costs booklet A booklet detailing the costs of settlement, required by the Real Estate Settlement Procedures Act, that must be given to a loan applicant at the time of, or within 3 business days after, loan application.

settlement date (1) The agreed date for transferring funds to complete a transaction. (2) The date on which a clearing member or authorized settlement agent prepares and processes a clearing draft as reimbursement for interchange transactions processed. (3) The date on which delivery of and payment for securities are expected as a result of a securities trade. The number of business days permitted between the trade and settlement date vary by type of security and nature of the transaction. *See also* cash settlement; regular-way settlement; seller's option; when-issued or when-distributed settlement. *Compare with* trade date.

settlement fail *See* fail.

settlement option (1) A plan usually found in insurance contracts in which the beneficiary of an insurance contract may receive payment in a lump sum, in installments, or both. The plan is usually for a fixed number of years, or for the life of the beneficiary with or without a fixed number of payments made if the beneficiary dies within the fixed period. (2) One of several methods used for securities trade settlement. *See also* balance-order settlement; confirm only comparison option; continuous net settlement (CNS); trade-for-trade (TFT) settlement.

settlement point In interchange, a bank or bank card association that pays by draft or draws a draft against another bank or association for payment of interchange transactions.

settlement price The price of the financial instrument underlying the option contract at the time the contract is exercised. Where necessary, option contracts specify objective standards for determining the settlement price.

settlement risk The possibility that operational difficulties interrupt delivery of funds even where the counterparty is able to perform.

settlement statement A report that must be given to each buyer and seller under the Real Estate Settlement Procedures Act.

settlor A person who creates a trust, such as a living trust, to become operative during his or her lifetime. *Also called* donor, grantor, *and* trustor. *Compare with* testator.

severalty Ownership by one person.

severance tax A duty levied on the owner of forests or mines when the timber is cut or the minerals removed.

share account A savings account at a credit union.

shared appreciation mortgage (SAM) A mortgage in which the lender provides a below-market interest rate and lower monthly payments in exchange for a share of the profits when the property is sold or at a specified date in the future.

share draft A bill payment device offered by some credit unions. Members of a credit union can write these checklike instruments against their savings share accounts.

shareholder *See* stockholder.

shareholder loan *See* share loan.

shareholders' equity *See* net worth.

share loan A simple interest loan secured by funds on deposit at a savings and loan association or a credit union. The purpose of this loan is to prevent the loss of dividends on a depositor's funds (shares) by withdrawal of the funds before the dividend payment date.

shares (1) Certificates that represent the ownership of a portion of interest in a business. *Synonymous with* stock. (2) The smallest unit of ownership in a business.

shelf registration Rule 415 of the Securities and Exchange Commission, which allows major corporations to go directly to the equity and debt markets to sell securities quickly. Previously rules, which had required companies to file registration notices with the SEC and wait at least 2 days for approval, had favored the formation of syndicates to sell securities. Rule 415 allows blanket registration of issues over the ensuing 2 years and encourages direct sale of blocks of securities.

shell A special envelope designed to hold bond coupons being presented for payment. Each shell must contain only the coupons from the same bond issue with the same payment date and owner. The name and address of the owner and the paying agent are written on the shell, and the shell is then presented to the paying agent for payment. A filled shell must be handled with the same care as cash.

shell office *See* representative office.

sheriff indemnity bond A bond that reimburses a sheriff who undertakes a seizure of goods if the sheriff is held liable for damages in an action brought against the sheriff for unlawful seizure.

sheriff's deed A deed conveying title, as a result of public sale, that includes no warranty or representations of title.

shipping The preparation of mortgage loan files and their transmittal to a purchasing investor.

shop (1) (Verb) To offer marketable securities to a wide variety of potential buyers. (2) (Verb) To pose as a customer or prospect of one's own firm or of a competitor to monitor sales and service levels. (3) (Noun) A workplace, for example, a dealer's or broker's office or a bank.

short (1) (Noun) A market position established when a person who has sold a futures contract or other financial instrument has not yet closed out this position through an offsetting purchase. (2) (Verb) To sell more than one owns or has contracted to buy (as in "to go short"). It is the opposite of long.

short bond A bond with a relatively short term to maturity.

short book *See* negative gap.

short certificate A certificate by the proper officer of a court as to the appointment and authority of a fiduciary, to be distinguished from a full certified copy of a letter testamentary, letter of administration, or letter of trusteeship.

short coupon A bond, bearer or registered, with an initial interest payment period shorter than the normal interest payment interval for the bond. For example, a bond that pays interest semianually is said to have a "short coupon" if the first interest payment is scheduled less than 6 months from the dated date of the bond.

short covering The purchase of a security or commodity to protect (cover) a short position.

short hedge The sale of a futures contract or other financial instrument to eliminate or lessen the possible decline in value of an approximately equal amount of the actual financial instrument owned.

short option position The position of a trader who has sold or written an option, regardless of whether it is a put or a call. The writer's maximum potential profit is the premium received.

short position The position of an investor who has sold more shares of a security or other asset than he or she owns.

short sale A sale of securities that the seller does not own at the time of sale but that he or she intends to purchase or borrow in time to make delivery.

short selling Selling an item that is not owned in the hope of buying it back at a lower price.

short squeeze A situation in which a lack of supply tends to force prices upward. A short squeeze causes losses for those who have a short position.

short term (1) In securities, generally 1 year or less. (2) For purposes of taxation, a time variously prescribed by law, usually 6 months or 1 year.

short-term capital gains Profits earned on the sale of assets held for less than the minimum period of time, prescribed by law and changed from time to time, that would qualify them as long-term capital gains and thereby subject to potentially favorable tax treatment. *See also* long-term capital gains.

short-term financing The process of securing funds for a business or other legal entity for a short period, usually less than 1 year.

short-term investment fund (STIF) A collective investment fund, consisting of highly liquid and readily marketable interest-bearing securities. Trust departments manage such funds and trust accounts purchase units of them.

short-term loan A loan to a business for less than 1 year, usually for operating needs.

short-term trust An irrevocable trust running for a period of 10 years or longer, which provides for the income to be paid to a person other than the settlor. At the end of the income term, the property returns to the settlor. Before enactment of the 1986 Tax Reform Act, the income from a trust of this kind was taxable to the income beneficiary and not to the settlor. The 1986 Tax Reform Act modified this income tax result for new short-term trusts created after March 1, 1986. Now the settlor will be taxed on the income if, at the time the trust is established, the settlor has a reversionary (future) interest in either corpus or income that exceeds 5 percent of the value of the trust.

short the board To sell futures on the Chicago Board of Trade.

short volatility position An option position designed to profit from an expected decline in the implied volatility component of the option's price. The position can take different forms. One form is to sell options and use delta-hedging techniques to protect against changes in the price level of the underlying instrument. Another position consists of selling a straddle.

siblings Children of the same parents.

sight In the body of a negotiable instrument, an indication that payment is due on presentation or demand.

sight draft A draft that is payable on sight (on demand) when presented to the drawee.

sight letter of credit A letter of credit that permits payment of funds to the seller immediately on presentation of the documents that satisfy the original requirements.

signature book A book containing facsimile signatures of officers authorized to make commitments for a bank. Banks establishing a correspondent relationship exchange such books.

signature card A card that is signed by a bank customer and held on file by the bank for purposes of identification.

signature field The field identifying the individual or department within the sending bank that created the message.

signature file department The bank department that has custody of all customers' signature cards.

signature guarantee A guarantee (normally obtained from a commercial bank or securities dealer) of the seller's endorsement, which appears on the stock or bond power accompanying the stock certificate being sold. The signature guarantee is a requirement of good delivery, unless the certificate is held in street name.

signature panel A small elongated rectangular strip, affixed to either side of a bank card during manufacture, that permits the cardholder to write his or her signature on the card.

simple capital structure Capital structure that exists when a corporation has no convertible securities that, if converted, would cause a material dilution of earnings per share.

simple interest (1) On deposits, interest computed by applying the stated percentage rate of interest to the principal only, and not to previously earned interest. (2) On loans, interest computed by applying a daily periodic interest rate to the amount of principal outstanding each day. *Compare with* rule of 78s.

simple trust In tax laws, a trust that is required to distribute all of its income currently and that does not provide for any charitable distribution. *Compare with* complex trust.

simplified employee pension plan (SEP) An arrangement, meeting the requirements of Section 408(k) of the Internal Revenue Code, under which an employer makes contributions to an employee's individual retirement account or individual retirement annuity. The employer deducts contributions made to the SEP as a salary expense and includes such amounts in the employee's gross income on Form W-2. The employee, in turn, is entitled to an offsetting tax deduction on his or her income tax return.

simulate To copy or mimic; to represent certain features of a physical or abstract system by using those of another system.

simulation A means of learning about something by making a copy of it and observing how the copy behaves. Simulation involves the representation of certain features of a physical or abstract system by those of another system. The representation of financial phenomena by computer operations or the representation of computer operations by those of another computer are examples of simulation.

simultaneous death The death of two or more people under such circumstances that the order of death cannot be proved.

simultaneous reserve requirements *See* contemporaneous reserve accounting.

single debt A system of mortgage accounting in which a servicer reports current installments as one total sum and gives a detailed payment analysis only on uncollected and unscheduled payments.

single-entry accounting A system of accounting in which each transaction is recorded only once. In this system, separate records showing amounts due and amounts owed are kept on customers, creditors, and cash. *See also* double-entry accounting.

single interest insurance Installment loan insurance that is provided only for the bank's interest in the collateral, with the owner or borrower subject to the loss of equity. *Also called* ultimate loss insurance.

single name account An account having only one owner.

single posting system A type of posting in which a bank's bookkeeping department posts only a depositor's statement. In this system, the ledger record is a copy of the depositor's statement rather than a separate posting.

single-purpose corporation A U.S. corporation set up to issue short-term paper in order to purchase assets of a certain type or to make loans and advances to a single firm. The stock of such corporations is sometimes donated to charitable institutions. The corporation usually issues commercial paper or preferred stock with a dividend reset at short intervals to reflect market rates. Examples of assets purchased include trade receivables and mortgages.

sinking fund (1) A provision in some bond issues that requires the issuer to set money aside during the life of the issue to retire the bonds. Periodically, some bonds are called and retired using the monies in the sinking fund. *Compare with* purchase funds. (2) An accumulation of amounts periodically set aside in escrow by municipalities or corporations that will be sufficient to satisfy a debt, such as a bond issue, at maturity.

sinking fund bond A bond that requires the issuer to set up a sinking fund for redemption purposes.

situation analysis The process of evaluating one's position in the existing internal and external environment, and identifying present and potential problems, opportunities, strengths, and weaknesses.

sixty-five day election In the case of distributions made during the first 65 days following the close of a complex trust's taxable year, the election by a fiduciary of the complex trust to treat part or all of the distribution as having been made on the last day of the preceding taxable year.

skimming A fraudulent reading of magnetically encoded data from a valid card; transferring such data to another card.

skimming pricing Using a high initial price for a new product.

skip account A borrower or cardholder with a past-due balance who cannot be found.

skip-day settlement A trade that is settled 1 day later than the normal settlement.

skip payment An option to skip the December payment, offered annually to cardholders who meet specified requirements.

skip person With respect to a generation-skipping transfer, a recipient or beneficiary who is at least two generation levels below that of the transferor.

skip tracing The process of locating borrowers who have stopped making their loan payments and cannot be located by their last known address or employer.

sleeper A security whose market price appears not to reflect some basic improvement in the company's position or some general upward movement of comparable securities in the market.

slow pay and unsatisfactory account A designation for an extension of credit indicating that it has not been paid as agreed or according to contract terms.

SLUGS (state and local government series) Special U.S. government securities that are sold by the Secretary of the Treasury to states, municipalities, and other local government bodies through individual subscription agreements. The interest rates and maturities of SLUGS are arranged to comply with arbitrage restrictions imposed under Section 103 of the Internal Revenue Code. SLUGS are most commonly used for deposit in escrow in connection with the issuance of refunding bonds.

Small Business Administration (SBA) An independent federal agency, created in 1953, to help small businesses. The SBA makes loans directly or guarantees loans made to small businesses.

Small Business Investment Act of 1958 Federal legislation that provides the current authority for the Small Business Administration to aid in financing small businesses.

small business investment company A private firm that provides equity financing, long-term loans, and managerial services to small businesses. These firms were established under the Small Business Investment Act of 1958 and are licensed, regulated, and partially subsidized by the Small Business Administration.

smart card A credit card imbedded with a microprocessor that gives the card the capacity to compute or to communicate information. For example, a smart card may include such information as a cardholder's secret code, which makes possible off-line authorization, with verification by the card's microprocessor.

Smithsonian Agreement (1971) An international agreement resulting in a devaluation of the U.S. dollar in relation to other currencies.

social responsibility The obligation of a company to conduct business activities in a way that does not adversely affect its customers or the community as a whole and to devote a portion of its resources to civic improvement efforts.

societal marketing As a result of the consumer movement, marketing by banks that involves public affairs programs, consumer financial counseling, and education in general.

Society for Worldwide Interbank Financial Telecommunication (S.W.I.F.T.) A nonprofit, cooperative organization of international banks that provides an international telecommunication system for the exchange of electronic information among banks.

software A set of programs, procedures, and possibly associated documentation, concerned with the operation of a computer. *Compare with* hardware.

sole corporation A one-person corporation whose authority, duties, and powers are attached to and vested in the office and not in the person who currently holds the office.

sole proprietorship A business owned and operated by one person.

solid logic technology Miniaturized modules, used in computers, that increase the speed of the circuitry by reducing the distance that currents travel.

sort The distribution of anything into particular groups, following a specified classification system (for example, grouping checks so they can be sent to the bank on which they are drawn). The classification can be alphabetic, numeric, by location, and so on.

source (1) Origin. (2) Original document.

source code The original program or language prepared by a computer before processing.

source data automation (SDA) The methods of recording coded data on paper tapes, punched cards, or tags that can be used repeatedly to produce other records without rewriting.

source language The language from which a statement is translated.

source program (1) A coded program that must be translated into machine language before being used. (2) A computer program written in a source language.

sovereign immunity A doctrine that a state cannot be sued against its will.

sovereign risk (1) The risk to a lender that the servicing of its loans to a foreign borrower may be abridged, frozen, or denied by acts of, or conditions in, the nation where the borrower is located. This risk, sometimes called "country risk," is unrelated to the actual borrower's capacity to repay. (2) In a more limited sense, the risk that a foreign government (as distinct from a business in that country) may default on its borrowings. *See also* country risk.

sovereign risk limit *See* country limit.

spaced maturities *See* laddered maturities.

span of control (1) The breadth of a particular supervisor's authority. On organizational charts, the lines of authority drawn from a person's position to various subunits indicate the span of that person's control. (2) The number of people who report to a supervisor.

special administrator An administrator appointed by a court to take over and safeguard an estate, pending the appointment of an executor or administrator. *Sometimes called* temporary administrator.

special assistance bond A bond payable from levies on properties for which an improvement was financed. The issuing government agrees to make the assessments and earmarks the proceeds for debt service on these bonds.

special character A character other than alphabetic or numeric characters (for example, *, +, %").

special drawing rights (SDRs) An international reserve asset created by the International Monetary Fund (IMF). Its value is based on a basket of currencies. IMF members may use SDRs in settlement of financial claims of other member nations.

special endorsement An endorsement that designates the party to whom the instrument will be transferred.

special guardian A guardian appointed by a court for a particular purpose connected with the affairs of a minor or an incompetent person. Sometimes a guardian ad litem is called a special guardian.

special handling code A code that indicates that a customer's statement requires special treatment by the mail room or that the statement should be routed to a specific department.

special interest account A term commercial banks use to describe a savings account in states where "savings accounts" by that name are prohibited.

specialist A firm that is a member of a stock exchange and is authorized by the exchange to maintain a fair and orderly market in the issues assigned to the firm. At its trading post on the exchange floor, the specialist receives bid and asked offers from buying and selling brokers. If buyers and sellers cannot agree on price and terms, the specialist sells from or buys for its own inventory.

specialized examination A limited examination of a bank by its regulator that is performed twice in a 2-year period between general examinations and focuses on specific departments, reviewing directors' and committee minutes, regulatory reports, and so on. *See also* general examination.

specialized funds Mutual funds that concentrate their portfolios in one particular industry or region.

special power of appointment *See* limited power of appointment; power of appointment.

special supervisory examination The examination of a bank with problems when conditions require more than one review in a year.

special tax bond Municipal bond backed by the proceeds of a specific related tax. For example, a highway bond issue can be repaid from gasoline taxes.

special use valuation The valuation for estate taxes of family-owned farms or other businesses involving real estate, based on actual use rather than the highest and best use. An executor may elect special use valuation, if certain conditions are met. These conditions are intended to ensure that the qualifying special use of the property continues after the decedent's death.

special warranty deed A deed in which the grantor agrees to protect the grantee against any claims that arise from actions that occurred during the grantor's period of ownership. The warranty does not extend further back than the date at which the grantor acquired the property.

specie Coins made from precious metal, usually gold or silver, as contrasted with paper money.

specific bequest *See* specific legacy.

specific devise A gift, by will, of a specific parcel of real property.

specific legacy A gift, by will, of a specific article of personal property, such as a watch. *Distinguish from* general legacy.

specific performance The actual accomplishment of a contract by the party bound to fulfill it. An action to compel the performance of a contract according to its terms is usually brought when the payment of damages would not adequately compensate the aggrieved party.

speculation The purchase or sale of an asset, sometimes on a forward basis, with the hope of making a profit later. The term is used in the foreign exchange, commodity, stock, and option markets.

speculative arbitrage Arbitrage (the simultaneous purchase of one asset and sale of another) undertaken to profit from expected changes in prices or price differentials.

speculative securities Securities that have an unusually high promise of capital gain or loss. For banks, fixed-income securities rated below the four highest ratings by rating agencies are assumed by examiners to be speculative.

speculator One who engages in financial transactions in order to benefit from expected movements in price. A speculator accepts greater risk to increase the opportunity for profit.

spendthrift clause The provision in a will or trust instrument that limits the right of a beneficiary to dispose of his or her interest, as by assignment, and the right of his or her creditors to reach it, as by attachment.

spendthrift trust A trust in which a beneficiary cannot assign or dispose of his or her interest; nor can creditors reach it.

spillover trust A type of trust that by its terms is merged with or added to another trust or estate when a certain event occurs. *See also* pour-over.

spin-off A corporation's severing of part of its operations to create a separate company. Shares in the new company are issued to the corporation's stockholders. Shares of the two companies can be traded separately.

split (1) The conversion of securities of one denomination into smaller units, generally for the purpose of a partial sale. (2) *See* stock split.

split balances Credit card balances requiring a split interest rate calculation. All credit card purchases made before a set date will be charged a certain rate until paid in full. New purchases made after the set date will be charged a different rate.

split deposit A deposit of one or more checks, with part of the total amount paid out in cash to the depositor.

split gift A gift made by a spouse to a third person and treated as one-half of the gift made by each spouse, if the other spouse consents to the gift.

split sale A condition in which one purchase is written up on two sales drafts, normally to avoid authorization.

sponsored American depository receipt (ADR) An American depository receipt issue sponsored by the foreign corporation whose securities the ADR represents. The sponsoring corporation pays the fees for the securities transaction, such as the transfer fee, dividend fee, cable charge, postage, and insurance.

spooling The reading and writing of input and output data on auxiliary storage devices, concurrent with job execution, in a format convenient for later processing or output operations.

spot deal *See* spot market.

spot delivery Immediate (as opposed to future) delivery. In foreign exchange, spot delivery is within 2 business days. It is distinguished from a forward contract, which is an agreement calling for a longer period (that is, in excess of spot or regular delivery).

spot market A market for buying or selling commodities or foreign exchange for cash payment and immediate delivery.

spot price The price of a commodity available for immediate sale and delivery. The term also refers to foreign exchange transactions.

spot rate The price or rate in the spot (cash or immediate delivery) market.

spousal remainder trust A trust established by the grantor to pay income to a beneficiary for a term of years, after which the assets pass to the grantor's spouse (or the spouse's estate).

spouse A husband or wife.

spouse's allowance An allowance made to the surviving spouse by a court having jurisdiction over a decedent's estate, usually to provide the spouse with funds for living expenses during the settlement of the estate.

spraying trust *See* sprinkling trust.

spread (1) The markup of a price, intended to cover a seller's selling expenses and provide profit on a transaction. A spread is the difference between the purchase and sale price. (2) The difference between the rate of return on assets and the costs of liabilities. (3) The difference between the buying and selling rates of a foreign currency. (4) The difference in prices of futures contracts of different maturities. It is a synonym for "basis." (5) The amount (for example, the number of basis points) by which a rate of interest exceeds a particular reference rate (for example, a spread of x above LIBOR). (6) The difference between the rate earned on an asset and the rate passed through to a purchaser of that asset. (7) (Verb) To go long on one futures contract and short on another contract of a different maturity, in the hope that the spread between them will change favorably.

spreading (1) Taking offsetting positions on different maturities in the futures market (long on one maturity and short on another), to benefit from expected changes in the spread (basis) between the two contracts. (2) Taking offsetting positions on different maturities or different strike prices in the options market. *Compare with* hedging.

sprinkling trust A trust in which the income or principal is distributed among the members of a designated class, in amounts and proportions determined by the trustee. *Also called* spraying trust.

squeeze A tight market, in which short sellers are relatively numerous and the supply of assets limited. Thus prices are under severe upward pressure in a squeeze, as the short sellers scramble to cover their positions by buying in the cash market.

stagflation An economic term used to describe the unusual situation of an economy that is experiencing severe inflation and unemployment simultaneously.

stale check Any check dated more than a reasonable time (a few months) before presentation. According to the Uniform Commercial Code, a bank is not required to pay on a check (other than a certified check) that is presented more than 6 months after its date. When a bank receives a stale check, it may call the writer for permission to pay the check, or it may return the check.

stale date (1) A date at the end of a designated period after a check or other item has been written that exceeds a reasonable time period for presentation. (2) A transaction that carries a date long since posted.

stamp duty A tax paid through the purchase of a stamp that must be affixed to a document.

stand-alone unit A terminal capable of functioning without connection to a computer system or terminal controller.

standard A criterion for a product or process usually expressed in terms of quality, quantity, cost, or time, against which other products or processes are compared.

Standard & Poor's (S&P) A financial services firm that provides bond ratings and other types of investment information.

standard cost The estimated cost of performing a service or manufacturing a product in the most efficient way possible. A forecast of standard cost serves as a basis of cost control and measures productive efficiency (or provides a standard of comparison) when ultimately aligned against actual cost. Actual cost will exceed standard cost because actual cost includes waste and inefficiencies.

standard deviation A statistical measure of the dispersion of observations on a variable.

standard industrial classification (SIC) code A standard system of numerical coding by type of industry, designed by the federal government.

standard metropolitan statistical area (SMSA) A defined geographical area of concentrated population for which the federal government compiles statistics relating to population and business.

standby application An application in which two or more computers are tied together as part of a single overall system and stand ready for appropriate action.

standby commitment (1) In the secondary mortgage market for single-family loans, a commitment issued by an investor or broker-dealer to purchase mortgages if offered. The purchaser of this commitment has the option of delivering or not delivering a specified amount of mortgages or mortgage-backed securities at a given rate within a specified time. (2) A commitment often used by a developer to secure a construction loan, thereby providing time to build, lease,

and qualify a project for a more favorable mandatory delivery commitment.

standby letter of credit A letter of credit normally written to be drawn on only in the case of nonperformance by the issuing bank's customer. Standby credits are often used to back up construction contracts or long-term sales contracts, and they can be used for a wide variety of purposes.

standby underwriting A service offered by an underwriter to an issuer planning the sale of additional shares of previously authorized stock to its present stockholders. Rights to those additional shares are issued to the stockholders. If the stockholders fail to absorb the entire issue, the underwriter purchases the surplus and sells it to the public.

standing committee An ongoing committee with continuing specific responsibilities.

standing instruction An instruction given by a customer or a bank for the special processing of recurring or specific transactions.

standing loan A loan on which no amortization payments are required. The loan, such as a construction loan, requires interest payments only and ultimate repayment of principal at the conclusion of the loan.

standing order An authority given by a customer to a bank to pay or transfer funds regularly from the customer's account.

start sentinel A start-of-text character that signals the start of data encoded on an information track within the magnetic stripe on a bank card.

state A term that has different meanings under different statutes. For example, it may or may not include Puerto Rico.

state and local government series *See* SLUGS.

state and municipal bonds Long-term debt issued by states and municipalities to finance public projects and facilities.

state bank A bank chartered by state banking authorities. A state bank may or may not be a Federal Reserve member and may or may not belong to the Federal Deposit Insurance Corporation.

state member bank A state-chartered bank that is a member of the Federal Reserve System.

statement A record prepared by a bank for a customer, listing all checks drawn and all deposits made for a given period, along with the balance in the account. *See also* monthly statement.

statement balance (1) The amount that represents the sum of the previous balance due plus cash advances and merchandise purchases for the billing period, less credit for payments and for merchandise returns, plus any appropriate finance and service charges. (2) The closing ledger balance in a depositor's account.

statement clerk An employee in a bank's bookkeeping department who usually performs one of two sets of duties, depending on the bank. In some banks, the statement clerk verifies all paid checks listed on a depositor's statement. In other banks, this clerk posts the statements for depositors' checking accounts.

statement cutoff date A predetermined date before the preparation of monthly statements after which no

further transactions will be posted to an account.

statement film A photocopy of the actual billing statement.

statement of condition A record, issued daily from the general ledger department, that condenses all of the general ledger accounts. This daily report is used to control the reserves required by law. *Also called* balance sheet.

statement of liability A statement of a cardholder's responsibilities appearing on the reverse side of credit cards, on cardholder agreements, or on other printed documents.

statement of record A report required by the developer of a subdivision regulated under the Interstate Land Sales Full Disclosure Act.

statement reconciliation An analysis that explains the difference between the balance of an account on a bank's books and a customer's books. Usually, most of the difference is due to outstanding checks and deposits in transit.

statement savings account A savings account for which the customer records his or her own balance and transactions. The customer then receives a periodic balance statement from the bank to reconcile his or her records.

statement stub The portion of a loan statement that the borrower or cardholder returns with the payment.

statewide banking The establishment of bank branches throughout a state, subject to individual state laws or regulations.

station plate *See* merchant plate.

statistical sampling A mathematical procedure in which a small group of items is selected for analysis from a much larger group, to maximize the information gained while minimizing the time and cost of the analysis.

statistics A branch of mathematics concerned with collecting, organizing, analyzing, and interpreting numerical data.

status code An alphanumeric code assigned to an account, either through manual input or by the computer system, indicating whether the account is in a restricted condition or requires special attention. *See also* block; blocked account.

"statused" account A cardholder record to which a status code has been posted, indicating that a cardholder may not use his or her account. *See also* block.

status report A hard-copy record of the status of all cardholder accounts or groups of accounts on which there has been activity.

Statute of Frauds A statute, first enacted in England in 1677, designed to prevent many fraudulent practices by requiring proof of a specific kind, usually in writing, of the important transactions of business. The Statute of Frauds declared that no action be brought or that no contract be allowed to be good when a transaction was not so evidenced. The original statute, for example, declared that all trusts of land be in writing. Although each state has its own statute of frauds designed to serve the same general purpose as the original statute, many of these statutes differ greatly from the original statute. However, the general purpose of all statutes of fraud is to prevent fraudulent transactions, by requiring that

obligations, to be enforceable, be in writing.

statute of limitations A statute that bars suits on valid claims after the expiration of a specified period. The period varies for different kinds of claims. In most states, there is a 20-year limitation on judgments; ordinarily, contract claims expire in 6 years; and claims for torts (injuries to people or property) expire within a shorter time. Each state has its own statute of limitations.

Statute of Uses An English statute enacted in 1536 that provided that the legal as well as the beneficial title to land held for the use of a person be vested in that person. There were certain exceptions to this vesting that opened the way for the development of the law of trusts.

statutes of descent Laws, rules, or statutes governing the descent of real property under intestacy.

statutes of distribution Laws, rules, or statutes governing the distribution of personal property under intestacy.

statutes of mortmain Several early English statutes, dating back as far as the thirteenth century, restricting the alienation of land to a corporation, particularly to an ecclesiastical corporation. Mortmain means "dead hand." In early English law, an ecclesiastic was deemed civilly dead, which explains the origin of the term "dead hand."

statutes of will Statutes (first passed in 1541) providing that no will, devise, or bequest is valid unless the will is in writing, signed, and attested as required by statute.

statutory exemptions Specified articles of personal property and a specified amount of cash left by a decedent, which are set apart for his or her immediate family and may not be subjected to the claims of creditors.

statutory investment An investment that a trustee is specifically authorized to make under the statutes of the state having jurisdiction over the trust. *See also* legal investment.

statutory law A statute passed by legislatures, such as enactments of Congress.

statutory right of redemption The right of a borrower to redeem mortgaged property after a foreclosure.

stochastic (process) Random changes that follow a predictable pattern. For example, when interest rates rise or fall, short-term rates change more than long-term rates. The relationship between the two is stochastic; the relative change in short-term rates follows a stochastic process. The term is particularly revelant in duration analysis, for one must either assume that short- and long-term rates will change by the same amount or make supplemental calculations to allow for stochastic changes by maturity, credit risk, or some other factor. *See also* duration.

stock A general term meaning common stock, preferred stock, and stock certificates. A stock is a certificate evidencing ownership in a corporate enterprise. The stock of a corporation is usually divided into two classes, common and preferred. The former represents the basic ownership; its holders' claims to income and assets are subordinate to the claims of bondholders, creditors, and preferred stockholders. Common stock usually has the voting privilege. The holder of preferred stock always enjoys priority as to income and generally to assets. However, his or her income is

usually limited to a definite percentage, regardless of earnings.

stock bonus A bonus paid in shares of stock.

stock-bonus trust A trust established by a corporation to enable its employees to receive the corporation's own stock as benefits. The purpose of a stock-bonus trust is to reward meritorious service by employees or to share the corporation's profits with employees.

stockbroker (1) An agent for the investor who acts as an intermediary between issuer and buyers in the initial offering of a security, and between buyers and sellers in the secondary market. Responsibilities of the stockbroker include actual exchange or book entry of securities and ensuring that transactions go through correctly. (2) An employee of a brokerage or broker-dealer firm who deals directly with the customer. Depending on his or her relationship with the customer, a stockbroker may or may not offer investment advice. *Also called* registered representative (registered rep.) *or* broker.

stock certificates Printed and signed certificates that are proof of an investor's ownership of the equity securities of a corporation.

stock company A company owned by stockholders.

stock discount The excess of a stock's par value over the capital paid into the stock.

stock dividend A dividend payable in stock rather than cash.

stock exchange (1) An organized, regulated marketplace, where officials of brokerage firms meet physically to buy and sell securities as directed by their customers, the investors; a centralized market for trading securities on the double-auction principle. (2) The association of brokerage firms and broker-dealers that provides such a marketplace and whose officials trade in it. (3) Because it is the largest exchange, the New York Stock Exchange is often referred to as "the stock exchange."

stock exchange seat A seat that entitles the bearer, and the firm with which he or she is affiliated, to trade on the stock exchange. Owning a seat on the exchange makes the purchaser a member of the stock exchange.

stockholder The owner of common or preferred stock of a corporation. *Often called* shareholder.

stockholder of record A stockholder whose name is registered on a corporation's books on the record date. The record date is so called because the person who is registered as the owner of the stock on this date will receive the dividend.

stock index futures A futures contract for the sale of a synthetic financial instrument designed to reflect the value of a specific stock index. Settlement is always in cash. *See also* financial futures.

stock ledger The book that records information about shares of a corporation's stock.

stock market (1) The market for stocks, usually in reference to the stock market in a particular country. (2) The market where stocks are traded, either over the counter or on an organized stock exchange. (3) An organized stock exchange.

stock option A document that gives the bearer the right to buy a specific stock at a stated price during a specified period, regardless of the prevailing market price. Stock options are traded in the same manner as other securities.

stock power A form of assignment executed by the owner of stock that contains an irrevocable appointment of an attorney-in-fact to make the actual transfer on the books of the corporation. *See also* bond power; power; power of attorney.

stock purchase option The right to buy stock from a company at a stated price within a specified time. A stock purchase option is usually issued as incentive compensation to corporate officers and other key employees for tax purposes and to encourage these employees to take an active interest in the company's performance.

stock-purchase trust A trust under which a surviving stockholder of a closely held corporation may purchase the stock of a deceased stockholder. A stock-purchase trust is usually, but not necessarily, an insurance trust.

stock registrar A corporate agent whose principal function is to prevent the issuance of more stock than the issuer's board of directors has authorized.

stock savings bank A savings bank set up as a profit-making corporation, with capital stock and stockholders. *See also* savings bank.

stock split The division of an outstanding issue of stock into a larger number of shares. The intent is to reduce the price per share, to make the stock more affordable for investors and to increase trading activity. Unlike a stock dividend, a stock split does not require the issuer to adjust its capital accounts. With a stock dividend, however, the capital account is credited and surplus is debited for the added shares.

stock transfer agent The agent of a corporation appointed to carry out the transfer of stock from one stockholder to another, by the actual cancellation of the surrendered certificates and the issuance of new certificates in the new stockholder's name.

stock transfer tax *See* transfer tax.

stock yield The rate of return on a stock, based on its market value as of a particular date and the dividend that the company is currently paying.

stolen securities *See* Rule 17f-1.

Stonier Graduate School of Banking (SGSB) A school for the advanced study of banking, conducted for bank officers by the American Bankers Association.

stop character *See* end-of-text character.

stop-loss order An order to a broker to sell an asset if the current market price declines to the level specified. The intent is to avoid large losses in a sharply declining market.

stop out The lowest price at which the U.S. Treasury sells Treasury bills for a particular auction.

stop payment (1) An order by a customer to his or her bank not to negotiate a previously issued check. (2) A notification sent immediately to the paying agent if a bearer bond or its coupon is lost or stolen. The owner, custodian bank, or depository that had the bond or coupon in its possession at the time of theft or loss issues the stop payment. Stop payments cannot be placed on U.S. Treasury obligations or certain municipals. Lost or stolen securities must also be reported to the Securities

Information Center, Inc. *See also* Rule 17f-1.

stop payment check A check that cannot be cashed because the writer has notified the bank that payment should not be honored.

storage (1) A device into which data can be entered and held, and from which it can later be retrieved. (2) Loosely, any device that can store data. *Also called* memory.

storage capacity The amount of data that can be stored in a computer storage system.

stored program A series of instructions in storage used to direct the step-by-step operation of a machine.

straddle An options position designed to profit from an expected increase in the price volatility of the underlying instrument. A straddle consists of the purchase of a put and a call with the same exercise date and exercise price.

straight credit A credit instrument under which the beneficiary is paid by a local bank designated by the bank opening the credit. The drafts are usually drawn in the currency of the exporter. The paying bank debits on its own books the payment to the account of the opening bank.

straight-line amortization A method of computing amortization (for example, of interest payments) that produces a constant amount of interest each year. *Compare with* level-yield amortization.

straight-line depreciation A method of depreciating an asset in which the value of the asset is reduced by a fixed (equal) amount each year throughout the expected life of the asset until only the salvage value remains. The amount of the charge is computed as follows: (cost minus estimated salvage) divided by estimated life.

straight reduction plan An amortization plan that provides for the payment of a fixed amount of principal at specified intervals, with interest payable on the remaining balance of the loan.

straight-term mortgage loan A mortgage loan granted for a fixed term of years, at the end of which the entire loan becomes due.

strap An options straddle position consisting of the purchase of more calls than puts, although all have the same exercise price and exercise date. While the trader expects an increase in price volatility, there is also an expectation that the price of the underlying instrument is more likely to rise than to fall. *Compare with* strip.

strategy development The broad statement of ways and means to achieve objectives.

stratified sampling A method used to segregate the population into individual strata using predetermined parameters. This technique allows the auditor to weight the sample among the different strata.

straw purchaser An individual who allows someone with a poor credit rating to use his or her name and credit report to obtain a loan.

street name Customers' securities held in the broker's name are said to be held in street name.

strict foreclosure A foreclosure that under state statutes terminates a borrower's rights after a given date. Title to the borrower's property vests with the lender once the court issues a decree terminating the borrower's rights.

strike price *See* exercise price.

strip An options straddle position consisting of the purchase of more puts than calls, although all have the same exercise date and exercise price. While the trader expects an increase in price volatility, there is also the expectation that the price of the underlying instrument is more likely to fall than to rise. *Compare with* strap.

strip loans Short-term loans sold under a long-term credit commitment. There is generally no recourse to the seller of the strip loan. *Also called* loan strips.

stripping Removing interest coupons from bonds or loans, with the intent of selling the interest separately from the principal.

STRIPS (separate trading of registered interest and principal of securities) The U.S. Treasury's acronym for zero-coupon instruments derived from selected long-term notes and bonds. At a bondholder's request, the Federal Reserve, as the Treasury's fiscal agent, will separate a designated security into its individual coupon components and corpus or principal payment. The pieces may be traded separately and must be maintained on the Treasury's book-entry system.

structural unemployment Unemployment caused by the mismatch of employees' job skills and employers' job requirements.

student loan *See* Guaranteed Student Loan Program.

Student Loan Marketing Association (SLMA or Sallie Mae) The leading financial intermediary to higher education, and the largest single source of funds for insured education loans. Federally chartered and stockholder owned, Sallie Mae provides a variety of financial products and services to all segments of the education market. Sallie Mae has two primary programs: (a) the purchase of guaranteed student loans from banks and other originators and (b) warehousing advances, which are collateralized financings to lenders for education-related loans.

sub-Chapter S corporation An election available to a corporation to be treated as a partnership for the purpose of income taxes. To be eligible for this election, a corporation must meet certain requirements as to the kind and number of shareholders, classes of stock, and sources of income.

subject Subject to confirmation.

subject to collection A situation in which, even though a bank has accepted a deposit for immediate credit to an account, funds that the bank cannot collect for some reason will be charged back to the account.

subject to count A deposit credited to an account but subject to adjustment if later accounting shows a discrepancy between the amount received and the amount claimed.

subject to mortgage The assignment of a mortgage to an assignee in which no personal liability for the debt is assumed.

subject to verification A situation in which, even though a particular deposit has been accepted for immediate credit to an account, if mathematical verification of the amount of the deposit differs from that shown on the deposit ticket, the appropriate adjustment will be made to the account.

subordinate A ranking lower than another ranking in terms of the priority of a claim on assets if default occurs.

subordinated A description of a security whose claim on the issuer's assets ranks below that of another class of security.

subordinated debenture A debt security that ranks lower than another security in the priority of its claim on the issuer's assets.

subordination A written instrument stating that a debt is subordinate to another's interest in the same property.

subordination agreement An agreement between two creditors of a particular borrower in which one party grants to the other a priority claim to the borrower's assets if default occurs.

sub right Literally, substitution right. A sub right is the right to substitute collateral in a repurchase agreement.

subrogation The substitution of one person for another with reference to a lawful claim or right. Subrogation is frequently called the doctrine of substitution. It is the assumption by a third party, such as a second creditor or an insurance company, of another's legal right to collect a debt or damages.

subscriber A person who agrees in writing to purchase particular securities, such as a specific number of stock shares or bonds.

subscribing witness One who sees a document signed or hears the signature acknowledged by the signer and then signs his or her own name to the document, such as the subscribing witness to a will. *Distinguish from* attesting witness.

subscription (1) An order for the purchase of new securities when, as, and if issued. (2) An amount of money contributed by each member of an international financial organization (for example, the International Monetary Fund).

subscription agent An agent that acts as a transfer agent when a stockholder exercises his or her rights or warrants.

subscription right *See* rights.

subsidiary A company that is owned by another company, either wholly or by holding a majority of the stock.

subsidiary account number (SAN) The encoded number identifying an individual account other than the primary account.

substantially-the-same Under generally accepted accounting principles (GAAP), no gain or loss is recognized on certain transactions in which the asset given up and the asset received are deemed to be subtantially-the-same as defined in GAAP. These transactions include certain exchanges to assets and certain sales of assets with the proceeds reinvested immediately in substantially-the-same assets.

substantive testing Audit testing whose objective is to provide an appropriate assurance of detecting a material total or monetary error.

substituted trustee A trustee appointed by a court, rather than by a trust instrument, to serve in the place of the original trustee or a prior trustee. *Distinguish from* successor trustee.

subvention A program by auto manufacturers to increase the volume of new car loans to their captive finance companies. The manufacturer subsidizes the loan rate, enabling the customer to benefit from a below-market-rate loan. An alternative program allows discounts on certain models if the buyer does not want the lower rate. Some manufacturers without captive finance subsidiaries make similar arrangements with the banks that handle their dealers' retail financing. *See also* buydown.

succession The act or fact of a person's becoming entitled to the property of a deceased person, whether by law if the person died intestate or by a provision in the deceased person's will.

succession tax (1) A tax on the transmission of a decedent's property that will be charged on the whole estate regardless of the manner in which the estate is distributed. This succession tax is called a probate or estate tax. (2) A tax on the privilege of taking property by will, by inheritance, or by succession in any other form upon the death of the owner, which is imposed on each legacy or distributive share of the estate as it is received. This is usually called a legacy, succession, or inheritance tax.

successive beneficiaries (1) Beneficiaries who follow one after another in succession. (2) The inheritance of property by descent or transmission to the next in succession, as from parent to child and so on down the direct line.

successor trustee A trustee, following the original or a prior trustee, appointed by a trust instrument. *Distinguish from* substituted trustee.

sum at disposal An amount of money held available in cash at the office of a bank for a beneficiary, at the instruction of another.

summary deposit ticket A special deposit ticket used by customers with many deposit items.

sum of amounts In a funds transfer environment, the sum of the transaction amounts in a multiple message.

sum of the digits *See* rule of 78s.

sum-of-the-years-digits depreciation (SYD) A method of depreciation in which the value of a fixed asset is reduced rapidly during its early years of use. With this method, annual depreciation is calculated as a fraction. The numerator of the fraction is the remaining years of the asset's life at the beginning of the year. The denominator of the fraction is the sum of the digits of the years of the asset's total useful life. This fraction, which changes every year, is multiplied by the cost of the asset to give the depreciation charged for a particular year.

supercheck A generic term for a multiple-bill-payment system.

superintendent of banks A name given to the state official who is responsible for chartering, examining, supervising, and, if necessary, liquidating state banks.

super NOW account A demand deposit account that is interest-bearing and similar to a money market deposit account, but (1) subjects the funds to reserve requirements, (2) is not available to corporations, and (3) has no limit on monthly transaction volume.

supervisor (1) The part of a control program that coordinates the use of resources and maintains the flow of central processing unit operations.

(2) The person who performs the task of supervision.

supplemental agreement An amendment to an agreement setting forth additional terms to the agreement.

supplementary details Information for an account owner bank that may be added to individual statement entries.

supply curve The representation on a graph of the quantities of a product or service that producers are willing to supply at various prices. Quantities of the product or service are usually shown on the horizontal axis and prices on the vertical axis of the graph.

supply-side economics A school of economic thought that holds that income taxes drive a wedge between workers and employers and reduce the incentive to produce. The cost of labor to employers is the amount they pay before taxes; the income to workers is what they receive after taxes. This school of thought assumes that substantial gains in output can come from cutting taxes.

Supreme Court of the United States The court of last resort in the U.S. federal judicial system.

surcharge (1) (Noun) An amount that a fiduciary is required by court decree to make good because of negligence or other failure of duty. (2) (Verb) To require by court decree that a fiduciary make good losses incurred because of negligence or other failure of duty.

surety A person or company that, at the request of another usually called the principal, agrees to be responsible for the performance of some act in favor of a third person if the principal fails to perform as agreed--such as the surety on an administrator's or a guardian's bond.

surety agreement A document, signed by an individual, that makes him or her liable for the obligations of another. If the debtor defaults, the signer (the surety) is liable for the debt.

surety bond A bond or guarantee usually given by a bonding company to answer for the debt, default, or miscarriage of another. The surety (company) binds itself to pay an obligation if the obligor defaults on the obligation.

surplus (1) A generic term referring to funds paid for stock in excess of par value. *Also called* paid-in surplus. (2) The balance of income in a trust that, at the end of the fiscal year, may be paid to the beneficiary.

surplus spending unit (SSU) An economic unit that currently spends less than its income.

surrender value The amount of a life insurance policy paid to a policyholder when he or she surrenders the policy. A portion of the surrender value may be loaned to the policyholder. *Also called* cash surrender value.

surrogate's court *See* probate court.

survey (1) A series of questions designed to elicit respondents' opinions about an issue, product, company, and so on. (2) A measurement of land, prepared by a registered land surveyor, showing the location of land with reference to known points, its dimensions, and the location and dimensions of any improvements.

suspense account A special classification for holding transactions and their related dollars until the issue necessi-

tating the suspense entry (such as a disputed transaction) is resolved. Suspense accounts must be funded by the bank on the balance sheet and, therefore, bear a funding cost.

sustainable growth The annual percentage increase in sales that a firm can experience while still maintaining a stable capital structure.

swap (1) (Verb) To sell an investment and reinvest the proceeds to gain a tax advantage, to change the timing of income flows, or to realize capital gains or losses. (2) (Noun) The purchase of foreign exchange for spot delivery, with the simultaneous sale of the equivalent exchange for forward delivery. (3) (Verb) To remove an active job temporarily from main storage, save it on disk, and process another job in the area of main storage formerly occupied by the first job. This process enables jobs to be executed when main storage has been overcommitted. *See also* currency swap; interest rate swap; loan swap.

swap line A mutual credit facility in which a government buys a foreign currency from a foreign central bank, uses the foreign currency to buy its own surplus currency held by foreigners, and agrees to sell the foreign currency back to the foreign central bank at the end of 3 to 6 months. A swap line is used to help peg a currency.

swap rate The difference between forward and spot rates for a currency.

sweep The prearranged, automatic transfer of temporary funds from a checking account into an interest-bearing account. A sweep is a function of an accounting system provided by some banks and brokerage houses to customers whose accounts receive funds (perhaps from securities sales) that temporarily await reinvestment.

Such funds may be "swept" into an interest-bearing account until the customer directs their investment.

S.W.I.F.T *See* Society for Worldwide Interbank Financial Telecommunication.

swingline A facility for short-term funds that can be drawn at short notice to cover the period between the offer of notes under a note issuance facility and the receipt of funds. *See also* note issuance facility (NIF).

swing loan A loan used to assist with a down payment on a property being purchased, to be repaid from the equity in a property being sold. *Also called* bridge loan.

switch A device, located in the offices of local exchange and interexchange carriers, that by opening or closing transmission circuits, first directs a call from its origin to its destination and then maintains the call's path until completed.

switching Liquidating an existing position and simultaneously reinstating that position in another future on the same financial instrument.

switching and processing center (SPC) The facilities that perform the rapid communications required in point-of-sale systems.

symbiotics Financial conglomerates controlling a large number of subsidiaries that offer financial as well as nonfinancial services to the public.

symmetallism A monetary standard in which a nation will redeem its currency in specified proportions of both gold and silver. *Compare with* bimetallism, in which a currency is redeemable in either gold or silver.

synchronous reserve requirements *See* contemporaneous reserve accounting.

syndicate (1) A group of individuals or companies that join together for some business enterprise. (2) A group of investment bankers organized to distribute a new issue of securities. (3) A group of banks involved in Eurocredit, Eurobond issues, and other joint ventures.

syndicated loan *See* syndication.

syndication (1) A loan made by a group of banks to one borrower. In most cases, the dollar amount requested exceeds the amount that the individual banks are either willing or able to lend. Each bank receives a pro rata share of the income based on its level of participation in the credit. (2) Generally accepted accounting principles generally distinguish between a syndication and a participation, which results in different accounting treatment for the recognition of fee income.

synergy product The combined action of products that, by working together, increase each other's effectiveness.

synthetic positions Combinations of options on the underlying instrument to produce a desired risk/gain position that cannot be obtained directly. Synthetic positions can be established in the following fashion: (1) long call --purchase put and purchase the underlying instrument; (2) long put--purchase call and sell the underlying instrument; (3) long position in the underlying instrument--purchase call and sell put with same strike price and same exercise date; (4) short position in the underlying instrument--sell call and purchase put with same strike price and exercise date.

systematic risk Risk that affects security prices in general and cannot be diversified away. It is caused by underlying national and international economic and political conditions. *See also* unsystematic risk.

system risk The possibility that the failure to settle by one participant in a private network would so jeopardize the financial condition of its net creditors on the network that they in turn would be unable to settle, possibly initiating a series of sequential failures.

systems analysis The examination of an activity, procedure, method, or technique of a business to determine what and how necessary operations may best be accomplished.

systems analyst A person skilled in defining and developing techniques for solving problems, especially on a computer.

systems selling The product strategy that consists of marketing coordinated solutions for a number of a customer's problems. It is based on the recognition that customers buy solutions to problems, not products. Package accounts are an example of systems selling.

10-K report An annual report that publicly held corporations must file with the Securities and Exchange Commission. Since 1974, corporations have been required to release this report, which generally contains more information than an annual report, to any interested stockholder that requests it.

10 percent tables *See* ten percent tables.

10-Q report A quarterly report that publicly held corporations must file with the Securities and Exchange Commission.

360-day year or 365-day year Two systems used for calculating daily interest paid on certain interest-bearing accounts. The difference in income as computed using the two different base years is substantial when large sums of money are involved.

tabulation system Any group of machines that can enter, convert, receive, classify, compute, record, store, and communicate data by means of tabulating cards.

take a loss To realize a loss by selling a security. *Distinguish from* paper loss.

take a position To purchase a block of a specific security as inventory, for resale at a profit. Usually a principal, dealer, or occasionally a broker acting as a principal makes the purchase.

takedown method An underwriting method in which the investment banker sells as much of an issue as possible and charges the issuer a commission per share. *Also called* best efforts.

takeout commitment A commitment issued by a permanent lender to purchase a mortgage loan from a mortgage loan originator or construction lender on completion of construction, thus "taking them out" of the loan.

takeover The acquisition of one business by another, accomplished by a purchase, exchange of capital stock, and so on. The takeover may be friendly or hostile. *See also* corporate raider; greenmail; poison pill; tender offer.

take profits To realize a gain by selling a security. *Distinguish from* paper gain, which is unrealized.

tandem loans A program in which the Government National Mortgage Association agrees to purchase government-insured or guaranteed mortgages from sellers, usually at subsidized terms to low-income borrowers, to provide funds for new loans made by the seller.

tangible assets Material resources that can be touched or recognized with the senses, such as cash, land, or machinery.

tangible net worth Ordinarily, the total capital accounts (equity) less intangibles.

tangible property Any property that can be perceived by the senses, such as a chair. *Compare with* intangible property.

tape (1) An information service provided by the New York Stock Exchange to brokers and major investors for a fee. The tape was originally a paper tape, produced by the ticker installed in a broker's office, but now the tape is usually an electronic display screen. During working hours of the exchange, the tape displays random facts of interest to investors: high trading activity in a major issue; a large change in prices; latest prices; national economic news; international disasters; and important news about an issuer. (2) A linear medium for storing data, which can be used as input to or output from a computer, for example, magnetic tape. (3) Magnetic tapes, punched paper, or paper loops that control the vertical formatting of printers or plastic tapes that control automatic typewriters.

tape-to-tape merchants Merchants who record and forward to the credit card processing centers their sales draft information on magnetic tapes for computer processing. The sales drafts are retained at the individual merchant outlets.

tariff (1) A tax levied by a government on imported goods. A government usually imposes a tariff to raise revenue (a revenue tariff) or to discourage a particular import to protect a domestic product or favor the nation's balance of payments (a protective tariff). (2) A schedule of rates, charges, services, and prohibitions (for example, those filed by a telecommunications carrier with a public utility commission or the Federal Communications Commission).

tax A compulsory charge levied by a local, state, or federal government against the income, wealth, or consumption of a person or corporation. Taxes are the principal source of government revenue. *See also* capital gains tax; death taxes; deferred tax; estate tax; excise tax; federal income tax; franchise tax; general property taxes; generation-skipping tax; income tax; inheritance tax; intangible tax; kiddie tax; organization tax; pick-up tax; privilege tax; progressive tax; proportional tax; regressive tax; regulatory tax; severance tax; stock transfer tax; succession tax; tax on net investment income; transfer tax; use tax; value added tax (VAT); withholding tax.

taxable distribution In general, any distribution that is reported as taxable income to the recipient.

taxable equivalent yield An adjustment that makes it possible to compare after-tax returns on taxable securities with the returns on tax-exempt securities. The taxable equivalent yield is the gross pretax yield on a taxable security that would be necessary to provide an after-tax yield equal to that available on a tax-exempt security. This yield is computed as follows: the nominal tax-free yield divided by 1 minus the marginal tax rate (expressed as a decimal).

taxable gift Property transferred by gift to the extent that its value exceeds allowable exemptions, exclusions, and deductions.

taxable termination For generation-skipping purposes, a taxable termination occurs upon the expiration of a beneficiary's interest in a trust unless (a) immediately after the termination a nonskip person has an interest in the trust, or (b) at no time after the termination may a distribution of any kind be made from the trust to a skip person.

tax anticipation bill A special class of Treasury bill, occasionally sold by the U.S. Treasury to corporations. A tax anticipation bill usually matures 1 week after a tax date but can be turned in at full value when taxes are paid, thus earning an extra week's interest.

tax anticipation note (TAN) The most common type of municipal note, sold in anticipation of tax receipts. It is a form of revenue anticipation note.

tax anticipation warrant A short-term municipal debt issued in anticipation of, and to be paid from, future tax receipts.

tax avoidance Minimizing tax liabilities by taking legally permitted actions. *Compare with* tax evasion.

tax base The object to which a tax is applied. This is usually income, wealth, or consumption.

tax bracket A term used to describe the rate at which a tax is imposed on various levels of an individual's

income. The rate structure of the U.S. income tax is progressive. This means that as income rises, a larger percentage of the incremental increase in income is taxed.

tax credit An expenditure that is deducted from a taxpayer's tax bill (that is, from the total sum owed to the government).

tax deduction An expenditure that may legally be deducted in calculating taxable income.

tax equalization An attempt by local governments to apportion property assessments equitably among their tax districts.

tax evasion Taking illegal actions to reduce tax payments. *Compare with* tax avoidance.

tax-exempt Not subject to federal or state income tax.

tax-exempt bond A bond, the interest income of which is not subject to federal income tax. Tax-exempt bonds are qualifying municipal bonds (bonds of state or local governments).

tax exemption An amount, determined by the federal or state government, that an individual can deduct from his or her taxable income for him or herself and for each dependent.

tax-exempts *See* municipal bond.

tax-exempt security An interest-bearing security, the earnings on which may be exempt from federal or state income tax. These securities are primarily municipal and state bonds, which are exempt from U.S. federal income tax.

tax-free rollover A provision by which a person, receiving a lump-sum distribution from a qualified pension or profit-sharing plan, can preserve the tax-deferred status of these funds by making a rollover into an individual retirement account or other qualified plan, if the rollover occurs within 60 days of receipt.

tax lien A claim against real property for unpaid taxes. Property tax liens usually take precedence over a first mortgage, while other tax liens (income, and so on) do not.

tax loophole A legal provision that can be used to reduce one's tax liability. Such provisions can be unintentional discrepancies in the tax laws or intentional special treatment for a particular group of taxpayers.

tax loss Any loss that serves as a deduction when one is computing taxable income.

tax-loss carryback, tax-loss carry-forward A legal provision allowing businesses to apply a particular year's taxable losses to a previous or future year's taxable income, thereby reducing the tax liability of the business in profitable years. *Also called* loss carryback, loss carryforward.

tax-loss credit *See* loss carryforward.

tax lot A block of identical securities bought at a certain price on a certain date by a trust account.

tax on net investment income An excise tax, generally of 2 percent, imposed on the net investment income of all tax-exempt private foundations, with the exception of certain operating private foundations. Net investment income of a private foundation is the amount by which the sum of gross investment income and capital gain net income exceeds certain allowable deductions. If a private founda-

tion makes sufficient charitable distributions in a given year, the excise tax rate is reduced to 1 percent.

tax shelter An investment made to take advantage of provisions within existing law that take different forms but usually have one or more of the following elements: tax deferral, leverage, and conversion of ordinary income to capital gain at the time of disposition.

tax swap Selling a security and reinvesting the proceeds in another security to gain a tax advantage.

tax waiver A written consent of a state tax department permitting the withdrawal of property belonging to a decedent's estate by the executor or administrator, to permit the assembling of assets and distribution.

T-bill futures Contracts for the delivery of Treasury bills of specified maturities at stated prices and on a stated future date. T-bill futures are sold through the International Money Market (IMM), the New York Futures Exchange (NYFE), and the Commodity Exchange (COMEX). T-bill futures are sold on a discount basis and are available for every month of the year.

teaser rate The first-period interest rate offered on an adjustable rate loan or adjustable rate deposit. This rate is set below market in the case of a loan or above market in the case of a deposit to attract customers. In the following periods, the rate is adjusted to market.

telephone order (TO) A direction that a merchant receives by telephone from a cardholder who wishes to charge the purchase amount to his or her bank card account without executing the resulting sales draft.

teller A bank employee who actually handles money, waiting on depositors and other bank customers. The teller receives deposits and pays out withdrawals. Large banks often have a separate teller for each specialized function.

teller machine A machine used by a teller to record transactions. The machine usually accumulates totals by transaction, for the purpose of verification and control.

teller proof A control system in which the individual teller balances and settles his or her own cash position each day.

teller's stamp A rubber stamp, bearing a teller's initials or number and the bank's name or transit number. The stamp is used for control purposes on each transaction to identify the particular teller who processed the transaction.

teller terminal A terminal specifically used for entering tellers' transactions in an on-line environment. The terminal also allows tellers to process inquiries about the status of accounts.

temporary administrator A person or trust institution appointed by a court to take over and safeguard an estate during a suit over an alleged will or over the right of appointment of an executor or administrator. A court will also appoint a temporary administrator during the period that probate is delayed for any reason, such as difficulty in finding or citing missing heirs. *Sometimes called* curator.

temporary bond A certificate, generally without coupon sheets, that serves as evidence of ownership until the printer has completed the final (definitive) bond. *Also called* interim bond. *Compare with* definitive bond.

temporary guardian *See* curator.

tenancy The holding of real property by any form of title.

tenancy at sufferance A tenancy in which the tenant comes into possession of real property under a lawful title or interest and continues to hold the property even after his or her title or interest has ended. A tenancy at sufferance involves a tenant who continues to occupy premises without the owner's permission.

tenancy at will A tenancy in which the tenant holds the real property at the will or pleasure of the owner. It may be canceled on proper notice.

tenancy by the entirety A tenancy by a husband and wife in which, except in concert with the other, neither husband nor wife has a disposable interest in the property during the other's lifetime. When either dies, the property goes to the survivor. *Also called* tenancy by entirety. *Distinguish from* joint tenancy *and* tenancy in common.

tenancy for years A tenancy for a definite period (for example, 1 year or 99 years).

tenancy from period to period A tenancy that continues from period to period, continuing automatically until legal notice of termination is given.

tenancy in common The holding of property by two or more persons in such a manner that each has an undivided interest that, on his or her death, passes as such to his or her heirs or devisees and not to the survivor(s). It is the same as an estate in common. *Distinguish from* joint tenancy *and* tenancy by the entirety.

tenant A person who holds or possesses real property.

tenants by the entirety *See* tenancy by the entirety.

tenants in common *See* tenancy in common.

tender offer (1) An offer to buy a controlling interest in a corporation by purchasing shares in the market at a stated price by a specified date. A tender offer is generally used when the management of the corporation opposes the takeover. *See also* corporate raider; greenmail. (2) An offer by a corporation to buy back a portion of its own shares. This is normally done when the corporation has excess cash and believes the market price of its stock is unreasonably low. The reduced share count may result in higher future dividends per share on the remaining shares.

tender panel A method for distributing notes issued under note issuance facilities. A group of financial institutions has the right to bid for the short-term notes issued under the facility on each issue date. *See also* note issuance facility.

tender rate security A type of preferred stock in which the dividend rate is reset by a remarketing agent at specified intervals, commonly 7 days or 49 days. On these dates, investors have the choice of selling or holding their shares. *Also called* remarketed preferred stock.

tenor The original maturity length of a loan or deposit.

ten percent tables The tables contained in Treasury Regulations SS20.2031-7 and 25.2512-5 that are used in most instances to value life estate, term, and remainder interests for estate and gift tax purposes. The tables are based on an assumption that all assets earn 10 percent after tax and do not appreciate in value.

term The time between the commencement and termination dates of a note, mortgage, legal document, or other contract. *Also called* tenure.

term bond A bond whose principal is repaid at the maturity date of the issue. An issue of term bonds has one maturity date for all bonds in the issue. *Compare with* serial bonds.

term fed funds Federal funds sold for a period longer than 1 day.

terminable interest An interest that will terminate or fail with the lapse of time, the occurrence of a contingency, or the failure of a contingency to occur.

terminal capture alliance program (TCAP) A program in the credit card industry offered to members to encourage the replacement of existing firstgeneration dial authorization terminals.

terminal digit control A system for filing serially numbered ledger cards into ten or more controls, to reduce the overall space requirements of the filing system and to simplify location of missing ledger cards.

terminal interchange reimbursement fee (TIRF) A fee defined by Visa U.S.A. as a special interchange reimbursement fee paid or received by a member for transactions authorized using the Loss Control Service. It is entered into interchange in a set period of days.

terminal migration program (TMP) A lower interchange rate offered to entice merchants to move from standard imprint to an electronic data capture system.

terminated merchant file A file of all potential problem merchants. This file is housed at the national system level.

term insurance *See* term life insurance.

term issue *See* term bond.

term life insurance A short-term insurance policy representing pure life insurance with no savings element. Under term life insurance, the insurer pays a stipulated sum of money when the insured party dies, provided the death occurs within a predetermined period. Premiums tend to be relatively low when a person is young but rise as he or she ages.

term loan A loan scheduled to run for more than 1 year, usually repayable in annual or more frequent installments.

term mortgage A mortgage that provides no periodic repayment of principal. The principal is due at the end of the term.

term repo A repurchase agreement with a maturity of more than 1 day.

terms of sale (1) The conditions of a sale, as laid down in a written sales contract. These conditions may include the time, place, and method of delivery and payment for the purchase. (2) The terms of payment for a sale, including the stipulation of any discount allowed for receipt of payment before a certain date.

terms of trade The relationship of a country's export prices to its import prices. A country's terms of trade are said to improve if the prices of its exports increase relative to the prices of its imports.

term structure of interest rates The relationship between interest rates on

the same securities with different maturities.

test A code in a message between the sender and the receiver used to validate the source of a message; it may also validate certain elements of the message such as amount, date, and sequence. The code is the result of a bilaterally agreed method of calculation.

testament Under early English law, a term that referred to the disposition of personal property by will. The words "and testament" are no longer necessary because a will now relates to both real and personal property.

testamentary capacity The mental capacity to make a valid will.

testamentary disposition The disposition of property by deed, will, or otherwise so that it will not take effect unless or until the grantor dies.

testamentary guardian A guardian of a minor or an incompetent person named in the decedent's will.

testamentary trust A trust established by the terms of a will. A testamentary trust empowers a trustee to manage assets for a beneficiary and becomes active after the maker's death and settlement of the estate. *Also called* trust under will.

testate (Adj.) Having made and left a valid will. *Compare with* intestate.

testator A man who has made and left a valid will at his death. *Compare with* settlor. *See also* trustor.

testatrix A woman who has made and left a valid will at her death. *See also* testator.

test key A code established between banks and used in transmitting financial messages by cable, telex, or telephone so that the recipient can authenticate the message.

theft of securities *See* Rule 17f-1.

thin market A securities market in which there are few transaction orders. Prices in a thin market are likely to be volatile.

third market When securities listed on a stock exchange are traded off the floor of that exchange, they are said to trade in the third market.

third party The party intended to receive funds immediately after the credit party has received them.

third-party payment A noncash payment made from a customer account at a financial institution to a payor other than that financial institution.

third-party transfer A transfer in favor of a party other than the sender or receiver.

thirty-second of a point One thirty-second (1/32) of 1 percent of the face value of a security; the fraction of a point used to express the bid and asked prices for government securities.

threat monitoring The analysis, assessment, and review of audit trails and other collected data to determine whether a system's security has been violated.

three-party paper A sales contract purchased from retail merchants by banks and other lenders.

thrift institution An organization that primarily accepts savings account deposits and invests most of the proceeds in mortgages. Savings

banks, savings and loan associations, and credit unions are examples of thrift institutions.

throat The area on the face of a certificate where the name of the registered holder and the par value of the certificate are imprinted.

throwback rule A rule stating that the distributions by a trust of previously accumulated income (with some exceptions) are taxed in theoretically the same way as the distributions would have been taxed when the income was earned by the trust, that is, "thrown back" to the year earned.

ticker tape Formerly, paper tape used in a ticker (a telegraphic device that records stock market quotations chronologically). Now the terms "ticker" and "ticker tape" are used to refer to the electronic displays that perform the same function.

ticket *See* sales draft.

tickler (1) A record of maturing obligations that is maintained to call attention daily to correspondence, financial transactions, or other obligations that must be handled on that day. (2) Any record established as a reminder of action to be taken on a fixed future date. A tickler is always arranged in the order of dates on which such action is to be taken. *Also called* duty card.

tickler system A reminder system, filed in chronological order, that informs the user of future actions to be taken, and the date required.

Tier One capital Under the risk-based capital framework initially adopted in January 1989, Tier One capital (also called core equity) consists of common stockholders' equity, qualifying noncumulative perpetual preferred stock, and minority interest in equity accounts of consolidated subsidiaries, less goodwill and other disallowed intangibles. In addition, perpetual preferred stock can be included up to 25 percent of Tier One capital. Banking regulators require Tier One capital to equate to a certain percentage of risk-weighted assets. There are also minimum requirements for total capital, which consists of Tier One plus Tier Two capital. Tier One and Tier Two capital replace the old components of primary and secondary capital, respectively. The banking regulators (that is, the Federal Reserve Board, Office of the Comptroller of the Currency, and Federal Deposit Insurance Corporation) each set forth risk-based capital guidelines. The guidelines should be referred to directly for current information. *See also* capital adequacy.

Tier Two capital Under the risk-based capital framework initially adopted in January 1989, Tier Two (also called supplementary) capital consists of the allowance for loan and lease losses (limited to a certain percentage of risk-weighted assets), perpetual and long-term preferred stock, hybrid capital instruments (including perpetual debt and mandatory convertible securities), and subordinated debt and intermediate-term preferred stock (subject to certain limitations). Banking regulators require total capital (Tier One plus Tier Two) to equate to a certain percent of risk-weighted assets. There are also minimum requirements applicable to Tier One capital alone. Tier One and Tier Two capital replace the old components of primary and secondary capital, respectively. The banking regulators (that is, the Federal Reserve Board, Office of the Comptroller of the Currency, and Federal Deposit Insurance Corporation) each set forth risk-based capital guidelines. The guidelines should be referred to directly for

current information. *See also* capital adequacy.

tight money A condition in which the supply of money is scarce, thereby causing interest rates to rise. Tight money often results from the conscious tightening of the money supply by the Federal Reserve System to fight inflation.

tight money market A condition in the money market characterized by relative strength in demand, which results in increasing interest rates. The term may also imply actions by the Federal Reserve System to restrict the availability of credit.

till money The currency banks keep on hand for cash transactions. Till money is allotted to tellers for use at their windows.

time-dependent password A password that is valid only at a certain time of the day or during a specified period.

time deposit Any deposit in a bank account that cannot be withdrawn before a specified date or without advance notice. Examples include savings deposits, time certificates of deposit, and time deposits (open account).

time deposit, open account (TDOA) Funds deposited by a business under an agreement that usually requires the funds to remain on deposit for some minimum period, or until some fixed maturity date.

time draft A draft that is payable at a fixed or determinable future time.

time loan A sum of money borrowed with interest for a specific period. A time loan differs from a demand loan in that a bank cannot recall the funds at any time but must wait until the maturity date.

time order An order for the purchase or sale of a security that, unless executed before the end of a certain day, expires automatically.

time-plan loan A loan for which interest payments are made monthly, in fixed regular amounts.

time-sale financing A form of indirect loan in which a lender, usually a bank, purchases a loan contract from a retailer. The contract is an installment loan agreement between the retailer and the purchaser of a product. The borrower makes payment to the bank or another indirect creditor.

time-series forecasting A prediction of future activity based on past trends. The term applies to a forecast of any series: economic, financial, sales.

time sharing (1) The sharing of a computer facility by several users for different purposes, at what appears to be the same time. The computer actually interacts with the users in sequence, but at such a high speed that it seems to serve all users simultaneously. (2) The exclusive right to occupy property for a specified period of time each year. Either the right or the ownership of the property may be purchased for a particular interval (such as a month) each year. An owner receives a deed, for example, for the right to occupy the unit forever during the month of February. The other months are sold to other purchasers. Time sharing is used primarily for condominiums in resort areas. *Sometimes called* "interval ownership."

times-interest-earned ratio A leverage ratio indicating the relationship between interest expense and net

profit, used to determine whether a business can meet its periodic interest payments.

time value The imputed monetary value of an option reflecting the possibility that the price of the underlying instrument will move so that the option will become more valuable. The total value of an option, or its price, is composed of its intrinsic value and its time value.

time value of money *See* present value.

title (1) The legal right to ownership of property, real or personal. (2) Legal evidence of ownership of real or personal property.

title binder Written evidence that a title insurance company has agreed to provide title insurance coverage. A title binder is valid only for a specified time, after which it must be replaced by a permanent policy.

title company A corporation organized for the purpose of issuing or insuring title to real property.

title exception A specific item in a title policy that a title company does not insure.

title insurance Insurance against financial loss resulting from claims arising out of defects in the title to real property, which exist but are undisclosed when the title company issues the policy.

Title I The section of the Federal Housing Administration Insurance Program that refers to home improvements and mobile homes.

title report A report issued by a title company before settlement of a real estate purchase. The report provides a legal description of the property and lists all restrictions and liens against the property.

title search A review of public records to disclose the past and current facts about the ownership of a piece of real estate.

to credit In the context of a payment order, an instruction to credit an account on the books of a paying bank, as distinct from actually remitting the payment.

to debit An instruction to charge an account on the books of a bank.

tombstone advertisement An advertisement announcing a new issue of securities and listing the underwriting firms.

tom next Literally, tomorrow next. Banks use this term for the delivery date on Eurodollar deposits and foreign exchange transactions to mean delivery on the next business day.

top management The highest-ranking officials of an organization, who are responsible for setting policy and making major long-range plans. *Also called* executive management.

Torrens registration A system of registering land title, as opposed to registering or recording evidence of such title. The originator of the system was Sir Robert Richard Torrens (1814-1884), a reformer of Australian land laws.

Torrens title certificate Under the Torrens system of registration of land titles, upon the entry of a decree of registration, the official registrar of titles must make and register what is called the original certificate of title in the public record. This official also furnishes a duplicate copy to the registered owner. Upon any registration of a transfer, the official furnishes the transferee with a new

duplicate certificate of title. Under the statutes for such a system of registration, the certificate of title is conclusive evidence of all matters contained therein.

tort Any wrongful act or omission that causes damage to the person, property, or reputation of another. It is commonly considered a private wrong, as opposed to a public wrong, which is called a crime.

total call The call for redemption of all outstanding bonds of an issue.

total-debt-to-total-assets ratio *See* debt ratio.

total lease obligation Under the Consumer Leasing Act, the total of (1) the scheduled periodic payments under a lease; (2) any nonrefundable cash payment required of the lessee or agreed to by the lessor and lessee, or any trade-in allowance made at consummation; and (3) the estimated value of leased property at the end of a lease term.

total proprietorship *See* equity.

total reserves Reserve balances with Federal Reserve banks plus vault cash used to satisfy reserve requirements.

Totten trust A trust created when a person deposits money in his or her own name as a trustee for another. Title is vested in the record owner (trustee), who during his or her life holds it in a revocable trust for the named beneficiary. When the depositor dies, a presumption arises that an absolute trust was created as to the balance on hand at the depositor's death.

track (1) A sequence of binary cells arranged so that data may be read or written serially from one cell at a time. For example, a track on a magnetic drum is a path one bit wide around the circumference of the drum. (2) The portion of a moving storage medium, such as a drum, tape, or disk, that is accessible to a given reading station. (3) An area on a magnetic stripe where data are recorded.

trade acceptance A draft drawn by the seller of goods directly on, and accepted by, the buyer, thereby obligating the buyer to pay the draft at maturity. *See also* draft.

trade association A nonprofit organization formed by companies or individuals in a particular field or business to promote their mutual interest, including the improvement of public relations, industrial consulting, government lobbying, and education.

trade balance The net balance of exports and imports of a country's merchandise (physical goods, not including services).

trade confirmation *See* broker confirmation.

trade credit Credit extended to a company by its suppliers, usually to cover inventory purchases or other normal operating expenses.

trade date The date on which a securities trade was actually executed. Trade date and settlement date are not necessarily the same. For example, regular-way settlement is generally 5 days for certain securities. Contractual settlement in excess of regular-way delivery is a forward contract.

trade discount A deduction from the stated price of merchandise given when payment is received by a specified date. Trade discounts are offered to encourage prompt payment of bills.

trade finance The financing of imports and exports. It is most often accomplished by means of letters of credit, bankers' acceptances, and documentary collections.

trade-for-trade (TFT) settlement A process for settling securities trades that allows trades to settle item by item in a depository environment using methods for automated book-entry settlement. TFT settlement is more restrictive than continuous net settlement (CNS). The seller must have the necessary position on the date of settlement or the trade will drop. A separate report on money settlement is produced as part of the settlement process. These trades settle on an individual basis and are not netted. *See also* balance-order settlement; continuous net settlement (CNS).

trade name A fictitious name adopted for business purposes, often indicating the nature of the business. For example, John Smith may operate a business under the trade name of "John's Diner."

trade price The price at which a securities transaction occurred.

trader A person who buys and sells securities.

TRADES (Treasury/Reserve Automated Debt-Entry System) The Treasury Department's commercial book-entry system, used to process marketable securities transactions. Securities are recorded at Federal Reserve banks as book-entry issues held at securities depositories. The system facilitates trading in the inter-dealer market by financial institutions and broker-dealers.

trade status changes report An interim notice provided by a depository to participants in the National Institutional Delivery System. This notice is issued each time a trade's status changes from unaffirmed or drops from the pending file.

trade ticket A record prepared by a bank for each trade, which reconciles the information received from its customer with the data provided in the broker confirmation.

trading account Securities (for example, U.S. Treasuries, agencies, and municipals) that are actively bought and sold for the purpose of making a profit. Trading-account positions are often tailored to current and anticipated customer needs, underwriting obligations, and trading strategies. *See also* investment account; market maker.

trading down (1) Selling securities from a portfolio and purchasing others of lesser quality as replacements. Securities are traded down either to increase income or to obtain greater potential for appreciation from more speculative securities. (2) The product strategy of adding a lower-priced item to a prestige line of products in the hope that people who are attracted to, but cannot afford, the original will buy the lower-priced item.

trading flat In bond trading, trading without accrued interest. Income bonds and bonds in default are usually quoted and traded flat.

trading on the equity *See* leverage.

trading post A U-shaped counter on the floor of an exchange where the traders of a small group of securities meet to transact their business.

trading up The product strategy of adding a high-priced or prestige item to a product line to attract customers for the lower-priced products.

trading volume The number of shares traded in a given period, usually a day, listed in terms of round lots (hundreds).

trailing edge The left edge of a check when viewed face up.

transaction (1) A trade or sale. (2) An action that leads to an entry in a bank's or other company's books. (3) An action that transforms information. (4) A specific action in support of a business activity. (5) An act between a cardholder and a merchant, or between a cardholder and a bank, that creates an obligation. *See also* funds transfer transaction.

transaction account Under the terms of the Monetary Control Act of 1980, an account with a financial institution that allows for transfers of funds to third parties.

transaction amount A data element in funds transfers that is the funds transferred between two parties in a transaction.

transaction date The date on which a transaction occurs. *See also* entry date.

transaction document (1) A form that (a) contains information pertaining to a transaction generated by a bank card and (b) evidences a transaction. (2) A check guaranteed by a bank card. Sales slips, refund slips, and cash advance/withdrawal slips are transaction documents.

transaction file A file containing relatively transient data to be processed along with a master file. For example, in payroll application, a transaction file indicating hours worked might be processed with a master file containing employees' names and rates of pay.

transaction inquiry An administrative message, generated by the issuer, that requests additional information regarding a transaction or verification that a particular transaction occurred as presented. Trace elements from the financial transaction in question must be included in the inquiry.

transaction report Usually a monthly report generated by a trust department detailing all transactions and the beginning and ending value of each account.

transaction type code A data element in funds transfers that is a code that further defines the purpose of the transaction, such as deposit, federal funds sold, or draw downs.

transaction velocity of money A measure of the average number of times during a certain period that the same dollar or other monetary unit is spent. The transaction velocity of money is calculated by dividing the total sales of goods and services by the total money supply.

transcript A summary of account activity for a designated period.

transfer (1) The routine necessary to record a change of ownership of stock or registered bonds, involving a cancellation of the old certificate and issuance of a new one. (2) *See also* funds transfer; payment order.

transferable letter of credit A letter of credit addressed to the beneficiary and/or transferee(s), enabling the beneficiary to transfer the credit to another party.

transfer agent An agent of a corporation that effects the transfer of its stock or bonds from one owner to another. A transfer agent for bonds is usually known as a registrar.

transfer agent custodian (TAC) program A depository service to speed the transfer process when new physical certificates must be issued. TAC is part of the depository's certificate on demand program. The depository sends all or part of its certificates for one issue to the transfer agent. The transfer agent cancels these certificates, prepares a matching large balance certificate in the nominee name of the depository, and holds the balance certificate in safekeeping. The depository can request the physical certificates when needed. The transfer agent then registers and forwards the certificates, and reduces the amount of the balance certificate. Turnaround for this TAC program is 72 hours. A refinement that speeds turnaround to 3 hours is called Fast/TAC.

transferee The person or corporation to whom property has been transferred.

transfer fee A fee collected from buyers and sellers of property to defray government costs of maintaining public records. *Also called* transfer tax.

transfer in contemplation of death A transfer of property by gift made in apprehension of death, arising from some existing bodily condition or impending peril and not the general expectation of eventual decease commonly held by all people.

transferor The person or corporation that conveys or transfers property.

transfer payments Payments, such as gifts or subsidies, that are not made in exchange for goods and services.

transferred account A cardholder account that has been transferred from one processing center to another, from one area to another within a processing center, or from one associate to another in the same bank card plan.

transfer risk The possibility that an asset cannot be serviced in the currency of payment because of a lack of, or restraints on the availability of, needed foreign exchange in the country of the obligor. *See also* allocated transfer risk reserve (ATRR); Interagency Country Exposure Review Committee (ICERC).

transfer service fee A service fee for an instant cash transaction.

transfer tax A tax imposed on the transfer of ownership of stocks and bonds, usually paid by affixing and canceling stamps to the certificates or other documents evidencing the transfer of ownership. *Also called* stock transfer tax.

transit check Any item that a bank chooses to classify as not payable locally; an out-of-town check.

transit department The department of a bank that clears checks. It receives items presented for payment and verifies their totals with deposit tickets, branch office settlements, and other data. This department proves the accuracy of the bank's transaction records and prepares the items for computer processing.

transit item A check drawn on an out-of-town bank. *See also* foreign items.

transit letter A form that lists, or is attached to a list of, checks and other cash items drawn on banks outside the city of a particular bank. A transit letter is sent to the bank on which the items are drawn for collection and payment.

transit machine A machine that sorts, proves, and lists transit items. *Also called* proof machine.

transit number (1) A numerical code originated by the American Bankers Association to facilitate the sorting and processing of checks. Each bank is assigned a unique number, made of two parts separated by a hyphen. The first part of the number identifies the state, city, or territory in which the bank is located, and the second part identifies the bank itself. *Also called* American Bankers Association (ABA) number, routing number, *or* routing transit number. (2) A number devised by the originator to identify a transaction uniquely.

transit number field A field that defines the boundaries within which the routing number of the drawee bank will appear.

transit routing number A number that identifies a particular bank. This number should appear twice on a check: once in the MICR line and once, for visual purposes, in the upper right-hand quadrant of the check.

transmittal letter A letter accompanying a shipment of securities, documents, or other property usually containing a brief description of the securities, documents, or property being forwarded and an explanation of the transaction.

transposition An error in the sequence of digits in a number, often made when numbers are copied. The transposition of two digits in a number always results in a net error that is divisible by nine.

traveler's check A special fixed-amount check issued by a well-known bank or other institution and sold at many franchise locations. It enables travelers to carry money without threat of loss or theft. The purchaser of these checks pays a fee for the convenience of guaranteed rapid replacement in the event of loss or theft. *Also called* traveler's cheque.

traveler's letter of credit A letter of credit issued to people as a source of cash while traveling. Correspondents of the issuing bank advance cash to the holder of the letter and post the amounts of the advances on the letter. Formerly widely used, it has mostly been replaced today by traveler's checks.

treasurer The officer of an organization who is charged with the receipt, custody, and disbursement of its funds.

treasurer's check *See* cashier's check.

treasurer's draft A check written on a corporation rather than a bank, but payable through a bank. Originally created to avoid a check tax in the 1930s, treasurer's drafts are used primarily for insurance settlements, payment of expenses for field sales-people, and, in some cases, for disbursements. Accounting practice dictates that the drafts be recognized as disbursements only after they clear rather than when they are written. *Also called* payable-through draft.

Treasury *See* Department of the Treasury.

Treasury bill A marketable U.S. Treasury security with a life of 1 year or less, sold to the public at weekly auctions on a discount basis in minimum denominations of $10,000 and in book-entry only form. *Also called* T-bill.

Treasury bond (1) A debt security of the federal government, with a maturity over 10 years. (2) A corporate bond that has been repurchased by

the issuing company and is held in its treasury.

Treasury currency The noninterest-bearing notes, paper money, silver certificates, and coins issued by the Department of the Treasury for use as a medium of exchange. Sometimes the term is used to describe paper currency, as distinguished from coins.

Treasury direct The book-entry system that enables individual investors to hold Treasury securities in a single account directly on the records of the Bureau of the Public Debt rather than buying them through a commercial bank or securities dealer. It is designed for investors who plan to retain their investment until maturity.

Treasury note An intermediate-term security issued by the Department of the Treasury, with an original maturity of 2 to 10 years.

treasury stock Stock issued by a corporation and later repurchased or in some way reacquired by the corporation. The shares are considered issued (that is, they are not automatically considered retired), but not outstanding.

Treasury tax and loan accounts (TT&Ls) Accounts in which tax deposits may be made through any authorized depository bank, where the deposits remain until the Treasury withdraws them according to a predetermined schedule.

trend analysis A technique that compares the results of an account balance or activity over equal intervals of time.

trial balance A list of the balances of all accounts within a given control group or ledger. A trial balance is determined periodically to check the control total established over the group of accounts in question.

trigger (interstate banking) A term referring to the period of limitation before banks can legally branch nationwide, or into a particular state or region.

trigger terms Phrases or figures used in advertising that will activate other Regulation Z disclosures. The following are trigger terms: the amount or percentage of any down payment, the payment period, the monthly payment, and the amount of the finance charge. The use of any of these terms requires the disclosure of all of the following: the down payment as a dollar amount, the repayment terms, and the annual percentage rate. An advertisement may use an example of a typical transaction for the disclosure.

troubled debt restructuring As defined by the Financial Accounting Standards Board (FASB), a troubled debt restructuring has occurred if the creditor, for economic or legal reasons related to the debtor's financial difficulties, grants a concession to the debtor it would not otherwise consider. A troubled debt restructuring may include such transactions as transfers from the debtor to the creditor of receivables from third parties, issuance or other granting of an equity interest to the creditor, or modification of terms of the debt. A debt restructuring is not necessarily a troubled debt restructuring. Generally, restructurings at fair value and/or market interest rates are not considered troubled debt restructurings.

true annual rate of interest See annual percentage rate.

true discount rate A method for computing the interest rate on the total installment note. The interest charge is deducted from the principal

when the loan is made. See also annual percentage rate.

true personal identification number (TPIN) The personal identification number used as a reference, as opposed to the number used and remembered by the cardholder. (The true personal identification number is related to the personal identification number by offset on the card.)

truncation See check safekeeping; check truncation.

trunk line (1) See bus line. (2) A telecommunication path that connects a private exchange to a telephone company's central office.

trust (1) A fiduciary relationship in which a person or corporation (the trustee) holds the legal title to property (the trust property). The trustee is subject to an obligation, enforceable in a court of equity, to keep or use the property for the benefit of another person (the beneficiary). (2) In business, a large corporation or group of corporations that has a monopoly or near-monopoly on the production or distribution of particular goods or services. (3) A plan in which the voting rights of a majority of two or more corporations are assigned to trustees, who then direct the affairs of the corporations.

trust account Any account in a trust department, including estates, guardianships, and agencies, as well as the actual trusts.

trust administrator A person employed by a trust institution to handle trust accounts and deal directly with trust customers and beneficiaries.

trust agreement A written agreement between a settlor and trustee setting forth the terms of a trust. See also trustor.

trust authority The legal right of a corporation to engage in trust business.

trust by declaration A living trust by which a person declares him- or herself the trustee of property for another person's benefit. *Also called* declaration of trust.

trust by order of court A trust created by the order of a court with competent jurisdiction.

trust charge The price fixed or demanded by a trust institution as compensation for a service. A trust institution has a legal right to fix a charge, in the form of either a commission or a fee, in contrast to an allowance, which is granted by a court. *See also* allowance; commission; fee.

trust committee A committee of directors, officers, or both of a trust institution, charged with general or specific duties relating to its trust business.

trust company A corporation charged by a state to engage in the trust business, serving both people and businesses. A trust company may or may not also perform bank functions, depending on the powers granted in its charter.

trust costs The costs to a trust institution of providing trust and agency services. *Compare with* trust charge.

trust deed A deed that conveys title to a third party (a trustee), who holds title for the benefit of a lender (the beneficiary of the trust). *See also* deed of trust.

trust department A banking unit that administers trust activities.

trustee A person or trust institution that holds the legal title to property for the benefit of someone else. A trustee is responsible for preserving and managing the assets of a trust.

trusteed Placed in trust, that is, in a trustee's care.

trusteed pension plan A pension plan in which the corporation's contributions to the plan are placed in a trust for investment and reinvestment, as distinguished from a plan in which the benefits are secured by life insurance.

trust estate All the property in a particular trust account.

trust for children A specific form of transfer for a minor's benefit that will qualify for tax purposes as a gift of a present interest, thus making available the annual gift tax exclusion.

trust for support A trust in which the trustee shall apply only so much of the income or principal as in his or her judgment is needed to support and educate the beneficiary.

trust function A fiduciary capacity in which a person or trust institution may act, such as executor, administrator, guardian, or trustee.

trust fund(s) (1) The cash held by a trust department for individual trust accounts. (2) The assets held in trust accounts. (3) Trust accounts.

trust indenture A written instrument describing all property originally placed in a trust.

Trust Indenture Act of 1939 Federal legislation that requires every debt security issue sold interstate to be issued under an indenture qualified by the Securities and Exchange Commission. The trustee appointed under the indenture must safeguard the bond-holders' interests.

trust institution A trust company, state bank, national bank, or other corporation engaged in trust business under authority of law. A company is a trust institution if any department is engaged in the trust business.

trust instrument Any written document, such as a will, trust agreement, declaration of trust, deed of trust, or order of court, under which a trust is created.

trust inter vivos *See* living trust; trust under agreement; voluntary trust.

trust investment committee A committee of directors, officers, or both of a trust institution, charged with specific duties relating to trust investments. A board of directors may also impose on a trust investment committee duties other than those relating to investments.

trust investments The property in which trust funds are invested, including securities and many other kinds of assets.

trust officer (1) A title given to certain officers of a trust institution. (2) Any official who manages trusts.

trustor A creator of a trust, who may also be called the settlor, grantor, or donor. A trustor may also be called a testator if the trust becomes operative after the death of the trustor.

trust powers As used in the Federal Reserve Act, the authority to engage in the trust business, to be distinguished from the powers of a trustee.

trust receipt (1) A formal receipt issued by a trustee for property held in trust. This receipt is used in certain commercial transactions. (2) A document that creates a special type of secured loan, often extended to an importer of merchandise. The borrower is allowed to take possession of the goods, while the lender holds legal title to them.

trust receipt financing *See* floor planning.

trust relationship The relationship between the trustee and the beneficiary of a trust.

trust risk *See* fiduciary risk.

trust under agreement A trust evidenced by an agreement between the settlor and the trustee. *Also called* trust inter vivos *or* living trust.

trust under decree A trust evidenced by a decree of a court of equity.

trust under deed A trust evidenced by a deed of conveyance, as distinguished from an agreement. This trust was originally confined to real property but now frequently also applies to personal property.

trust under will A trust created by a valid will, to become operative only at the testator's death. *Also called* testamentary trust. *Distinguish from* living trust.

Truth in Lending Act The popular name for the Consumer Credit Protection Act passed in 1969. This federal law requires disclosure of credit terms using a standard format.

Truth in Lending disclosures Information sent to customers at periodic intervals regarding finance charges, service charges, minimum payment schedule, customer obligations, and Fair Credit Billing Act requirements for items in dispute.

Truth in Lending Simplification and Reform Act A 1982 federal law designed to streamline the original Truth in Lending legislation by easing and simplifying disclosure requirements so that consumers can more easily understand disclosure statements.

TT&L account *See* Treasury tax and loan accounts.

turnaround The purchase and sale of securities for settlement on the same day.

turnaround document *See* remittance document.

turnaround time The time a computer takes to complete a job.

turnkey system A complete computer system, including all hardware and software, that is ready for use.

turnover (1) The number of times a complete stock of goods is sold in a given period. (2) The number of workers hired to replace those terminated in a particular industry, over a specific period.

turnover ratio The reciprocal of the average collection period (the average number of days required to collect accounts receivable).

tutor Under civil law, one who has been legally appointed to care for the person and property of a minor; the equivalent of a guardian.

twenty-four-hour banking A description of the availability for customer transactions provided by the presence of automated teller machines. Customers using these machines may access their accounts at any time.

two-sided market A market with good quotes on both the bid and asked side.

type code A data element in funds transfers that is a component of a message code indicating the action requested (for example, administrative message or funds transfer).

UBPR *See* Uniform Bank Performance Report.

ultimate beneficiary A beneficiary of a trust who is entitled to receive the principal of the trust property in final distribution. *Also called* principal beneficiary. *Compare with* beneficiary *and* income beneficiary.

ultimate loss insurance *See* single interest insurance.

unattended banking terminal *See* automated teller machine; cash dispenser.

unauthorized electronic funds transfer An electronic funds transfer from a customer's deposit account (a) that is initiated by a party other than the customer without actual authority to initiate such transfer and (b) from which the customer receives no benefit.

unauthorized investment A trust investment that is not authorized by the trust instrument. *Distinguish from* nonlegal investment.

unauthorized use The use of a credit card by a person other than the cardholder--a person who does not have actual, implied, or apparent authority to use the card--and a use from which the cardholder receives no benefit. A cardholder's liability for unauthorized use is limited to $50.

unbundled service A bank service that is not linked to any other service or service package and, thus, can be obtained separately. An unbundled service usually carries an explicit fee.

unclaimed balances Account balances that have not been legally debited or credited for a specific period. *See also* dormant account.

uncollected funds Funds consisting of the checks deposited and credited by a bank to its customers' accounts but not yet collected. The bank may impose a "hold" (withdrawal restriction) until the checks deposited have cleared. *Also called* float.

uncollectible and execution-proof accounts Accounts receivable that are not collectible, and for which there is no legal recourse because the debtors own no property.

unconfirmed letter of credit A letter of credit for which credit has been established but for which the correspondent (advising) bank does not guarantee payment of drafts against it.

uncovered writers Option sellers who do not attempt to reduce their market risk by taking offsetting positions in the underlying security or other options. This strategy is also called taking a "biased" view in option writing--that is, anticipating that the option will fall in value-thus reducing the chance that it will be exercised. *Also called* naked writers.

undercapitalized A business whose capital structure (debt plus equity) is insufficient for effective operation.

underemployment A form of hidden unemployment when an employee is working (that is, employed) but not to his or her capabilities.

underflow The condition that arises when a machine computation yields a nonzero result smaller than the smallest nonzero quantity that the intended unit of storage can store. *Compare with* overflow.

underlying The designated financial instruments that must be delivered in completion of an option contract or a futures contract. For example, the underlying may be fixed-income securities, foreign exchange, equities, or futures contracts (in the case of an option on a futures contract).

undertaker's receipt A document permitting the payment of a funeral bill directly from the decedent's account. The payment is made to the undertaker, to the person who paid the funeral bill, or in some cases to the surviving spouse.

underwriter A person or company who assumes a risk, for a fee, particularly in insurance or investment. By guaranteeing payment or cash to offset the loss, insurance firms underwrite casualties and losses. By purchasing the entire issue from a company and then selling it to the public, an investment underwriter guarantees the sale of a securities issue. An underwriter may also act on a best-efforts basis, in which the underwriter is not obligated to take down (purchase) any amount in excess of that which he or she can sell.

underwriting The assumption of a risk for a fee, particularly an insurance or investment risk. Insurance underwriting guarantees a cash payment in the event of a loss or casualty. Investment underwriting guarantees the sale of a securities issue.

underwriting syndicate A group of underwriters, working under contract together to guarantee the sale of a particular securities issue.

undistributed net income (UNI) The amount by which the distributable net income for the year exceeds the sum of any amount of income for the year required to be distributed currently; any other amounts properly paid, credited, or required to be distributed for such year; and the amount of taxes properly allocable to the undistributed portion of the distributable net income.

undivided profit An account in a bank's general ledger that is part of its capital structure. Undivided profits are profits that have not been paid out as dividends or transferred to the bank's surplus account.

undue influence The influence that one person exerts over another person to the point where the latter is prevented from exercising his or her own free will.

unearned discount Interest received by a bank in advance of the use of funds, by deduction from the face value of a note, that is "earned" as time passes.

unearned increment An increase in the value of land or other property that results from changing social or economic conditions rather than from the owner's efforts.

unemployment insurance Insurance that protects the employee against loss of income from unemployment.

unencumbered A description of property that is free and clear of any mortgages, liens, or debts of any type.

unfair competition A market situation characterized by dishonest, predatory pricing, collusion, price discrimination, and so on.

unfit currency Currency of such poor quality that it cannot be recirculated.

unfunded insurance trust An insurance trust in which the premiums on the policies are to be paid by the insured or by some third person during his or her lifetime. Assets are not provided to a trustee when the trust is created to ensure payment of future premiums. *Distinguish from* funded insurance trust.

unguaranteed residual value The portion of the residual value for which the lessor is at risk. It excludes the portion of the residual value that is either insured or guaranteed by the lessee.

unified credit An amount allocated to each taxpayer as a credit that can be applied against the gift tax, the estate tax, and, under certain circumstances, the generation-skipping tax.

uniform accounting system A system of accounts that is common to similar organizations, including systems promoted by a trade association for a particular industry or those promulgated by federal and state regulatory agencies.

uniform acts A series of acts drafted by the National Conference of Commissioners on Uniform State Laws and suggested for passage in the various states, with a view toward making the laws in the states uniform for the particular subjects covered.

Uniform Bank Performance Report (UBPR) A report based on data from bank call reports that is put together by the Federal Financial Institutions Examination Council. The report develops common data and ratios that allow standard comparisons of banks.

Members of the council include the
Federal Reserve Board, Office of the
Comptroller of the Currency, Federal
Deposit Insurance Corporation, Office
of Thrift Supervision, and National
Credit Union Administration.

Uniform Commercial Code (UCC) A
coordinated code of laws governing
the legal aspects of business and
financial transactions in the United
States (except Louisiana). It regulates
such topics as the sale of goods,
commercial paper, bank deposits and
collections, letters of credit, bulk
transfers, and documents of title.

Uniform Consumer Credit Code A
code passed at the state level that
attempts to standardize laws relating
to consumer credit throughout the
United States.

**uniform customs and practices for
documentary credits (UCP)** A standard code, issued by the International
Chamber of Commerce, that serves as
the primary guide for handling letters
of credit.

Uniform Gifts to Minors Act An act
adopted in certain states that provides
a means of transferring property to a
minor, in which the designated custodian has the legal right to act on
behalf of the minor without the necessity of a guardianship. A custodianship under the Uniform Gifts to
Minors Act is generally more restrictive than a custodianship under the
more recent Uniform Transfers to
Minors Act.

Uniform Simultaneous Death Act An
act providing that, in the event of
simultaneous death, each person is
presumed to be the survivor of the
other with respect to the testamentary
disposition of his or her property.
See also simultaneous death.

Uniform Small Loan Law A law
passed at the state level, that specifies
requirements relating to the interest
rates charged on small loans, maximum size of small loans, and licensing
and supervision of small loan companies.

Uniform Transfers to Minors Act An
act adopted in many states to replace
the more restrictive Uniform Gifts to
Minors Act. It provides a means of
transferring property to a minor, in
which the designated custodian has
the legal right to act on behalf of the
minor without the necessity of a
guardianship.

unissued stock Stock authorized by
the directors of a corporation and the
Securities and Exchange Commission
(SEC), but not yet sold.

unit bank A single-office banking
facility.

unit banking A requirement in some
states that banks operate without
branches. By 1988, 44 states had
enacted reciprocal branching agreements.

United States Code (U.S.C.) The
collection of federal statutes grouped
by subject area.

United States note A form of U.S.
currency issued by the U.S. Treasury.
These notes are no longer actively
circulated.

unit investment trust (UIT) An investment vehicle that buys and holds a
portfolio of securities--most commonly municipal bonds--and then sells
shares to investors. The investor then
receives a prorated share of interest
and principal payments.

**unit posting plan for checking
accounts** A system used in a bank's

commercial bookkeeping department in which the ledger, original statement, and original journal are posted simultaneously.

unit savings plan A system in which savings deposits and withdrawals are simultaneously machine posted to the customer's passbook, the bank's ledger card, and the audit tape.

unit teller A bank representative who handles both paying and receiving functions.

unit-value basis A method of determining the value of a beneficiary's share in a combined (or combination) pension plan.

universal account number A common number applicable to more than one type of account.

universal life insurance A life insurance policy that includes a savings element paying competitive market rates of interest. *See also* whole life insurance.

universal teller A teller who can handle all bank transactions without being assisted or leaving the teller window.

unlimited liability The status of an individual whose personal wealth beyond the amount of his or her investment in a firm is legally available to satisfy the claims of the firm's creditors. Both sole proprietors and full partners have unlimited liability for the debts of their firms.

unlimited tax bond A bond secured by the pledge of taxes that may be levied by the issuer in an unlimited rate or amount.

unlimited tax GO bond A municipal general obligation (GO) bond whose issuer has no ceiling on the taxes it

may levy to pay interest on, or repay principal of, the bond.

unliquidated claim A claim for which the debtor disputes the amount owed.

unlisted securities Securities that are not listed on a recognized exchange but are traded in over-the-counter markets.

unmatched book A gap, usually a negative gap. *See also* gap; negative gap.

unpack To recover the original data from packed data.

unrealized revenue Revenue that is attributed to a completed business transaction but has not yet been received in cash or a form that is readily convertible to cash.

unrecovered cost Uninsured losses from extraordinary obsolescence, fire, theft, or market fluctuations.

unsatisfactory account (1) An indication, for credit references, that a customer has not met the terms of his or her contract. (2) The irregular payment of a loan or frequent overdrawing of a checking account.

unsatisfied need A concept that assumes a buyer will not make a purchase unless he or she perceives a need for the product.

unseasoned securities New securities that have not been in the market long enough to establish a trading pattern.

unsecured debt A debt instrument not backed by the issuer's pledging of assets. Unsecured bonds are called debentures.

unsecured loan (1) Funds loaned with no pledge of collateral or with collateral worth less than the amount loaned. (2) A loan for which a lender does not physically control the security for the full term of the loan.

unsponsored American depository receipt (ADR) An American depository receipt (ADR) issue not sponsored by the foreign corporation whose securities underlie the ADR. The investor must pay the fees associated with issuing or canceling the ADR or collecting and paying dividends.

unsystematic risk Risk that is unique to a particular security, such as the possibility of bankruptcy. It can be reduced or even eliminated through efficient diversification. *Also called* avoidable *or* diversifiable risk. *See also* systematic risk.

update To modify a master file with current information according to a specified procedure.

upgrade To increase the credit limit.

upper error limit (UEL) A measure of the possible extent of errors in a population.

upset insurance A form of automobile collision insurance.

upstream correspondent *See* correspondent bank.

usable funds *See* collected balance.

U.S. dollar bond A bond denominated in U.S. dollars and sold overseas.

use (Noun) The beneficial ownership of property to which another person holds the legal title. Use is an early form of the modern trust.

use data The set of characters on bank cards used in off-line terminals

that records the most recent use of the card.

user-oriented language Language forms, syntax, and special words tailored to users who lack expertise in computers.

use tax A state sales tax levied on goods entering the state from another state. A use tax is an extension of a state sales tax, intended to tax goods bought in other states for use in the state levying the tax.

U.S. government securities The bonds, notes, and bills issued by the U.S. Treasury.

U.S. savings bond A nonmarketable U.S. Treasury bond. Several series are outstanding, including series E, H, EE, and HH. The U.S. Treasury no longer issues series E and H.

U.S. savings notes *See* freedom shares.

usury (1) A higher rate of interest than is allowed by law. (2) The act of charging a higher rate of interest for the use of funds than is legally allowed by a state.

usury laws Laws that stipulate the maximum rates of interest to be charged on different types of loans.

usury rate (1) The maximum rate of interest permitted by law. (2) Alternatively, interest in excess of the legal maximum. The usury rate is generally set by state law. *See also* legal rate of interest.

utility program A specialized program that instructs a computer to perform routine, regular functions, such as updating a file or generating a report outside the main processing stream.

vacation club account Funds deposited in a financial institution to accumulate money for a vacation. Deposits are generally made weekly to this account in small amounts.

VA guaranteed loan *See* Veterans Administration (VA) guaranteed loan.

validate To confirm, identify, or guarantee an amount appearing on an item by imprinting the date of confirmation and the amount on the item.

validation proceedings Legal proceedings required in some states by which the courts pass on the validity of proposed bond issues.

valid date A date (month and year) before which a bank card is not valid. The valid date may appear on the face of the card in embossed characters or in a magnetic stripe.

valuation The process of estimating the worth of property.

valuation account (or reserve) An account that either partly or wholly offsets one or more other accounts, for example, accumulated depreciation, allowance for possible credit losses, or unamortized debt discount. The valuation reserve is deducted from the stated value of an asset or liability to give its net value.

value The worth of a product or service, as expressed in money or a certain quantity of another product or service. When the worth of a product or service is expressed in terms of money, that is its price. *See also* replacement value.

value added The difference between the price of a manufactured or semi-manufactured product and the cost of the raw material used to produce the product.

value added tax (VAT) A tax placed on the value added to a good at each stage of production. It is also considered a national sales tax. It is the primary means of raising revenues in the European communities.

value at consummation As used in the Consumer Leasing Act, the cost to the lessor of the leased property, including, if applicable, any increase or markup by the lessor before consummation.

value compensated The purchase or sale of foreign exchange executed by cable in which the purchaser reimburses the seller for the value of the foreign currency on the date of actual payment abroad.

value date (1) The date on which a sum of money is officially transferred. (2) The date when a transferred sum of money is available to a beneficiary. (3) The date on which a transfer to an account is considered effective, either the day the instruction is received or some future date as stipulated by the sender. (4) A data element in funds transfers that is the date on which the funds are to be at the disposal of the receiving bank.

value of money What money will buy. The value of money declines as prices rise. The time value of money is called present value. *See also* present value.

variable amount note (1) A note evidencing the amount that a trust department lends to a borrower from cash held in various fiduciary accounts. The amount of the loan outstanding fluctuates, depending on the amount of cash on hand. (2) An annuity that pays income in units, the value of which fluctuates in relation to the underlying securities, primarily common stocks. *Also called* equity annuity. A variable annuity should be distinguished from the conventional annuity, which makes guaranteed fixed-dollar payments.

variable annuity *See* variable amount note.

variable cost A cost that varies in direct relation to the level of output.

variable income securities Securities that yield income depending on the issuer's ability to generate a profit. Thus dividend income on common stock often varies from year to year. Variable income securities differ from bonds, savings accounts, and preferred stocks that yield a fixed income to the holder.

variable rate certificate A savings certificate on which the interest rate varies, in consonance with the variance of some stated index, market rate, or condition.

variable rate demand obligations (VRDOs) Any municipal debt obligation with a variable rate of interest that can be redeemed by the holder at par value plus accrued interest.

variable rate loan *See* floating prime; floating rate; variable rate mortgage.

variable rate mortgage (VRM) A mortgage in which the interest rate varies according to changes in a specified index. *See also* adjustable rate mortgage.

variables sampling A method of sampling designed to estimate the dollar value of an account.

variance (1) The difference between corresponding items on comparative balance sheets or on income and other operating statements. (2) A measure of the dispersion of a frequency distribution. (3) The difference between standard and actual production costs.

vault A heavily guarded area of a bank or depository, protected against fire and theft and used to store cash, securities, or other assets.

vault cash (1) That portion of a bank's cash on hand that is left in its vault as an immediate reserve. (2) Cash on hand.

velocity of money The rate at which money circulates within the economy, either in terms of spending (transaction velocity) or income (income velocity).

vendee A person who purchases, or agrees to purchase, property.

vendor A person who sells, or agrees to sell, property.

venture capital *See* risk capital.

verification *See* confirmation.

verification factor A numeric factor used to prove transcribed balances or accounts.

verify To determine whether a transcription of data or other operation has been accomplished accurately.

vertical bear put spread A limited risk/limited gain options strategy involving the purchase of a put at one exercise price and sale of a put at a lower strike price.

vertical bull call spread A limited risk/limited gain options strategy involving the purchase of a call at one exercise price and the sale of a call at a higher strike price.

vertical combination The joining together of businesses involved at different levels in the production of one product. An example of vertical combination would be an automobile company joining with a steel company.

vertical integration The expansion of a firm to include new activities that involve earlier or later stages of production. Vertical integration occurs if the firm expands to produce a product that it previously bought from a supplier or that a customer of the firm previously manufactured.

vest To confer an immediate, fixed right of immediate or future possession and enjoyment of property.

vested interest (1) An immediate, fixed interest in real or personal property, although the right of possession and enjoyment may be postponed until some future date or until some event occurs. *Distinguish from* contingent interest. (2) A legal claim to the future of some property (for example, a company pension fund in which employees have a vested interest).

vested remainder A fixed interest in property, with the right of possession and enjoyment postponed until the termination of the prior estate. *Distinguish from* contingent remainder.

vesting With pension and profit-sharing plans, the attainment by a participant of a benefit right, attributable to an employer's contributions, that is not contingent on the participant's continued employment. Vesting may be total and immediate, be graduated over time, or occur on completion of the stated requirements for service or participation.

Veterans Administration (VA) A federal agency that administers laws covering the range of benefits available to former members of the U.S. Armed Forces. Some of these benefits are applicable also to the dependents and beneficiaries of veterans.

Veterans Administration (VA) guaranteed loan A loan to an eligible veteran, usually for housing or education, that is partially guaranteed by the Veterans Administration under the Servicemen's Readjustment Act of 1944, as amended.

Veterans Administration (VA) mortgage A mortgage that is partially guaranteed by the Veterans Administration.

video display terminal A display screen that allows stored or keyed information to be viewed for editing or manipulation.

virtual storage An operating system that divides a program into small segments so that only the active parts of the program are in main storage. This system allows many programs to be processed at the same time.

visible supply The total amount of municipal bond sales scheduled for sale in the next 30 days.

visible trade Exports and imports of merchandise.

voice-recognition system A system that permits a computer to respond to verbal instructions.

volatility Variability in the price of a financial instrument. Expected volatility is a variable used in pricing options.

volume (1) The total dollar amount of sales, new deposits, new loans, or sales or cash advances resulting from credit card use. (2) Figures quoted daily that refer to the number and dollar amount of shares traded each day on the New York Stock Exchange.

voluntary accumulation plan A method by which an investor can make deposits in some mutual funds after the initial deposit. The investor may add any amount above a stated minimum amount at any time, usually monthly or quarterly.

voluntary termination (swap market) The cancellation of a swap contract that is agreed to by both counterparties. A voluntary termination usually involves a lump-sum payment from one party to the other.

voluntary trust A trust created by the voluntary act of the settlor and not conditional on his or her death. *Also called* living trust *or* inter vivos trust. *Distinguish from* trust under will.

vostro account A term meaning "your account with us," used by a depository bank to describe one of its accounts maintained by a bank located in a foreign country. *Compare with* nostro account. *See also* due to account.

voting authority The power to vote a stock. A trustee may have sole, shared, or no authority to vote stock held in trust.

voting right The right of common stockholders and, in some instances, preferred stockholders to vote on major corporate issues and to elect the board of directors.

voting trust *See* business trust.

voting trust certificates Certificates (representing shares of stock) issued by trustees in whom voting rights are vested for a particular period, such as

the first few years after a company has been reorganized. *See also* business trust.

voucher Any written form proving that money has been paid or received. Vouchers include canceled checks, petty cash receipts, and receipted bills.

voucher audit Approval of a proposed disbursement by a bank's administrative authority.

voucher check A check to which a voucher is attached describing the purpose of the check. The seller of a product or service uses the voucher as a posting medium to show receipt of the check.

voucher system A system of internal control that uses vouchers as evidence of all payments in cash.

vouching The audit technique that involves examination of documentation supporting an account balance or performance of a control procedure.

wage earner An employee whose compensation is based on the number of hours worked.

wage-earner plan A plan proposed under Chapter 13 of the Bankruptcy Code.

Wage-Hour Law *See* Fair Labor Standards Act of 1938 (Wage-Hour Law).

wage incentive The compensation, in addition to base pay, offered to encourage workers to strive for exceptional performance in their work.

wage-price spiral A form of inflation (cost push) where higher prices lead to higher wages, which cause higher prices in a continuing process.

waiver (1) The voluntary relinquishment of a right, privilege, or advantage. (2) The document by which the relinquishment is evidenced.

ward A person who by reason of minority, mental incompetence, or other incapacity is under a court's protection, either directly or through a guardian, committee, curator, conservator, or tutor.

warehouse financing A form of inventory financing. Goods are held in trust as collateral for the loan. As the goods are sold, the trustee releases them to the purchaser and transmits the sale proceeds to the bank to repay the loan. There are two principal types of warehouse financing. In public warehouse financing, the goods financed are placed in a warehouse located away from the borrower's premises and are under the control of an independent third party. In field warehouse financing, a third party controls the goods in a location physically on the borrower's property. *See also* inventory financing.

warehouse receipt A document issued by a bonded storage facility, evidencing the fact that specific property has been placed there. A warehouse receipt is a document of title and may be issued in negotiable or nonnegotiable form.

warehousing The borrowing of short-term funds by a mortgage banker, using permanent mortgage loans as collateral. This interim financing is used to carry mortgages in inventory until they are sold and delivered to a permanent investor. *Distinguish from* warehouse financing.

warehousing advance program *See* Student Loan Marketing Association.

warning bulletin *See* restricted card list.

warrant (1) A certificate that gives the holder the right to purchase a certain number of shares of stock or bonds at a given price for a period of years or to perpetuity. Warrants are sometimes attached to securities. At other times, warrants are issued in connection with subscription privileges to stockholders. *See also* right. (2) A nonnegotiable draft that can be converted into a negotiable instrument by the payee under terms specified in the warrant. (3) A means of short-term borrowing by a government unit through issuance of a check against insufficient funds, which will be honored by the drawee bank on terms and interest rates that have been negotiated with the bank.

warranty A guarantee made by a seller as to the quality or suitability of the product or service for sale. *See also* express warranty; implied warranty.

warranty deed A deed conveying real property containing the usual covenants of warranty of title.

waste The spoilage or destruction of real property done or permitted by the tenant who possesses the property, to the prejudice of the heir or owner of the remainder or reversion.

wasting assets Assets that are exhausted through use or that lose their value over time, such as oil wells, mining claims, and patents.

wasting trust A trust composed of property that is gradually being consumed.

watch list A current record of loans that have received less than satisfactory risk ratings.

Wednesday scramble A situation that occurs because Wednesday is the settlement date for meeting reserve requirements. Because the reserve requirements are an average for the reserve computation period, an individual bank (or the banking system) may accumulate a short or long reserve position as Wednesday approaches. If many banks are short on Wednesday, a scramble for available reserves occurs, and the federal funds rate rises sharply. If many banks are over (long) on Wednesday, the federal funds rate will drop substantially. *See also* reporting days (Federal Reserve).

weekly reporting banks A group of banks that report data to the Federal Reserve each week.

weighted average (1) An average for a total series, obtained by multiplying data for the components by the ratio of each component to the total. (2) A method of inventory valuation in which the average cost of a particular item of inventory is calculated by dividing its total cost by the number of items purchased. This average cost is then assigned to all items of inventory in that class, and their inventory value is computed by summing all items.

weight list In shipping, a list that itemizes the weights of individual parcels or bales or, in the case of bulk commodities, that covers an entire cargo.

welfare economics A philosophy or school of economics concerned with attaining various goals of social welfare through specific economic policies.

when-issued basis (WIB) The trading of securities before they are issued, priced for delivery on issue.

when-issued or when-distributed settlement A settlement for the delivery of securities that depends on when the security will be issued or distributed.

white knight A party who launches a counter tender offer at the request of a takeover target. The purpose of the counter tender offer is to deter an unfriendly takeover.

white plastic A fraudulent merchant procedure involving the use of embossed plastic that is not a real credit card.

whole life insurance A level-premium type of life insurance policy that makes payment when the insured dies. This insurance usually contains a savings element and has a cash surrender value if the policy is canceled before death.

whole loan A loan sold in the secondary market. The full amount of the loan is available for sale; no portion or participation is retained by the seller.

wholesale banking The provision of bank services to large corporations and other nonretail entities.

wholesale financing The process of financing products sold to a dealer in goods.

wide-area telephone service (WATS) lines A telephone service for which a subscriber pays a flat rate for an unlimited number of telephone calls within a specified geographic area called a band.

widow's allowance The allowance of personal property made by a court or by statute to a widow for her immediate requirements after her husband's death.

widow's election *See* election.

widow's exemption The amount allowed as a deduction in computing the state inheritance tax on a widow's share of her husband's estate.

wildcat banking The banking system that existed in colonial times, under which banks designated remote locations as the only points at which their notes could be redeemed.

will A legally enforceable declaration of a person's wishes in writing regarding matters to be attended to after, but not operative until, his or her death. A will usually, but not always, relates to the testator's property, is revocable (or amendable by means of a codicil) up until the testator's death, and applies to the situation that exists when the testator dies. *See also* last will and testament.

windfall An unanticipated profit or other gain over which the recipient had little or no control (for example, an unexpected inheritance or rise in stock prices).

winding up Settling the accounts and liquidating the assets of a partnership or corporation in order to dissolve the firm and distribute its assets.

window (1) Access to a computer system at a time when the central processing unit is free to handle the required task. (2) A short period when the stock market or interest rates offer favorable conditions for launching a new issue or making a major investment.

window dressing An attempt to improve the appearance of a company's financial position or operating results, at the date on which financial results are reported, by using such techniques as not accounting for all expenses, anticipating sales, conceal-

ing liabilities, delaying write-offs, or underproviding for depreciation.

winning bid The successful bid for a particular issue of securities. A winning bid usually produces the lowest interest cost to a municipal borrower or offers the highest premium in the event of a single coupon bid.

wire A message sent over a wire service. *Also called* cable. *See also* wire service.

wire fate item A note sent for collection to out-of-town banks, accompanied by instructions to notify the collecting bank by wire whether the obligation will be honored.

wire house A firm that is a member of a stock exchange and maintains an electronic communications network linking its own branch offices and the offices of correspondent firms with one another and the exchange.

wire service (1) An organization that gathers and transmits news to clients, such as newspapers and radio and television stations. (2) Any telecommunication service over which messages or transmissions can be sent between subscribers (for example, telex, S.W.I.F.T., and Fedwire). (3) A means of transmitting information electronically between subcribers. *Also called* wire *or* service.

wire transfer *See* funds transfer.

withdrawal The removal of money or valuables from a bank or other place of deposit.

withdrawal by transfer A method by which a depository participant can obtain physical securities from the depository to forward to a buyer. The depository takes securities from inventory, has them registered in the name of the new owner, and sends the new certificates to the participant or the buyer.

withdrawal notice The written notice of intent to remove funds from an account on or after a specified date. Such notice is required for certain types of accounts.

withholding (1) The process of deducting a specific amount from a salary or wage payment of an individual. The amount deducted is the federal or state income tax that the individual expects to pay. It is withdrawn in small amounts from each paycheck. (2) The process of deducting a specific amount from interest or other payments in accordance with the tax law.

withholding tax (1) Tax money withheld from an employee's earnings by the employer for the purpose of remitting it to the government. (2) Amounts that a payor is required to withhold from interest or other payments.

without Literally, a shortened version of the expression "without an offer on the other side." This expression describes a one-way market in which there is a bid but no asked side, or vice versa.

without rights of survivorship An account for which the joint tenancy ends on the death of one of the parties.

WOR Without recourse. *See also* nonrecourse agreement.

word Any group of bits or bytes that a computer can treat as a single unit.

word length The number of bits in a computer word.

word processing The production of typewritten or printed words from a storage medium that permits informa-tion to be manipulated before being committed to final form.

working capital A firm's investment in current assets, namely, cash, marketable securities, accounts receivable, and inventory. The difference between a firm's current assets and current liabilities is known as net working capital.

working capital loan A short-term loan to provide money to purchase income-generating assets, such as inventory.

working conditions The environment in which a person works, including physical conditions, hours, compensation received, benefits, and treatment by superiors.

working interest A type of participation in mineral rights. The holder shares in the cost of developing and maintaining the mineral lease. This holder therefore receives a proportionally higher percentage return of income than a holder of a royalty interest, who does not share in costs.

working papers (1) The notes, memorandums, schedules, and other data used as the basis for a final report. (2) A statement giving a minor or immigrant permission to work, as required by some states. (3) For bank examiners, the written documentation of the procedures followed and the conclusion reached during a bank examination. The papers support the examiners' conclusions and may include examination and verification programs, memorandums, schedules, questionnaires, checklists, abstracts of documents, and analyses prepared or obtained by the examiner.

workmen's compensation A payment by employers to workers or their families for wages or salary missed because of work-related injuries, sickness, or death.

workmen's compensation insurance
Insurance that protects an employer
by paying employees or their families
for loss of income due to work-related
injuries, sickness, or death.

work-out loan A loan that requires
special repayment arrangements in
light of likely or actual default on a
portion or all of the debt.

work station A device or component
that allows communication between
the user and the computer. A display
station, a serial printer, or both
constitute a work station.

World Bank *See* International Bank
for Reconstruction and Development
(IBRD).

wraparound mortgage A second
mortgage "wrapped around" a first
mortgage. The second mortgage lender takes over the first mortgage and
makes payments on it. The payments
that the borrower makes to the
second lender include amounts due on
both the first and second mortgages.

writ An order or mandatory direction
in writing, under seal, issued in the
name of a state, court, or judicial officer commanding the person to whom
it is addressed to do or not to do
something specific. An example is a
legal order to hold or freeze the funds
in an account until some legal action
is concluded.

write To record data on a storage
device or a data medium. The recording may be permanent or temporary.

write-off The removal of a bad debt
or worthless asset from the books by
reducing its value to zero. A write-off
is usually charged to an allowance for
possible credit losses. *See also*
charge-off.

writer The party that sells an option.
The writer is required to carry out the
terms of the option at the choice of
the holder. *Also called* grantor.

write-up Increasing the value of an
asset as it is carried on the books.
Write-ups may be done to reflect the
rising market value of an asset or only
to present an apparently better financial position to stockholders.

writ of attachment A legal document
frequently served on a bank making a
debtor's assets subject to the terms of
a court order.

wrongful dishonor The failure to pay
a properly payable item.

Yankee bond A foreign bond sold in
the United States.

Yankee certificate of deposit A certificate of deposit issued in the United
States by a branch of a foreign bank.

year bill A Treasury bill with a maturity of 12 months. *See also* Treasury
bill.

year-end adjustment A modification
of a ledger account at the close of a
fiscal period arising from an accrual,
prepayment, change in physical inventory, reclassification, policy change,
audit adjustment, or other entry to
reflect the account's status as of that
date.

year-end dividend An extra dividend
paid by a company at the end of a
fiscal year, especially at the end of a
good fiscal year.

year totals In an annual report, the total amount of a given item (for example, revenue or sales) for a given year.

yellow sheets A daily publication that lists bonds traded over-the-counter. *See also* pink sheets.

yield (1) The annual percentage rate of return on capital, calculated by dividing annual return by the amount of an investment. (2) The annual rate of return from a security, expressed as a percentage of the amount invested. (3) The expected earnings to be realized from a mortgage loan, considering the stated interest rate and any discount or premium and assuming an average loan life for similar loans (usually a 12-year life for a 30-year conventional mortgage). *See also* current yield; nominal return; yield to maturity.

yield curve A chart showing the relationship among interest rates on substantially similar securities with different maturities.

yield to maturity The rate of return earned on a bond if it is held to maturity. The yield to maturity takes into account the present price, the coupon yield, the maturity value, and the timing of all interest and principal payments. In present-value terms, it is the discount rate that equates the present value of all future interest and principal payments to the present price of the bond.

younger generation beneficiaries For the purpose of the generation-skipping tax, beneficiaries who are assigned to a generation younger than the grantor's generation.

your account When used in funds transfer messages, "your account" refers to the account that is "due from " the sending bank.

zero-balance checking account An account that is part of a disbursement control system that consists of a master account and a number of zero-balance disbursement accounts. At the close of each business day, funds are transferred from the master account to cover the total amount of checks drawn on the zero-balance accounts. This system enables a firm to maintain control over its cash while allowing decentralized units to make disbursements from their own accounts.

zero-balance disbursement Multiple checking accounts kept with one or more banks for which there is one control or master account tied to the disbursing accounts. As individual checks clear the disbursing accounts, debit balances accumulate. Each day, after business hours, a credit from the master account is made to "zero out" each of the accumulated debit balances.

zero-base budgeting A budgeting procedure by which all expenditures are justified annually before being included in a budget. Zero-base budgeting strives to eliminate annual budget increases made habitually without considering whether the program, salary, and so on, should be continued.

zero basis A condition occurring when a convertible bond is valued so highly by investors that the premium paid to purchase the bond cancels the interest received.

zero-coupon bond A type of bond, either taxable or tax-exempt, sold at a deep discount from face value, that pays no current interest (as opposed to a coupon bond), but that pays face value on maturity. A key feature of zero-coupon bonds is that they provide the holder with a set yield throughout the term of the bond. Each year, an amount of interest is imputed to the holder. If the zero-coupon bond is taxable, income tax will be owed on the imputed interest.

zero defects A corporate program designed to strive for error-free performance. Objectives of such a program include improved product quality, increased employee morale, and decreased costs.

zeroization A method of degaussing (neutralizing the magnetic field), erasing, or overwriting electronically stored data.

zero proof A banking procedure in which all postings are successively subtracted from a control figure to arrive at a zero balance, thus indicating that all entries have been correctly posted.

zero-sum economy An economy in which there is no growth, and one person's income can increase only if another's falls. *Compare with* zero-sum market.

zero-sum market A market in which winners can gain only at the expense of losers. That is, gains by the winners exactly balance losses by the losers (ignoring transaction costs). The futures markets are zero-sum markets. *Compare with* zero-sum economy.

zeta analysis A model for identifying the bankruptcy risk of corporations.

zoning A government ordinance for the type of use, density of development, and other minimum standards for a given piece of property.

Z-score The mathematical result from applying zeta analysis.

Acronyms and Abbreviations

ABA	American Bankers Association
ABL	accepted batch listing
ACH	automated clearing house
AD&D	accidental death and dismemberment insurance
ADP	automatic data processing
ADR	American depository receipt
AIB	American Institute of Banking
AIBD	Association of International Bond Dealers
AIREA	American Institute of Real Estate Appraisers
ALTA	American Land Title Association
AMEX	American Stock Exchange
AML	alternative mortgage loan
ANSI	American National Standards Institute
APR	annual percentage rate
ARBL	assets repriced before liabilities
ARM	adjustable rate mortgage
ASCII	American Standard Code for Information Interchange
ASE	American Stock Exchange
ATM	automated teller machine
ATRR	allocated transfer risk reserve
ATS	automatic transfer service/system
AU	asset utilization
BA	bankers' acceptance
B.A.I.	Bank Administration Institute
BAN	bond anticipation note
BEO	book-entry only
BHC	bank holding company
BIC	bank investment contract
BIF	Bank Insurance Fund
BIN	bank identification number
BIS	Bank for International Settlements
b/l	bill of lading
bp	basis point

CAMEL	capital, assets, management, earnings, and liquidity
CAPM	capital asset pricing model
CARs	collateralized automobile receivables
CAT	computer-assisted training
CATS	certificates of accrual on Treasury securities
CBA	chartered bank auditor
CBCT	customer-bank communication terminal
CBOE	Chicago Board Options Exchange
CBT	Chicago Board of Trade
CBT	computer-based training
CCPA	Consumer Credit Protection Act
CD	certificate of deposit
C&F	cost and freight
CFR	Code of Federal Regulations
CFTC	Commodities Futures Trading Commission
CHAPS	Clearing House Automated Payments System
CHIPS	Clearing House Interbank Payments System
C&I	cost and insurance
CIA	certified internal auditor
CIF	central information file
CIF	cost, insurance, freight
CME	Chicago Mercantile Exchange
CMO	collateralized mortgage obligation
CNS	continuous net settlement
COBOL	common business-oriented language
COCO	confirm only comparison option
COD	certificate on demand
COM	computer output microfilm
COMEX	Commodity Exchange
CPA	certified public accountant
CPFF	cost plus fixed fee
CPI	consumer price index
CPU	central processing unit
CRA	Community Reinvestment Act
CRA	contemporaneous reserve accounting
CSN	card security number
CSV	cash surrender value

CTR	currency transaction report
CUSIP	Committee on Uniform Securities Identification Procedures
D/A	documents against acceptance (draft)
DBA	doing business as
DBMS	data base management system
DDA	demand deposit accounting
DDA	direct deposit account
DEA	data encryption algorithm
DFU	data file utility
DIDC	Depository Institutions Deregulation Committee
DIDMCA	Depository Institutions Deregulation and Monetary Control Act of 1980
DIF	Deposit Insurance Fund
dk	don't know
DNI	distributable net income
D&O	directors' and officers' (liability insurance)
D/P	documents against payment (draft)
DSU	deficit spending unit
DTC	depository transfer check
DTC	Depository Trust Company
DVP	delivery versus payment
ECOA	Equal Credit Opportunity Act
ECP	Eurocommercial paper
ECR	embossed character reader
ECU	European currency unit
ED draft	equipment dealer draft
EDI	electronic data interchange
EDP	electronic data processing
EDT	electronic data transfer
EFAA	Expedited Funds Availability Act
EFT	electronic funds transfer
EFTS	electronic funds transfer system
EITF	Emerging Issues Task Force
EM	equity multiplier
EPS	earnings per share

ERISA	Employee Retirement Income Security Act of 1974
ERTA	Economic Recovery Tax Act
ESOP	employee stock ownership plan
ETC	export trading company
Euro CD	Eurodollar certificate of deposit
Eximbank	Export-Import Bank of the United States
FAMC	Federal Agricultural Mortgage Corporation
Fannie Mae	Federal National Mortgage Association
F.A.S.	free alongside
FASB	Financial Accounting Standards Board
fax	facsimile transmission
FCA	Farm Credit Administration
FCM	futures commission merchant
FCRA	Fair Credit Reporting Act
FDIC	Federal Deposit Insurance Corporation
the Fed	Federal Reserve System
Fedwire	Federal Reserve Wire Network
FFB	Federal Financing Bank
FHA	Federal Housing Administration
FHFB	Federal Housing Finance Board
FHLB	Federal Home Loan Bank
FHLMC	Federal Home Loan Mortgage Corporation
FICB	Federal Intermediate Credit Bank
FIFO	first in, first out
FINS	Financial Industry Numbering Standard
FIRREA	Financial Institutions Reform, Recovery and Enforcement Act of 1989
FLB	Federal Land Bank
FmHA	Farmers Home Administration
FNMA	Federal National Mortgage Association
F.O.B.	free on board
FOMC	Federal Open Market Committee
FRA	future *or* forward rate agreement
FRB	Federal Reserve Board
Freddie Mac	Federal Home Loan Mortgage Corporation
FRN	floating rate note
FSLIC	Federal Savings and Loan Insurance Corporation

FTC	Federal Trade Commission
FX	foreign exchange
GAAP	generally accepted accounting principles
GAAS	generally accepted auditing standards
GAT	grantor annuity trust
GEM	growing equity mortgage
GIC	guaranteed interest certificate
GIC	guaranteed investment contract
Ginnie Mae	Government National Mortgage Association
GIT	grantor income trust
GNMA	Government National Mortgage Association
GNP	gross national product
GO bond	general obligation bond
GPM	graduated payment mortgage
GRIT	grantor retained income trust
GSL	Guaranteed Student Loan
HEL	home equity line
HMO	health maintenance organization
HUD	U.S. Department of Housing and Urban Development
IBAA	Independent Bankers Association of America
IBF	international banking facility
IBRD	International Bank for Reconstruction and Development (World Bank)
ICC	International Chamber of Commerce
ICERC	Interagency Country Exposure Review Committee
IIA	Institute of Internal Auditors
ILSA	International Lending Supervision Act of 1983
IMF	International Monetary Fund
IMM	International Money Market
IP	index of industrial production
IRA	individual retirement account
IRD	income in respect of a decedent
IRR	internal rate of return
IRS	Internal Revenue Service

I/S	inventory to sales (ratio)
ISDA	International Swap Dealers Association
ISIN	International Securities Identification Number
ISN	input sequence number
ISO	International Organization for Standardization
ITP	item of tax preference
KCBT	Kansas City Board of Trade
LBO	leveraged buyout
LC or L/C	letter of credit
LCM	lower of cost or market
LDC	less(er) developed country
LIBID	London interbank bid rate
LIBOR	London interbank offered rate
LIFFE	London International Financial Futures Exchange
LIFO	last in, first out
LIMEAN	mean of LIBID and LIBOR
LOCOM	lower of cost or market
LPO	loan production office
LRBA	liabilities repriced before assets
MAC	message authentication code
MAI	Member Appraisal Institute
MBO	management by objectives
MCCD	message cryptographic check digits
MDT	merchant deposit transmittal
MIC	mortgage insurance company
MICR	magnetic ink character recognition
MIP	mortgage insurance premium
MIS	management information system
MMC	money market certificate
MMDA	money market deposit account
MNC	multinational corporation
MO	mail order
MOD 10	modulus ten check digit
MODE	merchant-oriented data entry
MSRB	Municipal Securities Rulemaking Board

MSTC	Midwest Securities Trust Company
MUS	monetary unit sampling
N.A.	national association
NABAC	National Association of Bank Auditors and Comptrollers
NACHA	National Automated Clearing House Association
NACM	National Association of Credit Management
NAR	National Association of Realtors
NASD	National Association of Securities Dealers, Inc.
NASDAQ	National Association of Securities Dealers Automated Quotation system
NAV	net asset value
N.B.A.	national banking association
NBS	National Bureau of Standards
NBSS	National Bank Surveillance System
NCUA	National Credit Union Administration
N.G.	not good (designation on a check)
NIDS	National Institutional Delivery System
NIF	note issuance facility
NIM	net interest margin
NINOW	noninterest-bearing NOW account
NOI	net operating income
NOW	negotiable order of withdrawal
NPV	net present value
NQB	National Quotations Bureau
NSF	not sufficient funds
NYCHA	New York Clearing House Association
NYFE	New York Futures Exchange
NYSE	New York Stock Exchange
OCC	Office of the Comptroller of the Currency
OCC	Options Clearing Corporation
OCR	optical character recognition
OECD	Organization for Economic Cooperation and Development
OID	original issue discount
OR	operations research

ORE	other real estate
OREO	other real estate owned
OSN	output sequence number
OTC	over the counter
OTS	Office of Thrift Supervision
PAN	primary account number
PC	participation certificate
PCA	production credit association
PDate	pay date
P/E ratio	price-earnings ratio
PHILADEP	Philadelphia Depository Trust Company
PHLX	Philadelphia Stock Exchange
PIG	passive income generator
PIK	payment in kind
PIN	personal identification number
PITI	principal, interest, taxes, and insurance
P&L	profit and loss
PLAM	price level adjusted mortgage
PM	profit margin
PMI	private mortgage insurance
PO	preauthorization order
POS	point of sale
PPI	producer price index
PPS	probability proportional to size
P&S	purchase and sale
PUD	planned unit development
QDRO	qualified domestic relations order
QTIP	qualified terminable interest property
RAM	random access memory
RAM	reverse annuity mortgage
RAN	revenue anticipation note
RBC	risk-based capital
RCPC	regional check processing center
R&D	research and development
recap	recapitulation

RefCorp	Resolution Funding Corporation
REIT	real estate investment trust
REMIC	real estate mortgage and investment conduit
REO	real estate owned
repo	repurchase agreement
RESPA	Real Estate Settlement Procedures Act
RJE	remote job entry
ROA	return on assets
ROE	return on equity
ROI	return on investment
ROM	read only memory
RP	repurchase agreement
RPG	report program generator
RTC	Resolution Trust Corporation
RUF	revolving underwriting facility
SAIF	Savings Association Insurance Fund
Sallie Mae	Student Loan Marketing Association
SAM	shared appreciation mortgage
SAN	subsidiary account number
SBA	Small Business Administration
SDA	source data automation
SDR	special drawing right
SEC	Securities and Exchange Commission
SEP	simplified employee pension plan
SGSB	Stonier Graduate School of Banking
SIC	Securities Information Center, Inc.
SIC	standard industrial classification
SIPC	Securities Investor Protection Corporation
S&L	savings and loan association
SLMA	Student Loan Marketing Association
SLUGS	state and local government series (bond)
SMSA	standard metropolitan statistical area
S&P	Standard & Poor's
SPC	switching and processing center
SREA	Senior Real Estate Analyst
SREA	Society of Real Estate Appraisers

SRO	self-regulatory organization
SSU	surplus spending unit
STIF	short-term investment fund
STRIPS	separate trading of registered interest and principal of securities
S.W.I.F.T.	Society for Worldwide Interbank Financial Telecommunication
SYD	sum-of-the-years digits
TAB	tax anticipation bill
TAC	transfer agent custodian
TAN	tax anticipation note
T-bill	Treasury bill
TCAP	terminal capture alliance program
TDOA	time deposit, open account
TFT	trade-for-trade settlement
TIRF	terminal interchange reimbursement fee
TMP	terminal migration program
TO	telephone order
TPI	tax preference item
TPIN	true personal identification number
TRADES	Treasury/Reserve Automated Debt-Entry System
TT&L	Treasury tax and loan account
UBPR	Uniform Bank Performance Report
UCC	Uniform Commercial Code
UCP	uniform customs and practices for documentary credits
UEL	upper error limit
UIT	unit investment trust
UNI	undistributed net income
U.S.C.	United States Code
VA	Veterans Administration
VAT	value added tax
VRDO	variable rate demand obligation
VRM	variable rate mortgage
WIB	when-issued basis
WOR	without recourse

Bank Performance Ratios

The ratios listed below can be used to analyze the financial performance and general condition of commercial banks. This list is not intended to be all inclusive. Rather, it is designed to present in a simple format some of the more common bank performance ratios currently in use. It is organized under four main topic headings. Explanatory notes are presented at the end.

Profitability Ratios

$$\text{Return on Assets (ROA)} = \frac{\text{Net Income}}{\text{Average Total Assets}}$$

$$\text{Return on Equity (ROE)} = \frac{\text{Net Income}}{\text{Average Total Equity}}$$

$$\text{Net Interest Margin (NIM)} = \frac{\text{Net Interest Income}}{\text{Average Earning Assets}}$$

$$\text{Profit Margin (PM)} = \frac{\text{Net Income}}{\text{Total Operating Income}}$$

$$\text{Asset Utilization (AU)} = \frac{\text{Total Operating Income}}{\text{Average Total Assets}}$$

$$\text{Yield on Earning Assets} = \frac{\text{Total Operating Income}}{\text{Average Earning Assets}}$$

$$\text{Cost of Funding Earning Assets} = \frac{\text{Total Interest Expense}}{\text{Average Interest-Bearing Liabilities}}$$

$$\text{Net Overhead Ratio} = \frac{\text{Total Noninterest Expense Minus Total Noninterest Income}}{\text{Average Earning Assets}}$$

Asset Quality Ratios

Nonperforming Assets to Assets $= \dfrac{\text{The sum of loans past due 90 days or more, loans in nonaccrual status, and noninvestment real estate owned other than bank premises}}{\text{Total Assets}}$

Nonperforming Loans to Loans $= \dfrac{\text{Loans past due 90 days or more plus nonaccrual loans}}{\text{Total Loans}}$

Net Charge-Offs to Loans $= \dfrac{\text{Total loans charged off during the period minus amounts recovered}}{\text{Averaged Loans Outstanding}}$

Loss Allowance to Loans $= \dfrac{\text{Allowance for loan losses}}{\text{Total Loans}}$

General Condition Ratios

Earnings Base $= \dfrac{\text{Earning Assets}}{\text{Total Assets}}$

Loan to Asset Ratio $= \dfrac{\text{Total Loans}}{\text{Total Assets}}$

Loan to Deposit Ratio $= \dfrac{\text{Total Loans}}{\text{Total Deposits}}$

Primary Capital Ratio $= \dfrac{\text{Primary Capital}}{\text{Total Assets}}$

Equity Capital Ratio $= \dfrac{\text{Total Equity}}{\text{Total Assets}}$

Equity Multiplier (EM) $= \dfrac{\text{Average Total Assets}}{\text{Average Total Equity}}$

Gap Ratio $= \dfrac{\text{Rate-Sensitive Assets}}{\text{Rate-Sensitive Liabilities}}$

Market Valuation Ratios

$$\text{Market to Book Ratio} = \frac{\text{Market Price of Common Stock}}{\text{Book Value Per Share}}$$

$$\text{Price-Earnings Ratio} = \frac{\text{Market Price of Common Stock}}{\text{Earnings Per Share}}$$

Explanatory Notes

1. ROA = PM x AU

2. ROE = ROA x EM

3. Net interest income = Interest income adjusted to a tax-equivalent basis minus interest expense

4. Total operating income = Total interest income adjusted to a tax-equivalent basis plus total noninterest income

Glossary of Economic Indicators

Agricultural prices
An index of prices received by farmers in the market. The statistic is expressed as a percentage change from the previous month. It is a useful predictor of price changes on the grocery shelf, which are reflected in the consumer price index.

Capacity utilization
The ratio of actual output to full production capacity. Often called the operating rate, the ratio forecasts short-term business conditions. Capacity utilization tends to correlate closely with business profits and is sometimes used for estimating future business profits (high capacity utilization rate = higher profits). Inflationary pressures increase when the capacity utilization rate is high.

Car sales
The annual rate of retail sales of domestic cars, in millions. This figure provides data on the current state on the economy, but it tends to have little influence on the stock market.

Construction expenditures
The total amount of new construction spending expressed as a percentage change from the previous month. The total expenditure has two components: residential expenditures and nonresidential expenditures. The stock market tends to focus more on the data, usually employment and housing, that influence construction expenditures.

Consumer installment credit
The net change in billions from the previous month in consumer installment credit outstanding. The peaks and troughs in business and consumer credit historically precede business cycle extremes.

Consumer price index (CPI)
The index is based on the prices of several thousand goods and services in 56 cities around the United States. Price changes are captured by regularly repricing essentially the same basket of goods and services. Price changes are averaged together with weights that represent their importance in the needs and spending of the population group surveyed. The figure released is expressed as a seasonally adjusted and annualized percentage change from the previous month. The CPI is the most widely used indicator of inflation. It is also a measure of consumer purchasing power when compared to personal income changes.

Durable goods orders

New factory orders for durable goods are expressed as a percentage change from the previous period. Durable goods are items such as airplanes, appliances, cars, and furniture that are not considered to be short-lived. Changes in orders of durable goods are often viewed as precursors of production gains and economic growth in future months. Inflationary pressure increases when orders for durable goods and production capacity utilization are high.

Employees on nonagricultural payrolls

A coincident or lagging indicator of general economic conditions, this statistic is expressed as the net change in thousands from the previous month. Historically, employment is highest at or just after the peak of a business cycle, and lowest at or following the bottom of a business cycle trough.

Gross national product (GNP)

The total value of all currently produced goods and services sold during a particular timeframe. The statistic is presented as a percentage change from the previous quarter. Real GNP is the value of goods and services sold at 1982 prices; nominal GNP is expressed in current, or actual, prices.

Homes sold

The number, in thousands, of new single-family homes sold, seasonally adjusted and expressed as an annual rate. It is considered a lagging indicator of the housing industry and the economy.

Housing starts

The number of new single-family homes started during a specific period. The figure is expressed as an annual rate in millions. Housing starts represent about 5 percent of GNP and 30 percent of fixed investment (final goods not intended for resale).

Implicit price deflator

The ratio of nominal GNP (current market prices) to real GNP (1982 base year prices). When the implicit price deflator is rising, the inflation rate is positive, and vice versa. This is the third most widely used indicator of inflation, behind the consumer price index and the producer price index.

Index of industrial production (IP)

The IP is a measure of the output in the manufacturing, mining, and electric and gas utility industries. It is used as one of the two measures of the nation's output (the other being GNP). The figure is expressed as a percentage change in the index from the previous month. IP and GNP figures generally tend to complement each other and show similar cyclical movements. However, as a monthly release, the IP is available on a more timely basis than the GNP, which is published quarterly.

Index of leading economic indicators

The index is composed of 11 different components that historically reach their cyclical peaks and troughs earlier than business cycle turns. Business cycles are sequences of expansion and contraction in various economic processes that show up as major fluctuations in comprehensive measures of employment, income, production, and trade. The leading index is designed to predict monthly movements in aggregate activity. Typically, three consecutive monthly declines in the index signal a recession.

Inventory-to-sales ratio

The proportion of inventory to sales (I/S) during a month for all manufacturing and trade firms. A high ratio (large amounts of unsold inventory) indicates that production is exceeding sales and economic growth is slowing. A falling ratio indicates that production is not keeping up with demand and inflationary pressures may be increasing.

Manufacturing and trade inventories

The total value of inventories held by private businesses in current dollars, expressed as a percentage change from the previous month. An increase represents production in excess of current consumption, while a decrease indicates that production is not keeping pace with consumption. Business inventories may be a misleading indicator of economic activity because the figure may fall (or rise) at opposite ends of the business cycle. When the economy is growing, inventories soon become depleted. On the other hand, when business slackens, firms reduce inventories in anticipation of continued weak demand.

Merchandise trade balance

The total of all U.S. exports less the total of all U.S. imports. A trade surplus is an excess of exports over imports; a trade deficit is an excess of imports over exports. The figure is expressed in billions of dollars. Increases in exports relative to imports stimulate the economy because production and employment increase to meet the rise in demand for U.S. goods.

New orders, manufacturing

The total new factory orders received for durable and nondurable products expressed as a percentage change from the previous month. The statistic is a useful indicator of how new orders will affect the capacity utilization rate. When capacity utilization is already high, a large increase in new orders could place additional pressure on current production capacity, which in turn places upward pressure on prices.

Personal consumption expenditures
The purchase of goods and services by households expressed at an annual rate as a percentage change from the previous quarter. The statistic excludes payment of taxes or personal investments.

Personal income
The income received by households from all sources, such as interest on investments, wages, and government programs. The figure is expressed as a percentage change from the previous month and is compared with the CPI, PPI, and implicit price deflator to see whether consumer purchasing power has increased or decreased.

Producer price index (PPI)
The PPI measures the monthly changes in prices received by producers of commodities; it is expressed as a percentage change from the previous month. The PPI is prepared in three broad categories: (1) stage-of-processing goods, (2) farm and industrial commodities, and (3) mining and manufacturing outputs. The finished goods component in the stage-of-processing group is recognized as the key overall indicator of inflation in primary markets. Price transactions measured in the PPI occur early in the production process and typically herald changes in the consumer price index. The PPI is the second most widely used indicator of inflation.

Retail sales
The percentage change in total retail sales from the previous month. Although the financial markets pay little attention to this statistic, large changes in retail sales attract the stock market's attention due to the effect changes will have on inventories and, thus, production.

Unemployment rate
The number of people without jobs and looking for work, expressed as a percentage of those who are sixteen years or older. This monthly release is a lagging indicator of business conditions; economic activity normally reaches a peak (or trough) and passes it before the maximum (or minimum) number of workers are employed.

Federal Reserve Banks and Districts

District 1

Federal Reserve Bank of Boston
600 Atlantic Avenue
Boston, Massachusetts 02106
(617) 973-3000

District 2

Federal Reserve Bank of New York
33 Liberty Street
New York, New York 10045
(212) 720-5000

Federal Reserve Bank of New York
Buffalo Branch
160 Delaware Avenue
Buffalo, New York 14202
(716) 849-5000

District 3

Federal Reserve Bank of
  Philadelphia
10 Independence Mall
Philadelphia, Pennsylvania 19106
(215) 574-6000

District 4

Federal Reserve Bank of Cleveland
1455 East 6th Street
Cleveland, Ohio 44114
(216) 579-2000

Federal Reserve Bank of Cleveland
Cincinnati Branch
150 East 4th Street
Cincinnati, Ohio 45202
(513) 721-4787

Federal Reserve Bank of Cleveland
Pittsburgh Branch
717 Grant Street
P. O. Box 867
Pittsburgh, Pennsylvania 15230
(412) 261-7800

District 5

Federal Reserve Bank of
  Richmond
701 East Byrd Street
Richmond, Virginia 23219
(804) 697-8000

Federal Reserve Bank of
  Richmond
Baltimore Branch
502 South Sharp Street
Baltimore, Maryland 21201
(301) 576-3300

Federal Reserve Bank of
  Richmond
Charlotte Branch
401 South Tryon Street
P. O. Box 30248
Charlotte, North Carolina 28230
(704) 336-7100

Federal Reserve Bank of
  Richmond
Culpeper Communications and
  Record Center
P. O. Drawer 20
Culpeper, Virginia 22701
(703) 825-1261

District 6

Federal Reserve Bank of Atlanta
104 Marietta Street, N.W.
Atlanta, Georgia 30303
(404) 521-8500

Federal Reserve Bank of Atlanta
Birmingham Branch
1801 5th Avenue, North
Birmingham, Alabama 35203
(205) 252-3141

Federal Reserve Bank of Atlanta
Jacksonville Branch
800 Water Street
Jacksonville, Florida 32231-0044
(904) 632-1000

Federal Reserve Bank of Atlanta
Miami Branch
9100 Northwest 36 Street
Miami, Florida 33152
(305) 591-2065

Federal Reserve Bank of Atlanta
Nashville Branch
301 8th Avenue, North
Nashville, Tennessee 37203
(615) 251-7100

Federal Reserve Bank of Atlanta
New Orleans Branch
525 St. Charles Avenue
New Orleans, Louisiana 70160
(504) 586-1505

District 7

Federal Reserve Bank of Chicago
230 South LaSalle Street
P. O. Box 834
Chicago, Illinois 60690
(312) 322-5322

Federal Reserve Bank of Chicago
Detroit Branch
160 West Fort Street
P. O. Box 1059
Detroit, Michigan 48231
(313) 961-6880

District 8

Federal Reserve Bank of St. Louis
411 Locust Street
St. Louis, Missouri 63102
(314) 444-8444

Federal Reserve Bank of St. Louis
Little Rock Branch
325 West Capitol Avenue
Little Rock, Arkansas 72203
(501) 372-5451

Federal Reserve Bank of St. Louis
Louisville Branch
410 South 5th Street
Louisville, Kentucky 40202
(502) 568-9200

Federal Reserve Bank of St. Louis
Memphis Branch
200 North Main Street
Memphis, Tennessee 38101
(901) 523-7171

District 9

Federal Reserve Bank of
  Minneapolis
250 Marquette Avenue
Minneapolis, Minnesota 55480
(612) 340-2345

Federal Reserve Bank of
  Minneapolis
Helena Branch
400 North Park Avenue
Helena, Montana 59601
(406) 442-3860

District 10

Federal Reserve Bank of
  Kansas City
925 Grand Avenue
Kansas City, Missouri 64198
(816) 881-2000

Federal Reserve Bank of
  Kansas City
Denver Branch
1020 16th Street
Denver, Colorado 80202
(303) 572-2300

Federal Reserve Bank of
  Kansas City
Oklahoma City Branch
226 Dean A. McGee Avenue
P. O. Box 25129
Oklahoma City, Oklahoma 73125
(405) 270-8400

Federal Reserve Bank of
  Kansas City
Omaha Branch
2201 Farnam Street
Omaha, Nebraska 68102
(402) 221-5500

District 11

Federal Reserve Bank of Dallas
400 South Akard Street
Dallas, Texas 75202
(214) 651-6111

Federal Reserve Bank of Dallas
El Paso Branch
301 East Main Street
P. O. Box 100
El Paso, Texas 79999
(915) 544-4730

Federal Reserve Bank of Dallas
Houston Branch
1701 San Jacinto Street
Houston, Texas 77002
(713) 659-4433

Federal Reserve Bank of Dallas
San Antonio Branch
126 East Nueva Street
San Antonio, Texas 78204
(512) 224-2141

District 12

Federal Reserve Bank of
  San Francisco
101 Market Street
San Francisco, California 94105
(415) 974-2000

Federal Reserve Bank of
  San Francisco
Los Angeles Branch
950 South Grand Avenue
Los Angeles, California 90015
(213) 683-2300

Federal Reserve Bank of
  San Francisco
Portland Branch
915 Southwest Stark Street
Portland, Oregon 97205
(503) 221-5900

Federal Reserve Bank of
  San Francisco
Salt Lake City Branch
120 South State Street
Salt Lake City, Utah 84111
(801) 322-7900

Federal Reserve Bank of
  San Francisco
Seattle Branch
1015 Second Avenue
Seattle, Washington 98104
(206) 343-3600

Other Addresses Useful to Bankers

American Bankers Association
1120 Connecticut Avenue, N.W.
Washington, DC 20036
(202) 663-5221

American Institute of Banking
1120 Connecticut Avenue, N.W.
Washington, DC 20036
(202) 663-5221

Bank Marketing Association
309 W. Washington Street
Chicago, Illinois 60606
(312) 782-1442

Commodity Credit Corporation
U.S. Department of Agriculture
4th and Independence Avenue,
  S.W., Room 212A
Washington, DC 20250
(202) 447-3467

Commodity Futures Trading
  Commission
2033 K Street, N.W.
Washington, DC 20581
(202) 254-6387

Council of Economic Advisers
17th Street and Pennsylvania
  Avenue, N.W.
Washington, DC 20500
(202) 395-5034

Equal Employment Opportunity
  Commission
1801 L Street, N.W.
Washington, DC 20507
(202) 634-1947

Export-Import Bank of the United
  States
811 Vermont Avenue, N.W.
Washington, DC 20571
(202) 566-8990

Farm Credit Administration
1501 Farm Credit Drive
McLean, Virginia 22102
(703) 883-4000

Farmers Home Administration
U.S. Department of Agriculture
14th Street and Independence
  Avenue, S.W.
Washington, DC 20250
(202) 447-4323

Federal Agricultural Mortgage
  Corporation
1667 K Street, N.W., Suite 200
Washington, DC 20006
(202) 872-0049

Federal Deposit Insurance
  Corporation
550 17th Street, N.W.
Washington, DC 20429
(202) 393-8400

Federal Financial Institutions
  Examination Council
1776 G Street, N.W., Suite 701
Washington, DC 20006
(202) 357-0177

Federal Home Loan Mortgage
  Corporation
Building 5
1759 Business Center Drive
Reston, Virginia 22090
(703) 759-8000

Federal Housing Administration
U.S. Department of Housing and
  Urban Development
451 7th Street, S.W.
Washington, DC 20410
(202) 755-6422

Federal Insurance Administration
500 C Street, S.W.
Washington, DC 20472
(202) 646-2781

Federal National Mortgage
Association
3900 Wisconsin Avenue, N.W.
Washington, DC 20016
(202) 537-7000

Federal Reserve Board
20th Street and Constitution
Avenue, N.W.
Washington, DC 20551
(202) 452-3000

Federal Trade Commission
6th Street and Pennsylvania
Avenue, N.W.
Washington, DC 20580
(202) 326-2222

Government National Mortgage
Association
U.S. Department of Housing and
Urban Development
451 7th Street, S.W.
Washington, DC 20410
(202) 755-5926

House Committee on Agriculture
1301 Longworth House Office
Building
Independence and New Jersey
Avenues, S.E.
Washington, DC 20515
(202) 225-2171

House Committee on Banking,
Finance, and Urban Affairs
2129 Rayburn House Office
Building
Independence Avenue and South
Capitol Street, S.W.
Washington, DC 20515
(202) 225-4247

House Committee on Ways and
Means
1102 Longworth House Office
Building
Independence and New Jersey
Avenues, S.E.
Washington, DC 20515
(202) 225-3625

House Energy and Commerce
Committee
2125 Rayburn House Office
Building
Independence Avenue and South
Capitol Street, S.W.
Washington, DC 20515
(202) 225-2927

Interstate Commerce Commission
12th Street and Constitution
Avenue, N.W.
Washington, DC 20423
(202) 275-7119

International Monetary Fund
700 19th Street, N.W.
Washington, DC 20431
(202) 623-7000

Municipal Securities Rulemaking
Board
1818 N Street, N.W.
Washington, DC 20036
(202) 223-9347

National Credit Union
Administration
1776 G Street, N.W.
Washington, DC 20006
(202) 682-9600

National Automated Clearing
House Association
607 Herndon Parkway, Suite 200
Herndon, Virginia 22070
(703) 742-9190

National Labor Relations Board
1717 Pennsylvania Avenue, N.W.
Washington, DC 20570
(202) 254-8064

Office of Management and Budget
Old Executive Office Building
17th and Pennsylvania Avenue,
N.W.
Washington, DC 20500
(202) 395-3000

Office of the Comptroller
of the Currency
U.S. Department of the Treasury
490 L'Enfant Plaza East, S.W.
Washington, DC 20219
(202) 447-1810

Office of Thrift Supervision
1700 G Street, N.W.
Washington, DC 20552
(202) 906-6000

Overseas Private Investment
Corporation
1615 M Street, N.W.
Washington, DC 20527
(202) 457-7010

Resolution Trust Corporation
801 17th Street, N.W.
Washington, DC 20006
(202) 789-6313

Resolution Trust Corporation
Oversight Board
1825 Connecticut Avenue, N.W.
Washington, DC 20232
(202) 387-7667

Savings Association Insurance
Fund
1700 G Street, N.W.
Washington, DC 20552
(202) 906-6600

Securities and Exchange
Commission
450 5th Street, N.W.
Washington, DC 20549
(202) 272-3100

Securities Investor Protection
Corporation
805 15th Street, N.W., Suite 800
Washington, DC 20005
(202) 371-8300

Senate Banking, Housing, and
Urban Affairs Committee
534 Dirksen Senate Office Building
1st and C Streets, N.E.
Washington, DC 20510
(202) 224-7391

Senate Committee on Agriculture,
Nutrition, and Forestry
328A Russell Senate Office
Building
1st and C Streets, N.E.
Washington, DC 20510
(202) 224-2035

Senate Committee on Finance
205 Dirksen Senate Office Building
1st and C Streets, N.E.
Washington, DC 20510
(202) 224-4515

Small Business Administration
1441 L Street, N.W.
Washington, DC 20416
(202) 653-6365

Student Loan Marketing
Association
1050 Thomas Jefferson Street,
N.W.
Washington, DC 20007
(202) 333-8000

U.S. Department of Agriculture
14th Street and Independence
Avenue, S.W.
Washington, DC 20250
(202) 447-2791

U.S. Department of Commerce
14th Street and Constitution
Avenue, N.W.
Washington, DC 20230
(202) 377-2000

U.S. Department of Education
400 Maryland Avenue, S.W.
Washington, DC 20202
(202) 634-1947

U.S. Department of Housing and
  Urban Development
451 7th Street, S.W.
Washington, DC 20410
(202) 755-6422

U.S. Department of Justice
10th Street and Constitution
  Avenue, N.W.
Washington, DC 20530
(202) 633-2000

U.S. Department of Labor
200 Constitution Avenue, N.W.
Washington, DC 20210
(202) 523-6666

U.S. Department of the Treasury
15th Street and Pennsylvania
  Avenue, N.W.
Washington, DC 20220
(202) 566-2000

U.S. Internal Revenue Service
U.S. Department of the Treasury
1111 Constitution Avenue, N.W.
Washington, DC 20224
(202) 566-5000

U.S. International Trade
  Commission
500 E Street, S.W.
Washington, DC 20436
(202) 252-1000

World Bank (International Bank
  for Reconstruction and
  Development)
1818 H Street, N.W.
Washington, DC 20433
(202) 477-1234

American Bankers Association

Established in 1875, the American Bankers Association is the national trade association for commercial banks. The mission of the ABA is to enhance the role of commercial banks as the preeminent providers of financial services. This is accomplished through efforts such as federal legislative and regulatory activities, legal action, communications, research, and education and training programs.

Officers 1989-90

President

C.G. "Kelly" Holthus
President and CEO
The First National Bank of York
P.O. Box 69
York, NE 68467-0069
(402) 362-7411

President-Elect

Richard A. Kirk
Chairman of the Board and CEO
United Bank of Denver, N.A.
1700 Broadway
Denver, CO 80274-0005
(303) 863-6190

Immediate Past President

Thomas P. Rideout
Vice Chairman
First Union National Bank of
    North Carolina
Two First Union Center/GOVT. AFF.
Charlotte, NC 28288-0320
(704) 347-2308

Treasurer

Andrew J. Shepard
Chairman and CEO
Exchange Bank
P.O. Box 403
Santa Rosa, CA 95402
(707) 545-6220 ext. 224

Executive Vice President

Donald G. Ogilvie
American Bankers Association
1120 Connecticut Avenue, N.W.
Washington, DC 20036
(202) 663-5011